PATHS TO MODERN MUSIC

LAURENCE DAVIES

PATHS TO MODERN MUSIC

Aspects of Music from
Wagner to the Present Day

BARRIE & JENKINS
LONDON

© 1971 by Laurence Davies
First Published 1971 by
Barrie & Jenkins Ltd
2 Clement's Inn London WC2
Set in Monotype Imprint
Printed in Great Britain by
Butler & Tanner Ltd
Frome and London

ISBN 0.214.65249.1

Contents

		Pages
Preface		vii
Introduction		ix

PART ONE

The Legacy of Wagner
I	*Germany and the Art-Work of the Future*	3
II	*The French Wagnerians*	10
III	*Wagner's English Disciples*	17
IV	*A Postscript on Bayreuth—Yesterday and Today*	26

Romanticism in Decline
V	*Strauss, Hofmannsthal and the Opera Stage*	38
VI	*Mahler and the Beethoven Succession*	51
VII	*Schönberg or Webern?*	71
VIII	*'Wozzeck' as Satire and Prophecy*	87

French Ease and Versatility
IX	*A Century of Paris Opera*	100
X	*The Growth of the Mélodie*	113
XI	*Piano Music—Franck to Messiaen*	125
XII	*The Symphony in France*	139

PART TWO

From Nationalism to Cosmopolitanism
XIII	*The Sibelius Conspiracy*	155
XIV	*Busoni to Casella*	169
XV	*Roussel and Orientalism*	184
XVI	*Russia, Rachmaninov and the Exiled Virtuoso*	195
XVII	*De Falla in European Terms*	210
XVIII	*The Anguished Itinerary of Bartók*	223
XIX	*Stravinsky as Littérateur*	236
XX	*Martinů and the Brotherhood of Man*	247
XXI	*Prokofiev's Western Sojourn*	260
XXII	*A Note on Virgil Thomson*	274
XXIII	*Britten's American Operas*	287

PART THREE

| The Death and Re-Birth of an Art | 303 |

| *Index* | 323 |

Preface

The purposes that lie behind this book are set out as well as I am capable of expressing them in the Introduction that follows. All that can be required of this Preface, therefore, is that it should give the reader some idea of which things have previously been published, and convey my thanks to the various editors and publishers concerned.

Since it is essentially a book of essays, I must begin by separating the new from the not-so-new. In Part I, which deals with Austro-German and French music, quite a number of the pieces have already seen the printer's ink. Of the four essays on Wagner, those on 'The French Wagnerians' and 'Wagner's English Disciples' appeared, more or less unabridged, in the Magazine *Opera* in 1968 and 1969 respectively. I am accordingly indebted to the editor, Mr Harold Rosenthal, for permission to re-print them. The remaining two are new. As to the section on the late Romantics, the essays on Mahler, Strauss and Berg appeared in the official Journal of the Schools Music Association, entitled *Music*, edited by Mr Rudolph Sabor. However, owing to lack of space I had to reduce them drastically when submitting them for publication. As they stand in this book, each is longer by several thousand words. Hence they contain much that will be unfamiliar. I am grateful to Mr Sabor also for having commissioned the four French articles, and for allowing me to reproduce them here. Again, I have made extensive additions to these. Incidentally, none of these articles dates further back than the middle of 1968.

When it comes to Part II, there is a difference in that almost all the material is fresh. My aim here was to single out various countries of musical importance and discuss their respective contributions largely in terms of a typical representative and his problems. I was also very much concerned to debate the questions of nationalism versus internationalism that this task implied. The whole idea behind Part II should consequently be regarded as broadly cultural in intent. The essay on Stravinsky did appear in Sir Jack Westrup's *Music & Letters* in the second quarter of 1968; and the one on Roussel in Mr Frank Granville Barker's monthly

Music & Musicians in April 1969, at the time of that composer's centenary. None of the other nine essays have previously seen the light of day. Naturally, I should thank these editors for their willingness to assist me. Part III again, which consists of a more general, discursive summary, with briefer comments on a good many contemporary musicians whom it was never my intention to describe in any detail, was set down as a conclusion to the book and could not have existed in isolation from it. It has accordingly not been issued in any previous context.

Finally, I must take this opportunity to record a few other personal obligations. Robert Layton, Music Talks Producer for the B.B.C. Third Programme, gave me the benefit of his intelligent criticism of my style and presentation when I worked with him on programmes not related to the themes of this book. I am sure, however, that some of his advice has carried over into the book to its advantage. My sins, in this respect, naturally remain my own. Similarly, I have had helpful suggestions (many emanating from reviews of my previous books) from Rollo Myers, Edward Lockspeiser, Felix Aprahamian, Kenneth Loveland, Peter Gammond and a number of others. I wish to acknowledge a very special debt to Mr David Sharp of Barrie & Jenkins, who read through my book on 'César Franck and his Circle' and did an immense amount of valuable editorial work on it. His comments assisted me enormously when planning the present work. I found I also learnt much from the published notes of the late Theodore Steinway, former President of the famous piano manufacturing firm. His son, Mr John Steinway, the current Vice-President, was exceedingly kind in sending me material of interest about modern composers and their contribution to the piano. As usual, I find I owe the largest debt of gratitude to my wife, who not only helped me in the search for new material, but who suffered the agonies of watching the book being written. Everything I wrote was submitted to her for criticism before proceeding any further, and I made several alterations in consequence of her reactions. It would certainly be churlish not to acknowledge also the valuable lessons I have learnt from lecturing to my students in the University of Wales, whose attitudes have generally proved a sound guide as to what is or what is not acceptable to the reader.

To the staff of Barrie & Jenkins I owe a widespread obligation, which covers editorial advice, music copying, design and a host of lesser factors. My gratitude is a pleasure to express.

Introduction

Books get judged on their aims, and the extent to which they manage to achieve them, and confusion arises the moment these become misconstrued. This particular book is *not* aimed at providing another full-scale history of modern music. That task has already been accomplished with a surprising degree of thoroughness. William Austin's volume in the Norton History of Music Series appeared as recently as 1967 and runs to 700 pages. On a more modest scale, both Eric Saltzman and H. H. Stuckenschmidt have compressed a wealth of information into their respective contributions to the Prentice-Hall History of Music Series (1967) and the World University Library (1969). While books such as these remain in print, it hardly seems as if there is further need for chronology of the more obvious kind.

My own approach arose out of a different set of circumstances, and is consequently intended to satisfy a different demand. Setting myself to survey much the same period—roughly the last hundred years or so—I did so with the object of isolating certain themes, mainly to do with cultural or ideational influences on music. In the same way, I have assumed, perhaps recklessly, a reciprocal influence spreading outwards from music to affect the communal outlook of the age. Briefly, my attitude could be described as more sociological than musicological—though I hope this admission will not result in my being cast as a dilettante. I have studied all the composers chosen in the role of a senior university tutor in music, and I confess to being a regular, if inaccurate, player of the piano—a Steinway which it took years of savings and aeons of dreaming to possess. When writing these essays, I imagined they would form some sort of sequence leading from Wagner to Cage. But I felt certain that what they would really reflect was the strong interest I have always had in music's relations with society, including its relations with the other arts. Hence, the reader must do his best to forgive me if I seem to have omitted reference to composers whose work has been singularly independent, or whose extra-musical significance has been marginal. I apologize in advance, therefore, to artists who have had scant treatment because,

A*

in my view, their work exemplifies tendencies I have chosen to illustrate in another and broader fashion.

The Swiss composer Honegger was reported to have said on his deathbed, 'La Musique se meurt'—implying that the art would presently join him in the graveyard. No one who has read his book, *Je suis compositeur* (issued in English as *I am a composer* by Faber & Faber in 1966) could accept the view that the composer spoke out of malice or arrogance. He was among the most modest of men. It was simply that he could envisage no possible future for music, and had reached the conclusion that writing music was an impossible profession by which to try and live. That was fifteen years ago. In the meantime, a generation has grown up which claims far greater rapport with the avant-garde tendencies Honegger deplored, while a new patron has stepped forward in the person of the university to offer the composer the grants, commissions and fellowships he needs in order to survive financially. As for the older generation, or what is left of it, it has come to concur more and more forcefully, or regretfully in certain cases, in the dying Honegger's verdict. The question we should all like to see answered, therefore, can be put thus. Is modern music in for a new lease of life, or are its recent extremities (far more shocking than any Honegger could have predicted) merely to be considered in the light of death agonies? Phrasing it another way, has an old music silently died, and a new, unfamiliar one begun to issue its birth cries?

As things stand, there seems a clear division of opinion about the art's putative future, and what this division really reflects is a basic uncertainty about the premisses upon which art must rest. It will now be seen, I hope, why I have chosen to write my book in general, quasi-aesthetic language in preference to the strict language of music criticism. The reason is that the latter language no longer properly exists; or if it does it is competent to deal only with the music of the past, helping us hardly at all to understand the larger changes that have taken place since the first quarter of the century. Certainly it is unequal to the task of explaining how we reached the present impasse. On the one hand, it is easy to point to composers who confess quite openly that they are unable to make head or tail of that form of music which is being produced by computers, electronic generators and the like. On the other, there are unquestionably some young musicians who are already expressing themselves with the utmost confidence in the new medium. The cleavage seems in part a matter of what is being expressed, that is to say a matter of aesthetic substance; but at another level it is also a matter of what means of expression are being chosen, that is to say a matter of instrumentation, or more probably notation. The two issues should not be regarded as inseparable. Some theorists offer no objection to a change in the means as long as the ends of art are allowed to remain the same. Others claim that it is impossible to avoid promulgating new ends if one resorts to the kind of means now being proposed.

In an interview with Hans Keller, printed in the Winter 1966 issue of the journal, *Composer*, Sir Arthur Bliss had this to say:

> ... Music must convey to me some state of mind, or some emotional or intellectual stimulus. Some part of me must be moved by feeling I'm in contact with a superior mind that wishes to express itself to me ...

His point of view is one that reflects the attitude of a very large contingent of older musicians. Earlier in the interview, Sir Arthur described how intrigued he had been on hearing the sounds of a Messiaen organ piece; but he added that in the end sonority could not act as a substitute for personality. A mixed range of conductors and soloists has also been known to take this line, many of them a good deal younger than Sir Arthur. Guilini, Kertesz and Tortelier are three examples that come quickly to mind. All have complained of the engineering-like blue-prints which pass for scores, and all have regularly pleaded for a return to conventional means. Yet we must do justice to the tenacity of those who have committed themselves to a complex technological idiom. George Newson has recently described a new compositional device in the following terms:

> Synthesiser I is principally a collection of signal generators, that is sine, pulse, sawtooth and triangular oscillators and a white noise generator, reverberation unit, envelope generators and filters. It also has facilities for attenuating and mixing signals.

That description was made after a visit to the Independent Electronic Music Center, in up-state New York, undertaken as a result of a Winston Churchill travelling fellowship to the United States.

If Foundations of high-standing are prepared to subsidize music generated by the kind of machines Mr Newson describes (and it may be worth adding that the English composer, Roger Smalley, has recently been granted a six-year Fellowship at King's College, Cambridge, with a view to carrying out similar experiments), then it would seem that a new tradition is in the process of being launched. That this tradition will have to be based on a different kind of musical education appears to be obvious. The University of Surrey is indeed already advertising undergraduate

courses in which Physics plays as prominent a part in the training
as the old-style theory, harmony and counterpoint. Yet the public
continues to stay away from concerts of the new music; indeed
promoters tell us it is difficult enough to get people to attend when
works by such 'old masters' as Schönberg, Berg and Webern are
being played. *Opera* magazine recently conducted a survey in
which it was found that among the first forty-five operas readers
most wished to see performed only three were by composers that
could by any stretch of the imagination be called 'modern'—these
being Henze, Berg and Prokofiev.[1] In an earlier issue of the
journal, Pierre Boulez had announced confidently that the form
was dead anyway; a fact that has not prevented him from conducting *Parsifal* at Bayreuth, and *Pelléas et Mélisande* at Covent
Garden. Presumably, Boulez at least believes in conserving the
music of the past (or a rigorous selection from it). Otherwise, it is
significant that the most popular operas being written today are by
musicians like Britten, Menotti and Samuel Barber, who have
never made a secret of their adherence to the tonal system. The
same tends to be true of the other forms. Tonal symphonies are
still being written by men like Shostakovitch, Carlos Chávez and
William Schuman, and are proving tolerably popular.

When a dilemma of this sort imposes itself on an art, it is
reasonable to expect critics to do something to solve it. After all,
that is one of the main justifications of their existence. What we
find, however, if we examine the pronouncements of leading
writers on music during the last decade or so, is that they too
stand in bitter opposition to one another. In his notorious article,
'Who's Afraid of Pierre Boulez?' (printed in *Encounter*, February
1969, Vol. XXXII, No. 2, pp. 49–54), Henry Pleasants put forward the not-entirely-new thesis that the terms 'serious' and
'popular' have been responsible for a gulf in public taste that is
giving rise to dangerous misapprehensions. The former's connotations of superiority have led, in Mr Pleasants's view, to a mass
distrust and dislike of the highbrow forms, and that this in turn
has resulted in them becoming more and more highbrow and
hence more and more out of touch with the sensibilities of the
ordinary person. What we are now reaching, he argues, is the
ultimate phase of over-intellectualism—a phase he equates with
decadence and even, paradoxically, a kind of idiocy. Looked at
from the other end of the spectrum (an end Mr Pleasants tends to
view with a good deal more sympathy), there seems to be an
increasing ingenuity and status attaching to 'popular' music,

[1] For a full account of the results of the competition, see the March
1969 issue of *Opera* (Vol. 20, No. 3).

witnessed by the belated acclaim now accorded to jazz, the high praise bestowed on 'pop' groups, and the recognizable trend towards better training and aspirations on the part of, say, Hollywood composers. This is hardly the time or place in which to debate the merits of Mr Pleasants's thesis, but its very plausibility demands that we give it the most careful thought. At first glance, it has a decidedly truthful look about it, but the more we analyse it the more we can find to say against it. For instance, it assumes (tacitly, if not outrightly) that art should be a mass activity: it fails to take account of the manipulation of 'pop' tastes by tycoons and the more cowardly educationalists; and it does not do enough to convince us that the musicians who span both worlds (Leonard Bernstein and André Previn are, I suppose, the obvious examples) can achieve anything more than middlebrow esteem.

Literary critics have faced Mr Pleasants's arguments with considerably more combativeness than has so far been shown by music critics. Dwight Macdonald, for example, in his book *Against the American Grain* (Gollancz, 1962), has argued firmly against submitting to what he has christened 'mid-cult', or that form of art which sets out to please the majority without them having to think hard or really cultivate their tastes. It is a phenomenon he sees as distinctively American, having stemmed from the spread of mediocre schools and colleges for those who had previously been sub-literate, and, owing to the national treasonableness in education, will to some extent remain so. He also attributes it to the growth of the mass-media in which people are encouraged to regard even art as a branch of the entertainment industry. As instances of the tragic consequences of mid-cult for writers, Mr Macdonald cites the cases of Ernest Hemingway and John Steinbeck, who tried hard to please the masses while endeavouring to retain the place they had genuinely won for themselves in the sphere of literature. They were unable to have it both ways, and ended up coming perilously close to having it neither way. Similarly, the attempts recently made to up-date the Bible by putting it into committee English have failed to please the truly religious, while scarcely offering a very inspiring account of Christianity to the half-hearted. Meanwhile, the success of the U.S. Book Clubs shows how relieved many people are to hand over responsibility for their tastes to a panel. One does not need to be told that signs of these revolting cultural lapses are appearing simultaneously on this side of the Atlantic. On the other hand, it is undeniable that so-called 'serious' art was becoming highly esoteric, especially during the period between the wars. Artists like Picasso, Joyce and Stravinsky undoubtedly owed a measure of their success to snobbery, and their incomprehensibility acted as an invitation to charlatanism which they may or may not have succumbed to. The great difficulty (and it seems more of a difficulty than ever in the present age) is to discover forms of art that will preserve the element of subtlety without either baffling the common man or lulling him into a shameful sense of complacency. Music, like all the other arts, is meant to be enjoyed. But, like all lasting forms of enjoyment, it also needs to be pursued.

Perhaps one reason for the timidity of music critics lies in what Mr Felix Aprahamian has referred to as 'the Hanslick complex'. What he meant was the fear so many critics have of seeming to appear dull or bigoted in the gaze of posterity. Hanslick, it is well known, detested Wagner's music, and did his best to dissuade the public from listening to Bruckner and Hugo Wolf. Colin Wilson, in his book, *Brandy of the Damned* (Baker, 1964), has described him as 'one of the most loathsome figures of the nineteenth century', elsewhere adding that 'it would be impossible for posterity to forgive him for his part in driving Hugo Wolf insane'. Another typical comment is that Hanslick 'spent a lifetime stabbing genius in the back'. These charges certainly serve as an awesome reminder of the critic's responsibilities, and though there have been one or two attempts to rehabilitate Hanslick (notably by Stewart Deas and the retaliatory Mr Pleasants), he continues to seem an unlikeable, if not unsavoury, character. The point remains, however, that a critic is there to give his opinion, right or wrong, and even Hanslick was honest enough to read through the scores he was due to write about both before *and* after the performance— a form of conscientiousness the conditions of modern journalism usually prohibit. Nowadays, it is rare to find any single critic invested with the powers of a Hanslick. Instead, criticism gets its work done with the aid of a young, and frequently poorly equipped, circle of reviewers. Such persons are liable to lack the experience necessary for efficient comparison, and too often capitulate to the youthful desire to shock.[1] Hence, it is not uncommon to read that some untested composer is already 'the modern Beethoven' (André Hodeir on Jean Barraqué), or that a very experienced one is presented as 'a savage in awe before the symbols of an alien civilization' (Constant Lambert on Stravinsky). Such slashing pronouncements are bound to leave the ordinary listener in a dazed and bewildered state.

[1] I say nothing of the unscrupulousness of many editors who, in an effort to sell more copies of their magazines, encourage their employees to launch promotion drives on behalf of particular composers (or more often performers), using all the language of advertising. In the present age of 'half-tastes' and 'half-knowledge' this is likely to be as effective as it is delinquent.

By and large, contemporary critics err on the side of adulation rather than denunciation, even though Lambert (who has been dead for a decade and more) is as frequently reviled for his over-estimation of Sibelius as for his under-estimation of Stravinsky. It may be that the generation war—which is again an oldish phenomenon—tends to encourage an aspiring young critic to boost a composer from among his own age-group as a means of getting back at his conservative elders, without stopping to think that the terms 'progressive' and 'conservative' are treated equally ephemerally by history. A moment's reflection should also convince us that, while composers like Beethoven and Wagner were considered progressives, other giants like Handel and Mozart were widely imagined to be conservative. At least, they used the accepted musical language of their day; indeed they were virtually worshipped for their proficiency in it. A musician's stance towards the 'new' and the 'revolutionary' may consequently be less important, especially in the long run, than the quality of his gifts. The factor that really complicates musical criticism, and all other forms of artistic criticism, is that the expression of a person's gifts, like the expression of his character, can take a multitude of forms within a given language or framework. Also we have the same musical technique used to project, say, sensations of minute exquisiteness by one composer, and sensations of dramatic intensity by another.[1] Webern and Berg may be advanced to illustrate the point. What the critic should really be doing, therefore, is not so much examining the language in which a composer chooses to write, as describing and evaluating the content of what he has to say in that language. This means that he must be first of all a psychologist— that is to say, someone able to fathom a person's tensions and problems—and secondly a philosopher, in the sense of being able to know how much importance to attach to these things. A tall order, perhaps, to demand of a man society rates no higher than a superior journalist. But one that has to be fulfilled by at least a few figures in each period.

On this reckoning, it should hardly surprise us to discover that good critics are as rare, if not rarer, than good artists. The literary and pictorial arts have frequently had the modesty to acknowledge this fact. After all, it is only a small handful of critics of whom we think when we speak of the English literary tradition—Dryden, Johnson, Hazlitt, Coleridge, Arnold and perhaps Eliot or Leavis. Each no doubt presented a somewhat distorted view of his age, yet each is read for the uniqueness of his perceptions, for his

---

[1] At a still more obvious level, it is apparent that two different actors can impose different qualities on the same role, even on the same set of lines.

ability to penetrate to the heart of some individual or controversy. In fact, it is the successive evaluations of these men that have created the literary tradition—if we mean by that a select list of authors whose merits are fairly well agreed upon. By comparison, musical traditions have often been ill-defined, partly because there seems no clear relationship between creative and critical ability in music (it is significant that almost all the above literary critics were also novelists or poets of distinction, whereas there are scarcely any first-rate composer-critics belonging to any nation) and partly because it has been assumed too easily that music has nothing but itself to express. I believe it was Sir Neville Cardus who insisted that in Beethoven's music lay his 'actual juice and humours'—a proposition calculated to baffle those who are still looking for tonics and dominants. In the same way, we find in the music of Chopin signs of the anguished patriot and lover; in that of Schumann the incipient manic-depressive and romantic novelist manqué. No one would want to suggest that we throw away the scores of these composers and listen only for the 'confessional' element in their work. But it is for the *means* of expressing that element that we should be searching when we have their scores before us, and not for material out of which to write textbooks on harmony, form or counterpoint. Because music strikes us as so technical an art, it is tempting to concentrate on technique for its own sake. But it is only people that have sakes, and we ought by now to know enough to suspect the slogan 'art for art's sake'. Above all, we should avoid the assumption that music is a non-referential art that makes use of the same criteria for all.

What I am proposing to offer in this book, therefore, is a series of attempts to get at the philosophies and personalities of a number of modern musicians, and to enquire why they have taken the direction they have. It is also my wish to reveal to the reader, as far as I am capable of doing so, the extent of the influence wielded by these men, musical and extra-musical. To do this, I shall be forced to indulge in some technical analysis (I should not want it thought, despite the foregoing polemics, that I am out to lay the ghost of Sir Donald Tovey or some other exemplar of the orthodox criticism); but I also intend to allow myself the freedom to write out of that larger concern with art as a basic human activity that I have already spent so much time in defining. The sort of questions I hope the reader will ask himself, from time to time, are these. Why did the Romantic movement in music come to an end about when it did, and why did it seem to flourish longer and more tortuously in Germany or Austria than in some other countries? What does it mean when a nation prefers to interest itself in the intimate forms, and why is it that an unique fusion of the arts seemed to take place in countries like France at the time of the impressionist and symbolist revolutions? Is there a reason for the ardent nationalism experienced by some composers, and how is it that this nationalism has given way, in so many cases, to an equally insistent cosmopolitanism? What determines whether a composer is going to take up a particular genre, virtually to the exclusion of all others, and how does a composer decide on what path he will take through the jungle of modern music? Did the dodecaphonic movement appear as the only way out of a cul-de-sac, or was it inspired by more positive premisses? Finally, are we in at a funeral or a christening, musically speaking, or possibly both? Obviously, I intend to try to help the reader to answer these questions by giving him my views on them. But I shall be best pleased if he simply accepts my commentary as a foundation for another of his own. In that way, I hope that we can all ultimately learn from one book to the next.

PART ONE

The legacy
of Wagner

i Germany and the
Art-work of the Future

Every musician knows that Wagner's theory, based on the total
fusion of music, poetry and scene, was what brought the Romantic
movement to a head. Yet few understand, even today, how the
composer's views changed so much during the course of writing
the music-dramas that he caused these works to exhibit ambiguous
features of a most peculiar kind. *The Ring*, for example, was completed as a poetical text while Wagner was still obsessed by an
overall, Greek ideal of the theatre, and was still mildly enamoured
of the revolutionary politics in which he had indulged as a student.
In 1854, however, before he had written music for any part of the
tetralogy beyond *Das Rheingold*, he came under the influence of
Schopenhauer, who both turned him into a pessimist, politically,
and converted him to his well-known doctrine that 'all arts aspire
to the condition of music'. It is easy to imagine how radical was
the effect of these mental changes on the work the composer had
set himself to finish.

Not long ago, Peter Heyworth commented on the unsatisfactory
dénoûement of *The Ring* which, though it builds up the character
of Siegfried as hero, permits him to suffer a fate every bit as
inglorious as that of his precursor, Siegmund.[1] Germans who
regard the whole cycle as a triumph of nationalism must accordingly remain puzzled, if they are truthful with themselves, as to
why Wagner should have relapsed into such an untriumphant
ending. Considered as the allegory Shaw and others believed it to

[1] See his article 'Old Klingsor & New Bayreuth' in *Encounter* (July
1967, Vol. XXIX, No. I). The Barzun book is entitled *Darwin, Marx
and Wagner*, and was published in Britain by Secker & Warburg in
1942.

be, the work points no clear moral and appears to reach its climax in a return to the evolutionary slime of the Rhine. Jacques Barzun, another astute Wagnerian critic, sees this as an expression of the Darwinian fatalism of the period, viewing the complete drama as a life-like struggle for survival that culminates only in extinction and renewal. Ingenious though such an explanation may be, there is no evidence that Wagner was ever an admirer of Darwin, who likewise steered clear of artistic controversy. 'Social Darwinism' we associate less with the nineteenth-century biologist and more with such modern figures as H. G. Wells and Theodore Dreiser. It has, in any case, assumed a spurious quality in view of what sociologists tell us, and what emerges from the more scientific historians. Nonetheless, there are reasons for supposing that the composer turned allegory and fantasy into something more closely resembling tragedy. And the most positive of these reasons can be traced to the impact of Schopenhauer's teachings.

Concerning the musical basis of *The Ring* here again we encounter what seems like a contradiction between theory and practice. Many critics have argued that the 'leitmotiv' technique has a tendency to render events on the stage superfluous (Debussy ironically referred to the 'leitmotiv' as a form of visiting card, announcing the arrival of a character beforehand and thus spoiling his entry), while others have said that for long stretches it is the music alone that preserves the interest. This last allegation, if true, could reflect more on Wagner's discrepancies of ability as musician and poet respectively, than on the soundness of his theories. Yet there remains a strong suspicion that the cunning old hand knew very well what it was about; and that a decision to promote music to the topmost position had been secretly reached. Once more, if this was actually the case, then it almost certainly implies an acceptance on Wagner's part of Schopenhauer's precept. Musically, of course, the composer was slow to achieve his full potential, and his antecedents may not have been at all clear to him. Instead of basing his work on the accredited representatives of German opera—namely Gluck and Mozart—he had grown up with a preference for Beethoven and Weber. From Beethoven's Ninth Symphony, he derived the spiritual inspiration to embark on large-scale works. From Weber, whom he saw conduct *Der Freischütz* as a young man, he acquired the skills necessary to re-create that shadowy world of German romanticism associated with the Wolf's Glen in Act II of that composer's opera, and with the Walpurgisnacht forest scenes. On the pictorial level, one glimpses this world even more surely in the paintings of Karl Spitzweg, C. D. Friedrich and Moritz von Schwind.

It should not be forgotten, either, that Wagner borrowed from

Meyerbeer, Berlioz and Liszt the trappings of a formidable orchestral technique which, once he had thoroughly mastered, he indulged to the utmost. The result of all this was that *The Ring* came to embrace an enormous number of discrete and occasionally ill-assorted elements. There were the early theories of music-drama (derived to some extent from Gluck's 'sprachvermogen', and never entirely renounced); then came those influences picked up from men like Grétry ('La Musique est l'imitation de la parole'); there was Weber's fairy-tale world, re-inforced by his reading of the brothers Grimm and *Das Knaben Wunderhorn*; the example of the Greek theatre, and particularly, perhaps, the Orestes trilogy; and finally the pressures being exerted by Feuerbach, Schopen-hauer and the other German philosophers to whom the composer was constantly obliged. Add to this motley collection of influences the brassy virtuosity that went into pieces like the *Tannhaüser* overture and the Prelude to Act III of *Lohengrin*, and you have the real Wagner as distinct from the hero-worshipping portraits painted by his earliest biographers.[1] Anyone who examines *The Ring* carefully from every aspect (I am assuming people exist who are capable of this feat) is consequently likely to find the paradoxes as much accidental as deliberate. Honest literary scholars have stigmatized the poetry as mediocre (the mixing of lyric and drama-tic genres was only one of the complaints made by both Ruskin and Henry Adams); avant-garde producers, on the other hand, are apt to come up against sudden descents into 'grand opera' even in such late sections of the work as the chorus's tableaux of *Götter-dämmerung*; while there are certain characters—Siegfried himself is one—who, far from attaining a near-Shakespearian complexity, seem almost a reversion to the cardboard cavaliers of the French Second Empire. Alongside the variability of the music (inevitable, one would think, in a work spread over four evenings), these paradoxes are enough to account for any amount of public bafflement.

To say, nevertheless, that Wagner's ideas gave rise to widespread imitation in Germany would be an understatement. Simply be-cause they were so firmly rooted in both the history of the nation and the history of Romanticism, they were seen as the climax to centuries of endeavour. As John Warrack has so admirably put it:

> Wagner's genius was to distil in his gigantic creative act
> all the elements which Romanticism had uncovered and

[1] I am thinking, particularly, perhaps of the six enormous tomes of Karl Friedrich Glasenapp, completed in 1911, rather than the scrupulous work of Ernest Newman. But, according to one recent publisher's 'blurb', there have been almost as many biographies of Wagner as there have of Napoleon! It seems that 10,000 were written in his lifetime (1813–83).

isolated from Germany's artistic history since its renaissance at the close of the seventeenth century.[1]

In one sense, Schubert had tried to give expression to many of
these elements when he helped launch the lieder tradition; and it
was only his naivety and youthful death that probably prevented
him from anticipating the 'gesamtkunstwerk' on a more extended
scale. Schumann, too, as much in his piano pieces as his lieder,
managed to mingle literary with musical impulses in such a way
as to make them seem the natural expression of a single urge.
Indeed, it is arguable that nothing of this kind has ever surpassed
the brilliant musical marriages achieved in works like *Papillons*
and the *Kreisleriana*. It is only their miniaturism that can possibly
be held against them. But, as one might have imagined, once
Wagner reproduced these strivings on a truly spectacular level (and
one wonders if the modern generation really appreciates the cine-
matic effect his work must have had on his own contemporaries
and successors), then native composers lost no time in grovelling
at his feet in admiration and awe. Hugo Wolf's exhibition of self-
effacement at the Hotel Imperial in Vienna (where Wagner enjoyed
the luxury of a suite at King Ludwig II's expense) was only one
instance of this. Unfortunately, his opera, *Der Corregidor* (1896),
was later turned down by Mahler for production at the Court
Opera, and he would have done better to have stuck to those intimate forms of which he was already such a master. Even so, Wagner's chromaticism played its part in advancing Wolf's songs into
a new dimension. Peter Cornelius's *Barbier von Bagdad* was one
of the earliest fruits of Wagner's influence in the theatre, and was
unlucky in not being more widely acclaimed. After the composer's
death, Humperdinck's *Hansel und Gretel* (1893) and Pfitzner's
Palestrina (1917)—two very different works—renewed the influence.

The first real inkling of a reaction against Wagner in Germany
came with the publication of Nietzsche's two spirited pamphlets
in 1888—*The Wagner Case* and *Nietzsche contra Wagner*. The
irony lay in the fact that Nietzsche had once been a fervent disciple
of the master's, having made his way to Triebschen (the composer's
Lucerne home) in a fit of ecstasy when he was only twenty-five.
As a philologist and erudite Hellenist, Nietzsche was naturally
enchanted by Wagner's theory of a fusion of the arts. In practice,
however, he found Bayreuth (which had opened its doors in 1876)
far from a repository of old-world culture. Instead, it seemed to
him more of an entertainment palace, with overtones of beer-hall
sensuality. When he eventually attended a performance of *Parsi-*

[1] 'Old Germany & New Bayreuth' in *Opera* 1960, Vol. II, No. II,
pp. 729–37.

fal, this atheistic philosopher took bitter exception to the false religious genuflections he claimed to observe in the work. In *The Wagner Case* (by far the more damning of the two attacks) he went on to make other accusations: that Wagner had used music as a drug to amuse the middle classes, that he had permitted brutality and immorality to masquerade as life-affirming philosophy, and that he had turned the theatre into a giant spectacle aimed at enhancing his private ego. To the mature Nietzsche, the composer had degenerated into a mere actor. True or not, these charges possess a very modern ring. If they do not accurately describe Wagner, they place a finger unerringly on many of those who came after him, and to that extent Nietzsche's criticisms should really be construed as criticisms of what the twentieth century made of Wagner's ideas and influence, what they all amounted to for the generation ahead. Phrases like 'the pose in the end, the music and drama merely the means' and 'espressivo at any price' are singularly applicable to the arts as they stand today; while the charge 'sickly Christian obscurantism' is one the modern Church, as well as its pseudo-intellectual spokesmen, would do well to consider in the light of its own stumblings.[1] Oddly enough, Nietzsche never withdrew his admiration for *Tristan*—the one work which has brought Wagner into deepest disrepute with classicists and orthodox theologians.

The literary-philosophical impact of Wagner on Germans might have been greater had that nation maintained the supremacy it enjoyed in these sectors during the period of Goethe and Kant. But, as far as its writers were concerned, few figures of the first rank emerged during the age following Wagner's success. One of these was, of course, Thomas Mann, and it is to him that we have to look for a description of the composer's influence on such wider currents of thought. Throughout his long life, Mann maintained a profound interest in Wagner's work and personality, an interest that proclaims itself time and again in the author's novels and essays. As early as *Buddenbrooks* (1901), his first real success, we find Mann tentatively proposing his theory that, since Wagner, music has become a dangerous invitation to private and public anarchy. Young Hanno, the novel's hero, is presented as trembling with fear and excitement as he attends a performance of *Lohengrin*; while the old organ teacher, Edmund Pfühl, refuses to play excerpts from *Tristan* for Hanno's sister, Gerda, with the comments:

> That is not music—believe me! I have always flattered myself I knew something about music—but this is chaos.

[1] These are drawn from Walter Kaufmann's translations, issued in *The Portable Nietzsche* (Viking Press, 1954).

This is demagogy, blasphemy, insanity, madness! It is a
perfumed fog, shot through with lightning! It is the end
of all honesty in art.[1]

Three years later, in the short story *The Blood of the Walsungs*,
Mann shows us a brother and sister, undisguisedly named Siegmund and Sieglinde, committing incest on a bearskin rug—the
point once again being 'the music drives us in the direction of
madness'. (They had previously been to the opera to hear a
performance of *Die Walküre*.) One can hardly believe it a co-
incidence even, when the writer sets a later novel in Venice (the
city in which *Tristan* was finished), and makes his hero meet with
a kind of love-death as a result of a brush with a street singer.
Finally, in the essay *Leiden und Grosse Richard Wagners* (delivered
at Munich University in 1933), Mann expounds a complete view
of the composer, stressing his symbolism, pre-Freudianism, and
incarnation of the artist as alternately criminal and saint.

These last points are ones that were particularly slow to be
appreciated; they really had to await the spread of a new intellectual climate such as sprang up in the 1920's. Before that time,
symbolism was only half-understood (pre-war students did not
have the benefit of all those exegetical essays that now fill American
periodicals, neither had a scholarly industry grown up around
such figures as Kafka, Proust, Joyce and Mann himself), while sex
was still one of the great unmentionables. It is hardly surprising,
therefore, that Mann's essay did not appear at an earlier stage.
On the contrary, if the actual bringing out of symbolic and
psychological themes in Wagner's works is taken as the criterion,
this did not happen until after the Second World War, when
young Wieland Wagner became the first to present deliberately
anti-illusionist productions at Bayreuth. It is worth noting that
quite a number of sophisticated thinkers of the period between,
say, the Franco-Prussian War and the First World War utterly
failed in their efforts to see the more metaphysical aspects of
Wagner's achievements. Tolstoy, for example, in his book *What
is Art?* (1897), describes a performance of *Siegfried* which he
attended in terms that can only be considered obtuse. Treating the
whole thing as if it were intended as a piece of Russian verismo, he
spends so many pages tittering at the flimsiness of the dragon or
the poor acting on the part of the dwarfs that he altogether misses
any larger meaning the drama might have conveyed to him. Aside
from the fact that Tolstoy would probably have regarded all opera
as an over-civilized form of bourgeois entertainment, it is obvious

[1] Taken from the T. H. Lowe-Porter translation (1924) now available
in Penguin books (see p. 390 et seq.).

that he had come to the performance expecting the crudest kind of literalism. His questionable identification of himself and his work with the people also prevented him from seeing any merit in art that depended on subtlety and inference. Moussorgsky's *Boris* (in its original form) might have appealed to him, as might some of Borodin's more nationalistic works. But one can see, from the extent to which he regarded 'Westernized' Russians like Turgenev and Dostoievsky as 'betrayers of the folk', how limited were his powers of criticism.

Possibly the philosopher who understood Wagner best at that time when his work was being most obviously misjudged was Albert Schweitzer—a native of Alsace rather than Germany, but a man of decidedly Teutonic sympathies. Many people may think it odd that so great an authority on Bach, and so deeply religious and human a figure in his interests, should have developed an enthusiasm for Wagner. But Schweitzer's dualism enabled him to view art as both an objective and a subjective phenomenon. Bach, he considered, exemplified the former trend; Wagner the latter. As such, he saw nothing unseemly in Wagner's having made public the various personal and spiritual crises in his life. Indeed, it was only by giving the maximum possible expression to such crises that the more subjective artist could hope to break away from the plane of earthly existence, and experience some of the joys and sorrows of transcendence. Schweitzer attended *The Ring* as early as 1896, and had seen *Parsifal* only a very few years after Wagner's death. Both experiences remained fresh and vivid in his memory right up to that decade, following the Second World War, when he wrote from Lambaréné in Africa encouraging the composer's grandsons to discover a way of presenting Wagner's works so that their superhuman (or mystical) qualities could be made plain to a new generation used to such non-naturalistic arts as the cinema. As he himself put it in his letter:

> . . . Bayreuth is not music, but the experience of emotion and exaltation through ideas above earthly existence, ideas which have been given form in the dramas of Richard Wagner. To preserve this heritage in its pure state for the world, to keep Bayreuth alive as the Bayreuth which it became—that is the great and difficult task which has been allotted to you.

In these carefully-chosen words, a man of wisdom and insight—notable for the reverence he had for life and not for any desire to exploit it egotistically—fixed on the particular attributes in Wagner which will continue to make him a great artist for all those peoples in Europe willing to learn from him.

ii The French Wagnerians

To the majority of opera-goers, Wagner remains the supreme
instance of nationalist conceit in music, so that to speak of his
influence on the French might almost seem to be talking in riddles.
Yet a moment's reflection should convince us that some of the
composer's strongest and most vociferous supporters had their
headquarters in Paris. It is often acknowledged, for example, that
Vincent d'Indy was at the centre of a strenuous campaign to
promote his work, and was even inveigled into writing a pastiche
in his opera, *Fervaal*. If Wagner had this effect on so embattled an
individualist as d'Indy, it is only reasonable to suppose that his
impact on the more irresolute French musician must have been
staggering. A brief analysis of the situation reveals that this was
indeed the case.

Everyone knows the story of Wagner's earliest years in Paris,
when he was compelled to bow the knee to the great Meyerbeer.
It may not be so readily understood how prurient was the air of
expectation that came to surround each of the composer's subsequent assaults on the capital, assaults that quickly excited the
progressives whose fate it had been merely to stand and wait.
When the notorious production of *Tannhäuser* also backfired in
1861—owing to the mischievousness of the Jockey Club—Wagner
was forced to undertake a second retreat. Foolishly for him, he
could not resist taking his revenge for this slur at the time of the
Franco-Prussian War, when he published a silly lampoon mocking
the agonies of the occupation. It was scarcely to be wondered that
by the time he came to make his final attack on the city, feelings
had mounted to fever pitch. The sensible course for those who
could afford it was to invest in a prior trip to Munich, where the

operas could be heard in a more peaceable atmosphere; or after 1876 to Bayreuth, a shrine that was visited by a host of Frenchmen including Saint-Saëns, Chausson, Dukas and Debussy.

In Paris itself, a good deal of propaganda was put out by Pasdeloup in 1873, and a concert was entirely given over to Wagner's work by Lamoureux in 1885. It was not until 1887, however, that the next attempt was made at staging a complete opera. This was when *Lohengrin* was admitted to the Eden Theatre. The performance was given in French, and it was to be a further four years before the German version took to the boards at the Opéra. It seems astonishing to recollect that it was not until 1914 that Parisians had their first chance of hearing *Tristan*, since it was the case that the mature music-dramas aroused even more controversy. Debussy himself did not survive to hear the first German language production of *The Ring*. Knowing these facts, it may seem difficult to credit the enormous influence which we have said Wagner exercised over the composers of the Third Republic. What must be realized is that just because his music assumed the quality of forbidden fruit it aroused an exaggerated response in the minds of most listeners. Those who had made the pilgrimage to Germany returned with vivid anecdotes about both the man and his music. To the less adventurous spirits who had stayed at home, on the other hand, the sense of frustration flourished from gaining no relief. Surmounting it all was the hysterical behaviour of the anti-Wagnerites, men whose policies merely had the effect of stirring up curiosity where none had previously existed. In such a situation, it became ironical that the only pieces of Wagner's music to make their way to the capital were sensational transcriptions like the *Chevauchée des Walkyries*.

The unique fascination exerted by the German composer hardly rested with his music alone. Hundreds who had never heard a note of it were won over by his revolutionary artistic philosophy. Poets who had already succumbed to the Baudelairean theory of 'correspondances' could be excused for seeing in the Wagnerian gesamtkunstwerk a larger and more powerful vehicle for their ideas.[1] Likewise, the notion of a synthesis of the arts appealed strongly to many Platonists, as well as those ex-Romantics whose reading had been confined more to Hoffmann and Jean-Paul. Also there remained a sprinkling of dilettantes, like Catulle Mendès and Judith Gautier, to whom the name Wagner had become synonymous with a variety of avant-garde spectacles. Mendès had started

[1] This theory, familiar to students of French literature, was based on the poet's discovery of 'an intimate analogy between colours, sounds and perfumes'. The analogy is made explicit in *Spleen et Idéal*.

out as a symbolist poet, soon discovering a second career for himself as a polemical journalist. Judith was the daughter of Théophile Gautier, author of the classic *Mademoiselle de Maupin* and erstwhile music critic. These two were married in 1867 and afterwards took to visiting Wagner at his villa Triebschen, near Lucerne. In August 1869, the couple were accompanied by César Franck's future pupil, Augusta Holmès, on their expedition to Munich to hear *Das Rheingold*. Whether it was on account of Catulle's sudden infatuation with Augusta (herself said to have been the illegitimate daughter of yet another French poet, the sardonic Alfred de Vigny), or merely because of the effect wrought by the music, Judith soon began taking a warmer interest in Wagner than seemed proper. It may be supposed that the composer did not need the excuse of flattery in order to respond to her advances. Though less overwhelmed by his personality, Augusta could not resist paying her own form of homage by going on to write a series of Wagnerian operas, the best known of which was *La Montagne Noire*—a tale of Ottoman insurrection that secured a dozen performances at the Paris Opéra in 1895. Meanwhile, all three pilgrims suffered a setback to their admiration when Wagner issued his playlet *Eine Kapitulation*, a nasty little tirade that made all Frenchmen see red. Saint-Saëns was another musician who found it impossible to condone the crude mixture of nationalism and anti-Semitism contained in this work.

During the years following the armistice with Germany, Mendès gradually accommodated himself to the terms of Wagner's genius, realizing that it was necessary to overlook a certain amount of personal misconduct. He got his revenge for the slight to his own honour by writing a satirical novel entitled *Le Roi Vierge* (1881), which ridiculed King Ludwig II of Bavaria (Wagner's chief patron) in the guise of King Frederick II of Thuringia. The composer himself is said to have been the original of another character who is portrayed, the egotistical Hans Hammer. (Readers may recall, in this connection, André Gill's well-known cartoon of Wagner hammering a huge crotchet into one of his listener's ears.) But by the time this book had appeared in print, Wagner was nearing the end of his long life. In the intervening period, Mendès preached a watered-down version of the gospel, praising all those innovations which the composer had introduced while being very careful to avoid a Teutonic bias. What he really wanted was for a young Frenchman to come forward and write a Wagnerian masterpiece for the Paris theatre:

> Whoever creates such a work will be a great man and will
> earn our love. For, even though he borrows his forms

from Germany, he will modify them and, in his inspiration, he will remain a Frenchman.

Sentiments of a rather similar kind were later to be uttered by Romain Rolland and others who came to regret the absence of a major talent in their country. Of course, France failed to throw up anyone with gifts remotely resembling Wagner's. Debussy came nearest to him in stature, but his terms of reference were deliberately differentiated. The vogue which Wagner acquired in France was in the meantime dissipated to some degree by the attacks Nietzsche mounted on his memory. These attacks had a peculiar significance for the French, not so much because they hastened to endorse them, as because it was to the traditional Gallic ideals of wit and charm that their author had looked when casting around for an antidote to Bayreuth. Drawing much of their sting from the fact that the writer had once counted himself among the most ardent of Wagnerites, Nietzsche's sallies were aimed at convincing people of all nationalities that the Bayreuth philosophy was specious and rhetorical. True dramatic flair he now held to be the prerogative of men like Bizet. This was too facile a judgment to stand much scrutiny, but it was one that appealed greatly to those who had grown tired of hearing about the new Jerusalem. Hence by 1906, when Debussy came to write his *Children's Corner* suite for piano, it had become possible to poke fun at the dying Tristan in musical quotation.

But before this process of disenchantment took shape, there was a lengthy period of Wagner-worship throughout France. All through the closing decades of the nineteenth century, a motley collection of Wagnerian novels, guide-books and manifestoes kept on appearing. Baudelaire's own essays, grouped together under the title *L'Art Romantique* in 1868, had been an immense spur to the movement, which was still going strong at the time of Albert Lavignac's *Voyage Artistique à Bayreuth* in 1897. In between there came the founding of the *Revue Wagnérienne* by Edouard Dujardin (better known for his 'stream-of-consciousness' novel, *Les Lauriers sont coupés*) and the long-drawn battles of thinkers like Mallarmé, Téodor de Wyzewa (the Mozart scholar), Villiers de l'Isle-Adam and J. K. Huysmans. Not content with having stirred up a literary hornet's nest, the French Wagnerians attracted the attention of painters and poster-artists. Fantin-Latour's famous picture of *Petit Bayreuth* was only one expression of the interest they aroused, others stemming from the sketches done by Degas, Whistler and Odilon Redon. Several of these artists issued lithographs depicting favourite scenes from the operas, much as Beardsley was to do in England.

It is essential at this point to distinguish the ideological furore started by the composer from its purely musical ramifications. By and large, the aesthetic cliques were not interested in defining Wagner's status as a musician. They saw in him nothing more than a stupendous cultural entrepreneur. To the musical faction, on the contrary, he appeared as a fascinating new exponent of harmony and orchestration. It is scarcely surprising that the writers and philosophers spent all their time discussing *The Ring*, leaving the musicians to respond in their closer fashion to the intricacies of *Parsifal* or *Tristan*. The last of these operas was particularly catastrophic in its effect on a whole generation of French musicians. This is apparent from the fact that during the 1889 season at Bayreuth young Guillaume Lekeu had to be hauled out of the Festspielhaus unconscious, while Chabrier was reported to have burst into tears.

What effect did all this unhealthy clamour have on the native urge? Were there any important French operas written under the spell of Wagner? To answer these questions properly, we must first look at the attitudes that older and more wily musicians took up. César Franck, who was certainly one of the most influential of these, was careful to preserve a certain ambiguity of approach. Never choosing to embark for Bayreuth (pleading poverty as the ostensible reason) and maintaining a somewhat stony indifference towards ideas, Franck contented himself with a study of the scores, none of which secured his unmixed blessing. His attitude to *Tristan* may be summed up in the story of how he once scrawled the word 'poison' across the title-page of his copy. One would have thought the two composers had much in common, especially in view of their chromatic leaning. But it is quite likely that Franck never really grasped what Wagner was trying to do with the language of music, failing to understand that to the dramatic composer academic laws are of little consequence. The second of Franck's three operas—the tedious and unrevived *Hulda* (1882)—might just pass as Wagnerian. At least, its Marche Royale hints at the influence of *Tannhäuser*.

Gabriel Fauré was another French musician who managed to keep Wagner at bay—at any rate he made rich fun of him in his hilarious quadrille on themes from *The Ring*. Keen students may perhaps detect a less disrespectful tribute in the opera *Pénélope*. But by 1913, when this was produced, the fever had vanished from nearly everyone's veins. If we want to look for the artists who were completely overcome by the toxic effects of Wagner's music, we are more likely to find them among the pupils of these men, especially among those who made up the Franck circle. One of the first to get lost 'dans la forêt Wagnérienne' was the unhappy Henri

Duparc, whose song *Extase* (written in imitation of the Wesendonck lieder) was a bitter reminder of how difficult he had found it to get the German composer out of his system. His sole opera *Roussalka* was burned in a fit of self-destruction. Wagner wielded a similar power of intimidation over yet another of 'la bande à Franck'—the diffident and wealthy Ernest Chausson. For years this dedicated amateur slaved away at his drama *Le Roi Arthus*—a round-table romance which ends in a Tristanesque betrayal of the King by the lovers Lancelot and Guinevere—while all the time fearing what he described as 'the red spectre' of his predecessor.

By comparison, some of the most unabashed Wagnerizing sprang from the pen of Chabrier, whose Danish opera *Gwendoline* exhibited all the customary tricks—including a spinning song, several love-duets, and an immensely flammable immolation scene. As befitted his more sober outlook, d'Indy contrived to make his debts seem less obvious. He, too, indulged in a number of extraordinary parallels nevertheless. His early lyric drama *Le Chant de la Cloche* (1885) fell back on a guild of craftsmen and a rigged competition very much after the manner of *Die Meistersinger*; while the later *Fervaal* (1895) employed an oath of chastity and a magic garden both of which must have aroused a glint of recognition from producers like Appia and Tietjen. In fact, this last-named work made use of a whole host of Wagnerian devices, ranging from the leit-motif to the idea of a passing kingdom which it becomes the hero's destiny to efface. D'Indy was easily the most learned and uncompromising of the French Wagnerians, an irritatingly perverse man who insisted upon attacking what he called 'Boche art' at the same time as he was propagandizing madly for his idol. His later works generally played down the influence, but even the next opera which he wrote—the gloomy *L'Etranger*—contained ample evidence of his involvement. In it the figure of the Stranger who refuses the consolation of earthly love, and who ends by giving his life to save a party of shipwrecked villagers, carries unmistakable overtones of Wotan.

Other French operas which bore the stamp of Wagner's influence included Reyer's seldom-heard *Sigurd* (1883)—in which the plot was almost identical with Act III of *Siegfried* and parts of *Götterdämmerung*—and Lalo's legendary *Le Roi d'Ys* (1888), where the action was conducted in Brittany. Neither of these works was Wagnerian in style as much as in subject-matter. As far as the master's sensational use of stage effects went, the influence spread itself still more widely. Since these effects had been derived to some extent from Meyerbeer, it was understandable that they should have appealed to a later generation of French composers. Bruneau's presentation of a typhoon on the stage in his *L'Ouragan*

(1901) almost certainly owed something to Wagner's daring example, though the aim was more naturalistic than symbolic. An even more obvious instance where Wagner's technique made itself felt was in the ending of Lazzari's *La Tour de Feu* (1928) in which the immolation took place in a blazing lighthouse, all filmed in a kind of primitive cinemascope.

But certain of these men were reacting to what might be termed the Cecil B. de Mille aspects of the composer's genius. The subtler and more musical aspects were what struck serious artists of the rank of Dukas and Debussy. The latter's *Pelléas et Mélisande* (1902) remains the classic example of how fructifying Wagner's achievement became at the point of being properly perceived. No one listening to this masterpiece can continue to share the myth that nothing good came out of his French acclaim. If it is true that Debussy, no less than his feebler fellow countrymen, felt himself pursued by 'the ghost of old Klingsor', this was because he was determined not to be driven into adopting the simplest forms of imitation. In merging Wagner's uninterrupted 'melos' with his own equally revolutionary tendency towards 'speech-song', he brought together all that was best in two rival traditions. The debts which Dukas owed to the German composer were similarly explicit, and gave rise to music of the same high calibre. In his *Ariane et Barbe-bleue* (1907), the theme of the 'cinq filles d'Orlamonde' is subjected to continuous change and recall in the fashion originally set by Wagner. As was the case with *Tristan*, the work threatens at times to turn into a gigantic divertimento for orchestra, leaving the singers free to bewail their limitations. Each of these dramas strives to express a sorrow too great for human utterance. For this reason, possibly, it was difficult to look beyond them towards a new conception of the art. What ultimately killed Wagner's influence in France (aside from the chauvinism sparked off during the First World War) was exactly that which helped to end it in other countries—namely, the utter impossibility of realizing his intentions. The solution proposed by Schönberg and Alban Berg, as we can see only too clearly today, involved a degree of introversion that was repugnant to the French muse. In the last resort, most of his compatriots agreed with Saint-Saëns when he remarked 'La Wagnéromanie est un ridicule excusable; la Wagnérophobie est un maladie.'

iii Wagner's English Disciples

To judge from the amount of parody they inspired, Wagner's operas aroused a more urgent response in France than in England, where the musical impulse modelled itself strictly on Handel and Mendelssohn. As Bernard Shaw never ceased repeating, English composers formed a timid crew, their senses dulled by too much theory and counterpoint. It seems hardly possible to credit them with an awareness of the ideas contained in *Opera and Drama*— especially since that revolutionary treatise was still awaiting its translator in Edwin Evans. The great Victorian public, on the contrary, seldom objected to a new theatrical experience, particularly so long as furtive conversational habits were permitted to continue. At any rate, it was compliant enough to welcome several of Wagner's earliest masterpieces at a time when these unsettling works were being banned across the channel.

Lohengrin—characteristically sung in Italian—was the first of the operas to become known in London, and on reflection it does not seem to have been a bad choice for stimulating interest. Its appearance in 1868 probably seemed belated to those who knew the date of Liszt's Weimar production (1850), but national pride recovered when it emerged that Frenchmen had to wait a further nineteen years before being able to see the work in one of their own theatres. *Der Fliegende Holländer* and *Rienzi* also got off to a comparatively early start, being staged in England by the enterprising Carl Rosa in 1876 and 1879 respectively. *The Illustrated London News* carried a full page print of the apotheosis of Senta and the Dutchman, etched in the tremulous fashion of the day. What is so amazing to us in the present age is that not one of these productions provoked the sort of demonstration which had, for example, sunk the Paris *Tannhaüser* of 1861, and which had been almost a regular feature of Wagnerian first-nights abroad. Patrons at Drury Lane and other English opera-houses seemed quite satisfied to express their opinions through the medium of their daily newspaper. At least, this was how it looked before the various claques took a hand in changing things.

Not surprisingly, perhaps, it was a German who assumed responsibility for stirring up Wagnerian passions in England. He was Franz Hueffer, music editor of *The Times* and father of the novelist Ford Madox Ford. Married to a daughter of one of the most famous Pre-Raphaelite painters, Heuffer had access to a wide circle of literary and artistic friends, and he had no difficulty in transmitting his enthusiasm along the broadest of fronts. A Ph.D. in philology, and an ardent follower of Schopenhauer, he seemed the very model of a Teutonic scholar. It was through his writings that George Eliot and Edward Burne-Jones were converted to the cause. Though he died in 1889, Hueffer's expertness and tenacity went a long way towards laying the foundation for English Wagnerism. In particular, he helped to inspire the Wagner Society, founded by the conductor Edward Danreuther in 1873. Unfortunately, this society never fully recovered from its shaky start. Its trouble was that it leaned too heavily on its continental cousins, lacking the courage to become anglicized. Shaw was always attacking its members for failing to erect an English Bayreuth on Richmond Hill!

Once it had passed through its moribund phase, the society galvanized itself to the extent of issuing a quarterly periodical entitled *The Meister*. This continued to appear from 1888 to 1895. It also undertook to publish all Wagner's prose works in English translation by W. Ashton Ellis, a venture that never quite reached completion. Ellis deserves to be counted among the foremost of English Wagnerians for all that. His influence on the generation of Shaw and Beardsley could not have been more considerable. The last named artist strove to represent Wagner in pictorial forms, his erotic illustrations to *Tannhaüser* becoming a guarded pornographic treasure.[1] Arthur Rackham and T. W. Rolleston were others who derived employment from decorating the pages of Wagnerian editions, over a hundred of which appeared during the decade 1890–1900. It is easy to imagine how eagerly such literary offerings were devoured by a public brought up to revere the printed word. Swinburne, George Moore and Arthur Symons were just a

---

[1] John Glascso's recent completion of Beardsley's unfinished novel, *Under the Hill* (1959) shows that the notorious *Yellow Book* artist also wrote his own version of the *Tannhaüser* story; though it reads more like an up-dated Restoration comedy than anything Wagnerian. It is now available in the New English Library series.

few of the eminent men of letters who took it upon themselves to assist the movement.

Meantime, there had been a major musical onslaught with the London productions of *The Ring*, *Die Meistersinger* and *Tristan*. By a curious co-incidence, all three works were heard during one and the same season in 1882. Two complete cycles of *The Ring* were given at Her Majesty's Theatre under the management of Angelo Neumann, to whom Wagner owed most of his foreign success, while the remaining operas were sponsored by Pollini at Drury Lane. Both ventures were exceedingly ambitious in scope, the former reproducing many of the features which had attached to the original Bayreuth Festival of 1876; and the latter calling upon the formidable Hans Richter as conductor. The response to these productions was very mixed indeed. Some disappointment made itself felt when the house chandeliers were allowed to remain on for *The Ring*; and when it became obvious that no sound barriers would be installed for the orchestra. Nevertheless, the singing came as a distinct revelation, with Vogl's Loge and Niemann's Siegmund carrying off the honours. Far less enthusiasm was expressed over the visual aspects of the drama—which were evidently rather crudely conceived. Fricka's rams were described in one paper as being 'all too plainly of the toyshop breed'; while the fight with Hunding was assessed as 'the feeblest combat ever witnessed on the stage'.

Unhappily, the production of *Siegfried* coincided with the Phoenix Park murders, so that review comments were virtually squeezed out by sensationalism of a more realistic kind. *The Times* managed a brief paean of praise, but could not refrain from a sneer at the pantomime dragon. Journalists on the whole found it a penance to sit through the whole of *Götterdämmerung*, and the correspondent of *The Standard* was probably writing on behalf of his profession when he complained that the piling up of corpses had not taken place soon enough. At the rival theatre, *Tristan* caused another round of head-shaking, *Punch* comparing it to a 'long, dull sermon in a stuffy church on a hot August afternoon' and deploring its connection with what was typically described as 'the higher cultchaw'. But the same paper acclaimed *Die Meistersinger*, finding it pleasantly free from 'hobgoblins, hippopotami, demons and spirits'.

During the last years of Queen Victoria's reign, the case discovered a new champion in the redoubtable G.B.S. Adopting the pseudonym 'Corno di Bassetto', Shaw covered an enormous range of musical events in his capacity as critic. His running feud with Sir Augustus Harris, then artistic director of Covent Garden, spanned the period 1890 to 1894 and makes diverting reading even today. Savagely censorious of the 'diamond-show' that passed for opera under Harris's management, this tart young Irishman proved that he was already determined to see music and drama properly united in a single, spectacular art-form. His constant urging of Wagner's ideas sprang from first-hand acquaintance with the Bayreuth scene, and was backed by uncompromising convictions about the nature of the composer's genius. The notices he submitted of the famous Wagner nights at Covent Garden were remarkable, not simply for the good sense they exuded on matters of staging and singing, but for their quite unusual theoretical insights.

For example, Noufflard's study *Wagner d'après lui-même* was made the occasion of a valuable aside in January 1894, when Shaw pointed to the error of assuming that Wagner had 'reformed' romantic opera in much the same manner as Gluck had done during the previous century. 'Music-drama is no more reformed opera,' he indignantly fumed, 'than a cathedral is a reformed stone quarry.' He was also quick to stress that Wagner's music made dramatic points even when no action was being prescribed on the stage. Absolute music, in his view, did not exist in Wagner, the composer's poetic textures notwithstanding. This opinion must be seen as especially astute when it is remembered how widespread the delusion was to become that Wagner's works were really nothing but gigantic symphonic poems. Shaw's greatest contribution to the movement was not to come until 1898, however, some years after he had relinquished his role as critic. It took the form of his essay 'The Perfect Wagnerite', which poses the idea that *The Ring* is a political myth, dealing with the rise and fall of the capitalist system.

Knowing what we do about Shaw's background and beliefs, it is tempting to dismiss his theory as a wild piece of literary guesswork; or an attempt at socialist pleading. But this would be to ignore the extent to which Wagner's tetralogy was actually sketched while the composer was an active revolutionary. During his Dresden days, before he withdrew into pessimism and luxury, Wagner had been the comrade of Bakunin and had even gone through a period of being wanted by the police. This alone makes it plausible to suppose that he planned *The Ring* as a social allegory of some kind. When we add to these facts the knowledge that greed for gold and lust for power are indisputable themes of the tragedy, the explanation put forward by Shaw takes on powerful force. Certainly, it is no disservice to the truth to argue, as he does, that the dwarfs embody the spirit of industry, the giants that of perspiring humanity, and the gods that of uneasy officialdom. The character of Wotan, in particular, seems to cry out for interpretation along such lines, Shaw casting him in the role of a typical church leader caught between the forces of Law (Fricka) and State (Loge).

Despite the pointedness of this reasoning, Shaw failed to persuade the Fabian Society to participate in the work of disseminating the composer's opinions—which only goes to show how open these opinions were to an entirely different construction. In this sense, it is worth noting that many of Shaw's literary contemporaries and successors held a contrasting view of his significance. Hardy, for instance, saw Wagner as the poet of rural Germany—a role the composer would surely have been embarrassed to acknowledge. Bennett and Galsworthy, on the other hand, took him to be a pioneer of the more freethinking, naturalistic drama, placing him in rather the same camp as Ibsen and Strindberg. This, too, seems an altogether unconvincing piece of typecasting. D. H. Lawrence who, with his friend Helen Corke, wrote a steamingly Wagnerian novel called *The Trespasser* (one of the characters in it is actually named Siegmund) naturally imbued the composer with some of his own philosophy of sexual submission. Perhaps he was the least wide of the mark, in view of the moral of *Tristan*, though one can hardly credit the 'life-affirming' Lawrence with 'liebestod' tendencies even if the protagonists of *The Trespasser* do decide upon suicide as the only way out of their dilemma. Still further interpretations of Wagner's work gained currency among the 'Decadents' and 'Sensualists', and it was evident that very soon every crank, charlatan and theosophist would have his own special exegesis to impart. Not surprisingly, a reaction set in after the 1914-18 War, and public attention was strenuously re-directed to the music.

One of the most freakish of Wagner's pre-war supporters was David Irvine, whose tract *The Ring of the Nibelung and the Condition of Ideal Manhood* appeared slightly in advance of Shaw's essay in 1897. A second volume, entitled *Parsifal and Wagner's Christianity*, followed some two years later. Both books preached the gospel in perfervid terms. Unlike Shaw, Irvine rejected all political overtones in favour of what he took to be Wagner's moral teachings! Incredible though it seems, he regarded *The Ring* as an attack on the Church of England, sensing in the figure of Mime the archetypal conniving priest. The position of the clergy *vis-à-vis* Wagner was indeed somewhat delicate throughout this entire period. Ernest Newman reported the case of one anxious cleric who demanded re-assurance that Siegfried and Brunnhilde were formally engaged. Others are known to have fretted over the incestuous element in *Die Walküre*, not having observed the same phenomenon in those works of Byron and Wordsworth that lay

open on the shelves of their parish libraries. *Parsifal*, when it was
once performed in London in February 1914, was execrated by
ecclesiastical authorities for daring to present aspects of the Last
Supper on the stage. Hardly anyone stopped to consider how
Wagner's religious mythologizing might have been turned to the
church's advantage.

Clearly, nothing like the awe that had been observable among
French viewers was to be seen in England, and it is perhaps worth
emphasizing the different uses to which Wagnerism was put in the
two countries. Each attached a gratuitous meaning to the composer's work, but in France this tended to be mystical-symbolic,
whereas in England it was social-philosophical. The standard
British reaction to *Parsifal* was furnished by J. F. Runciman,
whose influential book on Wagner had made its appearance in
1913. In his estimation, the work was both blasphemous and
immoral, and he lost no time in denouncing it before a large body
of readers. It is true that the novelist Virginia Woolf later caused
Mrs Dalloway to swoon with ecstasy on attending a Bayreuth
performance of the drama, but she was presumably more sophisticated than the majority of her countrywomen. At all events, there
were few other signs of a loss of balance on this side of the
water.

If one thinker was more responsible than any other for implant-
ing a common-sensical approach to Wagner, it was surely Ernest
Newman, whose scholarly writings helped to clear away mountains
of ill-digested propaganda. Ferdinand Praeger's book *Wagner as I
Knew Him*—which Longmans had brought out as early as 1891—
was of course available to those who were determined to seek out
for themselves the true facts of the composer's existence. But
Newman, who had been busy on his researches since the turn of
the century, went one better in laying before the public unim-
peachable evidence relating to every nook and cranny of his
subject's life. His *Wagner as Man and Artist* (1925) and *Fact and
Fiction about Richard Wagner* (1931) proved mere preludes to
what was to become a superb four volume study, appearing between the years 1933 and 1947, and was to remain the finest
musical biography in the language. What set Newman apart from
the other commentators was his rigid avoidance of speculation.
From the outset, he refused to let himself become weighed down
by political or religious ties. If his work appears to possess any
fault today, it is that of seeming to exalt the music at the expense
of the ideas. For Newman belonged to that northern school of
symphonic addicts (it also came to include Samuel Langford and
Sir Neville Cardus) and had made his way up as an insurance
clerk in Liverpool. Nurtured on the glorious excesses of men like

Richter and Nikisch, Newman could hardly help expressing his powerful musical chauvinism. This made itself felt in his habit of dragging the reader relentlessly back to the scores. Towards Wagner's ideological presumptions, and particularly his pan-Germanism, he preserved an attitude of calm contempt. At least, this was the position from which he started out. Writing of the religious element in the composer's work, he began by arguing:

> The word redemption has no meaning for me in the sense in which Wagner and the theologians use it. I can believe that redemption is a concrete reality in the pawnbroking business; but if anyone tells me that men's souls are to be bought and sold, or lost and found again, without any volition of their own, I can only say that all this conveys about as much to my intelligence as talk about a quadrilateral triangle . . .

Later on, however, Newman came to accept a less restricted view of his brief.

The task of tracing the changes in this author's outlook—beginning with his preliminary *Study of Wagner* (1899) and going on to embrace *Wagner Nights* (1949)—really demands a monograph to itself. After all, it covers fifty years of a critic's life. All that need be said here is that his opinions generally evolved to meet the complexity of his factual investigations. As a rule, the later books dispense with that irritatingly English frivolity that so often disfigures the early writings. They reveal more willingness to appreciate the composer's extra-musical importance. Newman nevertheless continued to underplay the symbolic and mythological aspects of Wagner's work to an extent that cannot very well serve us today. Though he survived to applaud Wieland Wagner's 1951 production of *Parsifal*, it can scarcely be imagined that he shared that lamented genius's feeling for the psychological symbolism of the music-dramas. How he would have reacted to Robert Donington's Jungian criticism (contained in *Wagner's 'Ring' and its Symbols*, Faber, 1963) remains hard to guess. What Newman *did* have the stamina to do was to examine the opera plots as stories rather than as myths; and in the process he provided the best extant account of their literary and historical origins.

Otherwise, his belief in the autonomy of Wagner's music never wavered. Dramatic and pictorial representations remained for him a mere confirmation of what the music was projecting. To that degree, he upheld the notion that all Wagner's music was programme music—a point of view that places the composer as a strict disciple of Liszt and Berlioz. But it should not be assumed from this that Newman's contribution was primarily negative and

destructive. It was due to his initiative that regular Wagner
seasons became obligatory in England and that wartime prejudice
against the composer was so quickly discounted. Perhaps, also, it
is no coincidence that the period in which his views flourished gave
rise to a marvellous range of Wagnerian musicians, as opposed to
producers or designers. One is thinking particularly of figures like
Furtwängler, Kirsten Flagstad, Lauritz Melchior.

Yet with all the stress placed on Wagner's *musical* legacy, it
cannot be said that Britain, like France, produced a large crop of
native imitators. Edward Dent once went on record as saying that
English composers of the nineteenth century 'turned away from
opera as if it were an unclean trade'. Assuming this to have been
the case, it is still surprising that so little of Wagner's musical imprint is detectable in the concert music of British composers. Gustav
Holst, it is true, went through a long and painful Wagner phase,
and so did Josef Holbrooke. Bantock had a brief flirtation with
Wagner, producing works which, according to Peter Pirie, were
'Babylonian in orchestration and catastrophic in economic effect'.[1]
Otherwise, one is left with Havergal Brian—whose colossal symphonies must surely have owed something to Wagner's example—
and he remained largely unperformed until very recent times. The
case of Elgar is much the most complicated, since his debts have
always proved difficult to establish. Certain passages in *The Dream
of Gerontius* undeniably possess Wagnerian associations—'O Jesu,
help' is one example. Also, there seem to be occasional reminiscences in the First Symphony and the Cello Concerto.

Probably on account of their expatriate leanings, Delius and
Ethel Smyth remain the two British composers most influenced
by Wagner in their operas. The former's *A Village Romeo and
Juliet*, despite its Swiss libretto, almost passes for an English
Tristan—which may be one of the reasons it has not enjoyed the
success it deserves. The latter's seldom played *The Wreckers* is
even more overtly Wagnerian, but has certainly exerted little
interest either here or in Germany. Rutland Boughton, who had
ideas of opera at Glastonbury not very far removed from those
Wagner implemented at Bayreuth, lacked the talent and support
to put them into practice, ending up as the purveyor of a lighter
style. In investigating the causes which led other nations to
abandon their interest in Wagner (and here one can single out the
French in particular) prime importance should be attached to the
counter-impact of the Russian school. The comparable factor in

---

[1] For a full account of Bantock's debts to Wagner, see Pirie's essay,
'Bantock and his Generation' in *The Musical Times* (August, 1968,
No. 1506, Vol. 109), pp. 715-19.

England, on the other hand, was the persistence of a folk-song tradition such as found its way into the work of men like Vaughan Williams and Arnold Bax, each of whom might otherwise have developed more along Wagnerian lines; Bax's chromaticism is certainly derived from Wagner. During the 1920's and '30's, England looked inward at her own forgotten heritage, leading her, in the view of the latest generation of critics, to become provincial and retrospective. By the time she turned her face to the Continent once again, all sign of that cataclysm Wagner brought about had vanished, or else had been absorbed into the machine-like forces of the new Viennese school.

iv   Postscript on Bayreuth— Yesterday and Today

The enmities Wagner left in his wake in Germany and France (he scarcely regarded England a musical country!) rebounded on him heavily when he was put in the position of finding a permanent home for his 'total work of art'. For almost thirty years, he had allowed himself to be hounded from one country to another, always supremely confident of his powers, but unwittingly cutting off source after source as far as the revenue he needed to build the theatre of his dreams was concerned. His subsequent father-in-law, Liszt, encouraged him to erect such a building at Weimar, where he had ruled as music director. But the various revolutionary activities in which he had indulged at Dresden prevented Wagner from returning to Germany without incurring reprisals from the police. Similarly, the arrogant attitude he had taken up after *Tannhäuser's* failure in Paris, and during the Franco-Prussian War, rendered the composer even less persona grata in France. Baudelaire had tried to raise the subscription necessary to put up a suitable theatre, but had been met with stark opposition in all quarters. It seemed, therefore, as if the composer would never realize the ambition his work had increasingly marked out for him, and that he would die a disappointed man.

At this point, the unexpected happened, and King Ludwig II invited him from Switzerland—where he had been living amid a rising tide of debts—and offered him patronage on a scale even his egotistical dreams could not have predicted. With a royal pardon in his pocket, the composer accordingly made a triumphant return to Munich, where he supposed that the King's architect, Gottfried Semper, would build him the sort of opera house he demanded. Unfortunately, the men in control of Bavaria's modest treasury were not as burning to part with public money as had been the King himself; they had already had a taste of his profligacy. The upshot was that Wagner was compelled to retire once more to Switzerland, and think anew about the various schemes he could adopt. Meanwhile, Wullner conducted *Das Rheingold* at Munich without his presence or approval. There followed six further years of wrangling and intrigue, most of it designed to put pressure on the court to re-consider its decision not to lend him the money he needed. It was at this time, 1872 or thereabouts, that the composer became enamoured of the small Franconian town of Bayreuth, where the former Margrave's baroque theatre was still reputed to be in reasonable condition. Wagner decided to go and see for himself whether it could be converted into something close to his requirements. As it happened, he soon saw it would be much too slender an edifice to support the colossal *Ring des Nibelungen*, his masterwork and the one he most dearly wanted to see properly staged. On the other hand, he was much taken with the town itself, since it had attractive historic associations and was sufficiently removed from the major cities to constitute an ideal setting for an annual Festival. As may be imagined, the townspeople, who had no cause to bear the composer any ill-will, were only too happy to fall in with his project and began by making him a gift of some land.

At first, Wagner selected a meadow (as he had once thought of doing at Zürich) as the site for his theatre; but on account of the dangerous water level re-cast his request so as to take possession of the present ground high up on a hill just outside the town. Here, on the composer's fifty-ninth birthday, he laid the foundation stone of his Festspielhaus, inscribing on it the words:

> Hier schliess ich ein Geheimnis ein,
> Da ruh es viele hundert Jahr.
> So lange es verwahrt der Stein,
> Macht es der Welt sich offenbar.[1]

Once it became known that his intentions were serious, money began to trickle in. Musicians and rich music lovers responded to the calls made on their purses, and many of them were residents of the very same cities that Wagner had abused during his extensive travels abroad—for instance, London, Budapest and Vienna. Despite this encouraging start, there was still not enough in his coffers to move beyond the planning stage. At last, Ludwig came through with a massive sum, his final and most damning piece of

---

[1] In translation: 'Here is a secret that I hope will last a hundred years. So long as the stone remains, so long will it speak to the world.'

extravagance outside of the palatial mini-Versailles he was dreaming up for himself at, first of all Linderhof, then Herrenchiemsee.

Even when in the funds, Wagner had seemingly insuperable problems to solve over the shape his building would take. While finance had been confined to his imagination, he had proposed to himself several unique and costly features. Now that it was a reality, some of these had to be abandoned. True to his artist's inclinations, however, the composer chose to inflict his economies on the exterior of the building, and its seating, rather than on more fundamental objects. Hence, the long trudge up the tree-lined avenue leads, not to some gaudy, sculptured *palais Garnier*, but to a grim, red-brick structure reminiscent of a half-finished Town Hall somewhere in the Midlands. Likewise, the seats (except for a few rows of plush-covered armchairs at the rear) are hard, wooden contraptions capable of almost unbelievable discomfort. To sit on one of these throughout the whole of *Götterdämmerung* is a fate that cannot adequately be described; it must be experienced. Loyal Wagnerites continue to explain the Master's parsimony on grounds of acoustics, and it has to be admitted that the building is almost unrivalled in Europe from this angle. But I have also heard it said that Wagner's conceit was so mountainous that he believed only those who were experiencing acute unrest were capable of the attention his works demanded. Where he did lavish his money was on the stage—very large and steeply inclined so as to position singers in illusory ways—and on the immense orchestral pit, comprising an under-stage cavity masked by a leather cowl somewhat like that mounted over the dashboard of a giant car. This device was intended to direct the sound more accurately into the auditorium, and enable the singers to be heard without having to penetrate a barrier of instruments. To anyone who has heard the opening preludes to works like *Lohengrin* and *Das Rheingold*, the effectiveness of the first of these functions cannot be in doubt. The sound appears to float, almost as if by magic, to all parts of the theatre, its source being vaguely if at all located.

The première of *The Ring* in 1876 was accordingly an event that was not forgotten by those who attended it. They included a good many musicians from other parts of the world, and the news soon spread that an artistic venture of the greatest experimental importance had been launched. Such a venture naturally raised issues quite remote from the problems of theatrical design that had occupied so much of Wagner's attention during the actual building. Foremost among these secondary issues was possibly the acting/singing dilemma. Since the composer held uncompromising views about the equality of drama with music, it became necessary to find singers who could really act, and who were prepared to regard their respective roles as complementary and not as vehicles for stardom. On this issue, it might be mentioned, in Wagner's vindication, that Bayreuth still continues to be one of the very few opera-houses in the world where well-known singers are content to appear in minor roles. The composer's views on acting had been much influenced by his meeting with Wilhelmine Schröder-Devrient, whose performance as Leonora in *Fidelio* had moved him dramatically as much, if not more, than it had vocally. Her example usually lay at the back of his mind when he coached the singers for the opening of *The Ring*, and for *Parsifal*, the only one of the music-dramas to have been written *after* the construction of the new theatre. Costumes posed another difficulty, and so did scenery. On these questions, Wagner had originally thought on the lines of the Greek theatre, but as the element of German nationalism intensified he began to plan more in the direction of romantic naturalism. In practice, this term meant using scenic designers of the type of Böcklin and Feuerbach, whose sets were far more of an agglomeration of trees, rocks, castles, river-beds and the like than one would have supposed from reading the composer's early strictures on the subject. Later on, other designers, like Hoffmann, the Bruckner brothers and Emil Doepler all took a hand in the Bayreuth productions, though none of these seemed to arouse Wagner's unqualified enthusiasm. He still appeared to be looking for something like an amalgam of Greek and German principles at the time of his death in 1883.

From then on, the composer's widow, Cosima, was left with the unenviable task of clarifying her late husband's wishes on all matters connected with the music-dramas, and also with the job of running the Festival itself. Her approach to each of these responsibilities was firm to the point of being dogmatic. Many of the questions Wagner had failed to resolve, she regarded as settled. Being Liszt's daughter (as well as von Bülow's former wife) her musical understanding was not easy to impugn without exposing the impugner to ridicule. The remarkable powers of characterization she evidently possessed likewise convinced theatrically-minded 'doubters' that she was probably the best person to settle all disputes. An immensely forceful woman, Cosima lived to be over ninety, thus virtually determining the shape the Festival was to take right up to the end of the First World War and even after. In theory, her son Siegfried assumed control in 1907, but the shadow of Cosima in the background prevented anyone from pressing through any radical changes. Siegfried was unfortunately a particularly weak and conservative figure (Chausson was shocked at the reactionary attitudes he held when he paid a visit to Wahnfried, the Wagner family home, in the 1890's). He could not have

been more different, in this sense, from his father. His master had
been Humperdinck, who inspired him to write a glut of fairy-tale
operas that quickly fell into oblivion. As a producer, Siegfried
allowed his singers a good deal of latitude, more perhaps than was
wise. In the same fashion, he showed little appreciation of style
in stage-design, his sets being if anything even more cluttered than
those Cosima had demanded. He *did* have a good conductor in
Karl Muck, and was fortunate in attracting an even better one in
Toscanini—though the latter only put in an appearance right at
the end of Siegfried's reign. What he lacked was a first-rate authority to help him over his general production difficulties. In Cosima's
day, for example, each gesture on the stage had signified a particular emotional response, as in classical drama. Also, some effort
had been made to prevent the wilder pieces of stage machinery
from looking too ridiculous. The problems of doing this in dramas
involving underwater scenes in the Rhine, horses plunging into
the flames and the ultimate crumbling of Valhalla may be vividly
imagined. Perhaps these were what caused Siegfried to submit so
ingloriously to the demands of his singers.

When Siegfried himself died (only a short while after his
mother in 1930) the management of the Festival reverted yet
again to the mercies of a comparatively inexperienced young lady.
This time, she was English and not German, and hence even more
ill-versed in the tradition she was expected to uphold. Perhaps the
second part of this statement needs modifying, however, since
Winifred Williams (as she had then been) was brought out from
England by Klindworth and schooled rather rigorously in the
appreciation of Wagner. Her marriage to Siegfried was a trifle
unexpected, in view of the discrepancies in their ages, but she
provided him with two sons who would continue to bear the
Wagner name, which was possibly why Cosima appeared so ready
to give her blessing to the union. One suspects, in fact, that the
old lady was aware of her son's deficiencies, for she also privately
urged Muck to stick by him after her death, seeing to it that the
musical side would remain in capable hands. What she did not
foresee is Siegfried's comparatively early death, and Muck's
quick appeciation of the fact that this released him from the pledge
he had given. Winifred was accordingly left very much on her
own when it came to planning the 1931 Festival, except for the
jealous intrusions of her sisters-in-law, Eva and Daniela, who
were neither of them pleased at the prospect of seeing their
father's works suddenly dumped in the lap of a young foreigner.
But Winifred was no ordinary young girl, as she proved by her
astute handling of the various crises that sprung up to greet her
immediately on assuming office. Her first disaster had been

Muck's resignation (he *was* an old man, however, and perhaps should not be blamed for wishing to choose this moment to depart), yet she surmounted this by dividing the musical responsibility between Toscanini and Furtwängler, probably the two finest conductors of the century. Unfortunately, the former severed his new connection almost at once (originally over a trifling matter to do with Siegfried's memorial concert, but later on political grounds), while the latter found himself encumbered by the submerging of the orchestra, one of Wagner's holiest precepts. In the end, Winifred lost both her brilliant catches (Furtwängler returned during the 1939–45 War) and she was quickly back where she had started.

At this point, she gave further evidence of her resourcefulness by throwing herself on the mercies of Richard Strauss, who had once been a regular Bayreuth conductor, but had since been out of favour. In the meantime, of course, he had added greatly to his reputation as a composer, so that an invitation to return as the artistic director of an opera-house was not exactly an irrepressible ambition for which he had been longing. Out of a certain sympathy for Winifred's position, however, he acceded. (The very late obsession Strauss evidently had with *Tristan*—Solti and others having related that this was all the old man could talk about in his final years at Garmisch—suggests also that he always felt more drawn to Wagner's music than is sometimes alleged.) The next step was to ensure a first-class stage producer, and here Winifred again scored a success by engaging Heinz Tietjen, a man of decided visual gifts who was also an extremely competent musician. Of the two, Tietjen proved the more loyal, participating in all the Festivals that led up to the Second World War and turning his hand to everything from designing to dramatic coaching to conducting. Strauss dropped out as soon as he became unacceptable to the Nazis, and even before that his other commitments were too considerable to have permitted full-time attendance. At the end of the 'thirties, a variety of guest conductors appeared, including Victor de Sabata, on the face of it an unlikely Wagnerian. But it is still a point for debate whether or not an Italianate approach to Wagner pays dividends. (Wieland Wagner evidently thought the music-dramas could be made to sound too German, and he has remarked at length, in his book of *Entretiens avec Antoine Golea* (Belfond, 1966) how much he looked forward to the more luminous style of conductors like Alberto Erede, who was to conduct *Lohengrin* at Bayreuth, after Wieland's death, in 1968.) But what really broke new ground in the 1930's was Winifred's decision to invite Hitler to Bayreuth and so seek state subsidies from a government already becoming notorious for its persecution of Jewish artists. This was an astute move financially, but the effect it had on the singers and on the image of the Festival throughout the world was nothing short of disastrous.

Now that the Nazi era is closed, it is perhaps easier to see how deep Hitler's association with Wagner really went. He certainly admired works like *The Ring* and *Die Meistersinger*, and regarded Siegfried (the character, that is, and not the man—whose reaction to Fascism was fortunately never put to the test) as the embodiment of the German warrior-hero. It is *not* true that he ordered swastikas to be painted on the Gibichungs' shields, but unhappily it is very much the case that he and his party caused most of the best singers to quit Bayreuth, never to return... Among these may be counted Alexander Kipnis, Emanuel List and Herbert Janssen. Frieda Leider, the greatest Brunnhilde of the period, was more divided in her attitudes. She took the music-dramas seriously as dramas, and received much of her coaching from outsiders like Professor Golther. So she was perhaps less involved in the internal unrest that permeated the theatre. Nevertheless, when her own husband, the Jewish Rudolph Deman, came under suspicion from the Nazis, she had no option but to withdraw. That was in 1938, a rather late date to have made so crucial a decision. Flagstad, contrary to what is generally believed, sang very few times at Bayreuth, the engagements she accepted causing her to feel she might be compromising herself with British and American managements. Hence the mixed feelings aroused by her Covent Garden appearances in 1948. Hers and Leider's partner, the redoubtable Lauritz Melchior, *did* contract over a longish period, but turned his back on the whole enterprise once he became aware of what was happening. Again, in opposition to what one has often heard said, performances went on throughout the war, though with a limited repertoire. Furtwängler directed *Die Meistersinger* in 1943 and 1944, for example, and the present writer recalls him being booed in London when he gave the *Prelude und Leibestod* from *Tristan* with the Philharmonic Orchestra in 1947. It was not until after the Armistice that American troops occupied the Festspielhaus, committing an act of vandalism in German eyes, though the principles underlying their forms of entertainment could hardly have been more loathsome than those which had informed the entire Bayreuth venture in the immediate pre-war years.[1]

The style of production favoured in the 1930's veered towards the monumental, as may be imagined. Tietjen dispensed with

---

[1] For a detailed account of the performances and casts throughout the whole period 1876 to 1965, see Geoffrey Skelton's illuminating study, *Wagner at Bayreuth* (Barrie & Rockliff, 1965).

many of the trappings of 'romantic naturalism' only to replace them with sets that looked almost Roman in their vulgarity and grandiosity. His choruses grew to a gigantic size, and were obviously intended to impress. Probably the closing scene of *Götterdämmerung* under his supervision resembled one of D. W. Griffiths's film sets more than it did anything Wagner might have envisaged. But Winifred also acquired a more avant-garde producer and designer in the person of Emil Preetorius, a man of far more than average far-sightedness. The idea of depending on light and positioning instead of heavy draperies was one that had been advanced early in the century by Adolphe Appia, a brilliant Swiss dismissed by Cosima as 'revisionist'. Now that the climate was more favourable to experiment, Appia's ideas were raised again in a different form. Preetorius, for instance, designed quite bare and stark sets that looked forward to Wieland Wagner as well as backward to Appia. His design for *Die Walküre* Act III (1933) shows all the modern tendency towards de-localization, if it does not actually suggest a symbolic approach to the drama. Preetorius's book *Bild und Vision* was unfortunately not published until 1949, only two years before the grandsons began the Festival's postwar run. But this influence was felt throughout the earlier period, never displacing the traditional line of thought but hovering in the background as a possible new approach. It is inconceivable that Wieland Wagner, especially, was not very much indebted to him in arriving at his own revolutionary strategies. Once the War was over, of course, Winifred Wagner was relieved of her position as administrator and made to face a tribunal. It took six years of negotiating to get the Festival started once more, and then only by permitting the grandsons (who had not been old enough to have taken part in any of the pre-war productions) to exercise complete control.

For the third time, then, the family firm (if one may so describe it) gravitated into the hands of youth. This time, it expressed itself most forcibly through the presence of Wieland, the senior of the two brothers. (A sister, Friedelinde, had gone to the United States, but has since returned to Europe and lectured on the music-dramas both at Bayreuth and elsewhere.) Wieland, on his own admission, never had a great deal of musical training, but as all the world knows inherited some measure of his grandfather's genius for the theatre. The reforms he introduced were accordingly mainly theatrical, although his liberalism has also prevented the German character of the Festival from being further intensified; so that it has more than ever, in the past two decades, assumed the shape of an international event. From his first production of *Parsifal* in 1951, it became clear that in Wieland Bayreuth had at last found a mentor worthy of restoring the drama to its rightful standing. The astonishing fact is that he achieved this feat by going to the extremes of anti-naturalism. At first, this must have seemed the wrong policy to adopt, in view of the fact that it had been the decline of naturalism that had led to the singers' excesses of the 1930's. But no one had reckoned with Wieland's uncanny power of extracting from the music-dramas psychological symbols of a kind that were familiar to Germans in the works of Freud and Jung (and perhaps also in the novels of Mann, Kafka and Hesse) but had not previously been much associated with Wagner. Using the minimum of scenery, Wieland emphasized the role of a 'light-organ' and avoided anything that looked too literal a personification of the object concerned, whether it were sword, dragon or horse. His sets were considered dark (even front-row stall ticket holders had their work cut out to see what was going on) and gloomy; but this may again have reflected the attempt he made to see his grandfather's work through the eyes of those psychologists and psycho-analysts who had been enquiring, ever since Hitler's demise, into the sources of the German character.[1]

Those who saw for themselves Wieland Wagner's innovations will generally admit that much, if not all, of what he did made sense. The introduction of ambiguous sculptural forms led audiences to project, as they would in response to a series of Rorschach blots, the inner meanings they attached to certain scenes. Some of these forms were vaguely sexual or anatomical (the Mime's cave scene in the 1965 *Siegfried*, for example, had the shape of a human brain, even down to the contours of the cerebral cortex), others were so explicit that their meaning could scarcely have been misinterpreted. The towers in *Tristan*, for instance, were raised to phallic proportions, and the unimportance of geography stressed by removing all clues to country or location. What this clearly implied was that the scenery should help support the notion of guilt and repression upon which the drama was based. The empty disc-shaped stage for the love-scenes again concentrated the spectator's mind on the single emotion being dealt with. Sometimes this anti-illusionist approach went too far, as perhaps in the scene in Hunding's hut in *Die Walküre*, in which audiences saw nothing either of the sword or the door that finally swings back to let in the day. Wieland Wagner, then, made certain miscalculations, or else carried his principle of 'psychologism' too far. Sir Victor Gollancz

---

[1] Wieland had no objection to using the exegeses provided by these men as programme notes for his productions. Jungians like Dr Anton Orel (also known as a Christian believer) were often chosen for this honour, and the 1966 programmes which I have in my hand contain long and baffling analyses by Dr Gerhard Kohl and Dr Karl Worner.

has recounted, inimitably, the various sins of omission of which Wieland seemed either unaware or unrepentant.[1] The non-arrival of Siegfried and Gutrune at the end of Act II of *Götterdämmerung*; the 'descent' rather than 'ascent' into Valhalla; the unwillingness to render visible the scene in which Wotan's spear is shattered by a blow from Siegfried's sword—these are just a few of the charges brought by Sir Victor in his book, and it would be easy enough to point to others that would have angered staunch Wagnerians of the old school, such as Hans Pfitzner. It is symptomatic, perhaps, that Wieland's conductor, Hans Knappertsbusch, finally gave up working with him out of a lack of sympathy for his ideas. By contrast, Wolfgang Wagner's productions (and he *did* produce most of the operas before he became administrator and sole guardian of Bayreuth) have always struck audiences as more traditional. Though Wieland died in 1966, therefore, it was his bold experimentalism that gave a fresh twist to his grandfather's achievements, keeping them alive at a time when they were closely threatened with extinction.

The question that has posed itself most insistently over the past few years is therefore that of what is going to happen to Bayreuth now that another change of leadership has taken place. Some critics have not hesitated to predict a flashback to the old régime, and the 1968 productions that I saw of Wolfgang's certainly had all the appearance of realism once more. (One even saw the Swan in *Lohengrin* and the brightness of lighting and costumes made one think of Salzburg or Vienna, an almost too dreadful heresy to mention!) More significant still was the chilly reception accorded to East German performers (also one or two of the new Czechs recently imported), implying an additional return to the nationalism of pre-war years. But it is only fair to qualify this assumption by saying that it very likely reflected the feelings of a small group who had always resented Wieland's liberal, interbreeding of German with foreign talent. As far as one can judge, box-office receipts have not fallen (it still remains difficult to get tickets for Bayreuth from the day the booking office opens onwards), and rumours of a family feud over policy have so far not been confirmed to the extent of one suggestion—that the Festspielhaus be put up for sale, and run by another operatic company! No doubt some time will have to elapse before we can see clearly where the next move is coming from. The appointment of Pierre Boulez to conduct *Parsifal* in 1967 and 1968 (a suggestion that emanated originally

---

[1] See his book *The Ring at Bayreuth* (Gollancz, 1965), which arose out of a series of articles for *The Observer*. The book contains an interview with Wieland in which the case for the defence is also stated.

from Wieland Wagner) has undoubtedly caused a great stir of interest. M. Boulez is known to have stinging views on opera generally, and has frequently stated his position that all but Mozart, Debussy and Berg would be suspect if he were in charge of the repertoire. The fact that he has agreed to conduct Wagner may mean he has perceived new merits in this composer (though he was always ready to admit to a preference for *Parsifal*, like most Frenchmen). In an interesting article on the similarities between Boulez and Wagner, John Greenlagh has recently disclaimed any likelihood that the former will in some way 'resurrect' the latter; preferring to argue that a new collaborator for Boulez (Genet, perhaps, or Günter Grass?) would result in a new kind of opera.[1]

Looked at from a purely British angle, it is noticeable that, despite the anti-foreign brigade at Bayreuth, more and more singers are being asked to go out from Covent Garden or Sadler's Wells and participate in the annual Festival there. That they are not being invited for minor roles, but for some of the chief parts the music-dramas have to offer, is quite a new and exciting development. Gwyneth Jones has, for example, sung both Sieglinde and Eva with considerable success; while Amy Shuard replaced Marie Collier last year as Kundry in what seemed a pointed gesture of interest. Whether British singers are really ready for this kind of task is more problematic. It is evident that a generation of major Bayreuth singers is nearing the end of its reign, in that many who have sung there for years have recently showed signs of wanting to retire.[2] Wolfgang Windgassen has probably sung his last *Tristan* at Bayreuth, without there being any obvious successor in sight. (Jess Thomas and Jean Cox have been mentioned as possible great 'heldentenors' of the future, though it will take a long time for either to convince discriminating members of the public that they can fulfil what will be demanded of them.) Similarly, Martha Modl and Astrid Varnay may soon be expected to retire, leaving the remarkable Nilsson even more completely in possession of the field as far as the parts of Brunnhilde and Isolde are concerned. Here Ludmilla Dvorakova impressed large sections of the audience in 1966, 1967 and 1968, though one imagined she would be too diminutive in stature to make a convincing heroine for the tetralogy. As things stand, therefore, a musical re-adjustment might precede any further changes in stagecraft and production, and this could

---

[1] See 'Boulez 1969 and Wagner 1850' by John Greenlagh in *Music & Musicians*, May, 1969, Vol. XVII, No. 9, pp. 30–1.

[2] For a good recent estimate of the quality of singing shown by this generation, see *The New Bayreuth* by Penelope Turing (Neville Spearman, 1969). This book also paints a charming picture of Bayreuth itself, and would constitute an admirable handbook for the visitor.

take any imaginable direction. It would be pleasant—if a trifle optimistic—to believe that the next step needed to keep this nonagenarian patient alive and kicking would be a stiff injection of singers from the country that Germans once described as 'das land ohne musik'.

Romanticism
in Decline

v   Strauss, Hofmannsthal
    and the Opera Stage

Strauss has been presented to us in so many guises that even at this late stage in the history of music his place is regarded with some uncertainty. It is not that anyone disputes his right to a place. That is something even his detractors admit he earned by the sheer panache of his youthful tone-poems, surpassing those of both Liszt and Saint-Saëns in orchestral virtuosity, and by the evocativeness that continues to be aroused by every good performance of *Der Rosenkavalier* and *Arabella*. What still causes anxiety, and perhaps even dismay, is the extent to which Strauss lagged behind his master Wagner in his appreciation of the functions of opera, and how far he may in the end have to be considered an anachronistic composer. For someone who poured out a stream of operatic successes throughout the first half of the twentieth century, the composer has already assumed an odd kind of mental corpulence faintly reminiscent of Meyerbeer. Put beside his juniors, like Alban Berg and Kurt Weill, he seems almost antediluvian. Indeed, one cannot help seeing the point of view of those who consider his operas a disappointing series of regressions, each one coming to seem more old-fashioned than the last.

Naturally, we should beware of supposing that the new and the revolutionary are the necessary stigmata of genius. But equally there is something peculiar about a composer who evidently wanted to retreat further and further away from the ideals of his period. Gervase Hughes has, I suppose, expressed the typical reaction to Strauss when he wrote:

> . . . this one time enfant terrible, as things turned out, was the last great composer to fly the flag of nineteenth

century romanticism in an age of realism, atonality, and
pseudo-jazz—and he flew it to the end.[1]

A number of substantial biographies of the composer that have
appeared recently have proposed a half-hearted challenge to this
reaction in that they have attempted to show more clearly the
concealed innovations contained in the later works. But most
critics have been prepared to laugh with Lord Berners when he
called one of his satirical piano pieces 'Strauss, Strauss et Strauss'
—seeing bourgeois taste as having proceeded from Johann to
Richard to Oscar. We are also becoming over-familiar with the
jibe (recently repeated by that most punitive of Strauss baiters,
Igor Stravinsky) which runs: 'If Strauss, then Johann; if Richard,
then Wagner.' Presumably, each of these little digs is intended to
point up the composer's gradual capitulation to middle-class
ideals, and his ultimate musical, if not technical, deterioration.
Possibly Strauss's character (revealed to us by the conductors and
singers with whom he worked) has contributed much to the disrepute in which his music is sometimes held. Knappertsbusch, for
example, who conducted his operas regularly between the wars,
referred to him as 'a pig' whose only extra-musical interests lay in
gambling and salacious conversation. Singers like Lotte Lehmann
and Elizabeth Schumann, on the other hand, have given us a
portrait not lacking in modesty and charm, but one bleakly overshadowed by the figure of the composer's shrewish wife, Pauline.

There can hardly be any doubt (especially in view of the savage
political indictments made against him recently by Georg Marek)[2]
that Strauss was a much less heroic man than the audacities of
Don Juan and *Ein Heldenleben* might imply. Not only did he lack
that all-consuming passion for the arts that rendered Wagner such
a powerful object of curiosity (and redeemed him from some of his
more blatantly indulgent sins), but there lay deeply embedded in
his character elements of that beer-loving laxity so much associated
with his native city of Munich. On one plane, Strauss's life may be
construed as 'a tale of two cities'—the other being Vienna—in that
all he did was to exchange one, typically German, form of sensuality for another, typically Austrian, version of the same vice. To
say, however, as Cecil Gray once did, that whereas Wagner only
seduced the Muse, Strauss actually raped her, is to do a considerable

---

[1] See *The Pan Book of Great Composers* (Pan Books, London, 1964).
[2] These are contained in the writer's book, *Richard Strauss: the life
of a non-hero* (Gollancz, 1968), but they need to be offset by evidence
for the defence, such as is provided in Peter Heyworth's charitable study,
'The Rise & Fall of Richard Strauss' (*Encounter*, August, 1968,
Vol. XXXI, No. 2, pp. 49–53).

injustice to both composers. Gray's argument that *Der Rosen-kavalier* is no *Figaro* (even though the composer was temporarily bemused into thinking it the equivalent) hardly needs refuting. Either it is more of a compliment than it was intended to be, or Strauss had every right to retract without loss of honour. In any case, there is evidence that Mozart's life had its crude episodes. What is perhaps more to the point is that these episodes did not succeed in obscuring the vital dramatic genius which revealed itself in the earlier composer's manipulation of his characters; whereas in Strauss's case one is never quite sure that he does not have to depend entirely on his musical talents to see him through.

This brings us to the heart of the dilemma, since the extent to which a composer has to rely on the advice of his librettist is one measure of deficiencies. An averagely good librettist, like da Ponte, can still inspire Mozart ('filthy Mozart', as Kingsley Amis once called him) to create characters of Shakespearian depth and subtlety, because he has far higher than average powers of musico-dramatic delineation. Strauss, with a distinctly superior librettist in the person of the formidable Hofmannsthal, was placed in the position of having to have the dramatic implications of a scene spelled out for him, with results that were not invariably compelling. Was this because he was pressed into too narrowly theatrical conception of his role, or was he merely unable to write the sort of music that would give an extra dimension to things? This is a singularly difficult question to answer. Almost all critics have conceded that Strauss and Hofmannsthal ran into frequent disagreements. Indeed, ever since the publication of the *Briefwechsel Hugo von Hofmannsthal* (edited by Franz and Alice Strauss) in 1952, and its English translation issued by Collins in 1961, the evidence of their quarrels is plain for all to see, But the interpretations put upon these continue to vary in an astonishing degree. For many years before the publication of the correspondence, and in certain quarters afterwards, it was the fashion to cast Strauss as the conservative partner, obtuse in his appreciation of the deeper levels of characterization and determined in his desire to do down drama in the name of his brilliant and succulent music. Lately, however, the other side of the case has been presented, and Strauss revealed to us as the long-suffering victim of a literary conspiracy. William Mann, in his authoritative work, *Richard Strauss: a critical study of the operas*, has been notable for giving us the composer's angle on his collaborators and for revealing and even asserting the superior wisdom he frequently displayed over theatrical matters.[1]

---

[1] For the precise references, see the author's book, published by Cassell in 1964, especially Chapters IV to XI.

Hofmannsthal, on this count, is made to seem something much less than the dramatic genius he was previously taken for.

A quotation from Mr Mann's essay on *Elektra* will suffice to pinpoint the objections he lodges:

> Strauss, in his early forties already Germany's outstanding progressive composer, was destined to be influenced for the rest of his life by his work with Hofmannsthal—influenced, it may be argued, detrimentally: since Hofmannsthal dragged Strauss away from the vanguard of influential musical thought towards a product less provocative and, not only less admired, but curiously less popular.

To assess the truth of these allegations, it is essential to understand something of the respective backgrounds of both musician and writer. Strauss's early triumph with *Salome* was a 'succès de scandale' for 1905. Oscar Wilde's obscene play aroused the censor in every city in which the opera was first performed—Dresden, Berlin, Vienna, New York and London. What it did for Strauss, therefore, was to establish him as an extreme artist, the sort of revolutionary figure who might well go on to convert typical German expressionist dramas, like those of Buchner and Wedekind, into operatic masterpieces. This task, as it transpired, fell to Alban Berg to fulfil. Hofmannsthal, on the other hand, was a poet of dream-like classical cast, whose aristocratic connections (his family had been silk-merchants ennobled by Franz I as far back as Biedermeier times) seemed remote from the earthy, blood-ridden world from which Strauss was confidently expected to choose his next text. Well, *Elektra* turned out to be as blood-ridden as any arriviste could have desired; but the significant fact many overlooked was that it had been based, ultimately, on a Greek and not a German play. Later, Hofmannsthal made it clearer still that his interests lay in the past and not the present, and that he was quite the opposite of seditious. Ilse Barea, in her book on 'Vienna' (Secker & Warburg, 1966), draws a delicate sketch of the young Hugo as an anti-modernist who failed to fit in with his contemporaries, the socially-minded Schnitzler and Hermann Bahr, and who lived very much in poetic isolation.

Elektra (1909) was, of course, based on a German-language version of the Sophocles play, and Hofmannsthal did not write it specifically as the libretto of Strauss's opera. He had first put it on the stage as a kind of re-creation, in purely dramatic terms, of the Greek tragedy. This was in 1903, while Strauss was working on *Salome* and it was the composer's infatuation with Hofmannsthal's play, which he chanced to see in 1906, that led him to initiate the long collaboration. As a matter of fact, the two men were not unknown to one another; they had met at the turn of the century and even toyed, unconvincingly, with the idea of doing a ballet together. It had been Strauss who had let this project fall through, but equally it was the composer who now insisted on a joint operatic concoction. The more he thought about it, however, the more Strauss felt that perhaps he had been too hasty; that to follow *Salome* he should look around for a more charming subject. Indeed, Mozart had begun to exert some fascination for him, and it remains probable that it was he and not Hofmannsthal who had the stronger leaning towards the past at the precise moment when they came together. Still, they went through with *Elektra*, despite all doubts, and most critics regard it as not only the first but one of the best of their enterprises. However much Strauss was beginning to admire the early Viennese masters in his private tastes, there are few signs of their influence in the music of this lurid opera. Polytonality and even atonality appear for long stretches as the dominant modes, with lyrical episodes in conventional keys intervening to provide the heavy, romantic sensuality sometimes needed. Wagner is clearly the chief source of musical inspiration in the work, as he had been in *Salome*, since it is full of the typically Wagnerian habit of half-resolution, of building up tension by dissonance only to relieve it by further dissonance. Strauss's modernism, then, was still much to the fore.

It is a different story entirely with the next opera upon which the two men exercised their talents. This was the immortal *Der Rosenkavalier* (1911), as rococo a work—or so it seemed at the time—as any by the eighteenth-century composers. That Strauss himself wanted it to sound rococo is proved by his damaging remark that at last he had written an opera like Mozart's. But *Der Rosenkavalier* is no more all charm and sentimentality than *Figaro*, and it contains elements that shocked pre-First World War audiences as much as some of Beaumarchais's ideas must have shocked the rulers of the principalities in Mozart's day. The prelude, for example, enacts in musical terms the scene just prior to the one that confronts us as the curtains draw apart—a scene in which the Marschallin and her lover, Octavian, are rising from a double-bed in which they have spent the night. As Lotte Lehmann frankly put it:

> . . . a riotous prelude describes with truly remarkable
> lack of reticence the pleasures of a night of love . . . [1]

Apparently this was not how Hofmannsthal had wanted it; though he was not so prudish as to suggest a cut. As it transpired, the

[1] See *Singing with Richard Strauss* (Hamish Hamilton, 1964), p. 111.

censor did the job for him, a more decorous version having to be presented for the first productions. Berlin, hardly famed for its puritanism, even retained this tame beginning up until 1924, only a few years before Kurt Weill and Bert Brecht were dominating the scene. The intriguing feature that marks off *Der Rosenkavalier* from the former Strauss-Hofmannsthal venture was Strauss's decision to take it into his own hands to write a good deal of the music before Hofmannsthal was ready with the libretto. This was a bad habit into which he constantly relapsed during most of their later works. Undoubtedly it was one factor in accounting for the hurtful, at times abusive, tone of the latter's correspondence. He was afraid Strauss would commit him to scenes he had no wish to write, or would 'describe' a character musically before that character had properly taken shape in the dramatist's head.

This was invariably what happened to some degree. Yet it is not sufficient of an indictment to convict Strauss of having ill-served his librettist; neither is it sufficient of an excuse to exempt the composer from any failings he may have been responsible for. Both artists were occasionally to blame. The nineteenth-century waltzes Strauss intruded into *Rosenkavalier* were his own idea; all that Hofmannsthal had asked for was 'an old-fashioned Viennese waltz, sweet and yet saucy', presumably having in mind something like the divertimenti played by serenade ensembles during Maria Theresa's time. He must have been stunned to hear how close the finished products came to those strident Ländler so beloved of Franz Joseph and his family. Were they a deliberate parody on Strauss's part, or merely an expression of natural kinship? Was it his intention to tease Hofmannsthal, or merely to slip a trump-card up his sleeve at the box-office? Probably all these motives would have been regarded as equally discreditable by the composer's humourless collaborator, who very likely viewed the whole opera as a banal transmogrification. It continues to be questionable how far such vivid intrusions add to, or detract from, the listener's enjoyment. Similarly, the 'chimes' of the prelude and Act III can be viewed as vulgar or effective according to one's taste. Baron Ochs's music is unarguably vulgar; but then it was meant to be. The question there is whether some singers have not rendered it doubly so in virtue of their exaggerated histrionics. What stands everlastingly to the credit of Strauss as a musical dramatist is his handling of the Marschallin's character, which surely becomes more touchingly resigned, more truly aristocratic even, than Hofmannsthal would otherwise have allowed it to be. The conclusion we must draw, therefore, is that whereas Strauss unquestionably possessed a common streak—a Meyerbeer-like power of winning over the mass—he also harboured a true dramatic

flair that occasionally resulted in his being able to add a whole new
dimension to a character or scene.[1]

Four more operas were written by these ill-matched partners—
in many ways even more unalike than Gilbert and Sullivan—and
they all exhibit in varying degrees the paradoxes to which we have
pointed. *Der Rosenkavalier* became a gigantic success, the greatest
Strauss ever had. Hence, he should have shown the utmost care
over his next opera, so as to avoid disappointing his public. Instead,
he rushed to Hofmannsthal in search of another and immediate
libretto; so that those who are inclined to see *Ariadne auf Naxos*
(1916) as the beginning of the end should not be too quick to lay
all the blame on the poor poet. Yet again, there was a misunderstanding on both sides. Hofmannsthal began by paying very little
attention to *Ariadne*, working on the assumption that it would
constitute a kind of intermezzo between *Der Rosenkavalier* and the
next *large* undertaking he had in mind, which was a version of the
fairy-tale, *Die Frau ohne Schatten*. Unfortunately, however, his
libretto turned out to be a complex affair, involving set tableaux,
recitativo secco, arias with variations and all the other machinery
of the old opera that Wagner, and following him, Strauss had tried
to depart from. The upshot was that the composer was given a
number of more or less independent (and not easily reconcilable)
scenes to set to music. The over-long instrumental prologue became
a tiresome opera seria business; the first Act, involving the figure
of the Komponist, a successful piece of realism, even though it
harked back to an earlier period; the commedia dell' arte scenes
with Zerbinetta marvellously adroit comedy showing how brilliantly
Strauss could still write for both voice and orchestra; and the
ending a slightly glutinous love-duet more reminiscent of Puccini
than Wagner. That it all added up to a fairly ravishing evening out
—especially if sung by a Lehmann or a Jurinac as the Komponist
and a Selma Kurtz as Zerbinetta—was not denied. And even today,
there is no opera calculated to give more pleasure to the opulently-
clad audiences of the summer music festivals at Salzburg and
Munich. Possibly Strauss would have produced something more
controversial and progressive had he jettisoned Hofmannsthal for
d'Annunzio, as seemed a real possibility at one point during the
war years. But who will be brave enough to say he regrets *Ariadne*
was written?

When we reach *Die Frau ohne Schatten* (1919), on the other

---

[1] It is perhaps worth observing, too, that Strauss alone shaped most of
Act III of the opera, in which the exquisite Trio, the Marschallin's
heart-breaking farewell to Octavian, and the Negro page's discovery of
the handkerchief—all major dramatic moments—take place.

hand, there would doubtless be legions who would decline to shed a tear over its loss. I doubt if this is because the music is any worse than that of the previous operas—on the contrary, Strauss addicts claim that it represents him at his most consummate—but would prefer to concede that the plot is too complex and the difficulties of staging too insurmountable.[1] To begin with, it is an exceptionally long opera, and one is surprised to learn that it was selected to launch the re-built National Theatre at Munich, an event that lost most of its glamour by coinciding with the Kennedy assassination. A fable that exists astride a number of different planes—a realistic, peasant plane inhabited by Barak, the Dyer, and his wife, and a symbolic, courtly plane occupied by the Emperor and Empress are merely the main ones—its moral is that marriage without children tends to be materialistic and that it is only in the act of giving birth that one bridges the gulf between world and spirit. If, therefore, we are inclined to label *Der Rosenkavalier* as Strauss's *Figaro*, the temptation imposes itself to consider *Die Frau ohne Schatten* as his *Magic Flute*. Actually, the comparison is not just a slick one, since Hofmannsthal loaded his story with almost as much abstruse allegory and folk-lore as Schikaneder had done more than a century earlier. This time Strauss was obliged to show a saintly degree of patience in waiting for his partner to develop the story to its ridiculous pitch of complexity. That he could not stick out his ordeal is proved by the side-tracking work he put in on *Intermezzo* to Hermann Bahr's libretto. In the outcome, it was obvious that *Die Frau* would have to wait until after the war for its première but when this came about it received a glittering performance under Schalk at the Vienna Staatsoper.

The fact that the work did not go on to repeat its success elsewhere must be attributed to its unprecedented difficulties of staging. The 1932 Salzburg performance, for instance, almost ended in disaster as a result of trying to get it on to the stage of the little Festspielhaus (the new Gross Festspielhaus, with its fantastically wide stage, was not of course erected until after the Second World War). A similar situation occurred at other opera houses more used to dealing with the baroque or Mozartian repertory. In fact, *Die Frau* is, in contradiction to what has just been said, the most Wagnerian of Strauss's operas when it comes to size and musico-dramatic aim. Its music is at times indescribably beautiful, as in the cavernous scenes of the last Act, where the dark instrumental colours of the bassoon and lower brass blend ecstatically with high violin tremolos and the soaring timbres of the voices.

[1] Norman del Mar, in Volume II of his biography of Strauss (Barrie & Rockliff, 1969) is more ambivalent about the music of *Die Frau* than most. He concedes that much of it is banal.

It is well known that Strauss developed a 'love-affair' with the
soprano voice (Pauline had been an operatic soprano before their
marriage) and tended to give all his best parts to it. *Der Rosenkavalier*, for instance, contains two incredibly difficult but rewarding soprano parts. On the other side of the coin, most of the male
roles are allotted, as in this opera and *Die Frau*, to a bass or baritone.
Whether this preference has been partly responsible for gaining
the composer his reputation for 'lushness' is another moot point.
But the orchestration in *Die Frau*, even more than in any other of
the operas, proclaims Strauss's title to being the master craftsman
of his age. As in *Don Quixote* and the other symphonic poems, the
orchestra constantly performs miracles of ingenuity. The reason he
is still treated with suspicion in some quarters is that such a high
level of ingenuity is apt to leave the listener staggered and perhaps
ultimately bored. For one can no more be continuously miraculous
than one can be continuously simple or functional. There has to
be variety of effect. After listening to a work like *Die Frau* one can
appreciate Stravinsky's complaint about the 'endless six-four
chords'. Even he, however, admitted after hearing Strauss conduct
a rehearsal of *The Legend of Joseph* that 'his ears and musicianship
were impregnable'. The Russian's sympathies in the matter of
words and music lay very much with Hofmannsthal, partly out of
friendship and partly out of a detestation of that form of German
opera which he said gave him 'the green horrors', for which he held
Strauss responsible. Presumably, he was thinking more of works
like *Salome* and *Elektra*.

The modern element in *Die Frau ohne Schatten* is hardly of this
order, and does not seem too far removed from the music for *Le
Rossignol*—or that part of it that Stravinsky himself classed as
'opera-pageant-ballet'. Up to this point in his development, therefore, it was still just about possible to view Strauss as a composer of
further avant-garde possibilities. The suggestions which Hofmannsthal proposed in 1923 for an opera based on *Die Ägyptische
Helena* (it is noticeable that the initiative came from him and not
Strauss from this stage on, reversing the earlier trend) were really
what put paid to any more storming of the barricades. For here
was a truly classical subject—what could be more so than the
story of Helen of Troy—and one that would inevitably give rise to
a good deal of old-fashioned paraphernalia. Indeed, Strauss himself added the idea that ballets might be introduced, and that an
element of lightness be maintained. Actually, he was better
acquainted with Offenbach's *La Belle Hélène* (a comic skit on the
deeds of Paris and Menelaus) than with the original sources of the
myth, and apparently expected Hofmannsthal to provide him with
plentiful opportunities for witty and mildly satirical dialogue. He

even wanted this presented in spoken form, like the old Singspiel, though in the end it was replaced by a rather drab kind of speech-song, written as if it were Strauss's object merely to lift the work that necessary inch or two above the pedestrian. Also, this opera was conceived in a curiously artificial way as a vehicle for the soprano, Maria Jeritza, who as it happened demanded too high a fee. That Hofmannsthal was just as subservient in his attitude to personalities as Strauss is proved by the fact that he wrote out the names of the cast himself and was deeply incensed when Jeritza decided to withdraw. Strauss's advocacy of Elisabeth Rethberg (who ultimately created the part at the Dresden première in 1928) did little to calm his feelings, and one cannot help sympathizing with the composer, who at least knew something of the difficulties of casting operatic parts and was far more tactful in his approach to singers than most members of his profession. Eventually, *Die Ägyptische Helena* was sung all over the world, but it contains some of Strauss's weakest music and a libretto that W. J. Henderson did not scruple to describe as 'puerile and futile'.

If the collaboration between musician and poet had ended there, it would indeed have been a most unfortunate conclusion. Luckily, one more try was allowed them in *Arabella*, which had its first performance in 1933. The events leading up to this production were on the whole extremely promising and harmonious. The scenario was a novel called *Lucidor* which Hofmannsthal had written as far back as 1910, and it was turned with very little effort into an excellent, if somewhat facile, libretto. Both artists liked the work and both wrote frank, if not always sensible, letters about how it should be produced. The story has a novellette air about it that sharply distinguishes it from any of the pair's previous efforts. It concerns the penury of a certain Count Waldner, who is forced to live off credit at a Viennese hotel (the period is around 1860) and who becomes saddled with the task of marrying off his daughter Arabella to a landowner named Mandryka. The situation is complicated by the presence of a younger daughter, Zdenka, who develops into a rival with a lesser chance of success. A hackneyed scene of mistaken identity threatens to turn the whole thing into tragedy; but in the end the comic and romantic elements triumph. Not surprisingly, then, *Arabella* is probably the most fetching of all the Strauss operas to the man in the street. A fair amount of friendly banter went on between the creators of the work before a clear decision on the treatment accorded to the story was reached, Strauss taking an unexpectedly tough line on characterization and Hofmannsthal insisting on his right to insert wittier, more incisive dialogue. The finished script represented the best each man could do, but was unfortunately never vetted by Hofmannsthal, who

died of a stroke, following the news of his son's suicide, on July
15th, 1929. Thus Strauss was left to cope with all the problems of
casting and planning that had caused so much confusion in the
previous opera.

The reaction to *Arabella*—not excessively favourable at first—
eventually grew into something close to deep affection on the
public's part. The slowness of response can be explained in several
ways. First of all, it must be admitted that the opera requires to be
verbally understood in order to make its full effect. Thus non-
German speakers were placed at a distinct disadvantage, failing to
appreciate the numerous shafts of local humour contained in the
work. Some of these even take in special dialects, making the opera
more 'echt-Viennese' than any in the repertory. This is one case,
then, where the claims of opera critics like Harold Rosenthal to
have operas sung in a language intelligible to the audience carry a
great deal of conviction. Furthermore, despite the luscious music
in which the work abounds, it remains an opera that can be, and
nowadays usually is, enhanced by a spectacular or lavish production. Those who have seen the sumptuous sets designed by
Rudolf Hartmann for this work at Munich, with Lisa della Casa
displaying ravishing costumes as Arabella, will scarcely have
grumbled at the price of a ticket. Like *Der Rosenkavalier*—with
which many critics are inclined to compare it—*Arabella* pulls out
all the stops and is quite probably the last really grand, tuneful
opera to have been written. It requires singing of a tremendously
high order, as do all the Strauss operas, hence one cannot see it
being mounted as often as, say, *Carmen* or *La Traviata*. But it was
a wonderful note on which to have ended a great operatic partnership, and, along with the *Four Last Songs*, remains the best reminder of how unflawed was the composer's gift for melody, even
in old age. No doubt, ultra-modernists will continue to look on
Strauss as the rich man's Franz Lehár, using *Arabella* as their chief
weapon. But what composer of nearly seventy, except perhaps
Verdi, has ever poured out a comparable elixir of sound?

Now that we have reached the end of the Strauss–Hofmannsthal
story, how can we best sum up the present problems that arise out
of their operas as a whole? I believe one serious dilemma still
resides in the production factor, to which we have so many times
alluded. This dilemma can be stated in two ways. Firstly, why has
there been no serious attempt to produce Strauss's works as if they
were post-Wagnerian music dramas? And secondly, is it possible
that a means of production can be found for them that would con-
fer on them a wider significance than they presently enjoy? On the
first count, it must be said that Strauss has suffered more than
Wagner ever did from being a product of the 'age of the producer'.

Wagner, after all, produced his own works; or else delegated the task to someone in whom he had implicit trust. The entire Bayreuth venture—from 1876 to the present—has remained in family hands. Strauss, on the contrary, has been the sacrificial lamb on the altar of every new theatrical religion from Max Reinhardt's expressionism to the unabashed egoism of today.[1] In a way, the attempts he made to see everything through a 'period lens' (e.g. the eighteenth century through nineteenth-century eyes in *Der Rosenkavalier* and the age of baroque and rococo through a variety of lenses in *Ariadne*) was an invitation to the producer to try his hand at the sort of anachronisms in which Visconti and Zeffirelli are only too prone to indulge today. Strauss's music, being in itself frequently unlocated as to time and period, renders the invitation that much more accessible. It is true that much of Wagner implies 'stylized' production, but then Wagner's music-dramas bear the weight of universal myths in a way that Strauss's do not. Aside from the spurious mythology of *Die Ägyptische Helena*, there is nothing much in Strauss that can be placed in this category. What he offers us are plays set to superb music.[2]

Probably Hartmann has done best by Strauss in approaching him in a broadly-based fashion, risking no Wieland Wagner-like experiments in symbolism, but going beyond the 'straight' theatre of more conventional producers. For, if Strauss is not truly mytho-logical (he certainly adds nothing to German mythology, let alone the wider Jungian or Freudian kind certain producers like to play with), neither is he just a playwright's collaborator, like Debussy professed to be. To begin with, Hofmannsthal was always more of a poet than a playwright (*Arabella* notwithstanding) and Strauss always more of a musician than a man of the theatre. They each demand an element of fantasy, or super-realism, which should nevertheless not be pressed too far. The 'silver' set Hartmann designed for the Presentation of the Rose scene in *Der Rosen-kavalier* comes nearest to realizing the vision the two men set out, albeit unconsciously, to achieve. It is true, real and touching. Yet it also carries us into a world of luxury, chivalry and ultimate make-believe. The white spotlight on Octavian, coupled with the F sharp harmonies that float upwards from the orchestra, together symbolize the respective worlds of the poet and the musician— near enough to reality to stir our hearts, yet never so close to it to

[1] From this it may be inferred that I consider *too much* emphasis is being placed on production in general at the present time. This is prob-ably the result of singers accepting too many engagements to do them-selves justice, and a certain penchant for lavish sets that has no doubt arisen out of the public's willingness to pay high prices for seats.

[2] For a clear discussion of Strauss from a production standpoint, see J. S. Weissmann's 'Strauss on Stage' (*Music Review*, 1968, pp. 33–52).

blunt the shock we get when the curtain falls and we are thrown
back into a foyer full of perspiring people ready to tread the night
air or call for a taxi to whisk them back to their hotels and the
noisy confusion into which their lives already threaten to dissolve.

vi Mahler and the Beethoven Succession

Alongside the Austro-German tradition of opera and song went that of the classical symphony, which managed to maintain its hold over composers like Mendelssohn, Schumann, Brahms and Bruckner right through the period when romanticism was at its height. Indeed, in the cases of some of these men argument has never ceased to rage over whether they spent their lives trying on the mantle of Beethoven or capitulating to the desire to write attractive salon music for the mid-century amateur. Brahms and Mendelssohn are two particularly awkward figures to deal with in this respect. Were they classics or romantics? No doubt, the right answer is that they were both; but this only leaves us with the further conundrum of deciding on which was their best side. The term 'Beethoven succession' (which, as far as I know was coined by Mr Norman Suckling in his book on Fauré) is actually one that both compels and resists definition. On the one hand, it implies the notion of a dynasty, created presumably by the need for a continuing tradition of large, symphonic works of a spiritual as well as a classical cast. Yet, on the other, it hints at an idea of 'greatness' —an idea started by von Bülow's infamous dictum about the three B's of music (Bach, Beethoven and Brahms) and completed, retrospectively, by natural idolaters like Vincent d'Indy, Sir Donald Tovey and J. W. N. Sullivan. In case the reader is puzzled as to where all this is leading, let him pause for a moment and reflect on how very recent has been our abandonment of the belief that a generation's greatest composer is he who has written its greatest symphony.[1] Gustav Mahler, living from 1860 to 1911,

[1] One was surprised—even astonished—to read that so popular and fashionable a composer as John Dankworth was battling with an inner compulsion to write a symphony. One would have thought such an

certainly seemed obsessed with the symphony as the obvious vehicle for musical genius, and it is to his particular contribution to modernism that we must now turn.

In view of the foregoing remarks, he may not seem any more 'modern' than Strauss, inviting us to suspect a similar case of semi-conscious antiquarianism. But, as with Strauss, there are unsuspected complications. It goes without saying that these are of quite another kind from those we have been hearing about. For a long time, Mahler made no impression whatever on the musical public of this and numerous other European countries. Then, all of a sudden, he began to 'kick off his tombstones' in a fashion that surprised the few who knew of his existence and had heard some of his works. Delius made the only really clever prediction when he cynically remarked:

> . . . When the English grow tired of Sibelius, they will move on to Mahler or some other figure as their object of worship.

What led him to make this remark is obscure—perhaps he was giving vent to his customary scorn for fashion, or maybe the suspicion he always had that, as a nation, we prefer music of the grand, brassy variety to anything that calls for intimacy or subtlety. Anyway, he was right, since from about 1950 onwards Mahler's stock has continued to rise in Britain until we have reached the almost comical situation that confronts us today, in which the Albert Hall is filled to hear his Fifth Symphony conducted by Pierre Boulez; probably the man who more than anyone else has been responsible for relegating so-called 'out-of-date' forms to the museums he is often accused of wanting to blow up. At least we can point to more consistency on the part of Mr Deryck Cooke, and those who think like him, when they praise Mahler as an antidote to the arbitrary, shapeless 'aleatory' music of the present-day extremists. Or have we got it wrong somewhere, and Mahler is actually much more modern than we realize?

The present writer recalls attending what must have been the earliest, or one of the earliest, performances of the composer's Second Symphony (*The Resurrection*) given in London. It was during October 1949, and the programme also included the *Kindertotenlieder*, sung by the late Kathleen Ferrier. The main attraction was Bruno Walter's presence on the rostrum, most members of the audience quietly regretting that they were not being given an opportunity to hear the great conductor in a familiar masterpiece by Mozart or Beethoven. When it came to the

---

ancient ambition, on the part of a jazz musician, went out with the tearful Hollywood epics of the 1940's.

Andante of the Symphony, however, one could almost sense the change of heart. For what emerged was a lightly-scored idyll, permeated with Schubertian phraseology, that resulted in something close to the most enchanting chamber-music writ large. 'Were you resurrected?' asked someone playfully on the way out. I had to confess I had been faintly levitated, but hardly transported to the heavens. Sixteen years later, I chanced to hear the same work given by the Vienna Philharmonic at Salzburg (this time without Walter, alas!) and enjoyed it in much the same way as I had enjoyed the other tourist attractions of that pleasantly indulgent city. Even the 'Totenfeier' (or funeral rites) of the first movement seemed no more agonized than the death scene in Strauss's *Tod und Verklärung*, while the vocal finale sounded far more grandly operatic, and less spiritually jubilant, than I had expected. Perhaps I am merely recounting a case of musical obtuseness on the part of a single not very knowledgeable listener. But I have a feeling it illustrates a point of some importance in the appreciation of Mahler and his music. That point is that the composer's understanding of the term 'symphony' was totally at variance with that of most musicians, and that as a result he injected into the form so many improbable and conflicting features as to make it resemble a species of musical free association.

Mahler devotees may quite likely rise in wrath at this supposition on my part, and seek out chapter and verse to buttress their claim that the composer was actually acutely sensitive to the problems of architecture and long-range thinking. However, let me quote from his own ideas on the symphony as he expressed them to Sibelius when the two men met at Helsingfors in 1907. Sibelius having expounded his well-known view of the form as a logical, organic, tightly-knit entity, Mahler interrupted him to say:

> No, a symphony must be like the world, it must embrace everything . . .

That this reply was not merely an off-the-record rejoinder to keep the conversation from wilting is proved by the many other instances when the composer was cornered into outlining his theories for the benefit of friends and correspondents. These theories were all built on the principle that art was a microcosmic activity (sometimes with less emphasis on the 'micro-' than the 'cosmic') in which all happenings, whether good or bad, spiritual or material, were somehow to be incorporated. Such a conception later became known to us in literature through the anti-formalist aesthetics of a Proust or Joyce. It was utterly unknown in music until formulated by Mahler. We speak confidently of certain

writers—even before the present century—as having 'created a
world'. Dickens is a clear example of this sort of writer. What we
mean is that they peopled their books with all sorts of oddities,
many of them minute and unimportant in themselves, with the
object of building up a complete Gestalt or environment as seen
through a single pair of eyes. Sometimes this environment, by
virtue of the singularity of vision that has brought it into being,
becomes of more interest to us than the machinations of the
plot or the physiognomies of hero and heroine. At other times a
kind of order imposes itself after the event, conferring upon the
author a power of hindsight we did not suspect him of possessing.
Proust, I think, leaves us with this impression of having known,
after all, where the pieces of the jig-saw actually fitted. Indeed,
the title given to his last volume—*Le Temps Retrouvé*—implies as
much. It is my conviction that Mahler's music is best regarded
in the light of analogies like these.

In all he wrote nine complete symphonies, a work called *Das
Lied von der Erde* which only superstition prevented him from
titling in the same way, and sketches for a Tenth which have
recently been turned into a most convincing performing edition
by Mr Deryck Cooke.[1] The first of these mammoth works—they
vary in time from just over an hour to just under two hours—is
usually seen as one of a group of four, the so-called *Wunderhorn*
group which comprises the composer's first period output and
which taken together expresses the 'man-in-conjunction-with-
nature' theme celebrated in Beethoven's 'Pastoral' Symphony.
The simple folk-tune that breaks through the misty, impressionistic opening of No. I, with its Delius-like 'cuckoo calls', was
actually filched from the second song in the composer's earlier
Lieder eines fahrenden Gesellen. The whole exposition, if that is the
right term for it, sounds curiously unsymphonic, even for 1888.
If one were not told differently, one would say it was the beginning
of a symphonic poem inspired by Wagner's *Siegfried Idyll*. Of
course, one would be correct in imagining Wagner a potent influence on Mahler, as on the slightly younger Strauss. But the
Ländler of the second movement and the lugubrious *Frère Jacques*
theme of the third (said to have been inspired by a funeral-
scene engraving by the French artist, Jacques Callot) introduce
elements of irony and expressionism quite foreign to the outlook
of the German composer, and more indicative of an Eastern
European temperament. As it happens, Mahler's nationality is
difficult to define. He was born at Kalisch in what was then Bohemia, but was an Austrian subject. As he often liked to say, he was

[1] I am unable to take account, in such a brief essay, of Mahler's non-sym-
phonic work, such as the early cantata, *Das Klagende Lied*, and the songs.

in reality three times exiled—'as a Bohemian in Austria, an Austrian in Germany, and a Jew throughout all the world'.

This rootlessness from which the composer suffered is extremely important in any understanding of his work. His family knew the utmost poverty and misfortune, in that while Mahler was a child he had to compete with eleven brothers and sisters for the earnings of a drunken, coachman father, who eventually elevated himself to the level of proprietor of a wine-shop. Many of the children died in infancy, foreshadowing in a grisly way the stories recounted in the composer's *Kindertotenlieder*, a song-cycle on theme of child mortality set to poems by Rückert. I cannot resist quoting from Sir Neville Cardus's description of the conditions out of which this remarkably versatile genius emerged:

> The parents, though their marriage was not a love match, produced twelve children. Five of them succumbed to diphtheria at an early age; another succumbed to heart failure when he was sixteen. Leopoldine, a sister, succumbed at twenty-six to a tumour of the brain; brother Otto committed suicide, and brother Alois fled to America to escape creditors. In such a home, and a home isolated in a land of anti-Semitism, Mahler grew up. A coffin in his infancy must have seemed to him part of the domestic furniture.[1]

Clearly, this sort of background was not going to be productive of music with pure *Schmalz* as its basis. There are moments of joy and exuberance in his symphonies, but they are more often than not overlaid by a spectral, 'skull-and-crossbones' element or else end in a frenzied dance of death. Perhaps this accounts for some of the appeal he seems to have for the young, violence-driven generation of today. The *Wunderhorn* symphonies contain less nightmarish fever than the remainder; but they are just as full of sudden, grotesque allusions. They parody the street sounds of the towns in which the composer grew up, not in a fashionable intellectual way, but almost in the way a Daumier sketch parodies the urban landscape or caricatures the faces in a crowd.

Obviously, some psychological trauma lurks behind Mahler's constant intrusion of extraneous material into his symphonies. Their very sounds do not strike us as having been musically conceived as much as cacophonously overheard in some distant brawl. A story exists that the composer, after being brutally exacerbated by one of his parents' quarrels, ran straight out and collided with an organ-grinder who happened to be playing the popular air, *O du lieber Augustin*. When, much later in life, he had

[1] See *Gustav Mahler—Miracle of Artistic Creation* (RCA Records, 1964).

occasion to visit Freud about his neurasthenic tendencies, Mahler repeated this story to the great man as possibly having some significance. One scarcely needs to be a psycho-analyst to appreciate the relevance it could bear to the composer's peculiar ambiguity; his apparent inability ever to come up with an unqualified emotional response. The streets held the promise of gaiety for him (as did the barracks from which he heard many a rousing brass tune of the kind that recurs in his Fifth and Sixth Symphonies), while the home remained a continual source of terror and fear. By meeting with an incident of the type we have described, he quite probably got the two prospects mixed in his mind, so that alongside every expression of love or pleasure there went a suggestion of nerves being wrenched, shadows being cast. Even the dictatorial element in his character—and this emerged most fearsomely in his behaviour as Director of the Vienna Court Opera—may have stemmed from this experience, since it was often mollified by a show of sympathy for his problems as an artist; which were in reality problems in what Pasternak would have called 'his sister, Life'. Mahler's whole psychology is indeed a case-history that sheds constant rays of light on his work as an original exponent of a new kind of symphonic music—that based on social-clinical principles. Or else on a form of religious mania.

What should interest us most about this as musicians is the technique used to further it. Here it is essential to make the point that, contrary to what many listeners would have us believe, the composer rarely indulged in orchestral over-compensation. The huge orchestra he employed (frequently eight horns, four tubas, anything from three to seven tenor trombones and bass trombone, to say nothing of such exotic intruders as the xylophone, celeste, mandoline and guitar) was not assembled to act as a megaphone. Rather, it was by pitting one instrument against another (as in the Eighth Symphony and *Das Lied von der Erde*), or by forcing ordinary instruments into abnormal conjunction (as in the blaring F trumpets he frequently combined with shrieking E flat clarinets) that the composer proclaimed his uniqueness as an orchestrator. His habit of pitching a high, tenuous instrument like the oboe or flute against a low, rasping one such as the trombone reminds us far more of Berlioz than any other forerunner. In this sense, it is hard to see Mahler, as he is sometimes seen, as the link between Wagner and Strauss. He was admired by Strauss, it was even the case that Strauss learnt certain techniques from him. But their respective styles of instrumentation were never similar. Strauss actually *did* prefer the sound of the full orchestra, and such technical issues as he took up separately (like the famous trombone slide Stravinsky first discovered in *The Firebird*) interested him chiefly as accumulations to his 'special effects' repertoire. These effects—and I am thinking mainly of the use of oboes to suggest the bleating of sheep in *Don Quixote* or a high register clarinet for Till's execution—were intended to have a surface appeal only, and do not represent anything so fundamental as Mahler's singular intrusions. Instruments always stand out in Mahler—take the swooping horns to be found as early as the Ländler of Symphony No. I and as late as the Rondo Burleske of No. 9—yet as part of the design and not as vehicles for mimicry.

According to Hans Redlich, Symphones II, III and IV represent the composer's struggle to achieve religious repose.[1] If this was the case, he evidently sought that repose first of all in a rather simple belief in the after-life (which resulted in some of his most vulgar, over-written music); then a reversion to pantheism; and finally a child-like vision of paradise not unlike that familiar to us from the paintings of Fra Angelico. No doubt a theologian would regard these different beliefs as wildly irreconcilable. But Mahler knew little of theology, as his ultimate progress from Judaism to Catholicism seems to confirm. Bruno Walter, in a talk he once gave to accompany his final recording of the Ninth Symphony, cleverly differentiated Mahler from Bruckner (still too often bracketed in the public mind) by saying that whereas Mahler spent the whole of his life searching for God, Bruckner had the good fortune to begin by finding Him. If the works are anything to go by, there is much truth to this distinction. Mahler's Second, Third and Fourth Symphonies *do* all contain evidence of his troubled spiritual quest. The verses by Klopstock (to which he added some of his own) that occur in the finale of No. 2 provide unmistakable evidence of religious obsessions. So, in its more modest way, does the song from *Das Knaben Wunderhorn* that precedes them. Entitled 'Urlicht', it contains the following typical stanza:

> Then came I upon a broad, fair way,
> There came an angel and would turn aside me.
> Ah no, I would not turned aside be!
> I am of God, and again would to God!
> For loving God will give me light for seeing,
> Will light me onward to eternal, blissful being.[2]

Such words as these leave no room for doubt that the entire work is simply a prolonged meditation on the reason for life, on

---

[1] See *Bruckner & Mahler* in the Master Musicians Series (Dent, 1963).
[2] The translation is by Addie Funk, and is reproduced by kind permission of Boosey & Hawkes Ltd.

the need to accept a teleological view of existence. Enough has already been said as to *why* Mahler required this kind of assurance. What is unfortunately true is that neither this symphony nor its successor offers much hint as to *how* such assurance was to be vouchsafed him. In the Third Symphony, there seems to be a tacit assumption that it will come through unquestioning submission to nature. Here Mahler stands on familiar ground, expressing a philosophy very close to that of the early German Romantic poets in language not unlike that Schubert used for the 'Unfinished' Symphony. In six movements, the first of which lasts a full three quarters of an hour, Mahler's work labours what Schubert appears to have expressed almost epigrammatically—all the talk of the latter's 'heavenly length' notwithstanding. Most critics agree that the work is diffuse, despite the sharp division of its sections. A great deal of the first movement is boringly primordial (Stravinsky and Milhaud give us an exhilarating portrait of the dawn of life by comparison), while the mood of the Adagio seems too liturgical to fit the explicitly pastoral programme—entitled 'What the flowers on the meadows tell me'. The scherzo, as usual, is more of a success (one thing Mahler and Bruckner *did* have in common is that they could each write lively scherzi, Mahler's being occasionally too wild). It is based on an upper Austrian folk-dance. Loneliness returns for the interlude or fourth movement, while the concluding two movements alternate between the naivety of the Fourth Symphony (it is significant that the composer first considered using the last movement of the Fourth as an addition to the Third, but was dissuaded from doing so by reflecting on how much it would further extend the work's size) and the slightly bombastic quality of the Second.

The Fourth itself is on a far smaller scale than any of its predecessors, but easily supersedes them for all that. It is primarily a symphony for strings, a light near-Mozartian work that nevertheless employs a solo voice for the epilogue and some characteristically Mahleresque instrumental doublings for the other movements. (The effect of several flutes playing in unison against a double-bass counterpoint in the first movement is a good instance of how Mahler could remain Mahler even when trying hard to be delicate and classical.) Written during a comparatively happy phase in his life—he had just been appointed to the Directorship of the Vienna Opera after having served his apprenticeship at Hamburg and elsewhere—the symphony gives every appearance of being a release from the inner wrestlings that had gone into Nos. 1, 2 and 3. He was still single at this point in his life, having had a brief, abortive affair with a singer named Johanne Richter while at Hamburg; but the need for female companionship was never so acute that it affixed additional complications to his already overburdened character. Freud's diagnosis of a 'mother-fixation' is perhaps made more understandable by a work like this Fourth Symphony, where the emphasis all lies on a beatific vision of childhood. The opening sleigh-bells introduce us to a 'gemüt-lich' aspect to the composer's character which is certainly not in evidence in many of his other compositions. Similarly, the grazioso G major theme that forms the main subject (the first movement) is for once an expression of unalloyed charm and cheerfulness. It is the 'Death's Fiddle' movement, in which the violins are tuned scordatura (or a whole tone higher) that provides the macabre component in this symphony; but even that recalls the woodcuts of a child's picture-book rather than the horrifying encounter of a real-life skirmish. The two Trio sections, for example, are quite free of menace. A long Adagio then follows, in which sonata form and variation are ingeniously intermingled, and it is only in the shortish last movement that a simply-notated song, set in the shimmering tonality of E major, brings us within sight of the celestial city.

Thus the ending of Mahler's first period took the shape of 'a symphony without fortissimo'. It was to be very different in his next, second period, when marriage to a beautiful young girl and fame as a conductor combined to elicit from him more drive and worldliness. At least, the Fifth Symphony, written in 1901–2 though extensively revised between 1907 and 1909, seems easily the most confident and continuously splendid of all his works in the genre. In one way or another, every single one of his others has some eccentricity, blemish or leaning towards the bizarre. The Fifth is what one might risk calling a 'straight' symphony—conventional in its form, free of any complex programme, almost Beethovenian in its abstract power. It is best known, of course, for its Adagietto—a jewel of purely melodic string-writing that has too often been ripped from its setting and subjected to the over-sentimental 'portamenti' to which the anti-Mahlerites have unfairly objected. Despite this beautifully chamber-like episode, the composer entitled the whole work as a 'symphonie für grosses orchester'; and one gets a fine foretaste of what is to come from the brilliant brass fanfares with which the first movement kicks off. Mahler's young bride, the former Alma Schindler, was not pleased with her husband's efforts, however, finding them too much of an assault upon her ears. She was a spirited girl, with a good musical training and a laudable determination not to be over-awed by the man she had married. As it was she who was given the job of copying out the parts of the Fifth, she perhaps had the best opportunity possible to judge how far the composer had

over-scored the work. In her recently re-issued memoirs, we read
her casually writing:

> Mahler had over-scored the percussion instruments and
> kettle-drums so madly and persistently that little beyond
> the rhythm was recognizable.[1]

This criticism from his wife (few other people had the temerity to
stand up to Mahler, who enjoyed a reputation for quick and
vicious retaliation) probably did more to coerce the composer into
revisions than any amount of adverse comment in the press.
Whether he was right to accede to her in the way he did remains
debatable.

One of the immense difficulties that confronted Mahler as a
composer throughout the whole of his life was that of securing
proper performances of his works. Indeed, so few performances
of any kind were given that it was not uncommon for him to have
to wait many years for a première. (The Third Symphony, for
example, was not played until 1902, though it had been published
as early as 1898, while among the later works the composer never
lived to hear *Das Lied von der Erde* or the Ninth, given by Walter
in late 1911 and early 1912 respectively.) This meant that by the
time a work had some chance of being heard, Mahler's ideas about
orchestration—to say nothing of 'life', the real subject of all his
compositions—had frequently developed in a different direction.
His role as conductor at the Opera was one he took with unprecedented seriousness, and it was almost entirely his efforts that
weaned the Viennese away from their decadent 'post-biedermeier'
operatic habits towards a more modern conception of the form. His
re-establishment of Mozart's operas as the corner-stones of the
repertory, and his serious dedication to unfashionable works like
Fidelio, were major achievements, milestones in the history of
operatic production. If we are to place any faith in the testimony
of men like Walter and Klemperer, who worked with him, Mahler
was also a conductor of Toscanini-like stature. Walter has described him, in his book *Theme and Variations* (Hamilton, 1947) as
'the greatest performing musician' he had heard then or since.
Such gifts naturally enabled the composer to benefit from contact
with an orchestra in a way that a more theoretical figure could
never have done. To resort to an obvious analogy, it was the case

---

[1] The work, first issued in German under the title *Gustav Mahler:
Erinnerungen und Briefe* in 1940 (Albert de Lange, Amsterdam), was
produced in an English translation by Basil Creighton and published
by John Murray under the title *Gustav Mahler: Memories & Letters*
in 1946. In 1969, a new edition appeared, with an illuminating introduction by Donald Mitchell.

that most of the great piano composers of the nineteenth century were themselves tremendous virtuosi—Beethoven, Liszt and Chopin being the clearest cases. It seems more than likely that some of their mastery stemmed from purely neuro-muscular reactions acquired during the process of playing. In like fashion, much of Mahler's music must be interpreted in the context of his position; as a reflection of the day-to-day criss-crossing of instrumental timbres with which he was inevitably acquainted.

Symphonies VI, VII and VIII form another group on their own. This time the departure from orthodox ideas was sparked off, not by a prolonged religious crisis or a sudden elevation in his professional life, but by a gradual descent into pessimism followed by a courageous attempt to re-affirm his failing beliefs. The first of the group, dating from 1905–6, is widely regarded as the composer's greatest symphony, though there is nothing like the same general agreement as to the respective merits of Mahler's works as exists in the case of, say, Beethoven's or Sibelius's. Its greatness is perhaps most apparent in the opening March's fierce tread. The tension it generates is terrific; rather as if one were listening to a tighter-knit, less melodramatic Tschaikovsky. There is an intermezzo-like Andante, another favourite Mahler form, while the Scherzo makes use of equally characteristic leaps and trills to create a slightly diabolic atmosphere of a kind some critics find repulsive. The extended Finale (both this and the first movement are long beyond the average concertgoer's patience) reverts to the blunt hammer-strokes of the opening, but is broken up from time to time by episodes of slow, lyrical beauty. The entire work, like No. 5, disclaims the need for vocal intrusions. Possibly this fact will help potential listeners to decide whether or not they will take to the work, for Mahler addicts, even if they cannot agree on which is the composer's best work, usually discover a key to their preferences in his handling of the human voice. The Rückert lieder (especially, perhaps, the moving *Ich bin der Welt abhanden gekommen*), *Kindertotenlieder* and songs fron *Das Lied von der Erde* all contribute to the portrait of a composer who could, in the view of many, have rivalled Schubert, Schumann or Wolf in the setting of words to music. On the other hand, Mahler's songs are definitely orchestral, cosmic in aim and unable to subsist within the compact tradition of the Lied proper. It is accordingly a point of some consequence whether or not his songs enhance his symphonies.

Responses to Symphony No. 6 have also been conditioned, to some extent, by the listener's degree of acquiescence in Mahler's pessimism. For again, there is no question but that this is his most depressing work. It has been nicknamed 'The Tragic', just

like Schubert's No. 4, and really earns the title. More than any of
the remaining symphonies, it seems to have appealed to the
generation of Austro-German expressionists whose fate it was to
become Mahler's legatees. In Vienna itself, it was extravagantly
admired by Schönberg, Alban Berg and, surprisingly, Webern
—who described it as 'the only Sixth, despite the "Pastoral" '. It
should therefore be seen as a key work in setting the tone for
music written by the new Viennese school. Why Mahler gave
such particularly strong emphasis to the tragic side of his nature in
it remains enigmatic. Cliques were being organized against him
at the Opera at this stage; though they did not really become hurtful for another year or two. And though he and Alma lost a child,
this did not take place until 1907, a year after the symphony's
more or less ill-received première. By a ghastly unconscious premonition, he even wrote the Rückert songs *before* his child's
death, they being the next works he started on immediately on
finishing the symphony. One is left to conclude that the composer's religious doubts had returned to plague him, or else that
relations with Alma were not all they had promised to be. She
herself makes the somewhat ridiculous claim that Mahler was
jealous of her, and resented her complaints that her own career
was being sacrificed to his. It is true that Alexander von Zemlinsky had prophesied a brilliant career for Alma; but one can
hardly imagine it would have reached such heights. What seems
more likely, to judge from the tone of their letters and from Alma's
confidences, is that she enjoyed, in what was probably an innocent way, the company of great men, and filled their house with
important artists, musicians and writers who would not bow to
Mahler's superiority.[1]

However we may wish to explain the composer's despondency,
it was not to be very long before he had good cause to feel depressed. I am not referring as much to the death of his child as
to the diagnosis of heart-disease which was soon after returned in
respect of his own state of health. As it had been a family complaint, Mahler could not have been altogether surprised by this
news. But its impact on him was undoubtedly to hasten his
anxieties and make him feel all the more determined to arrive at
some kind of rapport with his Creator before it was too late. The
Seventh Symphony, however, had been completed during the
same summer as the Sixth, and had even been started before it.[2] It

---

[1] It is surely symptomatic that Alma had confessed to Mahler that she
'was only attracted to great men'; and that after the composer's death
she had a liaison with the painter Kokoschka, married the architect
Gropius and finally wed Franz Werfel, the novelist.

[2] Because of the strenuousness of his duties at the Opera, Mahler was
forced to regard himself as a 'summer composer'. This meant that

therefore bears no traces of added sadness, and could be said to have suffered from having been composed alongside a greater work. Repetition obviously becomes a dangerous addiction to a composer of Mahler's particular cast of mind, and there is no worse case of this in his canon than between these two symphonies. Redlich goes further and argues that, not only is there a similarity between the first themes of their respective opening movements, but that No. 7 harks back in patently imitative ways to Nos. 3 and 5. The most arresting feature of this seldom played work is probably the 'nachtmusik' which, taken with the thumping waltz-like scherzo, forms a sort of nocturnal triptych in its midst. By comparison, the outer movements are devoid of interest to such an extent that even the composer himself (usually very enthusiastic about his work, once completed) was 'torn by doubts' as to whether it should be performed. As he was allowed the customary long period in which to decide, he was able to make extensive alterations to the orchestral colouring. When eventually played in Prague in 1908, it secured a lukewarm reception, and continues to be the least often heard of all the symphonies, despite some recent protestations on its behalf by both Leonard Bernstein and Otto Klemperer. Possibly it is a work that holds more fascination for the conductor than for the listener, since its instrumental revisions have resulted in some rare sounds.

Most listeners, on the other hand, are familiar—either by hearing or repute—with the Eighth Symphony, the pretentiously labelled 'Symphony of a Thousand'. This work moves on to a higher spiritual plane than any the composer had previously inhabited, and takes for its text the hymn, *Veni, Creator Spiritus*. Impressive as is the final score, nothing demonstrates more palpably the strange philosophico-religious dilemma which Mahler continuously experienced from his early manhood right up to the time of his death. In a letter to Alma (dated June 1910) he attempted to explain how he had arrived at the work's odd programme. Having read Goethe and grasped his doctrine of love as a generative force, the composer somehow managed to equate this with the Platonic Eros—and then capped it all by relating his findings to orthodox Christian teachings! We know, from the cases of César Franck and d'Indy, how many late nineteenth-century musicians fell into the habit of choosing Greek texts as a means of adumbrating Christian subjects. But this accepted practice can scarcely account for Mahler's weird theological doctrines. It seems more likely that he was one of those minds (they still exist in large numbers today) whose natural bent is directed

he usually worked on a number of scores during the summer months, leaving the orchestration and copying to the winter.

towards detecting resemblances between apparently irreconcilable
faiths. The massive spiritual forces Mahler observed all around
him were things he took to be common property, as acceptable in
essence to the Christian as to the Jew, the Buddhist or even the
freethinker. On these problems, if not on his more personal ones,
the composer might have received better guidance from Jung
than from Freud. One mentions them because, in retrospect, they
seem to constitute yet another 'modern' influence that Mahler has
wielded, the 1950's seeing the beginning of a cult to unite East
and West, both spiritually and musically. Debussy and his successors obviously provided the clearest stimulus for this cult, but
Mahler's vaguely ecumenical attitudes (to say nothing of his
ultimate orientalism) were just as obviously another *point d'appui*.
Even as I write these words, the 'pop' musicians who have taken
firmest hold on the 'teenage imagination are taking a course in
Eastern Enlightenment.

The Eighth is too immense a work to describe, so staggering is
the array of singers and instrumentalists it demands for performance. Broadly, it falls into two sections, the first dealing with the
Veni, Creator hymn and the second with an adaptation of Part II
of Goethe's *Faust*. The opening section *is* in sonata form, if that
is a point in its favour, with a double fugue representing the
development and a foreshortened recapitulation. It does, however,
ask to be treated as a tableau on its own. The contrast between this
and the second section is so marked that almost all commentators
have drawn attention to it. Instead of the contrapuntal, essentially
Brucknerian style of the beginning (Mahler incidentally, was a
brilliant contrapuntist, as the Fifth and Ninth Symphonies especially reveal) we are now confronted with what seems like a romantic,
virtually operatic, scena. Perhaps it would be kinder to Mahler to
say that this section veers towards dramatic oratorio, with very
little effort put into thematic opposition and change. Faust is first
of all despatched from the scene in a strident choral flight, then
follows a long stretch of dialogue between Gretchen and the
Mater Gloriosa. Every so often this is punctuated by a further
choral invocation of tremendous force. Both these modes of expression are offset by certain purely instrumental interludes, involving celeste, piano, harp and similar unsymphonic aids. These
help to sustain a more ethereal note, and prepare the way for a
four-part chorale that in turn leads to the somewhat overwhelming
climax, consisting of the Chorus Mysticus theme in augmentation.
This was the last work Mahler actually saw through the press,
it being published by Universal Editions in 1910, the same year as
it secured its first performance at Munich. The first section had
taken him only three weeks to write, and the entire work had been

scored by the end of 1907. So that once again it was a case of having to exercise patience. This time, however, the composer's patience was amply rewarded, since the première was a colossal success, a fact that may have been due to his own conducting (he insisted on directing this work himself) or conversely to the new hall that was built especially to accommodate the work. Its influence, outside of the religious field, has been to direct composers towards vastness as an aim. Schönberg's *Gurrelieder*, for example, which demands an orchestra of one hundred and forty, four choirs and soloists, was surely a pointer to the same end, it having appeared a decade earlier. Both works, like some of Strauss's early symphonic poems, pushed the Wagnerian orchestra to its limits.

Nine tends to be a fatal number among symphonists, both Beethoven and Bruckner having expired on reaching it. Mahler, who was an extremely superstitious man, and by this time had incontrovertible reasons for believing he had only a short time to live, could not endure the prospect of embarking on a symphony with this grim numerical attachment. Instead, he wrote a work that differs little, if at all, from the kind of symphonies he had been writing, and called it *Das Lied von der Erde—The Song of the Earth*. Once again cast in six movements in place of the customary four, the work consisted of a series of settings from the ancient Chinese poets, presented in German translations by Hans Bethge. The mood of the poems, some of which were by Li-Po (who was later to appeal to such modern 'littérateurs' as Ezra Pound and Conrad Aiken), tended to be uniformly epicurean. The whole collection, known as *The Chinese Flute* had been sent to Mahler by a friend in 1907, and two years later he began their setting in a frame of mind that can only be viewed with deepest compassion. Writing to Walter, he grumbled resignedly:

> If I am to find my way back to myself, I have got to accept the horrors of loneliness. I speak in riddles, since you do not know what has gone on and is going on within me. It is, assuredly, no hypochondriac fear of death, as you suppose. I have long known that I have got to die . . .

The tragedy was, of course, that he was a mere forty-nine-years-old. And no man—least of all a genius with everything to give the world—is ready to face death working at the summit of his powers. 'Vis-à-vis de rien', as he once put it, what else could he do but relapse into a kind of wry fatalism? It could not possibly be otherwise. Hence, the new 'symphony' turned out to be grave and gay by turns, its moments of despair alternating rapidly with a mad, drunken hedonism. The juxtaposition was hardly foreign to Mahler the composer. What distinguished *Das Lied* was the

recklessness, the sheer abandonment of the writing in the drink-
ing episodes; and the slow, languishing finality of the *Abschied*.

Of the six movements, the first—entitled *Das Trinklied vom
Jammer der Erde* was set in driving, impetuous style and expressed sentiments very much of the Omar Khayam type. Its
opening horn call (using Mahler's well-known preference for the
interval of a fourth) compels attention in the way many do in
Wagner's *Ring*. But it is softened by climbing and falling motifs
only a second apart which announce the pentatonic element that
is to form the true basis of the work. Instrumental coloration in
this first movement exceeds anything even Mahler had previously
attempted, the 'flutter-tongue' trumpet and pointilliste harp effects
being only two of the devices he uses in superbly original fashion.
The second poem—*Der Einsame im Herbst*—reverts to a picture
of autumn loneliness and is thus sharply contrasted with the first.
It should be stressed, too, that the singers (usually tenor and
contralto) also alternate so as to give further differences of timbre
and mood. The main motives of the second poem are otherwise
divided between oboes and violins. After this brief expression of
resignation, movements III, IV and V all offer a spirit of gaiety,
ranging from delicate contentment to ebullient exuberance. *Von der
Jugend* has words very reminiscent of Pound's translations, or the
dandy-like diction of a Wallace Stevens lyric:

> In the middle of the little pool
> Stands a pavilion of green
> And of white porcelain
> Like the back of a tiger
> Arches the bridge of jade
> Over to the pavilion.

This tiny imagist poem is by far the most objective in the set, and
is accompanied by music that is quite unobtrusively 'chinoise' in
tone. No. IV is a sketch of young maidens picking lotus flowers by
the water's edge, and is notable for its picturesque use of mandoline and tambourine. By contrast, *Der Trunkene im Frühling*
returns us to the male singer, now overcome by the torrents of
Spring. But it is the very last poem (actually No. 6 is divided into
two) that has won for the composer his reputation as a singer of
swan-songs. Its gentle arabesques strike the authentic note of
Eastern pathos, and the final, repeated 'Ewig . . .' seems to mark
the close of all human endeavour.

That it was still not to be a close for Mahler is proved by the
actual Symphony No. 9 he wrote immediately he had got rid of his
deathly feeling of premonition. The fact that the composer again
worked more or less simultaneously on these scores meant that

'Das Lied von der Erde' provided him with the point of departure for the first movement of the Ninth. Listeners may judge for themselves whether or not this movement and the preceding *Abschied* spring from a like sense of disillusionment. The sinking phraseology of the beginning, with its slow harp accompaniment, may cause him to wonder if the symphony will ever gather enough momentum. The climax, when it comes, is nevertheless redolent of the old Mahler—brassy and stupendous in a way no other modern composer has ever been able to approach. A broad scherzo forms the second movement, fraught with tragic undertones, but it is the grotesque Rondo that follows that reveals to us most clearly how much energy was still left in this short, frail bespectacled man, who looked anything but the Titanic artist he has been designated. As with *Das Lied*—but in contrast to most of his other symphonies—Mahler this time reserved his slow movement for the end, propounding a long string Adagio of surpassing loveliness that ends by simply fading away into a subtle kind of perceptible silence. It is this movement, more than any in the unfinished Tenth, that contrives to be the 'threnody of German Romanticism' proclaimed by Professor Arthur Hutchings.[1] One is always suspicious about 'golden ages' or periods in history which come to constitute an apex of civilization in the minds of historians. But if I were asked to take one piece of music by which to symbolize the twilight of that great era that began in Vienna with the terse and witty symphonies of Haydn and Mozart, it would have to be the Adagio of Mahler's Ninth. I was never fortunate enough to have heard Walter (Mahler's principal assistant at Vienna) give this great work in the concert-hall, but hearing Klemperer's rendering, to a standing ovation, in the Royal Festival Hall in 1967 was endorsement of all that Berg and others have claimed for it. It is surely that culmination for which the composer spent his tortured life working.

'Tortured life' would be a justified phrase if Mahler's struggles had simply been confined to ill-health and religious doubts. But he had even more to contend with in the shape of dismissal from his post at the rostrum in Vienna. Attacks had been made on him from earliest days, most of them concerning his refurbishing of the repertoire and the ruthlessness by which he dispensed with the services of mediocre singers. Vienna has always been a trial to its musical directors (as von Karajan re-discovered in the 1950's and '60's), but in Mahler's case additional enmity was directed against

---

[1] See the *Pelican History of Music*, Vol. III. I should add, however, that the Tenth—in its brilliantly reconstructed version by Deryck Cooke —has now fully entered the repertory, and hence adds significantly to the Mahler canon.

him on account of his Jewishness. (Cosima Wagner, for instance tried hard to have him barred from the Court on this score.) Though few contested the brilliance of his conducting, there were many who resented his blasé attempts to interfere with tradition—a word he equated with 'sloppiness' and complacency. When told that Hans Richter had played Wagner at a slower tempo, the maestro tartly replied: 'Richter had no idea about tempi. Maybe he knew the right tempo for Wagner when he began. Since then he has forgotten.' This and similar cutting remarks earned him a certain notoriety among the older musicians. It must be admitted that the composer possessed a gift for being quarrelsome, even towards his most sympathetic associates. Both Mengelberg and Pfitzner were good friends with whom he broke so many lances that it does not surprise us to learn they had none left with which to defend him when his real enemies appeared on the horizon. By the end of the year in which these enemies really let fly at him, Mahler was accordingly forced to quit the city whose musical life he had upheld for a decade. An offer from the Metropolitan Opera, New York, gave everyone the excuse they were looking for, and in December 1907 Mahler and Alma crossed the Atlantic, leaving Vienna to the mercies of Felix Weingartner. Walter, who was deeply disappointed at not being given the post of successor, remained on until 1913, when he retired to Munich.

In America, the great conductor had the benefit of some of the world's finest voices, including those of Caruso, Chaliapin, Melba, Farrar and Lilli Lehmann. But he also encountered opposition from a young 'chef d'orchestre' who, for the first time in his life, struck him as a serious rival. His name was Arturo Toscanini, and when the two clashed over a production of *Tristan* it was Toscanini who emerged victorious, Mahler resigning to take over the directorship of the Philharmonic. Meanwhile, the composer's Eighth Symphony went some way towards rehabilitating him in Europe. It took the major heart-attack of 1911 to shock Vienna out of its complacency, however, and by then it was too late to do much beyond return for treatment, calling at Paris on the way. Knowing he was near the end, Mahler pleaded with his doctors to be allowed to die in his chosen capital; and this bleak privilege was not denied him. On May 18th, 1911, he had the expected fatal collapse, watched over by Alma, Walter and a few friends at the Loew Sanatorium. A couple of days later, these few, accompanied by a small contingent of orchestral players headed by the violinist Rosé, followed his coffin to its resting place in the Grinzing Cemetery, not far away from the abode of the great Schubert. After this there was seemingly nothing to do but mourn the passing of another colossus who might still have had wonderful music to give the world if only he had been allotted time to compose it. A glance through his effects first of all proved fruitless, and with the war so soon upon her Alma abandoned any search for unpublished material. There were some sketches for a Tenth Symphony nevertheless, and after the armistice serious thought was given to whether they could be pieced together. Movements one and three seemed fairly clearly laid out, and Schalk issued them in facsimile in 1924 on the assumption that the remainder could not be dealt with. This was not quite the case, however, and unorchestrated drafts of three other movements looked to some as if they were capable of some sort of realization. One of the difficulties was that no one knew precisely the order in which these skeletal movements were to be played. Richard Specht assumed, somewhat improbably, that the symphony had been intended as an Adagio followed by *four* Scherzi! Redlich could make no sense of the fragments at all. It is perhaps hardly any wonder that Alma thenceforward prohibited further attempts at completion.

As most listeners will know, the deadlock came to an end in 1960, when Deryck Cooke took it into his hands to reconstruct and where necessary amplify the entire work. He was supported in his project by Berthold Goldschmidt. A fascinating account of the venture is given by Mr Cooke in a recent book which reprints a selection of articles from *The Listener*.[1] It appears that Mr Cooke worked on the principle that, as most of the notes were decipherable, the main problem was one of realizing the harmonies they predicated and following through with a convincing imitation of Mahler's orchestral technique. The task was approached with modesty, and yet an intense determination not to see the world deprived of what appeared to be a masterpiece. That much ingenuity was expended may be gathered from the cleverness with which Mr Cooke cut the Gordian knot that had been bothering all his predecessors. By dividing the symphony into two— presumably on the model of the Eighth—he avoided the dilemma of deciding upon a strict sequence of movements. On first hearing of the scheme, Alma leapt in to exercise her veto; but after listening to what had been done she changed her mind and granted the necessary permission for public performance. The work has now become a part of Mahler's canon and has received countless performances both here and in America. Many Mahlerites are inclined to view it as another 'spiritually victorious' symphony, repealing the pessimism of the Ninth. The closing two sections (using the older terminology) certainly suggest a swing towards affirmation again. Other admirers of the composer—and Leonard

[1] 'Mahler's Unfinished Symphony' in *Essays on Music* ed. F. Apprahamian (Cassell, 1969).

Bernstein is perhaps the strongest spokesman for these—still re-
fuse to see the work as 'echt-Mahler', and have even gone so far
as to say they will never perform it. Possibly the most interesting
conclusion to be drawn from the experiment is that the composer
had evidently *not* moved away from the tonal style of the other
symphonies towards some kind of dodecaphonic adumbration.

In this sense, though Mahler's death was a terrible tragedy for
music, it is arguable that it came at a moment when he had said
all that was capable of being said in the language he knew best.
To envisage a post-war Mahler would be to conceive of a being
whose spiritual shell, so tough and yet so fragile, would have
been burst open by the actuality his music had predicted. As Egon
Gartenberg has expressed it:

> The drum and trumpet were among the main tools of
> Mahler. They relate the story of struggle and battle, and
> Mahler, enigma, dynamo, demon, creator and innovator,
> was first and foremost a fighter One must wonder how the
> guns and the trumpets, the holocaust of war would have
> affected Mahler and his music.[1]

[1] *Vienna: its musical heritage* (Pennsylvania State University Press,
1968).

vii Schönberg or Webern?

The deposition of Mahler from his post at the Vienna Opera, and
the gradual withering away of tradition to be observed in his later
works, brings us more or less directly up against what has been
termed 'the Second Viennese School'. The first thing we need to
settle about this expression is that only its middle term should be
allowed to stand unchallenged. It is an historical fact that Schönberg, Webern and Berg were all born in the Austrian capital, so
there is no possible dispute as to their origins. The adjective
'second', however, implies a break, a discontinuation, which
Schönberg, for a start, would have found offensive. For all his
startling procedures, he himself said:

> I personally hate to be called a revolutionary, which I am
> not. What I achieved was neither revolution nor anarchy.

Naturally, this does not dispose of the question of how the composer fitted in to the existing tradition—presumably that in-
augurated by the First Viennese School—and we shall ultimately
have to pay close attention to this qustion. There is a case for
stating that Webern began more ab ovo; but I am sure there will
be musicologists also willing to impugn that assumption. To move
on to the other disputable term, the noun 'school' poses the
suggestion that all three composers endorsed the same set of
principles and may truly be lumped together for listening purposes. Well, both Webern and Berg 'went to school' with Schönberg; but that is not quite the same as saying that they formed a
school. Going to school with a teacher does not imply acceptance
of his views any more than going to a resort for a holiday implies a
desire to go and live there. Indeed, if the current situation is

71

anything to go by, teachers and pupils are usually to be found on the opposite sides of the fence. If, then, we continue to use the expression 'Second Viennese School', it will accordingly be out of convenience (or bad habit) rather than a conscientious belief in the existence of such a unit.

Since the title of this essay was intended to be provocative, however, it may be that the reader is already primed to consider the proposition that at least two out of the three composers we shall be studying clung to divergent views regarding the future of modern music. The long neglect of Schönberg's music—which lasted virtually from the commencement of his career up until the early 1950's—has in any case now been accepted as a different sort of neglect from that which overtook Webern's. The former's neglect was restored almost as promptly as it was rectified in the advanced circles in which he was taken up; while Webern's reputation continues to grow through the '60's and even shows signs of having a strong appeal throughout the '70's for those composers who look as if they will be directing music's flow. The word 'traditionalist' has already been applied in a condescending, pejorative sense to Schönberg; even though such well-informed critics as Mr Deryck Cooke still say they cannot understand or abide his music. So far as Webern is concerned, however, he has earned the cachet of approval from both the youngest generation of critics and from such a sceptical old patriarch as Stravinsky. On the whole, Boulez too inclines to the Webern camp, though his attitude to the Viennese trio seems to vary appreciably from article to article, and he has been scathing in one respect or another about each of them, Berg particularly. One is left with the assumption that all three composers were shunned or misunderstood for a number of decades (the war incidentally cannot be made the scapegoat for this, since other difficult composers like Bartók and Stravinsky himself grew steadily in the public esteem through every kind of national and political disaster), and then it was suddenly discovered that one or two of them fitted particularly neatly into the general artistic climate of the mid-century. Indeed, to those of us who lived through the 1930's and '40's, it came as a distinct shock to see these composers raised up from the dead, so to speak, for we had smugly assumed their permanent demise along with the whole paraphernalia of 'serialism'.

As Schönberg was the originator and teacher of the methods they first set out to master, it is only just that we begin by considering the particular plight in which he found himself on coming of age. Born in 1874, he made his way with the minimum of musical training from Alexander von Zemlinsky, whose sister

he eventually married in 1902.[1] During the years which led up
to this event, he worked in a bank, missing that intensive musical
education that Webern, for example, was given at the University
of Vienna, under Guido Adler's guidance. But like so many self-
educated men, Schönberg outdid the formally educated in his
desire for knowledge, so that it was not long before he had absorbed the main influences that were to shape his ambitions. These,
surprisingly, were Beethoven, Brahms, Bruckner, Mahler and
Hugo Wolf—a formidable but not on the whole radical assortment. At the moment when he was switching to music as his chief
interest, however, Vienna had just been taken by storm by the
music of Wagner. *Tristan* was the 'ne plus ultra' in harmonic
audacity, and it was precisely this work's pushing of tonality to
its utmost limits, as it seemed, that caused the young composer to
ponder very carefully the position from which he could hope to
start out. Also the strongly 'expressive' character of this music
formed another possible *point d'appui*. Really it was the second
of these two musical developments that had the larger impact on
Schönberg at the outset of his career. Many listeners seem still
to associate the composer with the tone-row and the invention of
a new musical system. This is quite unsound from an historical
point of view, since he began by using the usual language of music,
as found in late Wagner and early Strauss, and did not get as far
as devising the twelve-tone method (he disliked the word 'system'
applied to it) until 1923. In fact, it is as well to clear up the terminology involved in Schönberg's work before we go any further. He
said, early on in his career, that he considered the term 'atonal'
meaningless; and the best words used to describe the kind of
music he wrote before the twelve-tone phase are 'non-tonal' or
merely 'expressionist'. The first of these suggested to the composer a transitional period when he was without tonality, but had
not yet found any substitute for it. The second is a word with
definable associations in all the arts, and does not necessarily
imply an element of bankruptcy as does the first.

It is better, I think, that we first of all tackle the implications
'expressionism' had for him. Briefly 'expressionism' is that form
of romanticism in which the self is presented in its most exacerbated and least controllable form. One hardly needs to point out
that Freud's classic, *The Interpretation of Dreams*, was completed
in 1899, the year in which Schönberg wrote his first important
composition, the *Verklärte Nacht* (Transfigured Night) for String
Sextet. Freud, moreover, was Viennese by adoption if not by

---

[1] An even more influential teacher was Oskar Adler, his sole guide
up to the age of eighteen.

birth, and his ideas were spreading rapidly through the city in
the years of Schönberg's expressionist phase. Of course, the projection of the libidinal elements in the personality—to resort to
psycho-analytic parlance—was not a new phenomenon. Painters
and dramatists, in particular, had made use of expressionist devices long before Freudian tenets gave them an air of scientific
respectability. Van Gogh's works were patently expressive of his
inner torments, and so were Strindberg's in plays like *The Father*
and *Miss Julie*. In Vienna, at about the point when Schönberg
was launching himself on a musical career, the painters Kandinsky,
Klee and Kokoschka (the last Alma Mahler's lover after the death
of the great composer) were each producing canvases with a
pronounced element of personal projection in them.[1] That they
deeply influenced the composer in his thinking about art is an
established fact. Schönberg himself was a surprisingly talented
painter (as his self-portrait and portrait of Alban Berg each
reveals) and there is a vividly accurate picture done of him by
Gershwin which emphasizes the man's near-psychotic intensity.
Music is usually slow to catch up with painting in any new discovery (a good example is impressionism, which was over in
painting by 1886, but did not begin in music till Debussy wrote
his *L'Après-midi d'un faune* between 1892 and 1894), and so it
was some time before Schönberg gave full vent to expressionism
in the manner of one or two of his pictorial colleagues.

Verklärte Nacht (1899) and *Pelléas et Mélisande* (1902) are the
first fruits of this phase of the composer's life. The former—which
describes the moonlit transfiguration of a man who has come to
acknowledge another's child as his own—was powerfully affected
by *Tristan* in its shifting harmonies and tender feelings of love.
The forest grove setting is also evoked in language not too remote
from that of Wagner's earlier works. *Pelléas*, on the other hand,
was an hour-long symphonic-poem, feverish in style and top-heavy
in its rich homophonic textures. It seems quite the opposite of
Debussy's more ethereal score, although the source was, of
course, the same in each case. It is intriguing that these early
pieces of Schönberg's seem to have lent themselves very ably to
the demands of the ballet, probably on account of the tensile
quality that so constantly emanates from them. The first was used

[1] It is worth defining in a little more detail the relationship between
art and depth psychology in this sense. Tests of personality, like the
Rorschach and Henry Murray's Thematic Apperception Test do not
scruple to make use of the individual's fantasies and interpretations of
situations as clues to his make-up. Such tests, in a way, only duplicate
in miniature the experience of writing a novel or play, which activities
can be a most potent guide to personality by means of projection.

as the basis for Anthony Tudor's famous *Pillar of Fire*, while the
second has just been pounced on as a vehicle for Fonteyn and
Nureyev by the French choreographer and ballet-master, Roland
Petit. It was played successfully in London during the Royal
Ballet's 1969 season. The other expressionist work at which
Schönberg almost tore himself apart at this period was the *Gur-
relieder*, an immense cantata which occupied him from the turn
of the new century virtually up to the day it was first performed in
Vienna under Franz Schreker in 1913.[1] This was the urge to-
wards the colossal expressing itself in the composer as it had done
previously in Mahler (we have already remarked on the similarity
of orchestral and vocal forces between this work and Mahler's
Eighth Symphony), and it stands at the opposite extreme from
Webern's mini-creations. *His* pieces rarely lasted longer than the
time formerly occupied by a short overture, and in his Five
Orchestral Pieces, Op. 10 there is not one that lasts more than a
minute! But we should not give the impression that Schönberg
became a victim of musical elephantiasis. On the contrary, once he
had chosen the chamber ensemble as his most natural medium,
his works were modestly scored and timed even when they
retained their difficulties of execution.

After the *Verklärte Nacht* and *Pelléas*, Schönberg settled for
the life of a teacher in Vienna (he had briefly flirted with the
theatre in Berlin, but had soon grown tired of it) and from about
1904 to 1910 he gave regular lessons to Webern, Alban Berg and
several others, including incidentally the pianist Rudolf Serkin
in their wake. As in the matter of his music, Schönberg's teaching
has been the occasion of much dispute. Tim Souster has recently
argued that the composer 'passed on his historical obsession to his
pupils Webern and Berg'.[2] There is enough truth in this to offer
us a firm clue as to his intentions. But one must remember that
Schönberg's historical *knowledge* was not by any means vast or
even substantial. How could it have been with so little formal
education to buttress it? It is more likely to have been intuitive and
inexact, but helped along by a decidedly ravenous appetite. To
this extent, what probably occurred was that, whereas the teacher
supplied most of the drive and enthusiasm, the pupils complied
by filling in certain gaps in his knowledge. It is unthinkable, for
instance, that Schönberg could have known as much as Webern
about the pre-baroque period in German music, the subject of the
latter's Ph.D. thesis submitted in 1906. Likewise, he could not

---

[1] This work, based on poems by the Danish poet Jens Peter Jacobsen,
tells the story of King Waldemar IV of Denmark and the seductive
Tove, who is finally poisoned by Waldemar's jealous Queen.
[2] See 'Schönberg and his Pupils' in *The Listener*, April 3rd, 1969.

have been as well-equipped as Berg to discuss the work of certain modern composers like Debussy. As a matter of fact, the French master was 'discovered' by Schönberg and Webern at about the same time in 1907. Wagner and Debussy were to be two especially profound influences on Webern (he had been to Bayreuth shortly after leaving the gymnasium, and had heard a good deal of Strauss and Mahler too), in that they led him to adopt the 'free' style, untrammelled by any deep consideration for the ancient sonata principle, so much admired by Boulez and the present-day extremists. Schönberg, on the other hand, maintained the closest respect for the classical forms as they had been put into practice by Beethoven and Brahms. The last composer was a particularly important source as far as he was concerned. Not only did he orchestrate one of Brahms's Piano Quartets (it does not sound very Brahmsian in Schönberg's version, however, the harmonies seeming a little too acid for that comfortable, romantically-inclined classicist), but he constantly modelled his work on the chamber-music techniques of that composer. Hence, the lessons Schönberg gave were mostly concerned with working out problems of form and orchestration selected from the period Bach to Brahms.

Perhaps it should be stressed, at this stage, that one of the great issues to present itself in the dodecaphonic (Greek for twelve tones) music Schönberg was to write much later was the need to acquire contrapuntal fluency. Clearly, if tonality is disbarred, and everything in the way of harmony disallowed, the sole means of movement left to a composer is that of linear crossing of 'rows'. This was best done, in Schönberg's view, by adopting devices like canon, inversion, retrogression. We shall see, a little later on, how these elements became fused into something resembling a 'system', however distasteful that word seems to have been to him. At this relatively immature stage in his thinking, chromatic harmony still appeared as the principal feature of his compositions; but there was already a marked element of anticipation in the importance the composer attached to contrapuntal exercises. Both Webern and Berg were made to do ricercari, cancrizans, double fugues and all the other teasing problems that make life so difficult for the non-mathematically-inclined musician. Despite the fact that he was not as erudite as, say, d'Indy, or as facile in part-writing as Franck, the bias of Schönberg's teaching was not thereby essentially different from theirs. The main difference was perhaps that it was a little more willing to come up to date, to risk reprehensible adventures no institution would have been pleased to endorse. But this habit sprang as much from the pupils as from the master, and it is very doubtful whether the French school ever produced young master-minds with the masticatory zeal for chewing over the orthodox lumps of harmony and counterpoint to be encountered in the classical works shown by Webern and Berg. Only Guillaume Lekeu can be compared with them in this respect, and he was dead at the age of twenty-four. What might be emphasized here is that, though the two pupils took equally unrebelliously to the hard, conventional tasks allotted to them, it was Berg, nowadays cast as the most conservative of the new Viennese, who was the keenest polemicist on behalf of non-tonal music. The meek Webern, who was actually the most revolutionary, had the kind of scholarly temperament which steers clear of argument, and he accordingly had little to say about his plans.

It must not be thought, either, that the Viennese trio were in quite such constant touch with one another as has sometimes been implied by advocates of the 'school' idea. In 1907, for example, Schönberg returned temporarily to Berlin to succeed Busoni at the Academy of Arts. It could also be said of him that he was at this time reaching the end of his first, non-tonal period. The Quartet No. 1 (1905) had preserved the tonal ambiguity of the first works; whilst the Chamber Symphony, Op. 9 (1906), written for fifteen instruments, had asserted the contrapuntal principles, predicated by the direction in which he was moving, in a curiously equivocal way. By the Quartet No. 2 (1908), however, Schönberg severed all tonal bonds more or less completely, producing a work in which the melodic lines are unprecedently angular and without vestigial harmonic support. The intervals between the notes are wider than before, and the suggestion of a new style is broached in the words of the vocal part which is introduced in the last movement. It begins: 'Ich fühle, Luft von anderen Planeten' (I feel the air of other spheres)—a prophetic quotation from Stefan George. This, incidentally, was the last composition to which the composer actually gave a key signature, being nominally cast in F sharp. The Three Piano Pieces Op. II (1909) which followed are normally regarded as ushering in the second period, typified by the total equation of consonance with dissonance; the abandonment of what might be described as the 'tortured lyricism' of the earlier period; and a more easily detectable preference for short, polyphonic forms. The cycle of songs based on George's poems, *Das Buch der hangenden Garten*, Op. 15, dating from much the same point in the composer's career, poses the fundamental difficulty which was to arise out of all Schönberg's subsequent music for voice—namely, that of finding singers with absolute pitch or with the willingness to attempt the zig-zag melodic lines such music embraced. Nowadays, singers seem better able to accept radical departures from the norm; but in the pre-First World War period vocal training was very often geared to the unusually tuneful standards of Schubert's lieder, which could be sung, albeit not very elegantly, by the ordinary domestic amateur.

All these developments were the result of Schönberg's own questing attitude, and they should be adduced as evidence for the defence when charges of traditionalism are hurled at him as they frequently are by young people now in their 'twenties or 'thirties. Particularly original and revolutionary were the next half-dozen or so of the composer's works—several of which present good claims to being his masterpiece. The Five Orchestral Pieces Op. 16 (1909) are amazing in their attempt to make colour perform the function of melody. The term used to describe this is 'Klangfarbenmelodie'. The idea was new and did not arise in any way out of the experiments both Franck and Debussy had made in harmonic 'synaesthesia'. What these composers had aimed at was the identification of colour with key, or with a particular chord—in the first instance only carrying a stage further Beethoven's preference for attaching emotional connotations to keys like C minor and A flat. Schönberg, in No. 3 of his Five Orchestral Pieces, begins with a chord, but moves away by permitting notes *of the same pitch* to be sounded in differing timbres. Chordal coloration was not something he dabbled with, since this would have had to depend on a primarily homophonic style, such as Debussy's, which had been abandoned along with the triadic element. What the composer did not bargain for was the extent to which 'tonal reminiscences' would occur by accidental production of triads and octave 'doublings'. In order to overcome these difficulties, Schönberg relied excessively, and perhaps somewhat artificially, on 'ostinato' and long pedal points, over which brief, dislocated motifs would suddenly appear. Consistent use of 'neighbour-notes', or displacements of the octave by the ninth and the tenth by the eleventh, assisted towards this end. In 1949, the composer revised this set of pieces so as to make them less of a task to performers, but most good orchestras of today can cope with them. The present writers recalls a strikingly good performance by the International Youth Orchestra, under Boulez, at the Bayreuth Staadhalle, which suggests that even youngsters at school are now equipped to deal with them.

It was with the vocal works of the period 1909–17 that Schönberg really came into his own, however, and the enormous gains he had made were perhaps best summarized in compositions like *Erwartung* (Expectancy) Op. 17, a monodrama of paramount importance in his 'œuvre'; *Pierrot Lunaire*, Op. 21, a chamber work for female reciter and five instruments; and *Die Glückliche Hand* (The Lucky Hand), a half-continuation of the colour-sound equation, more in the manner of the late Scriabin, for which Schönberg himself wrote the libretto. Of these exceedingly significant works, it is *Erwartung* that has excited the most attention in recent years; though for a long time *Pierrot Lunaire* was regarded as the greatest. Anthony Payne, in his recent study of the composer, has described *Erwartung* as 'one of the most remarkable examples of sustained, free composition in existence'.[1]

This is undoubtedly the reason for its great hold over the anti-Western modernists. Boulez, again, who has to some extent continued the tradition of melodic arabesque of the French orientalists, and who has been extremely critical of reversions to formal sonata-like procedures, has naturally responded to *Erwartung* as a gigantic improvisation. Generally speaking, the substance of Boulez's attack on Schönberg's music lies in the over-concern it shows with post-Brahmsian formalism and its relative unwillingness to indulge in fluid, plastic techniques. As he himself has phrased it:

> . . . there are no negative aspects of improvisation in Schönberg's music. He did not use something for a moment, then abandon it for something else.[2]

One can appreciate, from reasoning of this kind, how Boulez has arrived at his relatively poor estimate of works like the *Orchestral Variations* Op. 31 (1926–8), which he regards as 'too symmetrical' and not nearly as good as Webern's *Variations* Op. 30 (1940), which employ a far hazier mingling of forms. It is a fact, however, that even Webern's work is made up of traditional forms—overture, theme, recapitulation, development, coda and so on. What Boulez presumably admires is the comparatively unconstrained use of these forms, as opposed to Schönberg's straight, logical procedures. It is only a brief step from this position to the one that condemns Schönberg's twelve-tone interlude and that altogether vilifies that composer's last, American tendency to go back to a quasi-classical conception of music as an art of pre-ordained structures.

It is interesting that Boulez disapproves, less severely perhaps, of a like gravitation towards formalism in Webern's art, and would prefer the composer's earlier works to his latter. Of course, Webern never went as far in his acceptance of the structural element as Schönberg; but the shapes of his early works are more asymmetrical, more unclassifiable, than those of his later, and hence earn for them a certain imprimatur among the young.

---

[1] See *Schönberg* by Anthony Payne (O.U.P., 1968).
[2] Quoted from an interview, and reported in Tim Souster's article 'Boulez and the Second Viennese School' (*The Musical Times*, May, 1969, No. 1515, Vol. 110, pp. 473–6).

Boulez, in fact, has compared Webern's first efforts at composition
with Mondrian's famous series of 'Trees', done between 1909
and 1913. In a recent book on Mondrian, Frank Elgar has described these pictures as 'no more than geometric planes irregu-
larly assembled and high-lighted by only a few bright colours'.[1]

Irregular is the operative word here, for what they reveal is the
painter stripping away the language of Cubism (significantly
equated by Donald Mitchell, in his book *The Language of Modern
Music* (Faber, 1963), with Schönberg's 'serialism') and evolving a
dynamic, concave style of his own. Later on, much to Boulez's
disgust, Mondrian went back to the squares, triangles and straight
lines of the abstract school, thus depriving himself of a good deal
of his original freedom and adventurousness. I think the poet
Wallace Stevens has put better than anyone else the problem
involved in evaluating these styles, which are essentially modes of
rationalism and irrationalism respectively. In his usual gently
satirical vein he once wrote:

> Rationalists, wearing square hats,
> Think in square rooms,
> Looking at the floor,
> Looking at the ceiling,
> They confine themselves to right-angled triangles.
>
> If they tried rhomboids,
> Cones, waving lines, ellipses—
> As, for example, the ellipse of the half-moon—
> Rationalists would wear sombreros.[2]

In the *Six Bagatelles* for String Quartet, Op. 9 (1913), Webern
broke, much more effectively than he was to do later, with the
ideal of form. If one takes the view, therefore, that music should
be formless (or, at any rate, minimally determined by form) then
these represent his finest works, by comparison with which
Schönberg's seem conservative. To say, however, as Boulez has
done, that the latter was 'the Pétain of music' merely seems petu-
lant and insensitive to the virtues of a basic component in all
art.

In an early essay called *Trajectoires*, Boulez claimed that it was
only Debussy, in *Jeux*, who managed to cut completely free from
the pedantry and provincialism of most twentieth-century music.
The task for Debussy was getting out from beneath Wagner's
influence, something he accomplished together with Satie before

[1] *Mondrian* by Frank Elgar, trans. by Thomas Walton (Thames &
Hudson, 1969).
[2] *Collected Poems of Wallace Stevens* (Faber, 1955).

the turn of the century. In quite the opposite fashion, or so the story follows, Schönberg *failed* to disengage himself, not simply from Wagner (who was merely the most innocuous of his 'false gods') but from late Beethoven and Brahms, two thoroughly pernicious influences. Presumably Boulez and his juniors would therefore accept as proven Professor Machlis's version, which runs:

> Webern responded to the radical portion of Schönbergian doctrine, just as Berg exploited its more conservative elements. Of these three masters of the modern Viennese school, he was the one who cut himself off most completely from the tonal past.[1]

But mention of Debussy as the great innovator reminds us that it was Schönberg and not Webern who developed the method of 'sprechstimme' (or speech-song) in his cycle, *Pierrot Lunaire*—a device adumbrated in the French composer's operatic version of *Pelléas et Mélisande*. As a matter of fact, *Pierrot* has a good deal in common with that side of Debussy that has been described as 'harlequin-like'. It will be recalled that his Cello Sonata of 1915 was sub-titled 'Pierrot fâché avec la lune'; and that he had previously written songs like *Mandoline* based on the characters of the commedia dell 'arte. Schönberg's *Pierrot* was also a very formless work for its period. It has unequal barring, free rhythms and was actually referred to as 'musical prose' by no less a person than Webern himself. Egon Wellesz, writing in 1916, considered it the most advanced work imaginable in its invocation of primitivism and exoticism. That it is still regarded as such by many is suggested by Felix Aprahamian's remark—delivered at the 1969 symposium of the Cardiff Twentieth Century Festival of Music— that he would be happy to do without it altogether, and that it made no sense to him aside from its text. By comparison, few have followed Lambert in seeing it as a piece of aberrant Romanticism —'a Lieder recital that has taken a wrong turning'.

From 1915 to 1923, Schönberg remained virtually silent, having said all he could say with the materials in his possession and having no further ideas to inspire him. The war, too, imposed a certain inhibition on him, being a depressive type. When he did emerge from his mental cell, however, it was with the twelve-tone method at his disposal. Despite the complexity to which it has given rise, there is nothing fearfully mysterious about this method of composing. It merely assumes that each note in the chromatic scale possesses an equal value, and abjures the notion of an aural reversion to a tonic. Having made this assumption, the next step is

[1] *Introduction to Contemporary Music* (Norton, 1961).

to write a tone-row embracing all twelve notes in whatever order one wishes. One can then present this row as invented; invert it (that is to say, turn it upside down); use it in retrograde fashion (that is to say, play it backwards); and finally give it in the form of a retrograde inversion or combination of the last two arrangements. There are thus forty-eight ways in which a composer may project his material. The techniques of part-writing present no special departures, except that they are not bound by any harmonic rules. Canon, fugue, imitation and so on may be used (indeed they usually form the chief means of motion) but they must follow the principle of the row and no other. All sequences are accordingly versions of the row, at whatever point they enter, or on whatever instrument they happen to be played. What led Schönberg to devise such a method of composition is conjectural. He certainly did not intend it to be a final system by which composers would replace the tonal system. Rather, he thought of it as a fruitful limitation which he needed to impose on himself to rid his music of the element of disorder. Like Palestrina and the old masters, he knew the value of rules, and was aware that a challenge of the kind that might be introduced through this sort of method would be a spur to greater creative effort. Naturally, the method did not appear out of the blue to him, and there are transitional works, such as *Jacobsleiter* (1917), in which it begins to figure and then peters out. The *Serenade* Op. 24 (1923) is perhaps the first truly ordered 'twelve-tone' work, with the *Variations for Orchestra* Op. 31 (1926–8) representing the high-water mark of the style.

'Serialism', as the method was soon called, proposed certain aesthetic as well as technical questions. Was it, for instance, more expressive a method on account of its excessive dependence on the chromatic element? (Here it will be noted that nineteenth-century music, like Wagner's, generated tension in proportion to its degree of chromaticism, relaxation in proportion to its degree of diatonicism.) Or was it likely to lead to a bleakly intellectual music because all of its intervals were predetermined? Could untrained musicians really detect such things as retrograde inversions of the 'row'? And if not, was not this a serious fault in music expressly dependent on such factors? No one has answered these questions to the complete satisfaction of critics and public to this day. Some quite notable musicians, like Hindemith and Ansermet, have maintained that the human ear or brain is so constructed as to seek out a tonic, and hence twelve-tone music is a chimera. Others have argued, equally strenuously, that our desire for resolution is merely the consequence of years of conditioning. Oblivious to these controversies, Schönberg continued on the

course he had set for himself until 1933, when the Nazis decided
him to leave for the United States. There he taught at the University of Southern California and at Los Angeles right up to the time
of his death in 1951, having elected to become an American citizen
in 1940. His American works, while continuing the twelve-tone
method, did so without the dogmatism that had been attached to
his name in Europe. In a sense, they are a vindication of the
position to which he had always clung—namely, that his 'method'
was no more than a convenient aid to composition that might well
be modified in time. It is true that in the mid-thirties, he had
perversely delighted in a little inflexibility. (Of the Violin Concerto
of 1936, he had archly declaimed: 'I am delighted to add another
unplayable work to the repertoire'), but this was merely in order
to take a knock at one or two of his bitterest critics. In the Piano
Concerto (1945), we still find 'rows' but the music somehow
sounds more mellow; while in the final *Survivor from Warsaw*
(1948), for narrator, chorus and orchestra, there is almost a reversion to the expressionist period of forty years earlier. For this
reversion, some of the composer's admirers have found it hard to
forgive him.

Meanwhile, what was it precisely that Webern had achieved?
In terms of sheer bulk, it must be confessed, very little. Over the
whole of his life-span (1883–1945), he wrote no more than thirty-
one works, all of which can be got on to four gramophone records.[1]
Hence, prolixity is not a word one uses in connection with his art.
Similarly, avidity is not a word one uses in connection with his
character. In 1918, he retired from Vienna to the suburb of
Mödling, where he naturally saw a good deal less of his former
mentor. He took a few pupils himself (Humphrey Searle eventually became one of them) and acted as proofreader for a music
publishing house. Otherwise, he led an entirely uneventful life.
When the Second World War threatened to turn him out of his
home, he moved to Mittershill, near Salzburg, where he could
avoid the bombing. Musically, he had begun his career with a
Passacaglia, a most appropriate choice since one fundamental
principle in his music is that of 'perpetual variation'. Even with
greater assurance than Schönberg, he handled the subtle and
difficult alternatives proposed by the 'twelve-tone' method in such
a manner as to suggest acute powers of mental concentration.

[1] Assuming that the composer had a thirty-five year creative span, and
that his compositions work out at an average duration of about seven
minutes, it still does not indicate an annual output of more than about
five or six minutes! This must be the smallest on record, except for
occasional long-lived composers who dried up in their 'twenties or
'thirties.

Double canons in contrary motion came easily to him, yet all
emerged in a tight, aphoristic style in which there was no room at
all for repetition. Other features of his music also derive from
Schönberg, chiefly his preference for the single, sustained tone—
which we must attribute to the latter's principle of klangfarbenmelodie. However, I believe Debussy was also an influence in
this matter. If one listens to a song like *En Sourdine* from the first
set of the French composer's *Fêtes Galantes*, one can understand
what is meant. Webern's likeness for the extremes of dynamics
(more especially the extreme piano-pianissimo range) may again
have stemmed as much from Debussy as from Schönberg. The
composer's own innovations include the extension of the serial
principle to timbre and rhythm, and a tendency to place the
rhythmical emphasis on the off-beat, to indulge in rhythmical
suspension. All Webern's music is minuscule, and the second
quality one is apt to notice about it is its delicate 'pointilliste' scoring.

Perhaps the best of Webern's early music is contained in the
Five Pieces for Orchestra Op. 10 (1912), where seventeen instruments play without tutti. Every note is clearly enunciated and no
theme is allowed to dominate at the expense of its counterpoint.
Certain intervals occur more frequently than others and these
anticipate a general tendency in Webern's music—the major
seventh, the minor ninth, the tritone (almost essential for twelve-
tone composers if they are to avoid tonally euphonious associations) minor seventh and major ninth being the most familiar.
Rests also occur regularly, and these are not placed, as they are in
Mozart, to secure abrupt contrasts or as means to witticisms, but
in order to nullify tensions that arise. Webern's music never
becomes climactic for that reason. Robert Craft, who has recorded
all Webern's music, also draws attention to the composer's preference for triplet figures, refusal to engage in development, and
determination to obtain the utmost transparency of texture.[1] Yet
it would be a mistake to classify the composer as an abstractionist,
as some of his present-day disciples are inclined to do. He did in
fact write numerous songs, including some settings of George and
Rilke, and a good many of the poetess, Hildegarde Jone, with
whom he and his wife became friendly from about 1926 onwards.
An opera would, I think, have been outside the scope of his
interests and abilities; but he wrote a play *Tod* and held unexpectedly literary and philosophical interests. Kant and Schope-
hauer were, for example, favourite authors, and like Bruno Walter
he came under the influence of Rudolph Steiner. As may be
imagined, he took readily to Goethe's rather benevolent view of

[1] See 'Anton Webern' by Robert Craft and Kurt Stone in *The Score*
No. 13 (1955).

nature and spent much of his free time examining rocks, plants and various kinds of minerals. While at Mödling, he also acted as conductor of the Vienna Workers' Symphony Concerts (he had briefly done some theatre conducting at Danzig and Berlin just before the First World War) and became a convinced socialist. Although about half of his music is vocal, there are several important instrumental works, of which the Symphony Op. 21 (1928) and the Variations Op. 30 (1940) are the most formidable.

The former work is in two movements, the first in sonata form and the second a set of variations on a theme. It is strictly dodecaphonic, making use of inversions and retrograde motions. Presumably, it is the strictness of the sonata element—it includes exposition, development, recapitulation and coda—that is such a source of exasperation to the Boulez camp. But the fact must be faced that Webern could also be highly traditional; and if one is going to attack Schönberg on these grounds there is no possibility of letting Webern down all that lightly. The Variations Op. 30 call for largish forces—four woodwinds, four brass, celeste, harp, timpani and complete string section. In Webernian terms, this represents a mighty collocation, the equivalent of the orchestra Mahler chose for *Das Lied von der Erde*. Listeners who find these major works difficult of access (and I cannot believe that anyone finds them easy) might prefer to switch their attentions to the Piano Concerto Op. 24 (1934) where the presence of that instrument acts as a sort of focus even though there are no virtuoso intrusions. The chamber music contains a work for saxophone, piano and strings, the Quartet Op. 22 (1930) and a plainer specimen for strings alone, the Quartet Op. 28 (1938). These have been intelligently analysed by Colin Mason.[1] Webern also liked to think of himself as a writer of solo piano pieces—at least he enjoyed transcribing works (chiefly Schönberg's) for this instrument. His fairly well-known Variations Op. 27 (1937) are a trifle forbidding, and are not recommended to those who like their piano music to sound idiomatic. Other than that, there is not much to comment upon. A String Trio Op. 20 (1927)—which is considered by Adorno to be Webern's masterpiece—is so densely contrapuntal that one hesitates to draw attention to it. Webern himself continued to live at Mittershill till 1945, when he suddenly met his death at the hands of an American soldier. Out for a stroll after the curfew had sounded, he was unable to understand a command to halt, and was shot on the false assumption that he was engaged in guerilla activities. Thus ended the career of the most unmilitant musician of his generation.

[1] The reference is to 'Webern's Later Chamber Music' in *Tempo* XXXVIII (1957).

Answers to the question implicit in our title, then, are likely to depend, to a large extent, on one's reactions to such issues as size, scope and determination to remain within a given tradition. They may also be affected by the degree of emotion one expects from music. To a Stravinsky, obsessed (at least in his old age) by notions of clarity and compression, Webern has at last become the ideal for which his life has seemed a preparation. As he wrote of the composer in one of his most recent books of reminiscences:

> Doomed to total failure in a deaf world of ignorance and indifference, he inexorably kept on cutting out his diamonds, his dazzling diamonds, of whose mines he had such a perfect knowledge.[1]

On the other side of the coin, one cannot help admiring Schönberg's stand against both those who would destroy the tradition and those who would dilute it in the interests of middlebrow appreciation. Given his neurotic temperament, his acutely 'expressionist' attitude to art, there is something unutterably moving about his conviction, coming just when it did, that music was not for the masses, but for those who were driven by the desire for what Arnold called 'the pursuit of perfection'—his definition of culture, and a so much better definition than the anthropological cum-sociological definition which has since replaced it. As Schönberg truly said: 'If it is art, it is not for all, and if it is for all, it is not art.' Perhaps this sounds snobbish or condescending, but the composer knew when he wrote it that posterity would be the only audience who would ever give him unqualified applause, and that is a hard enough thought to live with. Today, when so many cheaper talents enjoy the easy fame that never came to him, it is absolutely necessary to listen to his words of wisdom:

> There are relatively few people who are capable of understanding, purely musically, what music has to say. Such trained listeners have probably never been very numerous, but that does not prevent the artist from creating only for them. Great art pre-supposes the alert mind of the educated listener.

Not sentiments to warm the hearts of the 'pop' managers, or even those educational Judases who would like to mould all our tastes to the same flabby image. But Art and Democracy are two different processes, and it is to the Schönbergs of this world that we owe our knowledge of this fact.

[1] *Memories and Commentaries* (Faber, 1960).

viii 'Wozzeck' as Satire and Prophecy

Schönberg's second great pupil, Alban Berg, was two years younger than Webern, having been born in 1885; and it would be hard to imagine two men more unalike in their outlook. The expression 'prince among men' has sometimes been used to describe Franz Liszt, presumably to convey an appreciation of that composer's superb generosity and commanding spirit. But it is just as applicable, in a quieter way, to Berg, whose nobility of feeling and gesture shine outwards from every act he undertook. To read his letters and articles (and he was a tireless defender of unpopular musical causes, even when they had little to do with his own unacceptable innovations) is to acquaint oneself with a human being who possessed as wide a range of fine qualities as any who ever walked this earth—genius, intellect, sensibility, judgment, self-understanding, humour and a veritable reservoir of compassion for all victims of persecution and injustice. What Schönberg himself wrote of him is so patently true that it may be confirmed on almost any page of the composer's life-story as presented by Reich, Wildgans, Redlich or any of the other standard authorities:

> What an easy thing it was to call forth his sympathy! I always had the impression that he had experienced beforehand what people close to him were going through, as though he had already suffered with them when they were suffering, so that when they came to tell him of it it did not catch him unawares but rather on the contrary re-opened old wounds. Wounds that he had already inflicted upon himself by his powerful sympathy.

We should do well to remember these wise words when we come to examine Berg's great opera, *Wozzeck*, which more than any

87

other work of this century underlines the brutality and sadness of human relations and comments, in a definitive fashion, on the moral condition of our age. But before going on to make this examination, it is essential that we should know a little more about the composer's background and aims.

The son of a fairly well-to-do salesman in the export business, Berg was one of a large family all of whom had inherited some musical talent from their mother, who kept a shop stocked with religious momentoes near St Stephens Cathedral. Ordinarily, the family would have prospered, but Berg's father died in 1900 and from then until they acquired some estates near Berghof, in the form of a legacy, in 1905, things went very poorly for them. This brief period of penury was not important in itself, except that it co-incided with the composer's need to choose a career and perhaps gave him a taste of how the other half was forced to live. The career he was obliged to select could not have been more un-suited to his gifts. It was a post in the Department of Inland Revenue which involved him in the computation and collection of taxes. Both these tasks were extremely distasteful to Berg, who typically wrote off a large number of debts as 'unrecoverable' when conditions permitted him to leave. Even after he had quitted this miserable profession, however, he found himself saddled with the management of the estates; and this occupied a good deal of the time he might otherwise have devoted to composition. As a scholar, he had not done especially well at school (again chiefly on account of domestic difficulties), but he seemed from the very first to possess exquisite taste and high literary ability. One suspects that it was the stupidity of his teachers, and his frequent absences through ill-health, that combined to mark him down as a very average pupil. The illnesses he had were asthmatic, and he went as far as to consult Freud about them in 1908 (during the midst of his Schönberg tuition), thus emulating his predecessor, Mahler, who had been given a diagnosis of 'mother-fixation', and his conductor colleague, Bruno Walter, who had gone to the famous psycho-analyst to try and arrest a mysterious hysterical paralysis that afflicted his baton arm. In Berg's case, Freud was able to do little to help, partly because the disorder was not entirely responsive to psycho-analytical treatment, and partly because Berg himself developed a strong superstition about it.[1]

---

[1] The superstition had to do with the number 23. This, as we have noted was the composer's age at the time of his severest attacks, and it was on July 23rd, 1908, that he had his appointment with Freud. Grisly conviction was given to his superstition when he died following the stroke of midnight on December 23rd, 1935. His last words were reputedly: 'Today is the 23rd. It will be the decisive day!'

Lessons with Schönberg had begun before Berg resigned from the government service, and it is worth mentioning that his teacher did not consider accepting a fee until his pupil's financial situation had improved. The earliest compositions to be written were surprisingly aphoristic in character, and redolent of Webern in their sheer brevity. They were mostly chamber-pieces and songs with orchestra. The minuscule song-cycle known as the *Altenberg-Lieder* (1910), which attempted to translate into music the tiny picture-postcard poems of the composer's friend and literary hero, Peter Altenberg, may be regarded as typical. Schönberg, though he admired his pupil's gifts as much as anyone, was strangely displeased with these efforts. It was not that he doubted Berg's capabilities. These had been proved time and time again in the perfection of the exercises he had submitted; and were suggested by the steadfast devotion he had always reserved for masters like Brahms, one of Schönberg's own heroes. A visit Berg paid to his teacher in Berlin during June, 1913 (*not*, incidentally, on the 23rd) was the occasion of a mild trauma. After he had shown Schönberg his Four Pieces for Clarinet and Piano, Op. 5, the master turned and berated him with unusual vehemence. The pieces were so slight as to have obstructed all possible development; they were mere jottings, suited for further expansion, perhaps, but useless as they stood. This was about the gist of his criticism, and since Berg tended to worship his teacher it was a criticism that cut to the quick. Immediately afterwards, Berg resolved to write less but to work on a more extended scale. The Three Orchestral Pieces, Op. 6 that followed were accordingly almost Mahleresque, taking two full years to complete. But the composer was altogether too mature a man to remain piqued at hostile criticism for long—especially if it came from a quarter he respected. It was only a short while, therefore, before good relations were restored. The reason we mention the incident is to show what a steely influence Schönberg managed to wield over his pupils, including Berg. It accounts, to some degree, for the conservatism latter-day critics have been inclined to attribute to the younger composer.

But only to some degree. We should not under-estimate the extent to which conservatism was a natural inclination to which Berg was mildly prone, a disposition he would not have been ashamed to acknowledge as his own. In an article—admittedly written later in his career—the composer cheerfully lambasted those who sought to equate all products of the new media with the utterances of genius:

The use of contemporary means—such as cinema,

revue, loudspeakers, jazz—guarantees only that such
a work is contemporary . . .[1]

Real development in art, according to Berg's way of thinking,
came about through the action of genius—a very individual and
unpredictable thing. Were he alive today, he would no doubt
find the all-mighty fuss going on over electronics, television opera
and so on of no significance whatever. Yet this point of view does
not make Berg truly a conservative. On the contrary, it may be that
the true conservative is to be found among the vociferous advocates of 'newness'—which on examination so often proves to be
anything but new. It might be worth while to draw attention, in
this sense, to the paradoxical attitude of Boulez who, after having
consistently attacked Berg for compromising with the tonal
system, and for clinging to the old set forms, has recently begun
to explain his own reservations to such a 'new' device as electronics:

> I do not find present-day electronics typical of music. I
> must first explain myself. Loudspeakers are used only for
> *reproduction* and not for *creation*. All is reduced to one di-
> mension, even with the best equipment.[2]

He then goes on to compare electronic music to acting if it were
all done through a Public Address System, with individual voices
all coming out the same. It is quite possible that Berg had similar
reservations about, not merely the new media of his day, but the
new compositional devices, including the twelve-tone method.
As a matter of fact, he wrote to Reich in 1929 that he genuinely
felt a tonal method might be combined fruitfully with a non-
tonal method if only there were a composer of genius able to do
it. This does not sound like the pronouncement of a betrayer
as much as a sceptic. It could also be interpreted as a modest
hint.

In May 1914, Berg went to the theatre to see a play entitled
Woyzeck (old spelling) by the dramatist George Büchner (1813–
37). The author had been a brilliant intellectual whose socialist
beliefs had brought him into conflict with the Metternich régime.
His works for the stage were few, the only other notable play of
his being *Danton's Tod* (Danton's Death). This was because he

---

[1] See Berg's article in the *Neue Musik-Zeitung* 1928. Year 49, No. 9,
Stuttgart.
[2] 'Boulez and the Second Viennese School' by Tim Souster, *Musical
Times*, May 1969, No. 1515, Vol. 110, pp. 473–6. It seems hardly necessary to add that Boulez renounced the 'twelve-tone' system as being
insufficiently individual to suit his *own* talents, and has pinned his faith
to the more flexible, melodic style derived from Debussy.

had devoted a large part of his activities to being a medical student, and had moreover died at the tragically premature age of twenty-four. On watching the play, Berg realized instantly that this could be made the vehicle for a powerful, emotionally expressive, opera. Its early date was a preliminary handicap, and so was the form in which it was cast. But as the composer himself was well endowed with literary abilities, and knew exactly the sort of operatic scenario he wanted, he had no compunction in adapting Büchner's play to his own requirements. The main obstacles were those of size and lack of contemporaneity. The first of these Berg overcame by dividing the original play into fifteen short scenes, five to each Act, and the second by introducing linguistic changes designed to bring the action more up to date.[1] Thus the final libretto, which was incidentally still unfinished in 1918 at the time of the composer's release from the army, coalesced into the ternary ABA form and each scene became fairly sharply marked off from the next. The last device offered the advantage of composing isolated character or situation portrayals, intended to contrast with one another. It absolved Berg from the need to write a continuous Wagnerian music-drama, and yet it also cleverly put out of court the old 'set number' procedure followed in Verdi and his imitators. When it came to the actual singing, Berg opted for his master Schönberg's 'Sprechstimme', so that the entire opera is presented in the form of heightened declamation, without arias or uninterrupted 'melos'. It should not be assumed from this, however, that *Wozzeck* is a twelve-tone opera. That technique, as we have had occasion to point out, was not invented until about 1923, by which time the work was complete. But there are remarkable anticipations of twelve-tone music in it, and the whole is couched in a non-tonal language that occasionally reverts to passages in recognizable keys (e.g. the D minor of the Interlude in Act III). Probably it is this combination of the tonal with the non-tonal that has made the opera acceptable as no other written by a member of the modern Viennese circle.

The story of *Wozzeck* is simply told. It is an account of the trials of an uneducated private soldier (a batman to a stupid, apoplectic Captain), who lives with his wife Marie and their child. At least, this appears to be the situation, but it transpires that the child was illegitimate and that Wozzeck has not sanctified the union by marriage. In Act I, we are shown the Captain, a sadistic

---

[1] Büchner's play had originally contained twenty-six scenes, and the text from which Berg made his adaptation was the Franzos edition of 1879 and not the earlier manuscript or the later Landau version dated 1909.

and unpleasant fellow, being shaved and engaging in patronizing remarks about the lower orders. After suffering these insults, Wozzeck retreats, with his friend Andres into the countryside outside the camp to cut firewood, finding the locale eerie and somehow ominous. Back in the barracks, Marie is singing a lullaby to her child, but is being distracted by the military band that passes her window; and especially by the charms of the Drum-Major, a typically conceited bully who has had his eye on her for some time. Another change of scene brings us into contact with the Doctor, an inhuman figure interested only in his scientific experiments relating to health and diet, who persuades Wozzeck to submit himself as a guinea-pig in certain tests. The act ends with a return to Marie's house, in which the Drum-Major has managed to effect his seduction. What follows in Act II is to some extent predictable. Wozzeck comes home and has his suspicions aroused by a set of earrings Marie has acquired from the Drum-Major. A second medical scene is enacted in which the Doctor now gives his attention to the Captain, whom he regards as an interesting case of grossness and over-indulgence. Later, at an Inn, Marie renews her affair with the Drum-Major in a more unashamed fashion; is watched by Wozzeck who returns to the soldiers' dormitory in a depressed state. When the Drum-Major wakens the whole platoon by bursting in drunk and boasting of his conquest, Wozzeck tackles him only to be knocked senseless by the big man's superior force. Act III begins with Marie in contrite mood, saying her prayers. But it is too late. Wozzeck invites her for a walk and stabs her in a fit of jealousy, afterwards attempting to work off his guilt by dancing in a nearby tavern. Burying the knife was something he had neglected to do, however, and he returns to the scene of the crime and throws it into a pond. Imagining he has not thrown it in deep enough, he then wades in after it and gets drowned. Meanwhile the Doctor and the Captain pass by, oblivious of the gasps they hear. In the very last scene, we witness the child of the victims playing hopscotch outside their house. Other children rush to impart the dreadful news, but the child fails to understand and goes on singing—'Hopp! Hopp!'— while the music fades into silence.

The most interesting fact about the music of *Wozzeck* is that it is cast almost entirely in ancient forms—though Berg expressly advised people at a lecture he once gave on the opera against listening for these forms as if they were pieces of absolute music. The point remains, however, that each scene contains music of a definite, strictly formal character. The opening Praeludium, with its rapid semi-quavers, has the function of depicting the Captain's silly chatter while being shaved. During the country scene with

Andres, a Rhapsody is employed to express the feelings of release on contact with nature.[1] The March of the third scene of Act I hardly needs explaining—it is the embodiment of the military strutting of the Drum-Major, having the same satirical function as the 'cannon' song in Kurt Weill's *Der Dreigroschenoper*. Marie's lullaby explains itself as a set piece demonstrating her feelings for her child, but the Passacaglia used for the scene between Wozzeck and the Doctor takes a bit more thought to elucidate. It is interesting to note that Berg actually looked this word up in a musical dictionary and found, to his surprise, that it meant a *fixed* theme with variations—exactly the artistic equivalent of the Doctor's *idée fixe* about diet and mental disorder, around which he constantly circles in his relations with Wozzeck and later the Captain. In Act II, the sonata forms used are meant to interlock the relations formed: firstly Marie with her child, then with Wozzeck. This could be interpreted as adopting a leit-motif technique, since the characters do have themes to themselves; but it is the manner in which these themes are fused that is significant. This gives Berg his opportunity to reveal them as the different components of a sonata exposition. Other unmistakable uses of this original procedure occur in the Fugue (where the voices are those of the Captain, the Doctor and Wozzeck) and the Rondo (intended to imitate the regularity of the snores of the soldiers' dormitory) from Act II. By comparison Act III consists of a series of six Inventions, and these again make various character-architectonic equations.

Looking at the literary aspects of the drama, it is obvious that Berg's sympathy lies chiefly with Wozzeck. This is most apparent in Act I, Sc. I, where the Captain's taunting eventually leads to an outburst on the soldier's part that gives rise, in a general way, to the grievances of the lower classes in a world in which they are chivied and bullied without being given any means to fight back. When, for example, the Captain upbraids his batman for not having married Marie and become respectable, Wozzeck turns on him and pleads:

> Poor folk like us! See now, need money! Look sir, always money. Let one of us try to bring one of his own kind into the world in a good moral way! We're all made of flesh and blood! If I were a lord, sir, and wore a silk-hat and had a watch and an eye-glass too, and could talk

[1] Incidentally, even within the confines of a single scene, old forms perform specific functions—like the Gigue used to mock Wozzeck in Act I, Sc. I or the Hunting tune meant to help evoke the countryside in Act I, Sc. II.

> genteel-like, then I'd be virtuous too! It must be fine in-
> deed to be virtuous, indeed, sir. And yet, I am a simple
> soul. Folk like us always are unfortunate in this world
> and in any other world. I think that if we go to heaven,
> then we shall be the thunder-makers!

This, without doubt, is the language of the Büchner who wrote the
pamphlet, *Peace to the hovel, strife to the Palace*, and it is the
language of Marx and Engels though they were born five and
seven years later than the author of *Woyzeck* and survived to
develop their ideas in connection with the mid-century factory
system. Communism, however, had not gained power until 1917
in Russia, by which time even Berg's work on the libretto of the
first Act had taken shape. One must therefore view the ferocity
of the class-conflict in *Wozzeck* as not merely satirical but prophetic. We have already noted Webern's attachment to socialist
doctrines in the 1920's, and while it is hard to see Berg as the
upholder of any mass philosophy (he was too much of a natural
aristocrat) there can be no doubt that much of his opera had been
prompted by his disgust for the arrogant officer-class of his day
and the instinctive urge he felt to do something to improve the
lot of the ordinary people.

One should not forget, either, that Berg had served in the army
throughout the War, first of all with the First Infantry Regiment
in Vienna and later (as a result of increased bronchial attacks) at
the War Office. It was during the earlier phase of his military
existence (1915–16) that he learned what it was like to lie awake
in a hut full of groaning, snoring soldiers—tired out but unable
to sleep for the noise and fear that surrounded him. When his
pupil Gottfried Kassowitz visited him at the Karalyhida barracks,
Berg remarked ruefully to him:

> Have you ever heard a lot of people all snoring at the
> same time? The polyphonic breathing gasping and groan-
> ing makes the strangest chorus I have ever heard. It is
> like a music of the primeval sounds that rises from the
> abysses of these people's souls.

What better evidence could one bring forward to account for the
Rondo Martiale's cacophony at the close of Act II? And how
valuable this and similar experiences must have been to Berg
when he came to create the unparalleled atmosphere of sinking
spirits that so pervades his whole opera? Militarism was, of
course, a distinct characteristic of the German-speaking nations
in the period which had led up to the War. It had been the target
of satirical attack from Schnitzler, the Austrian playwright, in

the earliest years of the century, especially in his masterly interior monologue *Leutnant Gustl* (1900), in which a young officer is forced by an out-dated code of honour to consider committing suicide because he has carelessly neglected to challenge a ruffian business man to a duel over some trifling insult. By the unexpected death of the business man, he is saved from making what was to all intents and purposes a hollow and pointless decision. The play, it is worth noting, cost Schnitzler his commission in the reserve, and is a perfect illustration of the idiotic style of behaviour current in the Vienna in which Berg himself had grown up. As it happened, one of the city's greatest socialist orators and critics, Karl Kraus, had for a long time been a minor hero of Berg's. Most of Kraus's ammunition came from the silly conversations of the officers who gathered at the corner of the Ringstrasse and the Kärntnerstrasse of an evening, and no doubt a good deal of this found its way into Berg's ears when he attended Kraus's well-known rallies prophesying 'the last days of mankind'.

Psychologically, too, Vienna was a city seething with hints of an unwelcome future. The character of the Doctor in *Wozzeck* was not intended, it seems to me, to personify the cold detachment of a Freud, who had after all treated Berg, despite the fact that Kraus was as anti-Freudian as he was anti-military. Rather, it may have been suggested by that other, somewhat more sinister, Viennese psychiatrist, Richard Krafft-Ebing, author of the notorious *Psychopathia Sexualis* and holder of a chair at the University since 1880. Far more than Freud's, Krafft-Ebing's work had a forensic basis; he was deeply interested, as Lombroso had been, in the formation of the criminal mind. Textbooks of this period made free use of photographs of putative criminal types, and it was widely assumed that these could be distinguished by various psycho-physical characteristics. Head form, shape of the ears, length of the little finger—these were some of the alleged stigmata of the conventional psychiatry of the age. It is not surprising that many doctors wished to investigate further along these lines, examining the relation between diet and psychosis (like the Doctor in *Wozzeck*) or seeking for a correlation between physiognomy and sadism. When watching the scene between the Captain and the Doctor in Act II of Berg's opera, it is difficult to know which of the two characters is the greater object of satirical scrutiny. The Captain is the familiar red-faced, alcoholic martinet, the kind of figure so marvellously depicted in Georg Grosz's brilliant caricatures. One can almost visualize the way Berg thought of him, heavy and sunken in his features with prognathous jaws and distended gorilla-like nostrils. Yet the Doctor, in his way, seems hardly less odious. He has the air of a typical ruthless experimentalist, almost Orwellian in his lack of interest in suffering:

> As for you! Hm! Bloated features, fat, thickish neck,
> apoplectic circulation there! Yes, dear Captain, you
> might well have an apoplexia cerebri someday; possibly
> you might have it just along the one side of your body.
> Yes! You might find you're only paralysed on the right
> side, perhaps—or, with the best of luck, just in the
> lower limbs.

In view of the experiments carried out by Nazi doctors on the
inmates of the concentration camps of the 1940's—to say nothing
of the present attitudes being expressed over transplant surgery—
Berg's sketch seems uncannily clairvoyant.

Another important element in *Wozzeck*—which helps to reinforce the satire and the prophesy—is the element of irony. This
often takes on a musico-dramatic form that seems indivisible.
A prime example occurs in Act I, Sc. 5 in which Marie is
seduced by the Drum-Major. Here the musical direction is
'andante effetuoso', which is suggestive both of the tenderness of
physical love and also its insidiousness as experienced in the
attraction the man has for the woman. The sub-title 'quasi-
rondo' again implies that every so often the spell which caused
Marie to capitulate re-asserts itself against her wishes. This
explanation is made more credible by the fact that Marie is not
entirely a slut. In Act III, she does show signs of repentence, and
what Berg seems to be telling us in the last scene of the first act is
that even a good woman can be magnetized into behaving badly if
conditions of military glamour (and, conversely in Wozzeck's case,
military humiliation) are allowed enough scope. The most striking
of all the instances of irony, however, occurs at the opera's close.
Here the child's innocent skipping, to the accompaniment of
fading 'folk' music, underlines the extremes of innocence and guilt
which stand at each end of the opera. The composer is reminding
us that the naivety of childhood is constantly being threatened, in
an unconscious fashion, by the horrors of adulthood; and this,
too, if one reflects on it, is a Freudian moral. At least, we are left,
when the curtain drops, with the feeling that the child will have
to grow up in the shadow of its parents' misdeeds; is happy at
present but is already committed to a terrible destiny. I am reminded very much, when thinking of this ending, of Chirico's
famous picture of a child bowling a hoop in what seems like a
deserted city (the picture is called 'The Mystery and Melancholy
of a Street' and was painted around 1914). As James Thrall Soby
has commented about the work: 'One has the impression that

even if she (the child) reaches the light, she is doomed.' The same oppression hangs over the male child at the conclusion of *Wozzeck*. He is a child of the age to have fought in the Second World War, or died in one of its horrible deportation camps, as Berg himself might have done had he lived to reach the holocaust.

Mention of folk-music also reminds us that Berg was not above introducing this sort of concrete reference if it aided his dramatic purpose. The hunting-song clearly had definite connotations for all inhabitants of Franz Joseph's Austria, many of whom were still alive when the opera had its Viennese première as late as 1930; while it had also been used by Schumann and others as a means of evoking the old Germany. Both the child's song and the military march again possessed local associations. It is significant that Mahler used such forms in his symphonies, which as we know were designed to embrace the ordinary world in consuming, pictorial detail. The 'gingerbread' ending of the Fourth Symphony and the fatalistic march of the Sixth can be seen as fulfilling the same sort of function within the symphonic context as Berg's intrusions fulfilled in the context of opera. It is even possible to believe that Mahler exercised a stronger influence over the composer than either of the two musicians with whom he has customarily been associated. Not that he failed to acknowledge his debt to his teacher in *Wozzeck*. The Largo—which forms the third scene of Act II—is actually a set piece for a chamber orchestra of identical dimensions to the one Schönberg used in his Chamber Symphony, and was explicitly intended as a tribute. The Inventions of Act III, however, are not to be explained in a similar fashion, all the two composers' work on Bach notwithstanding. The first is Marie's prayer, and its point is that it is monothematic. The second, on the other hand, is an invention on a single note—the tremendous fortissimo note struck by the timpani as the accompaniment to the murder. In the third scene, the invention is rhythmic, in illustration of Wozzeck's guilt-ridden waltz with Margaret. The death of Wozzeck again revolves around the invention of a hexachord B C F A D and E. This has been prepared for by the famous unison crescendo on a B which succeeded the death of Marie and created the change of atmosphere for the next scene. The only explanation for the term 'invention' in relation to the orchestral interlude that occurs after Wozzeck's death is tonal, it being the only part of the opera in a fixed key. Finally, the hopscotch scene is a perpetuum mobile, a strict triplet movement duplicating the repetitive patterns of the child at play. Thus throughout the entire opera nothing is the result of musical chance.

The getting of *Wozzeck* on to the stage forms a particularly long and harrowing tale in itself, too long to be told in entirety in this essay. Although completed in October 1921, Berg did not add the instrumentation until April of the following year. By that time, however, it was ready to be put into the hands of whatever company was prepared to receive it. Wisely, in view of his finances, he agreed to Alma Mahler's suggestion that the vocal score should be published in advance of production, so that singers and managers might have a better opportunity to acquaint themselves with the work, without having to commit themselves to a firm contract. Erwin Stein wrote enthusiastically about the opera in the hope of inducing a reaction. But the best that could be done with it at the initial stage was to perform it in the form of an orchestral and vocal triptych, a suggestion put forward by the conductor Hermann Scherchen. This version was performed under that conductor's direction in June 1924 at Frankfurt. One still occasionally hears it performed this way at concerts. The *Three Fragments* involve only Marie as soloist. The actual première of the entire opera had to wait a further year until Erich Kleiber performed the miraculous feat at the Berlin State Opera on December 14th, 1925, after no fewer than forty-eight rehearsals. Kleiber apparently did not care whether the venture cost him his job, so enamoured was he by the score. It hardly needs saying that this first performance caused a scandal not unlike that which had attended Stravinsky's *Le Sacre du Printemps* in the previous decade. Hans Heinscheimer has described the audience's feelings:

> At the première there were fisticuffs and verbal duels between the stalls and the boxes, derisive laughter, hissing and shrill whistling; for a time it seemed as though the enemies of the work might overwhelm the few—finally victorious—adherents of the composer.[1]

The following day, certain critics went as far as to say they had felt as if they had been locked up in a madhouse, and Berg himself was described in one paper as 'a master criminal'. The process of bringing the opera home, so to speak, was consequently a slow one. The *Three Fragments* were heard in Vienna in 1926, and another complete performance under Ostrčil at Prague brought the work into the light a little more. But it took two Berlin revivals (1929 and 1933) as well to clinch the acclaim.

To sum up one's reactions to *Wozzeck* is no easy task. Those who do not wish to be disturbed by art would do best to avoid it, for it resembles, far more than any work by either Schönberg or Webern, the hallucinatory worlds created by writers like Kafka, Hesse and Mann. It was a common criticism of Schönberg that

[1] See *Menagerie in F sharp* (Zürich, 1953).

he acted as the model for Adrian Leverkühn in Mann's novel *Doctor Faustus*; the composer who made a pact with the devil in exchange for perfect genius. Tempting though it may be to bring similar criticisms to bear on Berg, I cannot feel they would be really justified. His motives were altogether more humanitarian and his thirst for knowledge never became as Faustian as that of his teacher. What *is* true, however, is that Berg somehow presents us, in an entirely serious and admonitory fashion, with the sort of Europe that was about to evolve in the 1920's, a Europe bent on crude hedonism, social pessimism and utter indifference to suffering. Conservative critics of the arts, like the late Sir Winston Churchill, used to blame the more expressionist writers, painters and musicians for spreading the disease they were apparently intent on curing; and there is a question as to how far works like *Wozzeck contributed* to the climate of satire-cum-sensuality which dominated the later years of that decade. Certainly one associates Germany and Austria in the 1920's with a peculiarly acrid phase of cultural history—a phase that included the Marxist vitriol of Bert Brecht; the insulting lyrics and music of Lotte Lenya and Kurt Weill; Emil Jannings's pathos and Conrad Veidt's stylized arrogance; the films of Fritz Lang and the gruesome *Cabinet of Dr Caligari*, and a whole list of other 'art-forms', mostly stemming from the cabaret and night-club, which now seem to have been demeaning to man. It is not even as if such sadism has ceased, since during the 'thirties and 'forties it crossed the Atlantic to re-emerge in the theatre of Tennessee Williams and the novels of William Faulkner, each of whom has his present-day heir in Edward Albee and William Burroughs. But with all the savagery and fatalism to be encountered in the work of these artists, we must remember that it is part of the artist's role to inflict pain; to sting us into action that will right the grievances of the injured and alleviate the lot of the oppressed. It is for this reason that *Wozzeck*, for all its distastefulness, seems a greater work than any other of its time.

French Ease
and Versatility

ix A Century of Paris Opera

The founding of the Third Republic in 1871 marks a convenient
point from which to date the modern movement in France, since
new ideas in each of the arts chose this moment to make themselves visible. In terms of national pride, it was a moment of
bitter reckoning, the disastrous war with Prussia having convinced politicians of all shades that too much of the nation's time
had been spent on decadent pursuits. Whether or not opera should
be counted as one of these continues to be a matter of opinion.
What no one could possibly dispute is that French opera during
the Second Empire—that period when the works of Meyerbeer,
Auber and Halévy had reigned more or less unchallenged—had
been a bloated travesty of its better self, an occasion for middle-
class congratulation rather than artistic satisfaction.[1] However,
once Baron Haussmann's innovations in city-planning had been
accepted, the Emperor decreed that a vast new opera-house should
be built in the centre of the capital. The corner-stone of this
'grand palais' was laid as early as 1862, but completion did not
follow until 1875, some years after the monarchy had ceased to
exist. It was at this enormous theatre (still the largest in the world
in terms of acreage, if not seating capacity) that the most ambitious
composers of the last quarter of the nineteenth century strove to
get their works performed.

[1] An exception might be made for Gounod, whose *Faust* (1860)
proved an artistic, if unrepeatable, success. Even today, however, there
are critics who deplore the composer's sentimental distortion of Goethe's
play; and it is perhaps significant that Gounod bid a hasty retreat to
England once the war cleared the way for a more progressive spirit
in the arts. Though it has certainly had its day, *Faust* seems at present
to rate fairly low down in the operatic lists in Britain if not in the country
of its origin.

The situation that presented itself thus looked promising enough on paper—twenty miles of which had incidentally been used by Charles Garnier in his drawing-up of the new house's design! But precisely on account of the grandiosity of the place, and the sharp distinction made between 'opéra' and 'opéra-comique' (the latter characterized by its inclusion of spoken dialogue), it was inevitable that many talented musicians would be driven to seek a venue for their music elsewhere. For example, works so much the antithesis of comic as *Carmen* and *Pelléas et Mélisande* were placed in the position of having to begin life at the proletarian theatre in the Rue Favart, which had been built as a vehicle for the old 'spectacles de la foire' and had since become the home of Offenbach's hilarious parodies. If they failed to win a berth for themselves at this smaller institution, composers were obliged to settle for out-of-town premières at centres like Brussels or Monte Carlo. Indeed, it is remarkable, when examining the operatic careers of men like d'Indy and Chausson how seldom they were permitted a hearing in their own country. Even so dogged a patriot as Saint-Saëns, who seemed for the present to be Gounod's successor, was shocked to discover his *Samson et Dalila* rejected at the Opéra, and he was put in the humiliating position of having to ask for Liszt's aid at Weimar. Clearly, the cult of Italian music had something to do with France's unwillingness to laud her native musicians. Cherubini and Rossini (both huge successes in Paris, the former academically and the latter commercially) had sown the seeds of this cult, which somehow persisted in corrupting or disbarring the music of indigenous practitioners.

It is nonetheless idle to pretend that conspiracies were the sole cause of France's operatic torpor. Gounod was all set for a comeback immediately on his repatriation, and no one can say that he did not try hard to re-instate the native muse. His *Cinq-Mars* (1877), *Polyeuchte* (1878) and *Le Tribut de Zamora* (1881) represented a sustained burst of creative energy of which few operatic composers (Rossini aside) would have been capable. But with the possible exception of the last of these works—a rousingly combative piece that may have had some influence on the later operas of Augusta Holmès—Gounod produced nothing further of interest. Thus the man whose name was greeted all over the world as being almost synonymous with opera itself ended his career without additional acclaim, a fact he did his utmost to disguise by switching to church music and indulging in insincere bouts of high-mindedness. Almost the same fate overtook Saint-Saëns who, after he had finally got *Samson* on to the boards at Rouen in 1890, grasped the fact that he would have to be content with this single 'coup-de-théâtre' as the means of perpetuating his name. His other operas, including the large-scale *Etienne Marcel* (1879) had all been considered feeble or (unjustly) too Wagnerian. Fortunately for him, his more progressive disposition enabled him to achieve a high degree of renown in other spheres, notably those of the symphony and the symphonic poem. The truth is that the '70's and '80's were trying times for French opera generally. The older masters, those who had made their fortunes under Louis Napoléon, were practically a spent force, while the gradual process of raising opera from a profession to an art (a process that required some of the instrumental and theoretical reforms one associates with men like d'Indy and Fauré) had not got fully under way. Paradoxically, it needed the stimulus of the Société Nationale (a body set up to encourage chamber music!) and the orchestral pioneering of Colonne and Lamoureux to induce French composers to write more intelligently for the opera-house. Without these inducements, they remained at the mercy of unscrupulous managers and singers.

One young musician who was determined to compose realistically—without recourse to the creaking 'science des planches' of his seniors—was Georges Bizet. He, if anyone, was fitted to do what Gounod, despite all his good intentions, had actually failed to do. No one will dispute that he possessed all the necessary gifts. Even more than Gounod (who had flirted with sacred forms as early as his Prix de Rome days) Bizet was quite certain about what he had been sent into the world to achieve. He had none of the ambiguity that had hampered the career of his predecessor, and sentimentality had little place in his make-up. Though they had not attracted much notice, he had produced two operas before the war—*Les Pêcheurs de Perles* (1863) and *La Jolie Fille de Perth* (1866). These had proved graceful and accomplished works— vitiated slightly by their poor libretti—which remain in the repertory today. As Bizet was not born until 1838, it is hardly fair to judge him on these operas. They do not represent him at his most mature. The one-act *Djamilah* (1872) was a clear sign of how fast he was developing, and is an interesting work to consider in connection with the vogue for Oriental themes that came later. It will be recalled that, at a slightly later stage, there was a glut of Eastern operas produced in France—Reyer's *Salammbo* (1890), Henri Rabaud's *Marouf* (1914) and Gabriel Dupont's *Antar* (1921) being fairly typical specimens. Roussel's *Padmâvatî* (1923), described in some detail in Part II of this book, was certainly the pinnacle to this movement, if only on account of its authentic and scholarly approach. Bizet's most significant contribution, in terms of 'genre', was obviously *Carmen* (1875). In this unremitting tragedy, he single-handedly launched the style later to become known as 'verismo', thus helping to make the reputations of such non-French composers as Puccini and Leoncavallo.[1]

To us it seems almost unbelievable that a work so teeming with bright, popular tunes and starkly dramatic turns of plot should have been initially pronounced a failure. Yet this is exactly what happened to Bizet's magnum opus. The reasons underlying its failure are numerous and complex. Even though the composer had smoothed out some of the audacities of Merimée's tale, and had arrived at a spotless libretto with the aid of Meilhac and Halévy, the sexy gestures of the singer Galli-Marié were too much for the audience and critics, one of whom described them as 'the incarnation of vice'. The cigarette factory setting was also considered outrageous, all the more when the girls were portrayed smoking and hurling insults at one another. Other objections arose out of straight theatrical mishaps, such as the tenor Lherié's singing out of tune and the confused movement of the chorus. Among the composers who heard it, only Tschaikovsky had the insight to predict a great future for the work, Gounod finding it unmelodious in all respects except one—Michaèla's song in Act III, which he claimed Bizet had stolen from him! Some years after the composer's death, *Carmen* found its way back into the repertory, even reaching the sacred precincts of the Opéra once Guiraud had added a set of recitatives to transform it from the realms of opéra-comique to those of grand opera. In its latter form, it has recently been made into a film by Herbert von Karajan, using the sets of his Salzburg production and intruding some of the incidental music from *L'Arlésienne* as an added attraction. It was one of the supreme tragedies of French music that Bizet died within three months of the débâcle of *Carmen*; not, as legend would have it of a broken heart, but of a species of articular rheumatism that led to an unexpected cardiac arrest.

His place was occupied by a more cynical figure than any to have entered Parisian life since the time of Rossini. He was Jules Massenet, who inherited all Gounod's effeminacy (he was known to his enemies as 'Gounod's daughter') along with a far keener sense of theatrical premonition. Fourteen years younger than Bizet, it did not take him long to get into his stride, and by 1878 he had become so generally admired as to have been given the chair of composition at the Conservatoire, a plum usually reserved for much older men. From this time on, Massenet made full use of his

[1] For a lively and interesting account of the circumstances surrounding the première of *Carmen*, see Kenneth Wright's article 'From Flop to Pop' in *Music* (Vol. III, No. I, February, 1969). To appreciate Galli-Marié's character, it is necessary to consult the superb biography *Bizet and his World* by Mina Curtiss (Mercury Books, 1959).

prestige to influence young musicians, directing them to adopt a slick and histrionic style of writing while he himself enjoyed a long and profitable association with the Opéra. *Hérodiade* (1881) and *Manon* (1884) were probably the two most successful operas of the decade in which they appeared, and they were certainly sufficient to set their composer up as the model and authority for all around him. D'Indy remained furious at Massenet's triumphs, not merely because they enabled him to lord it over the modest and harder-working César Franck at the Conservatoire, but also on account of the appalling artistic surrender they pre-supposed. When the future Director of the Schola Cantorum (an institution devoted, among other things, to the study of church music) once asked Massenet what his attitude to oratorio was, he was shattered to receive the reply: 'Oh! I don't believe in all that creeping Jesus stuff, but the public likes it and one should always take note of public taste.' This was absolutely typical of the composer's approach to music, an art he judged exclusively in terms of the box-office receipts. *Le Cid* (1885) and the other operas he wrote were not quite so eagerly admired; but Massenet remained what Rimsky-Korsakov once called him— 'a crafty old fox'—to the very end of his days. No one ever succeeded in getting the better of him, and Saint-Saëns was about the only one of his contemporaries to outlive him. He had to be content for his revenge with a cross obituary notice in the *Echo de Paris*.

Those who had chosen the harder path by attaching themselves to Franck or d'Indy found that integrity frequently has to pay a heavy price. None of Franck's three operas made any sort of impression (rightly so, since he was not by nature suited to the theatre), but the crushing fate that befell operas by d'Indy, Duparc and Chausson should have acted as a fair warning to those who disbelieved in the 'vox populi, vox dei' principle. D'Indy's *Fervaal* (1897), which took many years to complete, was unconsciously influenced by Wagner, who was still being reviled for his attacks on the French during the time of the Prussian War. It was also too heavily scored a work, saturated with esoteric key-colour associations of a kind known only to Wagnerians and members of the Franck circle. His second opera, the shorter but much more impressive *L'Etranger* (1903), was greatly admired by Debussy, who devoted a chapter to it in his book *Monsieur Croche—anti-dilettante*. He saw the opera at Brussels just before writing *La Mer*, and there is every reason to think that the experience assisted him in his epoch-making task. Though still a shade Wagnerian (the leitmotif technique continues to be prominent and the figure of the Stranger seems to have stepped right out of *The Ring*), *L'Etranger* is actually very modern in its approach to stagecraft, and its only serious defect is its uniform dramatic tone, which makes it a difficult opera to sit through without a certain amount of boredom prevailing. The setting, the placing of the characters, the use of the chorus—all these things are forward-looking. But the plot is turgid and predictable, and there is no unexpected sub-plot to divert the audience's attention. The last of d'Indy's serious operas, *La Légende de Saint-Christophe* (1915), is really an ex-traordinary mixture of pantomime, passion-play and satirical comedy. Described in the official programme note as 'un drame sacré', it was actually referred to by the composer himself as 'un drame anti-juif'—and there are some nasty shafts of anti-Semitic innuendo in the work. The ultimate *Rêve de Cyniras* (1922-3) was at least less offensive in lampooning such pompous politicians as Clemenceau and Woodrow Wilson.

Plagued by the same noble musical standards as d'Indy—though thankfully not so vicious in his social and political opinions—Henri Duparc never got as far as finishing his one and only opera, based on Pushkin's *Roussalka*. As we have already noted, in our essay on the French Wagnerians, he burnt the manuscript in a fit of masochism. Chausson, on the other hand, *did* complete his *Le Roi Arthus*, but not until he had virtually cost him his health and stability of mind. The jinx on this opera—which turns on the love of Lancelot for Guinevere—was such that it was not merely rejected in Paris, but also in Italy, Spain and Germany. It eventually obtained its première at the Théâtre de la Monnaie in Brussels in 1903, four years after its composer's death. Albéric Magnard, who was a private pupil of d'Indy's and never knew Franck, had similarly excruciating experiences over his operas during the course of his short and tragic life (he was shot by the Germans, defending his property, in 1914). His score of *Yolande*, again first performed at Brussels, was destroyed in the raid on his home; but *Bérénice* (1911) had the satisfaction of being mounted in Paris itself, at the Opéra-Comique, probably in consequence of the ·influence of the composer's father, a prominent newspaper proprietor. It is a classical tragedy, very loosely based on Racine, which unashamedly employs the Wagnerian framework as its musico-dramatic basis. The same composer's *Guercœur* was also considered to have been destroyed, but two acts of it were pieced together by Guy Ropartz, who had in his possession a full vocal score of Act III, so that a partly apocryphal performing edition was put into circulation in the course of time and the opera actually given in 1931 in Paris. Neither it nor *Bérénice* has gained a foot-hold, however, either here or in France, possibly because of the very austere conceptions of melody and form to which the com-poser clung. Ropartz's own opera, *Le Pays* (1913), is less chilling, but suffers, like so many others of the period, from its regional bias. Modelled on the novel, *L'Islandaise*, by le Goffic, it revolves around three characters only, and derives such of the appeal as it possesses from the evocativeness of the soil.

It is astonishing how many other stage-works by members of the Franck–d'Indy school ended in disaster. Lazzari's *La Lépreuse* (1898) was a foolhardy undertaking to the extent that it made leprosy the subject of an opera; yet the manner in which it treated this theme ought to have compelled the greatest seriousness and respect. Instead, it was shelved by managements and shunned by the public, not securing its première till 1912. De Bréville's innocuous *Eros Vainqueur* (1910) was likewise still having battles with the censor after the First World War, and to my knowledge has never been presented outside France. Yet here again there was nothing particularly shocking or terrible—especially if one recalls what life was like in the 1920's. Its theme is vaguely reminiscent of Franck's *Eros et Psyché*—that is to say, an intellectual treatment of love. The public could take erotic stimulation from Massenet, on a fairly straightforward plane, but jibbed at having to cope with the Platonic element as well. Manon and Des Grieux could sing their way happily through the act of love on the stage, but Franck and de Bréville risked ecclesiastical and parliamentary disapproval. Such was the French attitude to one of life's fundamental problems, and it was not very different from the attitude in which every husband was allowed to have his mistress as long as he did not attempt to make her his wife. But perhaps the most regrettable failure of the Franck school was to be found in the inability of Charles Bordes to complete his magnificent skeleton of an opera, *Les Trois Vagues*. A half-surrealist work which introduced a 'lamia-like' creature of spellbinding seductiveness, it was broken off on the composer's sudden death in 1909. Attempts were made to finish it—as with *Guercœur* later on—but this time they all came to naught. Unhappily, Bordes had carried more of the score around with him in his head, and the sketches (which may be seen at the Bibliothéque de l'Opéra, in the Rue Scribe, along with a signed admission of defeat from the executors) were nowhere near comprehensive enough to be meddled with. The appearance of this opera—set in the Basque country and full of Latin exuberance despite its sinister implications—would have been a major achievement for French music. It would have fulfilled, far more effectively even than *Carmen*, the predictions Nietzsche made for it, in contrast to the false sensuousness of Bayreuth.

Bordes apart, it is no good pretending otherwise than that d'Indy and the rest of his colleagues at the Schola could have done with a little more of that Gallic charm they so affected to despise. There were middle-of-the-road composers in France who knew this and whose operas were consequently more immediately pleasing to the public. Chabrier's *Gwendoline* (1886) had been unrelievedly Wagnerian, but his *Le Roi malgré lui* (1887) contained far more of the native panâche. Its advanced treatment of harmony (using ninth chords without resolution, and making a less 'Tristanesque' use of chromaticism) paved the way for Satie and Debussy, to say nothing of the composer's 'spiritual grandson', Poulenc. Lalo's *Le Roi d'Ys* (1888)—though perhaps we ought not to be too insistent upon it being the product of a Frenchman— was another attractive work, with its 'mise-en-scène' in Brittany. All of these had to compete with Massenet's thundering successes, and none of them managed to do so quite as well as an opera composed slightly earlier in the decade by a musican whose associations were more balletic. As Professor Donald Grout says, in his authoritative study:

> The slight exotic flavour of *Carmen* and *Les Pêcheurs de Perles* is found again in *Lakmé* (1883), the best opera of Léo Delibes, with a Hindu locale and a tragic plot faintly reminiscent of Meyerbeer's *L'Africaine* and more than faintly foreshadowing *Madame Butterfly* of Puccini. Delibes's music is elegant, graceful and well orchestrated but lacks the intense quality of Bizet's. In *Lakmé* the oriental perfume is blended with an otherwise conventional idiom.[1]

Nevertheless, Delibes—who was incidentally beautifully parodied in the section called *Le Lion Amoreux* from Poulenc's ballet *Les Animaux Modèles*—brought to French opera a welcome lightness that offset the solemnity that too frequently spoilt the scores of the intellectual musicians of the age. If *Lakmé* is nowadays looked upon as a mere colourful excuse for coloratura singing on the part of some would-be diva, the same can surely be said for all those ridiculous Donizetti operas that have recently been dredged up from obscurity to titivate the expensively-oiled palates of Covent Garden socialites?

The most interesting development in realistic opera after Bizet was to come from the pen of Alfred Bruneau, a disciple of Maupassant and Zola, who was among the first to note the possibilities of literary naturalism as it was being practised by the

---

[1] See *A Short History of Opera* by Donald Jay Grout (Columbia University Press, 1947). A revised edition of this standard work appeared in 1967, and is recommended to those seeking a more documentary survey of opera as a whole.

better novelists and short-story writers of the period. Most opera-goers today have not even heard of Bruneau; yet in the 1890's he was widely assumed to be Wagner's successor. Certainly he was responsible for some significant experiments. One was the abandonment of verse libretti for prose. This was strictly in keeping with the composer's view that opera should reflect life as it was lived, but it posed a number of awkward musical problems arising out of the need for regular rhythmical accentuation. French, more than most languages, depends on natural stresses. One cannot *inflict* an accent as easily as one can in, say, Italian. Hence, Bruneau's ideal, while theoretically convincing, came to grief in practice. His music was forced to take its accents from the bar-lines, and assumed a character the American critic Alfred Kazin's university tutor once described as 'falsely robust'. Bruneau also lacked any substantial lyrical gift. Like d'Indy, he depended on short motifs, dramatically powerful, but unable to express emotions like tenderness and sensuality. This became a serious limitation to him, because it made his operas almost mechanical in their declamatory monotony. *Le Rêve* (1891), however, was a really stupendous success (it was performed in London within a few months of the première), and *L'Attacque du Moulin* (1893) gained him a further reputation for forthright engagement with current social issues. His *Messidor* (1897) would probably have put the seal on a great career amid the immortals had it not been for the backlash that descended on him through Zola's participation in the Dreyfus affair. From then on, he was considered a subversive influence; and although he continued to write on a prolific scale—*L'Ouragan* (1901) and *L'Enfant Roi* (1905) followed in support of his claims—he gradually died out as a serious force in French music. Parisians on the whole preferred the more spurious but emotionally touching naturalism of Charpentier's *Louise* (1900), with its passionate aria, *Depuis le jour*, to preserve the element of sentiment.

The composer who delivered the coup-de-grâce to both Bruneau (whom he found mildly distasteful) and Charpentier (whom he hated to the point of fury) was, of course, Claude Debussy, the writer of the greatest French opera since Berlioz's *Les Troyens*, if not of all time. The opera, *Pelléas et Mélisande*, was adapted from Maeterlinck's play with the author's full permission (he even helped in the sub-division into scenes) and took the best part of ten years to write. What makes it so special (aside from the quality of its music) is that it asserts that view of opera which Mr Joseph Kerman has designated as 'a sung play'. That is to say, in it the words are made to count for rather more than the music (reversing Mozart's famous dictum about words being 'the obedient daughter

of music') and the interest is meant to reside in a slight heighten-
ing of the action through the insertion of instrumental interludes.
Technically, the setting of the words is done in such a way as to
mirror the contours of the speaking voice. There is no forceful
declamation, neither are any luscious arias permitted to break
the flow. Really, it is a French equivalent of the German Sprecht-
stimme that Debussy sought to achieve, stopping short of the
extremes of the new Viennese school by maintaining sounds of
definite pitch and retaining the same quasi-tonal harmony as he
had used for his songs and piano pieces. Indeed, the songs are a
good introduction to *Pelléas* since they are not devoid of melody
yet depend to a higher than average degree on pauses and recitative. The story is fatalistic in a gentle-fairy-tale way, and describes
the love of Mélisande for the half-brother of the man she has
married. It ends in tragedy, the heroine dying in childbirth and
the two brothers faced with mortal confrontation. A key figure
in the drama is the world-weary king, Arkel, who rules over the
misty world in which everything takes place and who foresees
the conclusion in a curiously pessimistic and unreal fashion.
Debussy did not survive to write a successor to *Pelléas*, which
appeared in 1902, though he did work for long periods on a
version of Edgar Allan Poe's story, *The Fall of the House of Usher*.
This again would have suited his genius ideally, and it must
remain one of the profoundest sources of regret in all music that
the opera was never destined for completion.

Availing himself of the same librettist, Paul Dukas made an
almost equally splendid contribution to French opera with his
Ariane et Barbe-bleue (1907). In some respects, this was a more
Wagnerian work than Debussy's; the latter having got over his
Wagner period with the help of Satie before fully embarking on
Pelléas. The former's various leitmotifs proclaim this debt as
unmistakably as in the operas of d'Indy and the other French
Wagnerians. But Dukas had his own special merits, and these were
sufficient to place him well above the bulk of his competitors. For
instance, he was the possessor of a fabulous orchestral technique
and he was not in the least afraid to indulge it. It is the orchestra
which is the hero of *Ariane et Barbe-bleue*, despite the successes
numerous French sopranos have won for themselves in the name
part. Dukas's treatment of the theme is full-blooded but not
deliberately scarifying; and to that extent it may be compared with
that accorded to it by Bartók. The orchestral parts in Bartók's score
are a good deal more subdued, however, and impressionistic
in their effect. Dukas, despite his friendship with Debussy,
was never an impressionist, and, as listeners to his tone-poem,
L'Apprenti Sorcier, will be able to testify, uses instruments more

in the manner of Richard Strauss. Moreover, his score has none of Bartók's nocturnal sadness; it is not as overtly psychological. It is a great pity we do not get more chances to hear it in the theatre, and so get to know its undoubted individuality. The same might be said for Fauré's two operas, *Promethée* and *Pénélope*, the former receiving its première at the Béziers amphitheatre in 1900 and the latter at the Théâtre des Champs-Elysées in the autumn of 1913. Both deal with Greek themes, as one might have expected from so dedicated a Hellenist, but they are very different operas. The former really demanded the open-air performance it received (as the later travesty of it at the Hippodrome confirmed), since it imitated, as far as this was possible, the ancient sounds of the pagan world. Pandora's funeral music, with its distant trumpet refrain, perfectly exemplifies this tendency. *Pénélope*, on the other hand, is a magnificent singer's opera—as Claire Croiza knew when she placed it as one of the three she most wished to appear in— superbly original in its absorption of modal sequences into the new twentieth-century idiom.

Among the great names of French music, Ravel's is hardly known for his operas, since he never allowed his penchant for miniaturism to press him beyond the one-act form. His *L'Heure Espagnole* (1907) is important, however, for its employment of the same sort of 'parlando' devices as went into his collection of melodies called *Histoires Naturelles*. In other words, closing vowels are ellided and all kinds of semi-speech effects are reproduced. To call the result an opera would perhaps be a terminological error in any case; for the inclusion of ordinary spoken dialogue fixes it as an 'opéra-comique', so there is no problem. But the work is worth mentioning here for its uniqueness. It was based on a play by Franc-Nohain—so risky in its theme that Ernest Newman once humorously suggested it should be translated as 'The Immoral Hour'. The dramatist took no interest in Ravel's setting, taking out his watch at the end and merely remarking 'Fifty-three minutes' in the manner of the fathers of immigrant film composers when they have made it to Carnegie Hall. Set in a clockmaker's shop in Toledo, the story tells of the love-affair between the proprietor's wife, Concepcion, and the poet, Gonzalo. Complications arise when a muleteer named Ramiro enters the shop and compels the errant wife's affections by a display of strength. She invites him upstairs, leaving her former lover and her husband (who has returned, as he supposes, in time to catch the culprit) to argue out their rights. In total opposition to this rather lascivious work was Ravel's other mini-opera, *L'Enfant et les Sortilèges* (1925), which is a parable about childhood, and hence much more suited to the composer's genius. It describes a child (Ravel himself perhaps?)

who smashes up a grandfather clock, tears down the wallpaper, breaks the china and generally makes an infernal nuisance of himself. As in a dream, his misdeeds return to haunt him, the clock becoming Father Arithmetic chanting out the multiplication table, the figures on the wallpaper rising up to form a procession of nymphs and shepherds, and the china cup suddenly bursting into a risible conversation (conducted in a mixture of languages) and eventually dancing a jazz-age 'shimmy' with the Wedgewood teapot. The second scene turns the child out into the garden, where he becomes a similar victim to the dragonflies, bull-frogs and prowling felines.

Nothing like the humour (or the tender moral) of Ravel's last opera was observable in most of the other productions of the 1920's. Despite its reputation as a gay decade, it gave rise to few genuinely gay operas in France. Perhaps this was because opera, after the age of Diaghilev, fell into disrepute in favour of ballet. The works that really spring to mind in the period we are now discussing are the ballets of Stravinsky (a French citizen at this time) and the eccentric entertainments of Satie and Poulenc. No opera aroused the interest achieved by *Parade* or even *Les Biches*—and these, after all, were something of an anti-climax after the mighty dance epics of the pre-war years, like *Daphnis et Chloé* and *Le Sacre du Printemps*. What did emerge were a number of large vocal works from among the more serious-minded members of 'Les Six', and Honegger's *Antigone* (1927) and Milhaud's *Christophe Colomb* (1928) certainly deserve to be mentioned in this context. The last was termed an 'opéra sacrale' and was inspired by the composer's trip to South America as cultural attaché to the ambassador, Paul Claudel, who provided him with his libretto. As is obvious from the title, it depicts the arrival of Columbus in the New World. But it should not be assumed from this that it is an opera about hazardous sea journeys and manly heroics. On the contrary, it centres almost entirely around the feelings of wonder evoked by the new land and the need for prayer and guidance from above. It is therefore no less serious a work than Honegger's and seems strangely out of style with the decade in which it appeared. Milhaud went on to write another South American opera as late as 1952 in his *Bolivar*—this time assuredly more of an heroic theme. But Honegger added little to his operatic corpus, preferring to take the obvious step into oratorio and symphonic music. In the '30's, the work to make the biggest impact was possibly Henri Sauguet's opera on Stendhal's *La Chartreuse de Parme* (1939). This was a 'grand opera' with all the trimmings, and curiously old-fashioned to those who had expected something revolutionary. Sauguet (who is also significantly better known for his ballets, like *La Chatte* and

Les Forains) had written one previous opera—*Le Plumet du Colonel* in the period around 1924; but nothing much had come of it. He, too, has now taken a different direction.

It would be tedious, and beyond the scope of this essay, to go on listing the various operas to have attained some measure of acclaim in France since the Second World War. Most of the major composers—including men like Jolivet and Boulez, who have acted, respectively, as musical directors to the Comédie Française and to Jean-Louis Barrault—have avoided the form. In Boulez's case, he has frequently attacked the form as dead, referring to opera-houses as museums or mausoleums according to their repertoires. Again the principal theatrical impetus in France has come, not from the Opéra, but from such ventures as the Ballet Roland Petit, which has mounted a fair number of brilliant new successes. Dutilleux's *Le Loup* (1953) attracted far more notice than any new opera performed within the same period. Part of the trouble, it can now be said, lay with the management of the Opéra itself which, even more than the Metropolitan in New York, regarded itself more as the custodian of established works than the patron of new ones. Georges Auric's long reign as Director of the Opéra having come to an end in 1969, it is to be hoped that his successor will be given greater scope for 'avant-garde' works to be mounted. The colossal budget allows for this, and it is only government conservatism that appears to stand in the way. The well-known quarrel between the Minister for Culture, M. Malraux, and the intractable M. Boulez, has resulted in a deadlock no one seems capable of breaking. It is symptomatic that of all the operatic works to have been accepted into the repertory in France since the mid-century, the relatively archaic *Les Carmélites* of Poulenc (1957) has been the strongest in maintaining its position. Based on a novel by Bernanos, it is a conventional 'grand opera' again, dealing with the execution of a group of Carmelite nuns during the French Revolution. Since there have been at least three further revolutions in that country during the years between 1789 and the present, it hardly seems as if there has been a very determined attempt to come up to date. When we have a French opera about the events at the Sorbonne in May 1968, we may be sure that the form is still very much alive and kicking.

x   The Growth of the Mélodie

Song is a word that carries a host of connotations, and one that seems particularly inadequate when applied to French music. The term 'chanson', for example, which the average person would take to be the correct linguistic equivalent, only refers to a single species of French vocal composition, and that of the most general or popular kind. At least, that is how it is often regarded by French people today. However, it was used to cover a glut of other forms between the twelfth and sixteenth centuries, most of which have only a history book meaning for them. In the seventeenth century, a new expression arose out of the spread of courtly entertainment. This was the expression 'air'—and it attached itself as before to a number of different categories. The bergerette, the pastourelle, the ronde and even the vaudeville all existed as variants of the original 'air de cour' made popular by the Bourbons. When, in turn, the 'air' ceased to appeal, its place was taken by the 'romance', a more clear-cut form that had its heyday between the years 1770 and 1870. The best-known 'romance' in French music is probably Martini's *Pla sir d'Amour*, written in 1784, though the songs of Gounod, Bizet and Chabrier could all be considered as belonging to the form.

Just how the term 'mélodie'—first employed as a synonym for the 'lied artistique'—came into currency remains something of a mystery. For a long time, it was simply used to describe one of the products of the German or Viennese romantic school—a song like Schubert's *Serenade* or *Die Forelle*, for example. Saint-Saëns was possibly the first to appropriate it for French use in his 'Six Mélodies Persanes', Op. 6. But Berlioz is usually credited with having been the originator of what might be called the French 'art-song' in his cycle of Gautier songs of 1841, known as *Les Nuits d'Été*. That he wrote other, equally ingenious, specimens of the

113

genre is now gradually being recognized.[1] But though he made use
of some extraordinary rhythmic and harmonic progressions in his
work, it is no good pretending that he was able to transform the
genre into something equal to the German lied. For one thing,
Berlioz was not a pianist, and therefore had only a limited understanding of what could be done in the way of extending the role of
the accompanist. (He later orchestrated the *Nuits d'Été* cycle, and
it is almost always heard, and heard to best advantage, in this
version.) For another, he lived through the period of Hugo and
Lamartine, when French poetry was at its most rhetorical and
unsubtle. It is significant that when Liszt and others tried setting
the works of these poets, they produced only more complex
versions of the romance—which could be equated, if one wished
to be cynical, with the English drawing-room ballad. In any case,
it was pointless to try to imitate the German lied in France, since
there was a sharp difference in literary outlook between the two
countries. The German poets had drawn their inspiration more from
the soil, so that the tendency was for their work to have an earthy,
open-hearted sincerity. Müller, set by Schubert in his two greatest cycles, illustrates this quality very well. By comparison, French
poetry had always been more theatrical; and in the work of Hugo's
successors it was also to become more symbolic and paradoxical.

The first great master of the 'mélodie' was undoubtedly Gabriel
Fauré (1845–1924), whose settings of the Parnassian poets gave
rise to an altogether new and more refined type of lyricism.
Fauré wrote songs that were short (averaging about forty-eight
bars or so) and full of quaint modal twists. He was never a particularly romantic composer, and found it hard to invest his music
with those tearful qualities some of his audience wanted to hear.
Even so, the astonishing delicacy and 'souplesse' he created won
him the admiration of a wide and discriminating circle of connois-
seurs. By doing away with the old strophic habits of the romance
(that is to say, repeating the music for each stanza of a poem more
or less unchanged), and by cultivating an inimitable trick of legato,
he was able to breathe fresh life into the frail verses of men like
Albert Samain, Leconte de Lisle and Armand Silvestre. Early songs,
like the popular *Après un Rêve* managed to combine blandness with
a certain declamatory power. But almost all his later songs were less
assertive, more dependant on the subtleties of phrase and nuance
we have nowadays come to expect from the form. Even he, like his
predecessors, took a little time to find the poets who could offer him
material for his music, and in his case things were complicated by

[1] For an excellent review of Berlioz's complete output in this sphere,
the reader is referred to John Warrack's article, 'Berlioz's Mélodies' in
The Musical Times, March, 1969, No. 1513, Vol. 110.

his general dislike of the stage and anything that smacked of the histrionic. The only form of theatricality that was to have a distinct appeal for him was the old commedia dell' arte which had flourished very briefly in France during the seventeenth century—from about 1660 until the players were expelled from Versailles by Mme de Maintenon in 1697.[1] Thus he spent much of the middle period of his life attempting to re-capture in music those languid rococo gestures that had earlier been defined by Watteau on canvas.

The poet whose work enabled him to carry out these explorations was the indolent Verlaine. Such fruits of their alliance as *Clair de Lune, C'est l'extase* and *Mandoline* not only re-created that antique world of grace and refinement but also pointed the way the French 'mélodie' was to go in the years ahead. What they taught Fauré's contemporaries and pupils (he was Director of the Paris Conservatoire from 1905 to 1920) was how utterly sinuous and flexible the best vocal writing could afford to become, and how much more needed to be done in the way of devising ingenious piano accompaniments. In the finest of his Verlaine cycles—*La Bonne Chanson* and the *Cinq Mélodies de Venise*, with the odd individual poem picked at random added to the canon—the composer provided vivid proof of his theory that great music could be wedded to great literature as long as the conditions were right. Schumann had already confirmed this in his *Dichterliebe* and in the Eichendorf *Leiderkreis* Op. 39. Fauré was among the first to establish a similar musico-literary rapprochement in France. Not all of his songs were based on poetic rarities, however, and he occasionally relapsed into setting the work of more banal writers. To that extent, his taste was not as sure as that of, say, Debussy, and recent French song-writers have suspected him of having something less than an erudite knowledge of prosody. The poets he set towards the end of his career were all minor products of the 'fin-de-siècle', such as Jean de la Ville de Mirmont and the Belgian, Van Lerberghe. These men provided him with verses with a more pagan, pre-civilized theme; one to which his natural stoicism and impassivity inevitably drew him as the problems of retirement and death loomed near. The cycle, *L'Horizon Chimérique* typifies this final phase in his progress, and is perhaps the least arid of the works he wrote in his old age. One of its songs, the beautiful *Diane Séléné*, shows how much of the composer's uncomplicated lyrical gift still remained.

Quick to seize the torch from Fauré was the finicky and meticulous Henri Duparc (1848–1933), whose tragedy was of quite a

---

[1] I am exempting, for the purposes of this essay, the Greek forms of theatre which late in his life led Fauré to write operas like *Promethée* and *Pénélope*, the former for open-air performance.

different kind. In his case, his gifts were extinguished so early on in life that most of his days were spent as a kind of anguished spectator of other men's achievements. Having begun as a pupil of César Franck—who incidentally did little to stimulate his interest in song—Duparc proceeded to launch out in extremely original directions. Like another Franck pupil, the equally ill-fated Alexis de Castillon, everything he wrote in his first batch of songs proclaimed a German influence. But it was Wagner not Schubert who eventually claimed his allegiance. An ardent admirer of the Bayreuth composer's traits of style—enharmonic modulation, chromatic inflection and the evolving of a long, architectural perspective—Duparc was responsible for enlarging the compact world of the mélodie beyond the dimensions anyone had predicted for it. He introduced a rich, polyphonic texture into his accompaniments, and whipped up his melodies to a point of climax from which Fauré would have shrunk in horror. But then he was altogether more conventionally religious than Fauré (he was an occasional companion of Francis Jammes and Paul Claudel at Lourdes) and his sympathies as a song-writer lay with Baudelaire not Verlaine. His setting of *L'Invitation au Voyage* has as good a claim to perfection as any French song, so uplifting are its rhythms and so brilliant its harmonic chiaroscuro. Duparc was also notable for the variety of moods he mastered. The terrifying *La vague et le cloche*—a dream of being swept out to sea which passes into a surrealist-like sequence in which the poet imagines himself trapped in a belfry—shows what a pronounced sense of the grotesque he had. On the other hand, a song like the popular *Le Manoir de Rosamonde* is a tale of unrequited love and exploits emotions like loneliness and sorrow. What is perhaps common to all Duparc songs is the element of misery. He was not a writer of joyful music, even though it was said of him that he was frequently a joyful companion. One suspects that he forfeited all claims to normality the moment he sat down to write, since he had a genius for choosing insoluble problems, looked at from the musical angle. Almost all his difficulties as a composer stemmed from his inability to rest content with what he had done. A constant meddler, he went over everything he did a hundred times, creating endless perplexities by his decision to orchestrate several of his songs. From the standpoint of history, of course, this was an extremely interesting decision to have made, for what it confirmed was how capacious the new form had become. Ravel's orchestration of *Shéhérazade*—a setting of three poems by Tristan Klingsor—was thus anticipated in the many sumptuously scored accompaniments of Duparc; especially those he wrote for *Phidylé* and *La Vie Antérieure*.

Because of this interest in perfectionism, and his mysterious nervous breakdown in the middle of the 1880's, Duparc ended his career by leaving us a mere sixteen songs. Probably he would have disappeared into the limbo of musical history, along with so many other talented Frenchmen of the period, had these songs not been of such a remarkably high quality. Their small number has prevented him from acquiring the reputation of a Fauré or a Debussy (who in any case wrote large quantities of other music), but their tremendous finish and amplitude will ensure them a hearing wherever French song is studied and valued. In addition, they seem to possess an unique appeal for deeply religious sensibilities, particularly if they are both French and Catholic. Indeed, what Duparc's melodies share with the works of his master Franck is their tendency to use harmony as a means of quasi-spiritual illumination. The progress from darkness to light in many of Franck's larger compositions (the symphonic poem 'Les Djinns' forms a ready example) is an accepted principle which he originated, like the cyclic form. In Duparc, the principle reveals itself in his particular choice of key (again, like Franck, often falling within the circle E major, B major, F sharp major) and in his calculated changes of register. A song like *La Vie Antérieure*, for instance, which gives us another Baudelairean portrayal of a grotto beneath the waves, begins with heavy, sombre chords, presumably intended to suggest the cold darkness of the underwater scene, but moves as the sun's rays penetrate the surface towards a brighter, rippling tonality. *L'Invitation au Voyage*, with its dream of the sun breaking through Dutch mists, is an almost parallel case. No other French songs quite duplicate this mystical 'synaesthesia' of Duparc's.

In Debussy (1862–1918), whom many would regard as Fauré's chief rival for the title of master of French song, we encounter a more hedonistic artist. Yet he, too, is famous for having begun his most productive song-writing phase with settings of Baudelaire. The *Cinq Poèmes* of 1888 are in some ways an attempt to carry on from where Duparc left off, since they are equally saturated with Wagnerian sentiments and techniques. (The reader hardly needs to be reminded, in view of the essay on the French Wagnerians that Baudelaire was among the first of French writers to come under the German composer's spell.) The influence most easily detected in the Debussy songs is that of *Tristan* for they are full of unresolved chromatics. *La Mort des Amants* clearly mirrors the love-death yearnings of that opera, and is about as far as Debussy ever went in submitting to the more desolate, suicidal emotions. What saved him from a Duparc-like artistic collapse was his pleasure-loving nature, and the manner in which he was also responding to Russian influences. The song *Le Jet d'Eau*, also from this cycle, disperses its pessimism in a series of Borodin-type dissonances, making it artistically fresh and exciting even when the theme drags us in the direction of despair. The piano-writing in the *Cinq Poèmes* is another indication of Debussy's wider range of interests, suggestive as it is of the late, great Chopin. It pointed a way of escape for him in the brilliant series of keyboard compositions on which he was soon to embark. The fact that he never returned to Baudelaire is doubtless insufficient evidence in itself, but it tends to argue that once he had got over his Wagnerism (which he did by the time he got started on *Pelléas et Mélisande* around 1894), he had also summoned up the versatility to approach other poets through whom he could express different aspects of his personality.

As a matter of fact, Debussy had never been exclusively attached to Baudelaire. Even before he had set 'Recueillement' and the other poems, he had been experimenting fairly confidently with Verlaine. Like Fauré, he did not miss his chance to ransack the works of 'pauvre Lélian' more thoroughly when the occasion presented itself. *Green* from the *Ariettes Oubliées* was a poem eagerly filched by both composers, and a connoisseur would be needed to say which of their settings should be awarded the palm. Debussy's is certainly a triumph of naturalism, its whole-tone shimmers perfectly resurrecting the sounds of summer. Among the composer's other settings of this most musical of poets, the ghostly *Colloque Sentimentale* stands alone. A dialogue between the shades of parted lovers, it re-vamps an old serenade in accents both sad and recriminating. Less paradoxical were Debussy's experiments with the 'rondel' and other stylized forms (witness his settings of Charles d'Orléans and Tristan l'Hermite) and his wonderfully stark versions of the Villon 'ballades'. All these works carried him back to a much older France, and might have led him to take a deeper interest in classical literature had he lived longer. As it was, these settings were surely what led him to see himself at bottom as a 'musicien français' and not just a founder of the modern move-ment. Their scrupulous intrusion of recitative (something neither Fauré nor Duparc would have possessed the imagination to do) relate them closely to the nation's baroque operatic heritage, and does more to justify the title *Hommage à Rameau* (which attached to one of the piano pieces in the *Images*) than anything else in their composer's catalogue. It would be wrong to say that melody plays no part in a Debussy song, but what there is of it winds along in crepuscular fashion without a thought for shapely contours of the Fauré kind.[1] The piano, too, has to be satisfied with a good deal of sluggish chordal movement.

[1] In a recent television master-class, Gérard Souzay pointedly rebuked some of his students for their implicit assumption that Debussy's songs

Greater psychological dexterity attaches to the songs of Maurice Ravel (1875–1937), particularly the whimsical *Histoires Naturelles*, based on a collection of animal poems by Jules Renard. The flip, satirical harmonies and violent vowel skids contained in this cycle made it a work of revolutionary significance in the history of the mélodie. Typical of Ravel were those minute, realistic touches it gave him so much delight to add—the cricket winding up his watch (depicted by a series of appoggiaturas) and the peacock spreading his tail-feathers (an upward glissando on the keyboard). Whether on account of the scant respect he had for literature, or for some inscrutable reason yet to be revealed, Ravel failed to make the most of himself as a song-writer, returning to the 'genre' only a few times more during the course of his career. By a remarkable co-incidence, both he and Debussy chose the year 1913 in which to embark on a setting of three poems by Mallarmé. What is even more remarkable is that they ended up with two out of their three choices in common. Ravel's *Soupir* (not the same poem as Duparc set, or the same poet) and *Placet Futile* differ from Debussy's in being laid out for additional woodwind and string quartet; and also in being more directly influenced by Schönberg. Otherwise, there are many points of resemblance. Among the composer's later melodies, our greatest praise should be reserved for the *Chansons Madécasses* of 1926. Savage and paradisal by turns, these elaborate songs have struck critics as being peculiarly uncharacteristic of their author. In a sense, they should be attributed to the plunge of disillusionment that followed the signing of the armistice. Far easier to enjoy is the cycle, *Don Quichotte à Dulcinée*, commissioned for Chaliapin's famous film but in the last resort never used. The lively *Chanson à boire* with which it ends also marked a jovial conclusion to the thirty-five published works this gifted, though reticent, man contributed to the form.

With the demise of Ravel, the title of 'chef d'école' passed rapidly to Francis Poulenc, born in 1899 and died as recently as 1963. An extremely precocious—though as it turned out never erudite—figure, Poulenc began publishing songs in his twentieth year. Witty and decadent to begin with, he managed to bring together in his own person most of the qualities people assign to the French character. At times his work strikes us as burning with sincerity and candour; at other times uncommonly vulgar and 'aigu'. He was from the first drawn to the surrealist innovator and farceur Apollinaire, and a most interesting study could be made out of their partnership. It began in 1919 with *Le Bestiaire* and reached a peak of rapport in 1940 with the aptly-titled *Banalités*. Some of the

were unmelodious. On the other hand, Gerald Moore has made no secret of his preference for Fauré's more euphonious style.

songs from this last collection distil the essence of the composer's talent like nothing else he wrote. One thinks of the lazy *Hôtel*, with its bitter-sweet cocktail harmonies, and the Chevalieresque *Voyage à Paris*. But it would be unfair to assume that all Poulenc's melodies are content to exploit the more ephemeral sentiments. His collaboration with Paul Eluard resulted in two eminently serious works in which the city's shabbier backcloth—that most of us associate with Utrillo's paintings—is quietly brought to life. Thus *Tel Jour, Telle Nuit*, written in 1936, stands at the summit of the composer's vocal achievement and loses nothing by being compared with the best of Fauré or Debussy. Following Eluard's death, other attempts at literary rapprochement were made, but none completely succeeded. The Louise de Vilmorin settings are good in their way, though a shade precious and sentimental. Perhaps the most characteristic of the recent cycles is the riotous *La Courte Paille* (the title signifies a game of odd man out) set to verses by Maurice Carême in 1960. This work has moments that recall the composer's scandalous opéra-bouffe, *Les Mamelles de Tirésias*, and is full of typical recherché jokes and allusions. It has already come to seem almost as popular as the earlier, much earthier, *Chansons Villageoises* which likewise depends on its slightly salacious humour for its appeal.

Probably no other contributors to the mélodie have been as successful as those we have described. They, more or less to the exclusion of their contemporaries, comprise the tradition as expressed in the recital room. Yet so many neglected French composers interspersed fine songs among their larger enterprises that it would be less than just to pass over their achievements. Ernest Chausson, for example, who lived from 1855 to 1899, when he was killed in a bicycle accident, had a distinct aptitude for the medium. He might have attained greatness as a song-writer had he survived into the twentieth century and hence rid himself of those period pressures which, as things stand, do so much to vitiate even his best work. As Diana McVegh has said, his songs exude an aroma not unlike 'stale perfume'—a fact we must attribute to the nostalgic conditions under which they were written. The 'time of lilacs and roses'—which was that time during which the artist lamented the close of the Romantic era in a bout of self-pity and reminiscence—led Chausson to produce too indulgent an art. His Bouchor settings were moved by friendship as much as musical empathy, while the Maeterlinck cycle, *Serres Chaudes* is weighed down by the heavy textures he felt obliged to manipulate in order to rebut the charge of amateurism. Much better and lighter are the various settings of Camille Mauclair (author of *The City of Light* and several treatises on the aesthetics of music) which he made.

The backwardly-titled *Trois Lieder*, Op. 27 are worth reviving from time to time. Certain critics have complained that Chausson would really have done more to perpetuate Verlaine in music had that task been rendered unnecessary by the work of Fauré and Debussy. Perhaps this is so, since he was a singularly modest man. But Verlaine, it is worth noting, was set by a host of Frenchmen quite aside from those we have mentioned—for example, Charles Bordes, Gabriel Dupont, de Séverac, Sylvio Lazzari, Gustave Charpentier and René Lenormand.

Some beautifully descriptive songs, again, were left by Charles Koechlin (1867–1951), whose major interests unquestionably lay elsewhere. His setting of Leconte de Lisle's *Le Colibri* is not as well known as Chausson's—which forms No. 7 of the set listed as Opus 2—yet many judges would consider it the finer of the two.[1] It seems a pity that more of his work in this medium does not exist in published form. Pierre de Bréville is another musician, whose life spanned the period 1864–1949, whom it is possible to regard as a song-writer of greatly under-estimated powers. Martin Cooper, in his book *French Music from the Death of Berlioz to the Death of Fauré* (Oxford, 1951), goes as far as to say:

> Bréville's best and most original work lies in his songs, the earliest of which date from 1883. Here the influence of both Fauré and Massenet is plain ... The *Petites Litanies de Jésus* (1896), written for his children, have a simplicity quite unlike Gounod's maudlin piety, and the *Chanson d'Hamsavati* showed that Bréville could use the oriental convention with originality.

If these claims are true, they are all the more remarkable in view of the fact that de Bréville was in the main a disciple of Franck (who, aside from *La Procession* and *Nocturne*, wrote few 'mélodies' of interest), and later went on to assist d'Indy, who was notorious for omitting the solo song from the tuition meted out at the Schola Cantorum. Actually, de Bréville wrote about a hundred songs many of which, like Koechlin's, remain unpublished. Like Debussy, he went back to Charles d'Orléans for his *Douze Rondels* of 1931, though previously he had maintained the rather idle literary connections proclaimed in his partnership with Henri de Régnier (the monocled dandy to whom Ravel dedicated his *Valses Nobles et Sentimentales* and who was a regular companion of the young Proust). Perhaps it is rather unlikely that de Bréville's mélodies will enter the repertory at this late date; his correct

[1] The reader interested in comparing different settings of the same poet may be interested to know that Koechlin also set five *Chansons de Bilitis* by Pierre Louÿs, placing him in rivalry with Debussy.

counterpoint and meticulously regulated ornamentation would be enough to put them out of court with audiences more used to Poulenc's coarse humour or Boulez's mathematical Mallarmé.

What is more probable is that greater opportunities will arise to hear melodies written by contemporaries of 'Les Six'; or even other members of that arbitrarily composed band itself. Clearly Erik Satie—often described as the father of 'Les Six'—is being extensively revived, and though he concentrated his efforts chiefly on the piano there are examples of miniature songs of his that will undoubtedly add to his following. The *Trois Mélodies* of 1916—comprising *La Statue de Bronze, Daphénéo* and *Le Chapelier*—have all been heard in London recently. The first, set to words by Ravel's friend Léon-Paul Fargue, depicts an enormous carving of a frog to be found in a Parisian tea-garden; the second, by Cipa Godebski, a tree which mysteriously grows birds; and the third, by René Chalupt, a scene from *Alice in Wonderland* in which the Mad Hatter causes his watch to run three days slow by oiling it in butter. Each song gives Satie an excellent opportunity in which to indulge his Edward Lear-like talent for absurdity. Among the actual 'Groupe', Milhaud probably has the strongest claim, after Poulenc, partly because his output has been so large, But his setting of Gide's *Alissa* has been described by David Cox as 'a lyrical work of beauty and simplicity'.[1] The composer's *Catalogue des Fleurs* and *Machines Agricoles*—deliberately taken from seed and farming magazines with a view to shocking the literary pundits—simply recall the age of Dada without arousing any desire for a re-hearing. No doubt posterity will think better of the twenty-four *Tristesses* he wrote to verses by Francis Jammes in 1957. Pursuing the more symbolic trend in French literature, Henri Sauguet (not a member of 'Les Six', but a disciple of Satie in the school of Arcueil) began his mature phase as a song-writer by reverting to Laforgue, Max Jacob and Valéry as collaborators. But his œuvre, like Milhaud's, has grown to gigantic proportions, and it has now become difficult to see where his place will lie. Almost certainly he will be admired more for his ballets than for his songs.

It remains merely to re-inforce the point that the mélodie is by no means dead, or even dying. Living composers like Messiaen, Jaubert, Migot, Nigg, Jolivet and Dutilleux are all contributing, in various degrees of prolixity, to a medium for which the French, by virtue of their acknowledged literary prowess, ought to display

[1] See the illuminating chapter on 'France' in *A History of Song*, edited by Denis Stevens (Hutchinson, 1960). There are, of course, no poems by Gide under the title of *Alissa*. Milhaud selected lines spoken by a character of this name in the author's novel, *La Porte Étroite*, and set them in 1913. The cycle was revised in 1931.

a continuing aptitude. Messiaen's mother, Cécile Sauvage, was quite a distinguished poetess, her best-known work being *L'Âme en bourgeon*. While the composer was a member of the group calling itself 'La Jeune France' (the other members were Baudrier, Jolivet and Daniel-Lesur), he wrote his settings entitled *Poèmes pour Mi* as a tribute to his wife. By comparison, Jaubert has ranged more widely, using texts from more contemporary authors, including Giraudoux, Georges Neveux, Jean Giono and Jules Supervielle. He has not, however, written more, since he died in the war. Migot again has a very long list of mélodies to his credit, including some written to his own words and others to words by Tristan Klingsor, one of the turn-of-the-century cosmopolites and a member of the band of 'apaches'. Serge Nigg, born as late as 1924, has continued to look to Eluard for inspiration; while Jolivet, despite his theatrical interests, has chosen lesser-known poets, like Louis Emié, and has devoted the bulk of his efforts to instrumental music. The same may be said of Dutilleux who, despite a variety of successes in ballet, radio and film, has withheld the abilities many believe he would have in keeping alive the mélodie. Possibly Boulez, in his treatment of the single surrealist poet, René Char, has done more to advance the intimate vocal forms than any of these figures; though whether his use of several voices pitted against a chamber orchestra, as in *Le Soleil des Eaux*, really comes into the strict category we have set out to describe is problematic. The work named consists of two poems, the first portraying the vegetative life of a lizard as it gorges itself on a sunflower and gazes fascinated at a goldfinch which has settled nearby, and the second the rise and fall of the river Sorgue in flood.

What strikes the listener as of the greatest interest about Boulez's various vocal experiments is that they rely heavily on a more up-to-date version of the sort of recitative in which Debussy's songs were for the most part couched. It is well known, of course, that Boulez is an intense admirer of Debussy and has been much influenced by him in other spheres of composition. The long instrumental interludes and Sprechstimme of works like the Char settings call to mind, alternately, the technique of *Pelléas* and of *Pierrot Lunaire*; though the peculiar flautando effects demanded of the voice represent something new, just as the various sforzando effects which the pianist is expected to execute with aid of the elbow represent a departure from conventional piano idiom. If one were to classify Boulez, in terms of his approach to the music versus words dilemma (which occurs in song no less forcibly than in opera), one would have to range him alongside the upholders of the text; and to that degree he has come a long way from the essentially musical ends striven for by Fauré and his contemporaries.

At present, it seems more sensible to regard works like *Le Visage Nuptial* and *Le Marteau sans Maître* as either cantatas, miniature operas or poetic dramas according to one's understanding of these terms; and this despite their obvious similarities to the mélodie. The same may be said about the more recent set of 'Improvisations on Mallarmé' that goes by the title *Pli selon Pli*, in which the pitches and rhythmic intervals are almost scientifically determined by the syllabic structure and scansion of the verse. That this all portends something new and exciting for the fusion of French music and literature goes without saying. But whether it marks the logical end of the mélodie, or an unforeseen *point d'appui* destined to face it in a different direction, seems a question it is much too early to propose.

xi Piano Music—Franck to Messiaen

Though blessed with an unrivalled tradition of music for harpsi-chord, French composers proved slow to exploit the richer sonorities of the piano, allowing themselves to be overtaken by contemporaries in other lands. Having become far too enraptured with the theatre, they neglected to lay the foundations of a modern keyboard style similar to that Beethoven, Schumann and Liszt had forged in Germany. Indeed, it could be argued that without César Franck's adoption of these foreign composers as models, France might have contributed little to a sphere in which she had once led Europe.[1] In his majestic *Prélude, Choral et Fugue* of 1885, Franck belatedly took up from where Beethoven had left off, giving Parisians a long-deserved opportunity of hearing a great new piano work of classical dimensions.

Up to this time, the city had been content to applaud the never-ending procession of visiting virtuosi—including Chopin, Thal-berg and Liszt himself—as they thundered out the fantasias and transcriptions demanded of them by the salons. It was not until the the end of the century that Vincent d'Indy bore witness to shame-fulness of a situation which had permitted a noble instrument

[1] I am exempting from this charge the still obscure Valentin Morhange, better known as Alkan, who lived from 1813 to 1888 and wrote an incredible quantity of difficult music for the piano. His 48 *Esquisses* and 24 *Etudes* are, however, mainly technical exercises. The other works he wrote, including the interesting set of variations entitled 'Le Festin d'Esope', unfortunately remained largely unknown and are still not in the repertory, though ballets have been made of some of them. Alkan was a friend of Liszt's and a great scholar. Indeed, he met his death reach-ing for a copy of the Talmud and pulling the entire bookcase down on himself. Raymond Loewenthal has recently made a record of some of his works.

to be used for fashionable or imitative purposes. Unfortunately, Franck left only two important works for the piano, the second being the equally monumental *Prélude, Aria et Final* of 1887. And each happens to be cast in the severest intellectual language. They offer no hint of that Gallic sparkle so readily detectable in the compositions of Debussy and Ravel; and for that reason will continue to seem ill-chosen corner-stones with which to have initiated the nation's keyboard renaissance. Yet if it had not been for the 'high seriousness' of the Pater Seraphicus and his pupils, how much more burdened French piano music would have been with the products of a decadent Romanticism! In such a way does history operate.

As things turned out, the fin-de-siècle was distinguished not merely by its various tonal revolutions—including the Debussyiste and post-Debussyiste movements—but by a genuine resurgence of interest in the piano on the part of such sober figures as d'Indy, Dukas and de Bréville. Among these, d'Indy became by far the most unyielding in his pursuit of academic shibboleths. While a young man, he had been drawn to the picturesque element in German Romanticism, writing a series of *Tableaux de Voyage* (1889) to commemorate his travels in the Black Forest and along the banks of the Rhine. These delightful pieces merit exhumation if only to relieve musicians of the necessity for still further hearings of well-worn favourites like Mendelssohn's *Songs Without Words* and Schumann's *Waldscenen*. Thirteen pieces in all, Nos. 9 and 12, entitled respectively *Départ Matinal* and *La Pluie*, seem particularly fetching, the latter rather reminiscent of Fauré in its figuration. A much greater stumbling block to player and listener is the composer's mature Sonata in E—a forbidding work that takes on the most unpianistic shape, and whose relentless processing of motifs helps bring it more within the purview of the new Viennese school. But d'Indy kept alive his interests in all manner of sectors, including folk-music and pedagogical music. The contributions he made to these deserve the attention of pianists, young and old. His *Six Paraphrases sur des chansons enfantines de France*, Op. 95, for example, are well worth the effort of domestic performers; while the even later *Fantaisie sur un vieil air de ronde Française*, Op. 99, written within a year of his death in 1930, is an astonishingly vital and spontaneous work. It consists of a Préambule, an Intermède in the form of a cadenza, and a short series of Variations. No other works of his are quite as attractive as these, but for those interested in the more serious forms of neo-classicism his menuets, fugues and sarabandes, like those of the short-lived Alexis de Castillon, represent early attempts to adumbrate a style of music that was to become extremely popular in the 1920's.

Dukas, though he was not a pupil of Franck, was another artist who remained keenly alive to the possibilities of a French classical revival based on the piano. His sixty-minute Sonata in B flat minor (1901) preceded d'Indy's by the better part of a decade, and is considered by most good judges to be superior at every point. Indeed, it is hard to think of any other example of this form by a Frenchman—the contributions of Auric, Dutilleux and Boulez notwithstanding—that attains a comparable level of excellence. Its unpopularity stems from its refusal to indulge in any exhibitionism, even of the most innocuous kind. Also, its heavy textures are sometimes considered a burden to the player, a fact that tends to place the work in the same category as the least-often played compositions of Brahms and Reger. The same composer's *Variations, Interlude et Final sur un thème de Rameau* (1903) is another hefty proposition, shunned by the majority of pianists out of sheer sloth. Actually, it is one of the best sets of variations written for the piano since Beethoven's on a theme of Diabelli. Its organ-like chords and awkward stretches make it more reminiscent of Franck than Rameau, but there are also delicate touches of ornamentation that duplicate the 'agréments' of the clavecinistes who were at that time almost entirely forgotten. Dukas wrote nothing else for the piano—his entire output was among the smallest on record— probably because he set himself such a high standard. There is a transcription available of his charming *Villanelle* for horn and piano made by Samazeuilh, but this scarcely compensates for the absence of a wide range of original works for the instrument.[1] For some reason, Dukas has never been accepted as the superb artist that he was, and even his centenary in 1965 passed virtually unnoticed in Britain. Saint-Saëns, to whom his Piano Sonata was dedicated, did not even acknowledge the present of a copy, the only pianist ever to make a point of performing it regularly being Lélia Gousseau.

By contrast, de Bréville's works for the piano are infinitely more accessible, though they are not for the amateur. His suite *Stamboul* (1894, revised 1913) was inspired by his contacts with the Armenian musician, Astik Hammamdjian. It is in four movements, each of which depicts some quarter of that Turkish city. *Les Muézins de Ste-Sophie* portrays the Mohammedan criers whose job it is to proclaim prayers from the minarets surrounding that strange religious building (it was originally a Christian church under Justinian, but was converted into an Islamic mosque following the fall of Constantinople in 1453). The second movement,

---

[1] Again, I exclude trifles like *Prélude Elégiaque* (1909) and *La Plainte au loin du faune* (1921), since these were obviously written for salon or occasional purposes, and are of discouragingly modest dimensions.

Le Phanar, explores the Greek district of the city, and the third, entitled *Eyoub*, that area known as the Golden Horn wherein lie the catacombs. Finally, *La Galata* returns us to the business and shopping centre for a display of pianistic haste not unlike that to be found in Abram Chasins's parody, *Rush-Hour in Hong Kong*. The main difference between de Bréville's suite and most of the other noisy evocations of the clatter of the Orient is that he writes out of a greater sense of scholarly determination. *Stamboul* contains genuine Turkish rhythms—the Andante which follows the introduction to *Les Muézins* is, for instance, in 7/8 time—and is as modal in tonality as the piano allows it to be (quarter-tones being clearly impossible on the instrument). Otherwise, de Bréville added little more to the repertory beyond his Sonata of 1923 and the *Sept Esquisses* of 1925. The Sonata is much more grateful to play than either Dukas's or d'Indy's, being Franckist chiefly in its preference for 'bien-chanté' and determination to soften the edges of the musical phrase. For a player who wishes to extend his repertory by a longish, formally correct work, yet which abounds in lyrical cantabile, there could be no better choice, its comparative lack of modernism being its principal drawback. The *Esquisses* are the product of a similarly fastidious craftsman, and are more within the capacity of the average amateur.[1]

Camille Saint-Saëns (1835–1921) left a vast collection of piano music, which is hardly surprising since he was among the most agile performers France has ever produced. Aside from the Concertos, however, there are few things one would want especially to preserve. So much of what he wrote had a purely educational value that it is tempting to regard him as nothing more than a purveyor of graceful practice exercises for the examination-minded. There are books upon books of *Etudes* in the manner of Mozkowski (Op. 52, Op. III and Op. 135 being the main ones, the last entirely for the left-hand), and a huge collection of first-class transcriptions from Bach. At the other extreme, a good many of Saint-Saëns's pieces are in the various dance-forms made popular during the age of the salon, which persisted in a more or less beleaguered form till the end of the century. Thus we can point to a variety of gavottes, valses and mazurkas of the kind Chaminade wrote so prolifically. Possibly the most enticing of Saint-Saëns's trifles are the *Six Valses*, written at different stages in his long career, but published in a single volume. The *Valse Mignonne*, Op. 104 and the *Valse Langoureuse*, Op. 120, for example, con-

---

[1] So, for that matter are the *Quelques Danses* of Chausson, another talented Franck pupil who was admired wholeheartedly by Debussy. And further, the gay piano suites of de Séverac, who was d'Indy's lieutenant at the Schola.

stitute a definite inducement for those who are tempted by such morsels. Needless to say, they could not be more out of fashion today, and one hardly sees any prospect of them returning to general favour. Yet Saint-Saëns could really write for the piano—unlike some of his high-minded critics—and we should not forget that such a master technician as Ravel openly proclaimed his indebtedness to him on more than one occasion. Indeed, it is unlikely that the latter's Piano Concerto in G major could have been written without the mercurial example of his popular predecessor.

Alongside Saint-Saëns's easeful contributions to the repertory went the earliest experiments of his friend and pupil, Gabriel Fauré, whose links with the salon were at first similarly undisguised. Fauré conferred his greatest benefit on French music through his additions to the mélodie; but his large corpus of piano music should on no account be dismissed. On the contrary, it stands, along with those of Debussy and Ravel, at the very summit of his nation's achievements in that sphere. Taking his point of departure from Chopin (who in certain ways presented the appearance of a French composer) rather than Beethoven, Fauré quietly built up a collection of Nocturnes and Barcarolles that lose nothing whatever by being compared with those of the Polish master. In general, Frenchmen have preferred to lavish their ambitions on 'the piece' rather than 'the work', usually asserting their liking for the shadowy equivalent of the 'Nachtstück' as opposed to the formal sonata or étude. By upholding this preference, Fauré also confirmed the national fondness for pastel shades of expression. The gentle swerve of his melodies, the amazingly poised and delicate harmonies of which he was such a master, the apparently effortless flow of his scales and arpeggios—these features combined to make him a kind of musical Bonnard or Vuillard, and an unequalled exponent of his nation's graces. Readers anxious to come to terms with his achievement would do best to begin with the earliest Nocturnes, especially No. 2 (dearly beloved by Paul Dukas) and the near-popular No. 3, sometimes played by Artur Rubinstein. The latter is admittedly very Chopinesque, but is hardly the worse for that. Its lingering cross-rhythms help offset a characteristically modal plaint which develops, as the piece proceeds, into a magnificently expansive theme in octave chords, supported by rippling arpeggio accompaniment.

Fauré's middle-period piano music is of the same unmarred smoothness, as a rule, though slightly more difficult to play. Some critics attacked his Barcarolles for their blandness, attributing to them the same aqueous qualities as so many previous samples of the form. Too '*vaporeux*', they complained. But despite their similar flow, works the equivalent of the Fifth Barcarolle, Op. 66

are impossible to find in the output of Mendelssohn and his lesser contemporaries. That particular piece is a stormy, yet utterly romantic, effusion that has a good deal more in common with the last two Ballades of Chopin. Much the same claims could be made for the unquestionably great Sixth and Seventh Nocturnes (Op. 63 and 74 respectively), each amongst the finest single pieces ever written for a keyboard instrument.[1] Examined in detail, they would show Fauré's expert judge of sonorities (look at the winged middle section of Op. 63, and ask yourself where to find its equal); his piquant sense of modulation; his complete plasticity of form. For those who still doubt the composer's power to work on a larger, more heroic, plane, there remains the Theme and Variations, Op. 73, as strict and sober an achievement as any by Franck or Brahms. The solemnly proportionate theme has been likened by Charles Koechlin to the engraving on an old coin.[2] English listeners may be more reminded of Elgar's *Enigma*. The sequences are similar and so is the mood. What seems to be missing is Elgar's famous dying fall. But Fauré gives us a taste of something not too remote from that in his Ninth Variation, in which a gentle chain of thirds descends to meet the chord of the thirteenth to produce an effect Cortot once compared to the sinking of a star. Pianists curious enough to go on from this work to Nocturnes Nos. 9 and 10, and the late, sparsely-constructed *Préludes* Op. 103, will find themselves richly rewarded in terms of ideas, if not invariably in general excitement.

Fauré gave rise not so much to a school of piano composers, as Franck had done, but to a circle of independent imitators (a few had been pupils of the composer at the Conservatoire, of which he was the Director from 1905 to 1920). Louis Aubert, the player responsible for the première of Ravel's *Valses Nobles et Sentimentales* who died just recently at the age of ninety, was one who wrote a very beautiful Fauré-like triptych called *Les Sillages*. It comprises *Sur le rivage*, *Socorry* and *Dans la nuit*. This is a more advanced work than any of Fauré's in terms of virtuoso figuration, but it possesses qualities very similar in other ways. The chords are rich and full, the accompanying arpeggios touched with the shimmer of Fauré's peculiar brilliance—using that word in its exact, luminous meaning. Florent Schmitt represents another, almost forgotten, disciple who contributed generously to the piano repertory. His best pieces are probably those contained in *Chaîne brisée*, Op. 87, particularly the lilting *Barcarolle des Sept Vierges*.

---

[1] For further comments on Fauré's piano music, the reader may care to consult the present writer's book, *The Gallic Muse*, (Dent, 1967).

[2] See the biography *Gabriel Fauré* which Leslie Orrey translated and Dobson issued over here in 1946.

The ten preludes he collectively entitled *Soirs* are again worth a glance; but Schmitt was over-rated in his day, and his work commends itself more on the grounds of fluency and efficiency than anything else. More pleasure can be had from Grovlez's miniatures like the *Almanach aux Images*, the amusing *Impressions sur Londres* (containing a fugal imitation of the sounds emanating from Westminster Abbey on a Sunday morning) and the brief set of pieces called *Fancies*, which Augener brought out in Britain but which are now unfortunately out of print. My own preference among the works of the Fauré circle (though it really is a misnomer so to describe it, since its composer never worked under Fauré) is Jacques de la Presle's *Theme and Variations* (1944). The Franckist, chromatic influence is apparent in this exceptionally melodious composition, but Variations IV and VIII are unmistakably Fauréesque and an absolute delight to play.[1]

From Fauré and his followers, it is only a brief step to the work of the two composers who have done most to hasten the popularity of their country's keyboard music with amateur and professional alike. I refer, of course, to Claude Debussy and Maurice Ravel. Superficially alike in their musical philosophies, these two actually set themselves totally different aims. The piano tended to bring out dream-like elements in the former's imagination—one understands very well, after hearing some of his pieces for the instrument, why he called French music 'une fantaisie de la sensibilité'. Ravel, on the other hand, treated the piano more in the fashion of the seventeenth- and eighteenth-century masters—when he was not bent on using it as an exotic percussion instrument. Taking Debussy first, his attitude can best be demonstrated by the remark he is alleged to have made to a heavy-handed pupil: 'Let me imagine, when you play, that the piano has no hammers!' Only very rarely has any composer demanded of the instrument such a deliberately acquiescent function. Of course, it is easy to juxtapose *Jeux d'Eau* alongside *Reflets dans l'Eau* (or *Alborado del Gracioso* alongside *La Puerta de Vino*) with a view to emphasizing the two composers' common pre-occupation with impressionism. But this last term is one that suits Debussy (however much he objected to it!) better than it does Ravel. The former was essentially a scene-painter—the evidence of the *Etudes* notwithstanding—whereas his younger colleague was interested most of all in technical development and pastiche. What Debussy did was to 'break the circle of the Occident', to resort to Boulez's illuminating phraseology. He experimented with gong-like sonorities, mesmeric ostinati and

---

[1] It seems a pity not to mention, while considering Fauré's influence the richly sonorous pieces in Louis Vuillemin's *Soirs Armoricains*. Too difficult for the amateur, they should appear oftener in recital programmes.

a variety of unusual harmonies built up in towers of thirds. He also made extensive use of the whole-tone scale, as opposed to the predominantly modal approach of Fauré and Ravel. By imitating the imaginary tolling of a submerged cathedral's bell; stimulating the diving movements of goldfish in a bowl; comically duplicating the tumblings of a music-hall artist—and by a host of other naturalistic studies—Debussy gave to music a whole new encyclopedia of sensations and became the foremost innovator the instrument has ever inspired.

By contrast, Ravel's innovations were mechanically conceived, though one should not think too much the less of what he accomplished. The technique contained in works like *Gaspard de la Nuit* (1908) went so far beyond Lisztian requirements as to constitute the need for a new species of virtuoso. Fast-repeated seconds, glissandi in thirds, clanging, open fourths and fifths over rapidly changing accompaniment textures—all these devices were adapted to producing music of the most improbable degree of scintillation. Equally astonishing were the sustained pedal-effects, achieved with a bare minimum of notes, that he introduced into works like the *Valses Nobles et Sentimentales* (1911), inspired by nothing more serious than Henri de Régnier's essays in praise of idleness. The pastische element in this work comes in the penultimate waltz which, besides being 'plus Ravel' in the author's terminology, offers us something like the same kind of parody on the Viennese Ländler that the composer provided on a larger scale in his symphonic poem, *La Valse*. Otherwise, the work in which Ravel's powers of mimicking older musicians stand out most is the suite, *Le Tombeau de Couperin* (1918), in which there are not merely ancient dance-forms, like the Forlane and the Rigaudon, but in which there abound all sorts of subtle effects of ornamentation (trills, appoggiaturas, accents) that become deeply reminiscent of the great age of the harpsichordists. That this was at the back of Ravel's mind in most of his thinking about the piano is suggested by his habit of writing as if he had a double manual instrument at his disposal. This creates problems of placing hand upon hand (or the finger of one hand through the group of fingers of the other) that do not endear the composer to his interpreters. But there are a few easier compositions by Ravel, notably the *Sonatine* (1905), the little *Menuet sur le nom d'Haydn*, and the seldom heard *Prélude*, another minuscule piece written as a sight-reading test for the Conservatoire. All these, especially the last two, are recommended to those who love, but are dismayed by the difficulties of, the major works.

At the same time as these developments were proceeding, another and quite different line of pianism was reaching its apogee in a more southernly locale—a line it is tempting to call simply the line of wit, using that word in its serious *and* humorous connotations. Its benefactors have been the pianists Chabrier, Satie, Koechlin and Poulenc. The first of these was a native of Auvergne and the last of the Touraine, so that they brought certain rustic frivolities with them to add to those they picked up in Paris. Satie came from Honfleur, a seaport to the north, and Koechlin spread his regional interests so widely as to call one of his principal piano works *Paysages et Marines*. Despite this scattering of allegiances, all these managed to settle for large parts of their lives in the capital, and all exhibited a mixture of the rural and the cosmopolitan in their personalities. Chabrier was the old man of the group, having been born as far back as 1841, before the modern movement got under way. Yet, in a curious way, it was he who anticipated the popular element which is one of its features in the most conclusive manner. As a pianist, he acquired a hard-hitting style that made him known in the cafés and bistros, and which gained him the displeasure of instrument-makers all over France. Cortot describes how one Erard he knew bore the scars of what he called 'a fine hand to hand combat' in consequence of Chabrier's attentions.[1] The *Pièces Pittoresques* this composer wrote around 1880 illustrate very well the many-sidedness of his character. Some of them breathe the spirit of the French countryside in an utterly inimitable way, the *Idylle*, *Sous-bois* and *Tourbillon* being obvious instances. Others, like the rigid *Menuet Pompeux*, either fail to convey this rusticity, or were designed to cock a snook at the aristocratic traditions of French culture.

Erik Satie, born in 1866, came more closely into contact with the forces that have shaped the present-day world (the cinema, surrealism, socialism, anti-academicism) and had no hesitation in importing some of these into his music. Though best known for his clownish, and nowadays rather modish, ballets, Satie actually wrote a good deal for piano, mainly because he was inept at playing other instruments. Like Chabrier, he worked in the cafés, but unlike him he actually earned his living in them, much as Toulouse-Lautrec had to do in art. The 'Chat Noir', where the famous shadow-plays were performed, was his first venue after quitting the Conservatoire (where he had failed abysmally to take a Diploma), and a good many of his absurd parodies were doubtless conceived there. His first group of piano works were innocent enough—works like the *Gymnopédies* and the *Gnossiennes*. The former were simple diatonic tunes in 3/4 time, thought up as parodies of Greek callisthenic exercises, and the latter also a group

[1] The story appears in Volume I of his *French Piano Music* (O.U.P., English translation by Hilda Andrews, 1932).

of vaguely classical pieces, this time inspired by the story of Knossos in Crete. It was after returning from a second bout of academic training at the Schola Cantorum (more successful in every way than the first) that the composer commenced his more truly waggish experiments. Pieces like the *Véritables Préludes Flasques* (1912), the *Avant-dernières pensées* (1915) and the *Sonatine Bureaucratique* (1917) were scholastic exercises transformed into deliberately jokey terms, the last being a skit on Clementi. Most pianists still fight shy of such works, partly because they carry verbal commentaries that not everyone can understand or appreciate and partly because they are not especially well-suited to the piano as a medium. Notwithstanding his café-concert experiences, the fact is that Satie was *not* a particularly good player of the instrument (Poulenc has confirmed as much in his *Moi et mes amis*, La Palatine, Paris-Genève, 1963), and it was only in the *Cinq Nocturnes*, which were among the last works he wrote for it, that we get an inkling of real skill and refinement.

If one can stomach Satie, in terms of the simplicity of his writing, one should have no difficulty in taking to the numerous Sonatinas of Koechlin, whose wit is more like Ravel's—that is to say, less bumptious and more neat. The texture of his music stands about half way between late Fauré and Satie, being barer than the former but not as ostentatiously nude as the latter. The Sonatinas fall into two groups, the second being differentiated as *Nouvelles Sonatines* and being, on the whole, less rewarding. What gives the initial group its distinction is the expressive use of modality, the almost Mozartean clarity of outline, and the refusal to add parts simply to lend sumptuousness to the texture. They are easy to play and very French in feeling. So are the *Paysages et Marines*, which are more chromatic, with the harmony more filled out. The 'tessitura' (if one may be allowed such a term in relation to the piano) continues, however, to be very high up and 'harpsichordish'. The suite *L'Ancienne Maison de Campagne* (a copy of which I once picked up in a Paris second hand music shop, containing Koechlin's handwritten comments to Marcel Delannoy) is the most substantial-looking of his piano works. Written in 1932, the work illustrates both the topographical interests of the composer, and also his incorrigible eclecticism. Quotations appear in it from Fauré's song *Berceaux*, from Milhaud's *Foire de Bordeaux* and even from Debussy's *Pelléas et Mélisande* of which opera he was a devout admirer. The late Norman Demuth, in his study of *French Piano Music* (Museum Press, 1959) regards No. 10, *La Veille du départ*, as the real and only success of the set. But I am inclined to agree with David Drew that too much attention has been paid to *Paysages et Marines*, if not to the other Koechlin piano works, so that as a gesture of further interest in this gifted musician's work I would prefer to suggest that students make a start with the twelve *Préludes*, Op. 209, which, as far as I am aware, have never been publicly performed in this country and were the last piano pieces Koechlin wrote, coming just before his death in 1951.[1]

To turn from him to Poulenc is almost to renew a familiar friendship, since the *Mouvements Perpétuels* (1918) seem to be in the repertory of everyone who has passed his Grade V of the Associated Board's examinations. Nevertheless, there are whole collections of his work that are rarely if ever performed outside France. The sprightly *Improvisations* (1932/41) come near to being in that category, despite the composer's declared view that they were his best compositions in the medium. There are also *Huit Nocturnes*, again spread over the 'thirties in terms of writing, of which the first is unexpectedly graceful and flowing, without a trace of the 'wrong-note' harmony commonly employed. For those who prefer their Poulenc to sound irreverent and noisy, the *Promenades* (a title appropriated from Albéric Magnard?) offer some shattering experiences. The piece ironically labelled *En Bateau* may be profitably contrasted with Debussy's of the same title from his *Petite Suite*. Whereas the latter conjures up a peaceful afternoon at Argenteuil (it being a placid Barcarolle in thirds, with semiquaver accompaniment), Poulenc's piece might be described as the musical equivalent of sea-sickness. The direction 'Agité', followed by a fortissimo marking, leads one to expect the worst, and that is certainly what one gets. The whole collection, of course, ranges over the various locomotive cults then popular in Paris—train, aeroplane and bicycle included.[2] Despite the delightfully relaxed D flat Intermezzo and cleverly-contrived *Thème Varié* (1951), my favourite among Poulenc's piano works is the delectable *Les Soirées de Nazelles* (1936), a wonderful jumble of balletic variations in which the composer mixes his style with the mannerisms he had acquired from a galaxy of contemporaries ranging from Stravinsky to Prokofiev and Ravel. As a deliberate flaunting of the principle of plagiarism, it seems to sum up the French capacity for drawing nourishment from every practicable source —only to end by leaving the listener with a convinced sense of the nation's inimitableness and uniqueness.

---

[1] Drew's interesting essay on 'French Music', contained in the symposium *European Music in the Twentieth Century* (Pelican, 1961), has much to say on both Satie and Koechlin.

[2] This was the period when Honegger wrote his famous *Pacific 231* in imitation of the sounds of a railway engine, and Lindbergh made his Transatlantic crossing by air, celebrated in music by Martinů's *La Bagarre*.

Poulenc's colleagues in 'Les Six' did less to stimulate interest in the piano. Auric's Sonata is a formidable work in all senses, but hardly very typical of his fondest pre-occupations. More was done to further the instrument's potentialities by later musical *flâneurs* like Jean Françaix, Jacques Ibert and Jean-Michel Damase. The first-named, a star pupil of Nadia Boulanger, has tried his hand at a short Sonata, and is notable for a set of pieces inspired by Paul Valéry's theories of the dance. Ibert, known to all for his skit *Le Petit Âne Blanc*, actually wrote nine other miniatures of the same kind in a set collectively entitled *Histoires*. One of these, called *A Giddy Girl*, is an irresistable take-off on an English Edwardian waltz, slightly 'risqué' at the same time as it strives to be respectable. Lord Berners would have enjoyed it. Otherwise, the *Histoires* represent too much of an imitation of Debussy (the titles are added to the end of each piece in the manner of the two books of *Préludes*). The same composer's three *Escales*—though they are transcriptions of orchestral works—are so much more interesting that one is tempted to break a rule and play them as if they were originally conceived for the piano. They describe, Albéniz-fashion, various ports of call—Rome, Palermo, Tunis, Nefta and Valencia. Damase is much younger than either of the two composers with whom I have considered him, having been born as late as 1926. But his idiom is not much removed from theirs. Again, his music exudes the French *clarté* to enjoyable effect, and yet he always has something interesting to say. The *Féeries* is an album of sixteen shorter pieces for children, as also his *Pièces Brèves*. The best introduction to him for adults comes through either the Sonata (which is difficult and requires a few awkward stretches) or the Theme and Variations. To my mind, the latter shows the composer at his best. It is impossible to mention all the other French composers who have written lightly in the neo-classical vein for the piano. Jean-Jacques Grunenwald, who teaches at the Schola Cantorum, and Daniel-Lesur, who until fairly recently was that institution's Director, are two academics who have written particularly felicitously for the instrument. The former's *Suite de Danses* and the latter's *Pavane* are well within the scope of the persevering beginner.

By the time the neo-classical school had ceased to dominate, the Second World War had turned France upside down, and what emerged from the chaos was chiefly the musical renaissance we associate with the work of Leibowitz, Messiaen and their respective disciples. As things stand some twenty-five years later, it is the work of Messiaen that seems to have contributed most to the French tradition of piano writing. His eight *Préludes* (1930) were already a remarkable step forward towards the extreme use of harmony as coloration which was a feature of Debussy's works of the same title, albeit not so daring or pronounced in character.[1] The slow, sad harmonies of the *Chant d'extase dans un paysage triste*, particularly where the theme re-enters in octaves with fluent arpeggio support (page 9 of the Durand edition), are expressive of the natural world in a contemplative and quasi-religious fashion, and stand at the opposite pole from Chabrier's rusticity. Similarly, the song-like second section of *Le nombre léger* foreshadows the light, bird-like textures of some of the music for piano and orchestra the composer was to write in the years ahead. Professor Demuth singles out *Cloches d'angoisse et larmes d'adieu* as indicative of Messiaen's complex, chromatic idiom, and the succeeding *Plainte calme* as typical of his occasional naïve beauty of phrase. Other pieces, like the two designated *Île de Feu* from the *Neumes rhythmiques* (1949–50), are savagely intense, and though they were intended merely as studies in use of rhythm they give the impression of somehow asserting the frenetic force of nature. Almost certainly the piano work of the composer's most likely to become a classic—despite its prohibitive length—is the immense collection, *Vingt Regards sur L'Enfant Jésus*. This contains, as the title implies, twenty separate pieces and takes two and a half hours to play. Predictably, pianists have chosen favourites from it, like the *Regard de Père* and the *Regard de l'Esprit de Joie*, some of which can form attractive contrasts. As a whole, however, the work calls for virtuoso treatment of an unprecedented kind, and until recently only Yvonne Loriod, the composer's wife, made a habit of playing it in its entirety. Nowadays, John Ogdon, Michel Béroff and Thomas Rajna have all performed it creditably, and one must accept that it will become as much a part of the repertory as the Debussy *Images* or Ravel's *Gaspard de la Nuit*.

The *Vingt Regards* was written as early as 1944, however, and Messiaen's many admirers have been put out by the fact that he has since then concentrated much more fervently on orchestral works, like the *Chronochromie* and *Les Couleurs de la Cité Céleste* —which press the colour-sound equations a stage further again— or works for piano with orchestra, like the apparently endless *Catalogue d'Oiseaux*, in which a pantheistic infatuation with birdsong seems to have replaced all other interests. Despite his relative silence, however, Messiaen looks as if he may be the last composer to use the piano as a great impressionistic instrument. The sonatas of Boulez and Amy, while more immediately in tune with the current vogue for gamelan effects, obtain these effects by the use of new forearm positions and by essentially altering the character

[1] One of them bears the name *Un reflet dans le vent*, which could hardly be more Debussyan in its associations.

of the instrument. Finger-technique has become a thing of the past in them, and they disavow the intentions of piano-makers by striving for sounds of indeterminate pitch and uncertain tone-colour. This being the case, it is surprising that they do not abandon altogether an instrument which, after all, cannot properly obtain pitches less than a semi-tone apart and was never intended to produce the gong-like effects of certain types of percussion instruments like the marimba or the xylophone. To see the piano played 'à la Cage'—with strips of wood or metal inserted and with the pianist doing no more than strike an occasional isolated note at one or other of its extreme ends—is, paradoxically, to be a witness to a most old-fashioned kind of experiment. It is like using a microscope for a door-stop. If modern composers, with all their scientific know-how, cannot come up with a more effective means of expressing their obviously very different ideas about music—and leave the piano for those who were trained to play and compose for it—it argues an acute mental poverty of which one would hardly have considered them capable. Certainly it is better that the instrument should revert to the noble status enjoyed by the harpsichord or clavichord than become a mere wooden object to be attacked by mallets, chisels and other implements of the kind described by Mr Rollo Myers in his review of the Paris concerts of David Tudor and John Cage, when even the legs (exposed from beneath their Victorian coverage) were subjected to asexual assault.[1]

[1] Mr Myers's comments are summed up in a timely article entitled 'Towards a New Music?' published in the Winter 1966 edition of *Composer*.

xii The Symphony in France

It is commonly supposed that the symphony is a Viennese form, and that French composers have fared very badly at it. Part of this statement, if not all of it, is untrue, in so far as the original sources of the form were the 'sinfonia avanti l'opera' perfected by Alessandro Scarlatti and the French overture of Lully. Each of these sources was in being long before the series of three-movement Haydn works was begun in or around 1759, or the Mannheim school commenced its experiments with enlarged ensembles. There is nonetheless some sense behind the popular view in that it was only with Haydn, Mozart and Beethoven that history gave rise to a form of orchestral work that stood apart from any preludial, theatrical or entracte functions. The works they wrote, as we all know, varied enormously in aim and scope and contained grossly dissimilar approaches to tonality, form and instrumentation. Yet what they had in common was perhaps just enough to justify the use of the term 'symphony' as something essentially new and definable, however difficult that task proved itself to be.

Robert Simpson, in his introduction to the Pelican volume called *The Symphony: Haydn to Dvořák* (1966), has discovered common elements in the fusing of musical material into organic wholes; the use of tonality as a long-range governor, so to speak, of harmony; the careful control and juxtaposition of mood; and, finally, the impression of size and power. Many readers will recognize certain of these elements as having been singled out and emphasized by notable critics of symphonic form—the first two by Tovey in his approach to Beethoven and the last two by Deryck Cooke and Neville Cardus in their comments on Mahler. It nevertheless remains hard to find one single symphonic composer who satisfies all four of Mr Simpson's criteria equally

139

conscientiously. Moreover, what may be large-scale and tonally advanced for one age may seem miniature and platitudinous for the next. One is reminded, in this sense, of Constant Lambert's jibe about some listeners preferring Beethoven's symphonies to Mozart's in the way they would prefer a six- to a four-cylinder car. Most importantly of all, I feel, we should keep on reminding ourselves that, as in every tradition worthy of the name, permissible deviations occur as the natural expression of genius. It is accordingly stupid to consider each individual symphony against a common background of assumptions and judge its merits entirely on the extent to which it complies with these assumptions. Looked at from a more liberal position, as stated above, there is no reason why a work like Debussy's *La Mer* cannot be considered a great, if somewhat unconventional, symphony. As a matter of fact, it satisfies the criteria listed by Mr Simpson a good deal more efficiently than many works of the Viennese school.

Yet I suppose it remains true that, as far as modern music goes, the role of symphonist was first appropriated by those composers who lived and worked in Vienna in the early years of the nineteenth century. It then gradually became adopted by musicians in other lands, each of whom gave the form its own national twist. In a series of talks on American television, delivered some years ago, Leonard Bernstein elaborated on this thesis by saying that what really happened was that every nation followed Beethoven's example, including his own Germany and Austria, producing symphonies that were to all intents and purposes variations of the master's. At home, Schubert and Brahms strove to emulate his grandeur, while Mendelssohn added a Celtic touch in his 'Scotch' symphony and a southern one in his 'Italian'. Schumann was persuaded by Liszt, another contender, to try his hand, with results that sounded even more national than his most typical compatriots. In Czechoslovakia, Finland and Russia, the theme was taken up by Dvořák, Sibelius and Tschaikovsky—the last of whom proffered vodka to Beethoven's beer, as it were. Even England, a decided late-comer to the field if one excepts Sterndale Bennett and other overrated figures, produced in Elgar a man influenced far less by neo-Elizabethan polyphony than by the solidity and massiveness of the 'Eroica' and 'Rhenish' symphonies and the brassy symphonic orchestration of Wagner. What is interesting to us as students of the French tradition, is where that nation's composers fitted into this expanding circle, if at all. And here we must return to the second half of our opening sentence by re-stating our doubt as to whether they had any desire to fit in; or whether they gave the lie to Mr Bernstein's plausible thesis by hiving off in a different direction altogether.

First of all, let us admit that the symphony was introduced (or, if you prefer it, re-introduced) into France in good time for that country to have made its contribution alongside all the others. Gossec (1734–1829), who survived to be ninety-four and was an ardent if not especially gifted exponent of the form, ostensibly lived long enough to have established it as the reigning genre in the French capital. The trouble was that he lived *too* long, spending his earliest years amid the Baroque arcadia of the Bourbon kings and queens, and his last amid the heroic materialism of Napoléon. The traditional monarchs were not interested in abstract music, while we all know what the last tyrant did for the symphony through the splenetic reactions of Beethoven in ripping off the dedication page of his No. 3. No, unhappily Napoléon took his artistic vision, such as it was, from the Greeks and the Romans, and his tastes in music from the monumental operas of Spontini and Cherubini. Thus at a time when other nations were beginning to follow the lead given by Beethoven, France remained in the grip of an operatic charisma as disastrously wrong-headed as any in musical history. Nor was that all. When the rule of Bonaparte ended at St Helena, the establishment of a 'bourgeois' monarchy only resulted in the musical equivalent of Victorian commercialism and pomposity. Finally, when the coup d'état of 1851 brought 'the little corporal's' nephew to power and a Second Empire was formed, it predictably led to a feeble attempt at resuscitating the theatrical splendours of 1800, with Meyerbeer cast in the role of a more sensational Spontini. Instrumental music, where it existed, had the status accorded to entomology, or some other equally obscure and mildly distasteful pastime.

Undoubtedly the first substantial work in nineteenth-century France to carry the title of symphony was Berlioz's epic *Symphonie Fantastique* (1830), and this I am afraid poses all the questions about the nature of the form we hoped we had successfully dealt with. As an avowedly programmatic composition, with an ancestral effect on the symphonic poem, it is scarcely to be interpreted as a French adjunct to the Beethoven canon. Formally, the work is certainly tauter and more consistent than it has been made to appear by generations of wild conductors and wizened anti-Berliozians. Its employment of an *idée fixe* is not such a pronounced departure from the cyclical technique of Beethoven's Fifth (where the four-note 'Fate' theme re-appears more 'sotto voce' in the Scherzo), and looks forward to the now accepted procedures of the Franckists. It is accordingly a fairly unified work that meets the first (and perhaps the most important) of the criteria listed in the introduction. The *ampleur* of its orchestration and studied differentiation of mood help to satisfy other criteria too. But perhaps it was only in the later symphonies, like *Harold en Italie* (1834) and *Roméo et Juliette* (1839) that the vastly extended Berliozian melody properly adapted itself to the demands made on it, and the composer mastered his harmony in such a way as to comply with the tonal needs of the symphonic form. It should be remembered, even now that Berlioz has been re-instated as an important symphonist, that he was by nature a deeply histrionic individual; and that, whatever may be said on his behalf, the choral episodes and hybrid pictorialness threaten to turn *Roméo et Juliette* into an opera manqué. In the same way, the elevation of the solo viola part in *Harold en Italie* gives the work a concertante basis hardly compatible with the symphonic ideal. But the debate continues, both as to the composer's stature and métier, and it is interesting, for example, to observe a sharp difference of opinion between Professor John Manduell—who considers Berlioz an unsymphonic composer—and David Cairns and Robert Simpson, who evidently think otherwise. Berlioz himself, it is fascinating to record, proudly announced: 'I start where Beethoven left off!' While few would deny him the right to his claim, the real question is whether or not in so doing he 'burst the bounds of symphonic form', leaving us with great music but not necessarily great symphonies.

The position with Camille Saint-Saëns, perhaps the next candidate to propose himself for symphonic honours in France, was the very reverse in that it was said of him that he wrote 'de la mauvaise musique, bien écrite'. That is to say, he turned out symphonies that were models of clarity and form, but lacked the fire of genius. Being the most Gallic of the great French composers, it was only to be expected that Saint-Saëns would write pleasing symphonies, yet we do him an injustice if we imagine that his works had no more exalted aim. He tried hard to achieve the masterly sort of concision that one finds in late Mozart; and Fauré was probably right in seeing a connection between these two men. Where he went astray was in clinging to his belief that art equalled artifice carried to its extreme. Always opposed to the profundities of the Franckists (which admittedly were sometimes more solemn than really profound) Saint-Saëns raised up neatness of phrase, transparency of orchestral texture, professionalism of formal construction as his goals. They are fine goals, and should not be despised. But they were not the sort of goals a great symphonist sets himself. Gounod let the cat out of the bag by referring to Saint-Saëns as 'the French Beethoven'. This, of course, is exactly what he was not. Weight was what he most needed to fulfil that hallowed vocation, and it was a quality he was distinctly short on. His First Symphony, however, appeared as early as 1855, and no one can say of the composer that he was unprogressive in his attitude to instrumental forms. Both symphony and chamber music benefited incalculably from his boundless energies, and he was rightly critical of the tendency of French composers to slide into a commonplace acceptance of opera as the only worthwhile form. The Second Symphony in A minor (1878) was again written in the early part of the composer's career, some eighteen years before it was published, and even secured a grudging performance under Pasdeloup in manuscript. Why it was not more enthusiastically acclaimed is puzzling, for it is an irresistible effort with its idyllic adagio for flute and cor anglais, whirling scherzo and prestissimo finale.[1] Perhaps on account of the difficulties he had in getting it accepted Saint-Saëns waited twenty-five years before embarking on his Third Symphony (1886), which he intended as his pièce de resistance. It contains parts for organ and piano, and was warmly received at the St James's Hall, London, but it proved the point that, in the last resort, the symphony was not his strong suit.

If César Franck had possessed Saint-Saëns's ease and confidence, he would surely have gone down as one of the major symphonists of all time. As it is, the solitary specimen he did write is such a firm favourite with 'pops' audiences in Britain and the U.S.A. that it has more than once topped the polls in both countries. Like most of Franck's works, it is a sport of sorts, having only three movements in place of the usual four. The Allegretto manages to telescope slow movement and scherzo by combining the cor anglais section (which actually begins as a pizzicato introduction for strings) with an E flat dialogue between cello and clarinet. But it is obvious that it is the first movement's powerful 'faith' motif, blazoned forth on the full brass choir, that has done most to win the symphony its appeal. A most exciting swing also attaches to the concluding Allegro, but this movement, like so many others of Franck's, seems hampered by its constant weak-beat accentuation. The work's faults are in fact the expected ones—awkward pauses between the various episodes (caused possibly by the organist's habit of switching from 'swell' to 'great'); too frequent polarization around the same cluster of notes; occasional slithering chromatics; and a marked tendency towards vulgarity in the screeching last movement climax. One or two of the themes are also a bit mincing—notably the Finale's F sharp second subject—but these are amply offset by such happy inspirations as the main theme of the middle movement and the grave,

---

[1] It was a typical piece of French illogicality that César Frank was bitterly reproved from all quarters for including a cor anglais solo in his D minor Symphony of 1889. Yet no one even remarked on Saint-Saëns's use of it thirty years earlier.

Wagnerian introduction to the opening Allegro. Franck's contemporaries regarded his symphony with extreme condescension,
Gounod allegedly describing it as 'the affirmation of incompetence' and Ambroise Thomas, the Director of the Conservatoire
at which the composer was Organ Professor, expressing his disdain
by starchy silence. It took the sudden, posthumous inflation of
Franck's reputation around 1900 to bring the work into the forefront of the repertory; but even today its position is curiously
ambiguous. Cecil Gray first praised it then reviled it, while
Constant Lambert referred to it as 'a musical Minotaur'. Neither
of these judgments has affected the public's enjoyment of the
work very much, and despite the changing evaluations it continues
to arouse Franck's symphony was a milestone in the history of
the form and a real vindication of his nation's position.

This position might have been still more forcibly vindicated had
Georges Bizet lived to write a succession of symphonies instead
of his single Symphony in C (1855). True, Bizet was never a pupil
of Franck's, though he did take the rare step of becoming a
periodic 'auditeur' at the professor's classes in the last couple of
years of his life. The Symphony, of course, dates from a much
earlier period, and was incredibly written in the space of a month,
having been begun four days after the composer's seventeenth
birthday in October of 1855 and completed towards the end of
the succeeding November. Inspired by Gounod and not Franck,
it is a delicate, charming work, bereft of the element of size but
so melodious and adroit that one is amazed to learn that it remained
undiscovered until 1933 and unperformed until 1935. Today, it
is heard in broadcast concerts almost every week, such is the
inducement it offers to orchestras of modest dimensions and attain-
ments. A musicologist might quibble over its success, attributing
the work not simply to Gounod's influence but to Gounod's actual
notes, since there is a strong resemblance between the former's C
major and the latter's D major composition in the form. The
resemblance is structurally very close indeed, and for once the
older man might have had a strong case for pressing one of his
customary charges of plagiarism. But then plagiarism is a peculiar
thing in music, and most of the greatest composers—Handel and
Brahms stand out—were guilty of it in one way or another. In
this particular case, it would be hard to deny that Bizet's own
melodic gifts are in evidence, and perhaps this is all that really
matters. Had he written more works of the same kind, one would
have had to take the charge with greater seriousness. As it stands,
Bizet can hardly be counted a major force in the history of the
symphony, and his presence in these pages should be looked upon
more in the nature of an unexpected, but delightful, intrusion

of no greater significance than a visit from a pleasant young caller who found himself compelled to hurry away. The solid work French composers devoted to the symphony—and only the ignorant assume that no such work was done—was put in by the longer-living d'Indy, Ropartz and Dukas, to mention only the less avant-garde.

It is another nice question for the musicologist whether or not we should regard d'Indy's *Symphonie Cévenole* (the full title to this work was *Symphonie sur un chant montagnard Français*, which is rather too much of a mouthful for common usage) as a true symphony. Completed in 1886, it is another essay in the concertante style, like Berlioz's, this time using the piano as the chief instrument. The work is in three movements, and hence cannot be thought of as a mere *Fantaisie*. Yet it is questionable whether its fresh, airy use of Ardèche folk-song really puts it in the symphonic class. Since it was almost certainly influenced by Franck's *Les Djinns* (1884) and *Variations Symphoniques* (1885), which the composer knew about in their early stages of construction, we should possibly designate it, like them, as a symphonic poem with piano obligato or set of variations for piano with orchestra. Whatever we call it, it is a better piece than many of d'Indy's later and more dogmatic ventures, and it ought to be played much more often than it is. The present writer recalls Cortot, even in his unreliable old-age, giving a spendidly vibrant account of it which seemed to belie altogether the notion that d'Indy had no lyrical impulse. Yet by the time we reach that composer's Symphony No. 2 (1904), the Franckist obsession with cyclic form and the determined adulation of Beethoven had so much got the better of him as to have resulted in a work of stifling, intimidating character. A large work, it has an introduction; a substantial first movement made up of contrasting themes (one slow and solemn, the other more lively, and presumably intended to signify the characteristic struggle from darkness into light that was a feature of most of the circle's work); two intermediary movements of no great significance; and an epic final Allegro in which the cyclical recurrence takes the shape of a powerful chorale expressed in full orchestral tutti. Roussel always admired this symphony, and in conventional terms it is undoubtedly the most serious and important the composer wrote. Certainly it easily supersedes the dreadful 'Battle' Symphony d'Indy's militarism nudged him into writing during the First World War, with its almost blasphemous simulation of the thunder of the guns and the tramping of dying men's feet along the Marne.

In many ways, Ernest Chausson's Symphony in B flat (1889–91) was the best of the Franck circle's products in the form. It has its limitations, as the composer himself knew, but it is the only full-scale French symphony of its period to have escaped the dogmatisms or trivialities we have been describing. To begin with, Chausson was far more talented—though not more learned—than the rest of his comrades. His amateurism should not be mistaken for incompetence. As a rich man, to whom music could easily have become a mere avocation, he whipped up the envy of tired professionals, who frequently attacked his music on the flimsiest grounds. It was commonly alleged about him, as it was about Magnard, that he owed what little success he had to influential backers. This was the reverse of true in each case, since each composer went to extreme lengths to avoid calling upon the patronage open to them. Chausson certainly did more for others than anyone—except possibly Albéniz—ever did for him. The symphony is sensuous and flowing without ever descending to the occasional sickliness of the famous *Poème*, and it does not get itself blocked off into sections in quite the way Franck's does. Harmonically, it looks forward more to the age of Debussy (a young friend) without proposing anything blatantly revolutionary. The writing of the work cost Chausson neurotic obsessions of a quite shattering kind, and it is hard not to blame Duparc, in particular, for having exercised an inhibiting influence over him. At first, the dilemma was over whether to include a scherzo; but the real trouble caught up with him in the Finale, by far the weakest section of the whole composition. Here the composer's bad habit of filling-in broke loose, and his thematic material (always difficult to coerce) pivoted lamely around the same three or four notes. Chausson himself conducted his work at the Société Nationale's concert in April, 1891, and one might as well take this opportunity of saying that the Society's encouragement was probably the biggest single administrative factor in promoting French symphonic music in general. With its help, and the advocacy of Colonne and Lamoureux as conductors, the outlook for the orchestral (and chamber) musician began to seem a good deal healthier from this time onwards.

Other followers of Franck who devoted themselves strongly to the symphony included Guy Ropartz (1864–1955) and Charles Tournemire (1870–1939), the last succeeding Franck at the console of Saint-Clotilde. Ropartz was a prolific composer and dynamic teacher, a more benevolent and less dogmatic d'Indy. Most of his life was spent away from Paris, as Director of the Nancy then the Strasbourg Conservatoires. Unlike what one might expect from so academic a figure, his music is all light and ventilation, qualities he could hardly have picked up from Franck. He has sometimes been described as the last of the regional composers, and this seems true if one pauses to reflect on his life-span. But nearly all d'Indy's associates (especially those who taught at the Schola) were regionalists of one sort or another—Paul le Flem, Joseph Canteloube, Déodat de Sévérac being just a few. It is hardly surprising, in view of Ropartz's long family connections, that his works exude a Breton flavour very redolent of the province in which he was born. Of his five symphonies, the third (which contains parts for choir) gained him the most praise, but since he reached his peak as a composer at about the time of the impressionist revolution, he was made to suffer all the quips of the modernists who were against both folk-music and symphonic music. Debussy, for example, wrote scathingly about this work:

> I must confess that the words 'on a Breton chorale' (added to the title of a symphony) had led my thoughts in a direction opposite to that which Guy Ropartz has given them. I beheld Brittany, the fitful wildness of the sea, its harsh green more beautiful than any other, the Breton chorale—its soul deeply, religiously untamed and immutable as an old cathedral. And here I am presented with a little route map . . . Great Heavens! What do I care about symphonic form?[1]

One cannot help feeling this outburst a bit unfair to Ropartz who, after all, was not out to write another *La Mer* or *Cathédrale Engloutie*. The composer outlasted the Debussyistes, however, and fared a lot better in his late years. His Fifth Symphony (1946) was much admired by the late Charles Munch, who gave it its première in Paris. Tournemire, unfortunately for him, has still not had his turn, his nine symphonies having exercised a powerful influence over Messiaen without ever seeming to have been played in their entirety. He is a genuine case for investigation and possible revival.

We have already observed, in our essay on French opera, that Paul Dukas tended to take his directions from no particular party or creed. His post as Professor of Orchestration at the Conservatoire held him to a less-than-radical view of French music as a whole; but he was also a distinguished critic on the staff of *Le Revue Hebdomadaire* and hence had a more than averagely keen idea of what was happening in advanced circles. He was almost unique in the smallness of his output and the success he attained with each separate work (one opera, one symphony, two major piano works, one symphonic-poem, a 'poème dansé' and a villanelle for horn and piano), but much of this was the result of his fierce and unrelenting attitude of self-criticism. His Symphony in C

---

[1] For a fuller appraisal of Ropartz by Debussy, see *The Theories of Claude Debussy* ed. by Léon Vallas (Dover Books, 1966).

(beginning with a plain statement of that key's common chord, as if to prove how indifferent he was to fashion!) was conducted for the first time by Paul Vidal at one of the winter Concerts de l'Opéra in 1897. Like Franck's, the work contains only three movements—an andante is sandwiched between two allegros—but the whole edifice is built on a heroic scale. The themes are announced with characteristic clarity and vigour, and these only reach their first movement climax with the rising scale motif affirmed on the brass. Conversely, the andante is remarkable for its delicacy and purity. It is marked 'espressivo e sostenuto', and set in the key of E minor. To end, Dukas chose an allegro spiritoso' in 3/4 time, developing his ideas more rhythmically until he reaches a tremendous peroration—'de la puissance de l'esprit' as the poet Paul Valéry put it. Listeners may be puzzled as to why this formidable work has not made more of an impact. Obviously, it was somewhat overshadowed by the virtuoso tone-poem, *L'Apprenti Sorcier*, which quickly followed it, but there is more to it than that. Dukas never aimed at popularity and his fame deriving out of the last-named work was virtually accidental. His other works, though all marked by absolutely first-rank quality, are rarely heard. They were too intellectual for the audiences of their day, and ipso facto even more so for the audiences of our day—who can appreciate mental gimmickry but whose taste for 'works of art' is as mocking as it is for holy writ. If anything, there is more likelihood of a revival of *Ariane et Barbe-bleue* which at least has spectacle to recommend it.

When the impressionist movement drew to a close in France with the death of Debussy and the dispersal of his followers, the next change in the musical climate was that brought about by 'Les Six', whose symphonies tended to be shorter and patently neo-classical. Haydn became the model again and not Beethoven or Franck. Only d'Indy soldiered on as the custodian of the late nineteenth-century values, and he was met with derision from most of his cheeky juniors among the Cocteau set. Milhaud's two chamber symphonies (*Le Printemps* and *Pastorale*) embodied the typical interests of the 'twenties—bitonality, unusual instrumentation, brevity and escapism. Eventually, he went on to write six such symphonies, the third being a Serenade, the fourth and fifth scarcely more than divertissements for strings and woodwind, and the last really a chamber work in the exact sense, being scored only for oboe, cello and a quartet of voices.[1] Honegger proved far more serious in his symphonic intentions, and his five essays in the medium are all interesting in their different ways. The First was

[1] A Seventh Symphony of larger dimensions has recently been added to the canon, and there will doubtless be more to come.

commissioned by the Boston Symphony Orchestra, like Roussel's Third, and is perhaps the least important. The Second was delayed until 1941, by which time the composer was nearly fifty, and it expresses feelings of hope and despair emanating from the war-time atmosphere. Its trumpet Chorale in the Finale was presumably intended, as Norman Demuth suggests, to radiate 'a message of hope'; but Honegger was always a bit of a pessimist and it is hardly surprising to find that other critics have pointed more to the 'dance-of-death' elements contained in the work. The *Symphonie Liturgique* that forms No. 3 in the series also arose out of the war, though it was not issued until 1946. It includes *Dies Irae*, *De profundis clamavi* and *Dona nobis pacem* movements and has been compared in the first place to Beethoven's *Missa Solemnis* and in the second to Debussy's *Le Martyre de Saint Sébastien*. The Fourth was also given a very ambiguous sub-title—'Deliciae Basilienses'—and was written for the twentieth anniversary of the Basel Chamber Orchestra. Rather restrained in tone, it looks back even further than the classical period to the age of the baroque, and is a work that well deserves frequent hearings. Lastly, the Fifth is given the suffix 'Di tre re' and was composed in 1950. Its textures are again slim, but the keynote continues to be serious.

Poulenc, Auric and the remaining members of 'les Six' were not by nature or inclination symphonists, and they possessed the wit to acknowledge the fact.[1] The man who, above all, went straight to the heart of the symphony in France was Roussel, with whom we shall be dealing in greater detail in Part II. He shared the taste for brevity common in the 'twenties, but that was about all he did share. A composer of immense integrity and erudition, he stood above the chaos of contemporary 'sound-making' and wrote works that are both formally exact and yet thoroughly modern and exciting. There is nothing slender about them either, for although neo-classicism was also his ideal his temperament brought him much nearer to the brusque, strong stimulating young Beethoven than to any of his more facile colleagues. In purely French terms, he relates to the Franck–d'Indy tradition, and was, as it happens, an admiring but not totally uncritical pupil of the latter at the Schola. His first two symphonies do not amount to very much. No. 1 being a semi-programmatic work given the title *Pour une fête de printemps* and neither looking beyond the exotic-impression-istic phase through which the composer then seemed to be passing. With Symphonies 3 and 4, however (dating from 1930 and 1934 respectively), we enter a different world, in which the aim was

---

[1] Sauguet, though not a member of 'Les Six', was associated with the band via Satie; but his *Symphonie Expiatoire* and I.N.R. Symphony are hardly characteristic.

evidently to produce brief masterpieces of compressed musical planning. The Third is certainly successful in achieving this aim, its taut rhythms and springy, generative force causing Poulenc to dub it a 'Spring' Symphony. Its slow movement is nevertheless its greatest, containing longer stretches of melody which mount steadily to an unparalleled climax in the form of a brilliant fugato passage, in which all Roussel's special knowledge of counterpoint is put to magnificent use. Most critics have felt the Fourth a slight anticlimax after this, but the composer was rather a sick man by the time he wrote it. Even so, it contains ample evidence of Roussel's marvellous aural sensitivity in its free polytonal effects and its sharp feeling for instrumentation. Probably its last movement, the Allegro Molto, is the winner on this occasion; it is better than the corresponding movement in No. 3, which did not quite maintain the high standard set by that work as a whole. In Roussel, if no one else, the French symphony discovered a master.

Since his death in 1937, no composer has been able to match, let alone conquer, his achievements. Koechlin wrote a Second Symphony at the advanced age of seventy-three (1943–6), his first having been an early *Symphonie d'Hymnes* in which the movements depicted diurnal and nocturnal sensations in a more or less informal way. This later work is reminiscent of Bach in its preference for chorale, fugue and other contrapuntal forms, but it also proclaims Fauré's modal influence and is hence exceedingly eclectic, like most of the composer's work. Jolivet's *Symphonie de Danses* is again too extreme a departure from the norm, being a mere sixteen-minute exercise in the balletic style written in 1940. Since then, the composer has written two longer symphonies (1953 and 1959) for full orchestra which give rise in more characteristic fashion to his hypnotic, ritualistic and heavily discordant style of writing. The last work in the form to date, however, reverts to the string orchestra once more (1961) and has yet to make its way into the public mind. Easily the most traditional symphonies of recent years—and I have no wish to employ the term 'traditional' pejoratively here—are those of Henri Dutilleux, a much underestimated composer outside his own country. His First Symphony (1952) resembles those of Roussel, but the writing tends towards non-tonality to a greater degree. The first movement is a Passacaglia, the theme being announced pizzicato on cellos and doublebasses. It is easily the best movement in the work, though I believe David Drew goes too far when he describes the Scherzo as 'cheapjack' and cannot agree with him that the Finale is saved from a comparable banality only by Roussel's influence. On the contrary, it seems to me a good movement (it also makes use of variation form), comparable with the first, and a credit to its own composer's powers of invention. On the whole, however, I should be inclined to place the Second Symphony (1959) above the First. Its ingenious distribution of the orchestra (the work is sub-titled 'Le Double', and pits a 'grand orchestre' against a 'petit orchestre', the latter including a harpsichord and celeste) and brilliantly clear textures make it an astounding achievement. Possibly we should attribute the influence in this work to Franck more than Roussel, since the former's famous D minor Symphony—though the fact is not generally known—was planned as a 'double'.

It now simply remains to chronicle the contribution of Messiaen in his *Turangalîla-Symphonie* of 1946, a vitally important contribution to the avant-garde movement in France—despite its comparatively early date—on account of its abandonment of nearly all previous conceptions about the symphony. Using a set of Sanskrit writings, some of which were invented by the composer for purely sonorous purposes, it is a sort of massive Hindu love-song in ten movements. The composer himself gives this description of it:

> The three keyboard instruments, glockenspiel, celesta and vibraphone, have a special part similar to that of an East Indian gamelan as used in the islands of Sonde (Java and Bali). The percussion, amply furnished, performs true rhythmic counterpoints. In addition, an Ondes Martinot dominates the orchestra with its expressive voice. Finally, a part for piano solo, which is extremely difficult, is designed to make the orchestra shine with brilliance, with chord clusters and bird songs, almost transforming the *Turangalîla-Symphonie* into a concerto for piano and orchestra.

It will be gathered from this account that, as with Boulez's various cantatas, this symphony broke completely from the Westernized idea of the form, not simply by the giving to it of a special oriental locale, but by employing non-Western instruments and making full use of the athematic, rhythmic-ostinato, extended pedal-points and other devices of the East. Historians will recognize the origins of this break-away in the work of Debussy and the middle-period Roussel; but there is a transcendental element present too, which may perhaps owe something to the mysticism Franck introduced into French music. Not everyone can appreciate the complete freedom from form and tonal law expressed in a work of this kind, which seems as romantically incomprehensible to most of us as Berlioz's mammoth symphonies must have seemed to those nurtured on Gossec. The instrumentation again involves a total mental re-adjustment on the part of the listener, and even the instruments themselves, according to Stravinsky, run the risk of metal fatigue. But facetiousness of this sort will not get us very far. Messiaen's standing as a teacher and scholar is such that, whether or not his works will ever be classed as symphonies, his music will contribute significantly to that of the future.[1]

[1] Even Dutilleux has now succumbed to the vaguely supernatural forces at work in the aesthetics of Messiaen, to the extent that his latest symphonic work, entitled *Métaboles* (1964), has a movement explicitly called *Incantatoire*. The première of this interesting work took place in the U.S.A. under Szell and the Cleveland Orchestra. It received its British première as part of the C.B.S.O.'s 50th Anniversary concert in 1969.

PART TWO

PART TWO

From Nationalism
to Cosmopolitanism

xiii   The Sibelius Conspiracy

To state that nationalism was one of the great driving forces behind
the Romantic movement would be to utter a platitude. The very
existence of different 'folk' customs, different languages for singing, different and more separate political ambitions, all contributed
to making this so. No one can dispute that it was possible to tell,
say, Italian music from French music—or either from German
music—long before the rise of Romanticism. But as Alfred Einstein has neatly phrased it:

> The strengthening of the national character after 1800
> was unmistakable, even among the great and well-
> established nations. Rossini, we repeat, seems 'more
> Italian' than Paisiello or Cimarosa; Berlioz, 'more
> French' than Grétry, Méhul, or Lesueur; Schubert,
> 'more Austrian' than Haydn or Mozart; Schumann,
> 'more German' than Beethoven.[1]

If we accept these generalizations (and one detects a suggestion
of inaccuracy here and there; Grétry, for example, not being
French but Belgian!), we are led to pose another set of questions
arising out of them. The first, and most obvious, is whether the
passing of the Romantic movement and the rise in its place of the
so-called 'modern' movement has lessened or intensified this
nationalist element in art. The second, which is a more subtle
question, is whether, if a continuation of nationalism is detected,
it reflects sincere or inherent differences such as those in evidence
in the middle of the nineteenth century, or whether it does not
prefigure spurious qualities deliberately manufactured for the
purpose of gaining advantage. What I am trying to say is that

[1] *Music in the Romantic Era* by Alfred Einstein (Norton, 1947).

155

nationalism, as well as being a genuine and presumably admirable principle to uphold, now offers excellent opportunities for cultural (not to say political) conspiracies; opportunities unscrupulous artists and governments could be relied upon to seize with outstretched hands.

During this chapter, and those that follow, I shall be endeavouring to trace the effect of national sentiments on a wide range of post-romantic musicians, my object being to see if it is true that such sentiments still seem to be striving for expression in music. It will be another of my aims to probe a little more deeply into the *quality* of these sentiments, hoping to discover whether or not their credentials are in order. I do not wish to delve into the musical niceties or minutiae of the various national cultures with the intention of impugning what seems like a fake or an accretion. Such a task would, in any case, be quite beyond my qualifications. On the contrary, what I am interested in doing is to keep track, in a general way, of modern composers' allegiances, to note whether these have, for the most part, remained rooted in native soil or whether they have hived off in the direction of cosmopolitanism. If it should turn out that the former situation is the one that prevails, then we must go on, in each case, and ask why this should have been so and how much integrity or falsification is involved. An example will make my point for me more succinctly than anything else. In the capital of Wales, where I live, there is a circle of stones which most people associate with Druidic rites placed directly in front of the National Museum. It is quite pleasing to look at. However, a scholar of my acquaintance once referred to this as 'instant Stonehenge'—and I could see, after making a few discreet and not especially welcome enquiries, how he had arrived at his description. The circle is actually quite old, but apparently not much older than the hansom cab. Since the 1920's, all of us musicians have become familiar with 'instant Bach', and not so long ago it used to be fashionable to produce something that resembled 'instant Machaut or Dufay'—a form of music another colleague of mine used to call 'monastic skiffle'. I am not sufficiently up with the current trend to know whose turn it is this year; but I feel sure some musicianly corpse is somewhere in the process of being dissected in the cause of patriotism.

What all these preliminary attempts at sarcasm have to do with Sibelius may not be at all clear, and I should at once make plain the fact that they were not invoked as a preamble to a frontal assault on his music. There have been enough of such assaults in recent years. He is, however, a case—very similar to all the others we are about to investigate—where it would be useful to know more concerning motivation and aim. Is Sibelius a Finnish composer, for example, or are we to take seriously Cecil Gray's claim that he was to all intents and purposes Swedish? Does it matter what nationality he was? More to the point, what inspired Sibelius to become a composer—aside, that is, from his talent? Was it the prospect of becoming a national cultural hero? (One must remember that Finland had never before produced a musician of his calibre.) Or did he use national success as the springboard for the international acclaim he desired? It is often conceded (though not as often as it used to be in the 1930's) that the composer's Fourth Symphony is one of the greatest orchestral works in the repertory. Yet what do we think of *Finlandia*? Presumably, not very much. If so, why did the composer write it? There is a problem rather like Elgar's here, and the point I want to bring out is not the usual one about a man having the right to compose a few bars of lighter music now and again if he feels like it. It is that the lighter music in each case happens to have almost become the national anthem. If this is not regarded as significant, let me express it another way. Both Elgar and Sibelius travel well to certain countries, but seem to lack a passport as far as others go. A composer like Stravinsky, on the other hand, appears to be equally acceptable (or unacceptable, as the case may be) in all countries, even Soviet Russia about which he has said some exceedingly nasty things in his time. What I am trying to get at is that sometimes a composer has to succeed first of all in his own land—which may involve him in the adoption of one particular aesthetic. Then he may want to succeed in all countries—only to find that this will involve him in quite another. Whether he decides to change his philosophy or not at that point becomes crucial to his development, and may also become crucial to his integrity.

Composers unfortunately do not generally succeed by magic, à la Mozart. What they usually have to do is find some means of sponsorship, whether national, private, or otherwise. They may have to hawk around their scores for years before anyone is convinced of their merits. The temptation then intrudes itself to succeed by the most accessible means to hand. Then, once a name, proceed to do what they have always wanted to do. I think the story told about Ravel very instructive on this count. When the composer was once asked how he could have descended to writing such a banal piece as the *Bolero*, he tellingly replied: 'But you see, without it I would not have become Ravel!' Probably he was under-estimating the degree of fame he had already acquired; but one knows of other Ravels, as it were, who did *not* become Ravels (and whose names do not appear in the history books) because they assumed that all it took to be a great composer was to write great music. They failed to see that a large problem for many artists is to *convince* people that they have written great music. Literary-minded readers may recall a rather similar parable in one of Henry James's short stories called *The Next Time*. In it, the writer Ralph Limbert finds that every work he writes is a masterpiece, but he cannot sell any of them. When his friends suggest that he write a pot-boiler so as to get a market for his books, he tries but cannot manage it. All he can do is to write masterpieces. And so that is what he does, piling up a shelf full of unpublished and ultimately forgotten works of genius. As his sister puts it at the end of the story—reversing the old proverb—'You can't make a sow's ear out of a silk purse!' The moral to be drawn from these tales—and I think it should be borne in mind when it comes to evaluating the work of every composer treated in this section—is that most great artists have to try and produce a 'sow's ear' at some time in their careers, usually at the very beginning but sometimes, as we shall see in the cases of Bartók and Prokofiev, at the very end. Sibelius was no exception to this rule.

The feature that distinguished his case from most of the others was that he came from a country where a subtle form of apartheid was being practised. Throughout the eighteenth century Finland had been Swedish and Sibelius's ancestors were accordingly Swedes in the legal meaning of the term. (Hence Gray's rather misleading remarks.) But as far back as 1809, the country had become a province of Russia. It therefore makes just as much sense to say that the composer's family had been Russians—or even that he himself was a Russian, since Finnish independence was not granted until the time of the Revolution, when he was just turned fifty. Actually, each of these suppositions is a little foolish, because the Finns had their own distinctive forms of culture from an extremely early stage. Even the upper and upper-middle classes—who were expected to speak Swedish in their official business—were in fact very different from the Swedes who lived in Sweden. The case is a bit like that familiar to Englishmen who existed throughout the late nineteenth and early twentieth centuries, when an Anglo-Irish class ruled over Ireland and an Anglo-Welsh class over Wales. This did not prevent writers like Shaw, O'Casey, Joyce and Dylan Thomas (who, as far as I know, never wrote a word in any language but English) from constituting a Celtic literary revival that is still going on to this day. Indeed, there is a far more obvious case in the United States, which after all were originally English colonies and still make use of a language which, if it is not exactly identical with English, cannot be called by any other name. Yet no one would presumably have thought even Melville or Mark Twain English writers. And to suggest as much to a Norman Mailer would no doubt result in a

punch on the nose. The fact that Sibelius came from the bourgeoisie (his father was a doctor) meant that he spoke Swedish; yet
he also had enough Finnish to read the *Kalevala* in the original
and actually attended one of the few schools where Finnish was
encouraged.[1]

Born at Hameenlinna in 1865, Sibelius was a native of South-
Central Finland and he grew up in a rather ordinary provincial
home. His father died when he was only three, so that the family
did not become as affluent as it might otherwise have been. But
there was sufficient money to see the two brothers (Jan had a
brother Christian who later became a psychiatrist and hospital
superintendent) through university, and to provide a fair measure
of creature comfort. Young Sibelius was a poetical, wildly imagin-
ative child, given to strange fantasies. (There is a drawing of his,
reproduced in Harold E. Johnson's biography (Faber, 1959),
which was evidently done around 1887 to accompany a quartet for
violin, cello, piano and harmonium, and it seems wonderfully
expressive in a dark, Hoffmanesque way.) He was adept at music
at a prodigy's age, having lessons at the piano from the time he
was nine and embarking on his first composition (called *Votten-
droppar* or *Water-drops*) at around ten. But the role of prodigy
never became enacted, nor did he ever persevere very greatly with
the piano in later life. The many piano pieces he has left us (the
Sonatinas are perhaps the best) were written as occasional pieces,
or in order to earn money. It was the violin that captured his heart,
and that not until he was fifteen. The ambition to become a violin
virtuoso was an exceptionally real one with him, once he had
mastered the essentials of the instrument, and he must have been
a good, if not brilliant, player. At least, he led Quartets at home
and in the Conservatoire, and important professors and conductors
were not averse to accompanying him. But he lacked the quality
to make a soloist of the first-rank. However, he was not really
given much chance to try until rather late in his education, since
his mother packed him off to Law School in 1885 on the assumption that this was the safer career. Sibelius—like Chausson—
hated the Law, despite the good prospects it offered, and did not
even wait to graduate before transferring to the Conservatoire at
Helsinki to study music. His nature was far too poetical ever to
be tied to a desk.

[1] Finland was more fortunate than Wales, in this respect, since after
the infamous 'Blue Books' Welsh children had a wooden 'knot' tied round
their necks if they were caught speaking their native tongue at school.
Of course, reforms followed—as they did in consequence of the work of
Johan Snellmann in Finland—and today the situation looks like moving
in the opposite direction!

The Director of the Conservatoire was a man named Wegelius. Needless to say, he was impressed with his new student's capabilities, but could not help feeling that his musical outlook required to be broadened. One powerful liberalizing force residing there on the faculty happened to be Busoni, but of course he was a pianist and his ideas were in all probability too advanced for Sibelius at that time. Nevertheless, the two became friends and met again at intervals after they had each left the institution. It was Busoni who gave Sibelius a letter of introduction to Brahms in 1890, but the great man gave one of his customary exhibitions of bad manners by not acknowledging it. (As it happened, Brahms met Sibelius accidentally at the Leidinger café in Vienna; but it was with Fuchs and Goldmark that he was obliged to study there.) Before going to Vienna, however, Sibelius had been transformed by a major aesthetic experience nearer home. This was his hearing of the *Aino* Symphony by Robert Kajanus, a figure destined to play an immensely important role in his life. Kajanus was in reality more of a conductor than a composer (he later became famous as the supreme authority on the interpretation of Sibelius's symphonies), and in 1882 he had founded the Helsinki Philharmonic Society, an institution that was more of a rival than a friend to the Conservatoire. This was because Kajanus based his work on strong nationalist premisses, whereas Wegelius was a Wagnerian who never ceased to propagandize for that composer in Finland. He even persuaded Sibelius to make the trip to Bayreuth in 1894, and it is still a matter of conjecture how much benefit, if any, the young man derived from it. His letters to Wegelius are enthusiastic; but it is possible he was merely being polite. In later life, Sibelius proclaimed himself a staunch anti-Wagnerite, but that too is open to suspicion since his mature tendency was to reject the notion that he had ever been taught or influenced by anyone. There can be no question whatever, though, that he was bowled over by the *Aino* Symphony—which is based on Finnish legend. (It is significant that his last home at Järvenpää was named 'Ainola'.) After hearing that, the book of source-material, the *Kalevala*, was rarely out of his hands.

The years 1890 to 1892 were extremely fruitful ones for the composer in every way. During the first of them, he became engaged to a daughter of the very aristocratic Järnefelt family, and also began to develop a marked interest in the orchestra. In the next year, he made sketches for the work later to become known as 'En Saga' (an unprogrammatic piece, still in the repertory, which curiously enough did not produce the success the composer predicted for it), and also for a full-length symphony. Instead of following the precepts of Wegelius, this work evolved out of the

most ardent nationalist sentiments and became known as the
Kullervo Symphony. It was first played in 1892, and was a
tremendous success, even though it was omitted from the Sibelius
canon right throughout the years of his greatest fame.[1] Two
months after the première of this significant addition to his œuvre,
the composer married into the family whose militant Finnish
views must have had the effect of further enhancing his attitudes.
His fiancée, too, had been named Aino, after the same legend as
had inspired Kajanus. Her father was a Lieutenant-General in the
Finnish army, and her mother the former Baroness Elisabeth
Clodt von Jurgensburg. Among the sons of the family was a
musician, Armas, who had actually been the means of securing
this valuable, as well as pleasurable, introduction for Jan. His
marriage gave him influence, self-confidence and new horizons—
but not the automatic security one might have imagined. He still
had to pursue a career, and in one sense it was fortunate that on
the termination of his studies he was given a teaching post at the
Conservatoire under Wegelius. This might have restored him to
orthodox views.

The 1890's, however, saw a great swell in the nationalist feeling
against Russia, and rather than concentrate on his profession in
the way any ordinary young man of high abilities might do,
Sibelius joined in various semi-revolutionary groups designed to
stir up the desire for independence. His *Kullervo* Symphony had
marked him out as an artist whose work could be used for political
purposes, and there can be no question but that the composer
allowed this assumption to pass unchallenged. He became friendly
with the nationalist writers, Juhani Aho and his followers, and it
was Aino's brother, Arvid, who did much to engineer these
contacts. Their paper, *Päivälehti* was couched in the usual language of protest, and it won Sibelius's sympathies from the outset.
By 1897, the composer had established himself so well in the eyes
of Finns generally that he managed to induce the government to
grant him an annual pension, later increased to very sizeable
proportions. One cannot help seeing all this rapid rise to fame as a
reflection of the composer's beliefs as opposed to his musical
achievements; which at that time remained relatively slight. It is
true that *Kullervo* is a big work (five movements, including choir
and orchestra), but it is also a functional work in much the same
sense as the smaller choruses of Op. 23, Op. 28 and Op. 30, all of
which set out to be patriotic. That Sibelius did not think well

---

[1] It was only with Robert Layton's biography of Sibelius in the Master
Musicians Series (Dent, 1965) that English readers were given a detailed
analysis of this early work, which in reality was far more crucial to the
composer's future than many a later and more famous composition.

enough of any of these (including *Kullervo* itself, which remained in manuscript till 1958) to publish them in their entirety, may be taken as evidence of the way in which he regarded them. Perhaps one ought not to blame the composer for clutching at success in this apparently quasi-political fashion (all the more so in view of the stipulations we have made about genius and its difficulties of recognition), but it ought to be said quite openly and unequivocally that Sibelius—who incidentally soon developed aristocratic delusions, writing in his diary of 'the growing arrogance and savagery of the working classes'—was a man utterly dedicated to self-advancement. He was no Schubert or Bruckner, not by any stretch of imagination.[1]

That he continued to exploit his nationalist reputation throughout the 'nineties, and was only induced to look beyond it by circumstances other than musical, is proved, first of all by the work he put into the *Lemminkäinen* Suite (1895). This series of four legends sprang yet again from the *Kalevala*—drawing their material from the hero's journey described in the twenty-ninth canto; the description of the island, Saari, contained in the eleventh canto; the episode dealing with the Swan mentioned in cantos fourteen and fifteen; and finally the account of the resurrecting of the hero's body and his transformation into a god. Of the entire set, only the famous *Swan of Tuonela* is regularly heard in the concert-hall, its mournful cor anglais melody being familiar to thousands who have only the slightest knowledge of music. Considered in purely musical terms, this Suite is possibly the first real glimpse we are allowed into the authentic Sibelius—the notes of the pedal horn, the bass clarinet, the bassoon and lower muted strings providing us with a miniature spectrum of the dark instrumental colours used in the later symphonies. But the work's failure with the public was no doubt a conclusive factor in leading its composer away from the blatant nationalism of his first period towards the slight Russianism of his second and universalism of his third. He and Aino had gone to Karelia for their honeymoon, and the Suite bearing this title (with its popular and rousing March) was another

---

[1] It is true that Sibelius was not astute in his dealings with publishers (though this stemmed as often as not from his desire to settle for cash in preference to royalties). But he managed to coerce the government into raising his pension from 3,000 to 5,000 marks, and bargained with the Eastman School of Music (U.S.A.) for a 20,000 dollar a year salary in exchange for a professorship. Moreover, he was not above resorting to crude advertising devices (such as having his head put on stamps or getting streets—now about fifty such—named after him. Besides, *years* of his life went into the writing of other potential *Valses Tristes* —a method of fund-raising in which he was as unabashed as he was unsuccessful.

obvious product of the nationalist phase. So, in a more artistically commendable way, were the settings of Runeberg (Finland's greatest Romantic poet) he made—especially the beautiful *Se'n har jag ej frägat mera*, translatable as 'Since then I have asked no more'. Those who would like to know what Sibelius looked like at this period should make it their business to seek out the marvellous portrait of him by Gallén-Kallela, done in 1894.

The real change in style came about with the Symphony No. 1 in E minor, composed in 1899. This work, often attributed to the influence of Tschaikovsky, is both romantically tuneful in the manner of the Russian composer and sombre in the fashion of Sibelius's true self. The instrumentation is perhaps the most individual feature, the symphony opening with a low clarinet theme accompanied only by the almost inaudible roll of a drum. The rest of this first movement, however, is energetic and vivid in the style that Borodin, Tschaikovsky and many others had already made popular. For the slow movement, Sibelius chose gentle, melancholy string writing which, though melodious enough, hardly matches the concentration he was later to invest in this section of his works. It is the Scherzo—hammering away in Beethovenian vigour—that is possibly the finest inspiration in this, on the whole, very accomplished composition. People have been drawn to the Finale on account of the long, winding second subject. It is certainly one of the most memorable themes its composer was ever to invent, but as was his custom in the early symphonies he succumbed to the temptation to over-play it on its return. Whether the tuba which appears in this work was an original addition or not remains disputable. It could argue for a greater Wagnerian influence than Sibelius would have wished to admit. But, on the other hand, he did make such an expressive use of this awkward instrument in the slow movement of his Second Symphony (1902) that I think we must allow him full credit for its intrusion. This later work is also Russian-sounding, with the Finale again being the weakest section. Its main theme is a trifle vulgar and obvious, and is not improved by being given its famous ostinato-crescendo treatment.

Finlandia, which belongs to the same period as the First Symphony, is very different from it, and reverts (if one accepts the distinction Gerald Abraham and others have made between the nationalist works and the symphonies proper) to an older mode of approach. The tune, like that of *Land of Hope and Glory* is of the kind that Elgar himself said came to a composer only once in a lifetime. The question here is whether or not this one came to Sibelius in his lifetime. Harold Johnson is inclined to think not, despite the assurances the composer gave his English admirer, Rosa Newmarch, that it was all his own invention. According to Johnson:

> ... The opening bars are a note-for-note duplication of a composition that Emil Genetz had written for male chorus eighteen years earlier. It is the well-known *Arise, Finland!* (*Heraa Suomi!*), composed in 1881 and performed in Helsinki during April of the following year for the ceremonies celebrating Lonnrot's eightieth birthday. *Arise, Finland!* soon became extremely popular, and it is likely that Sibelius heard it many times during his student years in both Hameenlinna and Helsinki.

Obviously, this is a conundrum no one is going to resolve with any certainty. The flaunting of *Finlandia*, however, was something for which Sibelius was certainly responsible. In fact, it was commissioned as a straight political weapon by Baron Axel Carpelan, who wanted a kind of battle-hymn comparable to those Rubinstein and Liszt had written on behalf of Russia and Hungary respectively. It was Kajanus who drew the Baron's attention to the fact that the recently-written *Finlandia* would suit his purposes admirably. And suit them it did for a number of years, with its composer's heartiest approval. He even liked to boast, in his later years, that the work had been banned during the political troubles around about the time of the 1900 and First World Wars. Whether or not this was true, it seems an odd ambition for a serious composer to have wished upon himself.

The decade we recognize as Edwardian held somewhat different ambitions for Sibelius in that, by this time, he had made up his travel schedule for the conquest of Europe. The myth of the composer as a lone, craggy individual, confined to his forests and his fireside, is one that may have contained elements of truth if one is thinking exclusively of the later years. In the period 1900–10, no image could be more calculated to mislead. In 1900, Sibelius travelled to Paris where, despite his eventual award of the Légion d'Honneur, his music is still cordially detested. He therefore wasted no time in moving on to Prague in the following year, where the reception was far kinder. Dvořák and Suk each took a keen interest in him, and looked upon him as a kind of Finnish Grieg. The composer also conducted his own work in Germany at about this time, concluding his agreement with Breitkopf and Härtel, an agreement that unhappily did not take account of the Berne copyright. Hence, Sibelius was to lose money on it during the First World War, and until the Scandinavian firm of Hansen came to his rescue. During the winter of 1902, the composer took a villa at Rapallo and it was there that he composed most of the Second Symphony. On the whole, he liked extreme locations— that is to say, he preferred wild countryside, on the one hand, or busy city life on the other. Probably it was the anonymity each conferred that proved most conducive to composition; though he discovered shortly after this time that the invitations to high living in the big city could be a destructive force. His move from Helsinki to Järvenpää (where he remained for the rest of his days) was made in 1904, and apparently motivated by the ruinous effect on his music and his finances of *la dolce vita* as lived in the Finnish capital. This meant relinquishing his teaching post, but he hoped to re-coup his losses by regular tours to foreign countries. Up to a point, he was successful in this aim, paying a second visit to Berlin in 1905 (where Strauss conducted the revised version of his Violin Concerto, a new composition of great beauty spoilt only a little by the Wienawski-like virtuoso intrusions) and two profitable visits to England. By the second of these, he was quite well known to certain sympathizers in this country. Sir Henry Wood, for instance, who arranged for the Third Symphony to be performed at an R.P.O. concert in 1908, was among the foremost of these, though Rosa Newmarch, and Sir Granville Bantock were also very much on his side. Bantock's lavish hospitality was particularly appreciated.[1]

Though the Third Symphony is not generally considered among Sibelius's best, it had the function of paving the way for his finest works in the medium. By its more tightly-knit structure, its harsh tritonal effects and its further breaking-down of the music into small cellular units (both thematically and instrumentally), it made possible the revolutionary procedures that reached fulfil- ment in No. 4. (1910–11). This last work—which was roughly contemporary with the String Quartet, *Voces Intimae*—uses the linear methods of the chamber ensemble in combination with pointilliste techniques of orchestration which the composer may have appropriated from the French impressionists. It is odd that, though this is almost always regarded as his greatest work and its slow movement was chosen as the music for the composer's own funeral, Sibelius frequently went on record as despising the age's taste for counterpoint. Harmonic music was his declared ideal, and he reacted savagely to neo-classicism and the Hindemith type of ideal. The Fourth was unfairly deplored by critics, and audi- ences in most countries failed to make sense of it. Even in England

---

[1] It was while on this second tour, however, that Sibelius developed a throat infection which he imagined for a long time was due to cancer. An operation finally cured him; but having to forego cigars and alcohol was a penance to this most self-indulgent of artists.

(where the composer's stock has always stood higher than anywhere else, except perhaps the U.S.A. where his champions
Koussevitzsky and Stokowski raised his music to the top of the
poll in the 'thirties) listeners at Liverpool, Manchester and Birm-
ingham were at a loss as to the work's meaning. The Fifth
Symphony (1915) is perhaps for that reason infinitely more
accessible, though it cost the composer several rather lengthy
revisions. Of course, he had time to do these during the War,
when musical activities gradually came to a standstill.[1] After the
cessation of hostilities, Finland gained her long-awaited independence from Russia, and Sibelius had no further need for the national
styles he had evolved. Yet he continued, more than ever now that
his people were free, to be vaunted as the great Finnish composer,
the embodiment of his nation's virtues. Ironically, this role
imposed a much heavier burden on his talents than he could
have imagined, with the result that the last thirty-five years of
his life were, in one sense, a gigantic conspiracy to preserve his
fame.

At first, this scarcely needed preserving. After all, he had con-
quered in most of the capitals he had visited, and when the Fifth
was played in London in 1918 it dispersed the temporary feelings
of bafflement created by its predecessor. It was in the inter-war
years, in fact, that Sibelius's reputation was deliberately plugged
by critics like Cecil Gray and Constant Lambert in England, and
Olin Downes in America. The effect of their extravagant encomia
(Gray, in particular, practically wiped the slate clean of all composers between Beethoven and Sibelius; while he emerges as the
only artist to receive absolute acclaim in Lambert's influential
Music Ho!) was to convince the Finnish composer that he could
never hope to live up to his own publicity. His response was
accordingly guarded in the extreme. Though he wrote more
music—the tenebrous Sixth Symphony was added in 1923 and the
single movement Seventh a year later—it was from this point on
that the ominous Sibelius silence began to impose itself. Incidental
music (which he had written profusely at all stages of his career)
did not come to a halt, partly because it was treated in the lighter
fashion one would have expected. But the only great work to flow
from his pen after Symphony No. 7 (whose merits are still hotly
debated, some seeing it as a 'compressed sonata movement' and
others as a straight Rondo or Fantasia-sinfonia) was the tone-

---

[1] The revisions were partly to do with the number and order of the
movements; and it is still disputed as to whether the work is in three or
four movements. The composer's final word was that it should be taken as
four. Looked at either way, it is an immensely appealing and optimistic
work.

poem, *Tapiola*.[1] Sibelius had written a number of good tone-poems amid his other works, certain of which—like the *Oceanides* and *Pohjola's Daughter* deserve more frequent hearings—but this last was without doubt his masterpiece. If it is not the best piece of music he ever wrote, it certainly comes close to it, and does for the howling, inhuman forests of Finland what Debussy's *La Mer* does for the restless, uninhabited sea off the French coast. Both works are tremendous affirmations of the force of nature, chilling reminders of the puniness of man's existence on a planet ruled over by the anarchical commands of wind and water. Played first in New York under Walter Damrosch in 1926, it was the note on which Sibelius decided to end his claim on the attention of posterity, and who is to say he was unwise?

Rumours that circulated throughout the period 1932–57 regarding a possible Eighth Symphony came to naught. Explanations were advanced in a dozen different journals as to why none had appeared. Basil Cameron told the present writer in 1945 that he had actually seen a score, while several American conductors were known to have said they had been promised the task of giving the première. It remains feasible that some music was written and then discarded. But the real reason underlying the composer's refusal to publish anything further is surely the obvious one: that he knew he was unable to improve on what he had done and that the logical consummation of the symphony in his eyes had been reached with the Seventh. What is much more interesting is to reflect on why a man of his stature should have perpetuated a deception for so many years.[2] Bevies of critics and musicians, after all, made the trip to Järvenpää during these years, and the inevitable final question was 'When is the Eighth to appear?' Sibelius warded these enquiries off with persistent guile and dissimulation for a period longer than Mozart's entire lifetime. That he reached a point fairly early on when he knew nothing more would be written has now become clear. Harold Johnson relates the case of Professor Otto Anderson, Director of the Sibelius Museum, who visited his charge to try and get at the truth some years before the composer's death. Knowing how touchy the old man was on the subject, he began by discreetly remarking:

'If I return to America, what shall I tell them?'

[1] According to Nils-Eric Ringbom, in his book *Jean Sibelius: a Master and his Work* (University of Oklahoma Press, 1954), the composer himself first proposed the title 'Fantasia-sinfonia'—only to withdraw it later.

[2] The whole argument over whether there ever was an Eighth Symphony is discussed fully in Arnold Whittall's article 'Sibelius's Eighth Symphony' contained in the *Music Review*, Vol. XXV, 1964, pp. 239 et seq.

To this, Sibelius evidently replied as follows:

'Yes. What shall you tell them?', casting about nervously.

Finally, Aino looked up from her knitting and said:

'Why don't you tell Professor Anderson the truth? There
is no Eighth Symphony.'

The admission then came forth, the composer's face brightening
'as though a heavy weight had been removed from his shoulders'.

Shortly afterwards, on September 20th, 1957, while Sir Malcolm
Sargent was conducting a concert of his music at the Helsinki
Festival, Finland's greatest composer died quietly at the incredible age of ninety-one, having held the whole world in
suspense for as long as most musicians could remember. What
possible valediction does such a career merit? That Sibelius was a
charlatan? That he was no more than a gifted nationalist who
overreached himself in the search for wider acclaim? That he was
one of the century's greatest composers who nevertheless steered
himself into a deserved cul-de-sac? Of these possible obituaries
(and I can imagine others) I should be inclined to opt for the last.
I do not doubt for one moment that Sibelius began by using his
position as the leader of a minority culture to stake claims that
ordinary members of other nations were prevented from staking.
After all, it is an excellent ploy to be able to say that you are the
first of your race to do anything unusual. And you are almost
bound to receive the backing of your clan. But as well as being a
ploy, it is also a dangerous trap, since in the end it is harder to
make good one's claims than it is to stake them. That Sibelius
did make good his claims in works like the Fourth Symphony and
Tapiola I believe to be undeniable. With these works, he established himself as an artist of the calibre of Mahler, Debussy,
Bartók, Stravinsky, Schönberg and our other twentieth-century
masters. It was only by allowing it to appear that he was their
superior that he permitted himself to be caught in his own trap.
A tempting conspiracy to have set in motion, but one that a man
of Sibelius's intelligence should have had the sense and integrity
to expose.

xiv Busoni to Casella

Italian music, like German and French music, has had the advantage of a long and distinguished tradition. Yet unlike those of the two other countries mentioned, that tradition has been made up of widely disparate elements. True, a good deal of Italian music has remained faithful to the vocal forms. But this scarcely serves to unite the different aesthetic assumptions that seem to lie behind so much of what it comprises. Those who lobby enthusiastically for the operas of Monteverdi or Cavalli are unlikely to be among the most vociferous supporters of 'Cav' and 'Pag', to say nothing of the nation's less blatant masterpieces of theatrical sentimentality. Of course, one tries to account for such discrepancies first of all in historical terms. More than two hundred years, after all, separate the two types of work. Yet we know there is something else that accounts for the opposed partisanship. Sensibility is one name we could put to it. Another might be simply philosophy, or theory of dramaturgy. Whichever way we look at it, the discrepancies are fundamental, and are of much the same order that divide the admirers of, say, Michelangelo from those of Modigliani. Musically, even more than in painting, a lot took place between 1700 and 1900 within the minds of Italians. But many of these were expatriates, men like Cherubini, Spontini, Rossini and so on. Bellini and Donizetti also carried on a tradition involving the voice—that known as 'bel canto'—and this became exceedingly influential throughout Europe. But by the middle of the nineteenth century, all these earlier traditions were in danger of being swept aside in the tide of nationalist fervour set in motion by Cavour and powerfully assisted by Verdi's robust operas. The extent of that composer's commitment may be judged from the fact that after 1861 he actually became a member of the new Italian parliament for about four years. With Verdi's death in 1901, Italian music became even more conditioned by popular and national tastes (the baroque forms, it need hardly be added flourished under a system of papal states and hence could not have expressed national feeling to anything like the same extent) with results that might have been predicted.

The appearance of composers like Puccini (1858–1924), Leoncavallo (1858–1948), Mascagni (1863–1945), Ciléa (1866–1950) and Giordano (1867–1950) quite naturally paved the way for a reaction, having as its aim a return swing to the classical object-ivity of the ancients. Such men as these had all written increasingly subjective music, banal and over-emotional into the bargain. In some cases, it was their intention to inculcate a verismo style capable of projecting the violence and passion of the streets on to the stage. Otherwise, the object seemed to be merely to provide melodious music for singing which, instead of being corrupted Rossini-fashion by being subjected to excessive coloratura, became the vehicle for a great deal of unsubtle bellowing from artistically illiterate tenors. It was the identification of music with such works as *Tosca*—accurately described by Mr Joseph Kerman as 'a shabby little shocker'—and *Pagliacci* that triggered off the animadversions of that generation of Italian composers which sprung to fame in the period around the First World War and after. This generation in-cludes a very diverse assembly, some of whom were a good deal more critical of their immediate predecessors than others. Respighi (1879–1937) attacked modernism, while looking more towards impressionism than to the old cult of verismo. Pizzetti (1880–   ) has again been slow to condemn his seniors—Verdi at least he still reveres—and yet his own music has comparatively little in common with what preceded it. It was with Alfredo Casella (1883–1947) that an all-out attack was launched on the Puccini school, and *his* music has as much of theirs in it as Stravinsky's or Schönberg's, two of his chief idols. Malipiero (1882–   ) became a supporter of his, without perhaps going quite so far in his denunciations, having had to work his way through the older styles at the hands of his conservative teacher, Bossi, at Venice and Bologna, while Casella was emigrating to Paris. Castelnuovo-Tedesco (1895–1969), though obsessed all his life with classical subjects for operas and tone-poems, was much influenced by Hollywood, and has left a corpus of music of a rather traditionally romantic kind. Dallapicola (1904–   ) and Petrassi (1904–   ), on the other hand, have veered towards twelve-tone music and thus placed themselves at the opposite extreme from their parent generation. Maderna, Berio and Nono are still more avant-garde.

Clearly, it cannot be part of my aim to survey the development of Italian music from Verdi to Nono, nor would it help me in my task if I were to attempt such an exercise. What I shall do is to single out one strand of that nation's musical history—that represented by the reaction in favour of neo-classicism. This means that I shall have to by-pass the later operas of, say, Puccini, even though they would appear to come within the purview earlier laid down. The title of my book—*Paths to Modern Music*—must be invoked to protect me here; since whatever merits Puccini's operas possess, they can scarcely be regarded as helping to clear a road to the present. Whereas the response shown by Casella and his friends, cabbalistic though it may have been, did just that. Moreover, this particular section of the book is concerned chiefly with the fate of nationalism. And to pursue the line of Verdi and his operatic successors would be to concur in the view that Italy failed to penetrate its nationalist shell in music—an assumption that seems patently untrue. The question that really concerns us is whether this penetration has been quick and successful, or slow and relatively unsuccessful. As such, it may be that we shall need to look back even further than the Casella–Malipiero revolt to a time when the first expressions of discontent with the verismo style became observable. In support of this end, we ought to give much of our attention to a composer who is at present beginning to be treated with interest and respect by the avant-garde even though it is more than a century since he was born. I refer, of course, to Ferrucio Busoni (1866–1924). His writings have certainly come to seem the most important of any Italian's of the period, and his admirers have every right to claim him as the neo-classical movement's greatest and most articulate spokesman. Why Italian composers were so slow to model themselves on him is a mystery. I can suggest three possible reasons, none of which is definitive in itself. Firstly, Busoni spent very little of his life in Italy. Even his Italian parentage has been impugned, though his father, Ferdinando, was of pure Italian stock and his mother, the former Anna Weiss, Italian by descent. Secondly, the composer may have proved too profound a thinker and too tepid a democrat to have pleased his average countryman. Thirdly, there is the fact that, like Rachmaninov, he was a pianist and suffered the disadvantages of a dual career. Together, these factors placed the composer in a hermetic light.

Busoni's early years demonstrate quite unequivocally why he was not regarded with more seriousness in his native land. Gifted with a phenomenal piano technique, he was already playing works like the Mozart C minor Concerto (K 491) at the age of eight, and was being primed by a rather Mozartian father for an international career. Though Ferdinando was no Leopold Mozart in his abilities (his instrument was, in any case, the clarinet), he had some of the same pedantic devotion to his son's cause, and stood behind him for hours on end forcing him to repeat passages until they achieved an incredible quality of perfection. From 1879–81, young Ferrucio was also given lessons by the German, Wilhelm Mayer, a teacher probably recommended through the boy's mother and her friends.[1] She herself was a fine pianist, and did as much as anyone to create the mop-haired virtuoso who was to take city after city by storm with his brilliant recitals. As we have already observed in our essay on Sibelius, he went to Helsingfors and became professor of the piano for two years from 1888 to 1890, after which he married a local girl and moved on to take up similar positions at the Moscow Conservatory, and in Boston. Women were incidentally fascinated by him, and his marriage did not prevent him from having numerous extra-marital affairs—a fact not readily deducible from the cold logic of his books and his playing. The compositions he wrote in the 1890's are of no great consequence in his œuvre, probably on account of his dual career. Indeed, he later disavowed everything he had written before 1912, a quite late date in the story of his composing life. The chief works of this self-acknowledged apprentice period were a Violin Concerto (1897); a Piano Concerto with male chorus finale (1904); an opera entitled *Die Brautwahl* (*The Bridal Choice*) (1906–11), based on a story by E. T. A. Hoffmann; and the tremendous *Fantasia Contrappuntistica* (1910) which was an attempt to complete the final section of Bach's *Art of Fugue*. This last work cannot be set aside, whatever Busoni may have thought of it. It is a fugue with *five* subjects—three of which were originally supplied by Bach—and which involved the composer in over a hundred changes of position, without augmentation, diminution or transposition.

Before composing this work—which he did at the behest of Bernhard Ziehn of Chicago—Busoni had already completed his sketch *Towards a New Aesthetic of Music* (1907), in which nearly all his technical innovations were first proposed. Prophetically, he saw, like Saint-Saëns, that the music of the future might well be microtonal. He therefore spent much time working out a system that would free music of its former tonal limitations. The Major and Minor scales were the first objects to come under his lash, and he promptly worked out 113 versions of the tonal scale to which composers might have recourse. His attitude to Debussy (who, in

---

[1] These early years, incidentally, were spent chiefly in Trieste. It had been supposed that the boy would make his name in Paris, but the nearness of the Franco-Prussian War led the family to move to the Adriatic, where he remained for the time being away from the mainstream of European musical life.

his view, had merely stuck to the whole-tone scale) was that he lagged behind Bach and Brahms in adventurousness. One typical scale he used in his own music was C, D flat, E flat, F, G flat, A, B and C. Thus instead of resorting to the orthodox two tones and a semi-tone followed by three tones and a semi-tone, he sub-stituted a semi-tone and three tones followed by a semi-tone, a tone and a final semi-tone. As anyone who tries out these two scales on the piano will discover, the latter requires a modification of the orthodox fingering as well. The business of obtaining the micro-intervals he wanted he solved by getting an old instrument-maker to build him a piano with three manuals (it must have looked a bit like the Emanuel Moor duplex coupler, which only has two, but which has them interlocked in tiers as Busoni wanted), each being tuned so that the original tone could be divided into three—a trifurcation instead of the chromatic bifurcation, if you like. The instrument, like Moor's, has not found favour, even though the intervals on it could be easily distinguished from one another. Busoni's own music is incidentally mainly tonal. He was praised by Alois Hába and Sorabji, but other composers fought shy of the whole scheme. Twelve-tone work was not to be heard as such till about a year before Busoni's death, so he could not have heard much of it. But he did not care for Schönberg's 'non-tonal' music—describing it as 'suppressed tears, sighs, flutterings of grief' and so on. But this is possibly a fair comment on works like *Pierrot Lunaire* and those which came before it.

It is perhaps not apparent what this taste for experiment—how-ever interesting it was in itself—had to do with Busoni's approach to his native music. The answer is that it had three important implications:

1. It assumed that music was an affair of the intellect, and hence could not be expected to subsume such rhetorical attitudes as were implied in the work of Puccini and his followers.

2. It argued for experimentalism as the *basis* of art, i.e. Busoni wanted complete freedom from previous conventions, implying an avant-garde music of which only a few could be expected to show appreciation. As he himself neatly put it in his essay *How Long Will It Go On?*:

> If art should become absolutely accessible to all (which I personally am against) let us at least preserve a distance. Let it be in the middle of the people and yet separated from them, as becomes a monarch.[1]

3. It asserted the need for a theatre of illusion as opposed to a theatre of 'reality'. Reality he considered an impossibility in

[1] Written for the magazine *Signale für die Musikalische Weld*, 1910.

operatic terms, and thereof. Hence his acceptance of opera as
allegory, pantomime, almost as ballet. It is no accident that he
regarded *The Magic Flute* a far greater work than *Figaro*; the
former makes no attempt at realism, whereas the latter grapples,
albeit rather factitiously, with the social issues of the age, in the
same manner as Beaumarchais's play. To quote again from him:

> The sung word will always remain a convention of the
> stage, and a hindrance to any semblance of the truth; to
> overcome this deadlock with any success a plot would
> have to be devised in which the singers act what is in-
> credible, fictitious and improbable from the start, so that
> one impossibility supports the other . . . and both become
> possible and acceptable . . . It is for this reason and
> because it disregards this important principle from the
> beginning that I look upon the so-called Italian verismo
> for the musical stage as untenable.[1]

Such a view clearly puts out of court all operas bar the symbolic
creations of the 'advanced' composer. From this, Strauss's *Die
Frau* would seem much more his ideal than, say, Verdi's *Otello*,
even though he regarded the former as a 'mere orchestrator'.

One of Busoni's obsessions about opera was that it should above
all be a self-supporting form from the musical standpoint. What
he disliked so intensely about the older Italian operas was not,
oddly enough, their sketchy and absurd libretti. It was their poor
music. Writing about this belief, he claimed:

> For—and this seems to me essential—an opera score,
> whilst fitting the action, should show detached from it
> a complete musical picture; comparable to a suit of
> armour which, intended for the envelopment of human
> bodies, in itself exhibits a gratifying picture, a valuable
> work in material, form and artistic execution.[2]

Of course, this should not be taken to mean that the composer
approved of the more casual type of libretto—on the contrary,
he went to extreme lengths to secure the right choice for his own
operas—but it does mean that he regarded music as something
to be judged in its own right. The idea that music could be good
because it was a suitable adjunct to something else horrified him.
It was good or else it was bad, and there was nothing more to be
said about it. This point of view badly needs endorsing today,
when so many opera-goers seem to have been recruited from the

[1] From 'The Future of Opera' in the *Entwurf einer neuen Aestheitk
der Tonkunst*, 1913.
[2] 'The Oneness of Music' from *Concerning the Possibilities of Opera*,
1926.

theatrical fraternity and have had no musical experience or training. Quite apart from the recent tendency for producers to belittle the musical functions of opera, there has grown up a readiness on the part of the public to accept most music as long as it is accompanied by good acting, plenty of spectacle and all the appurtenances of expense visible amid the sets. Busoni would have castigated these tendencies in the firmest language; and for that reason his approach to opera was unusually stringent. The play that stood up well enough without music (like *La Dame aux Camélias*, or presumably even *Pelléas*) he considered unworthy of musical treatment. The defect of one form of cheap opera, therefore, was its dramatic completeness. Otherwise, what he demanded was a libretto which gave opportunities to the composer to add, by means of his music, some element of mysticism or super-realism. As he put it, in the same essay from which we last quoted:

> The people demand Life from the stage, as with justice
> it is demanded everywhere, but they demand the life that
> they themselves lead. Only they commit the error of also
> putting it to music. Even the greatest succumb to this
> error. Verdi also succumbs to it.[1]

The composer's own operas consisted of *Turandot* (1911), *Arlecchino* (1914–15) and *Doktor Faust* (1924), the last having to be completed by Phillip Jarnach, one of Busoni's pupils, after the master's death. Of the first, there is little that need be said. It is based on the same story of Gozzi's as Puccini was to use much later. The difference in treatment is striking, however, and illustrates very well the force of the comments we have recently been analysing. The play was clearly mystical enough to suit Busoni, but he had not at that time thoroughly developed his idea of music as something to be intertwined with the action. Hence, his purpose, as he saw it, was to add to the sinister, magical drama by providing musical interludes—dances, marches and so on—that would enhance the atmosphere of unreality. The reliance on spoken dialogue for other sections implies a determination to render unto the drama what was the drama's, so to speak, thus opening the way for a separation of functions which ultimately pointed in the direction of sterility. Naturally, Busoni avoided the false exoticism of Puccini, and to that extent his score possessed the integrity he always desired. It does not, however, employ oriental rhythms and forms with the genuine dramatic tension we find in, say, Roussel's *Padmâvatî*, which we shall be dealing with in the next chapter. In any case, the subject was ambiguous. The presence of Italian masked figures formed a 'bridge from the familiar Venetian locale

[1] Op. cit., p. 9.

to the fictitious Orient of the stage'; so that what Busoni was trying to do was to explore a terrain mid-way between life and fantasy. By comparison, Puccini (in this opera, at any rate) strove for pure fantasy; while Roussel presented the public with an authentic Orient. *Arlecchino* is a much better work, and far closer to Busoni's ideal. Its commedia dell'arte characters are virtually archetypes of the various human frailties—the Abbé personifying tolerance and smug forbearance; the tailor, Matteo, naïve idealism; Colombina the perennial feminine attribute of duplicity. Predictably, critics found the work cruel and inhuman; but Busoni's intention was more to create an ambiguous joke in which the element of mockery was not meant to hurt. It is an indication of his critics' lack of objectivity that they failed to see this. For them, even archetypes were made of flesh and blood.

Doktor Faust, which is widely assumed to have been Busoni's masterpiece, is not quite the standard realization of Goethe's play we might have been led to expect, even allowing for the composer's dogged musical chauvinism. For one thing, it deals only with one single episode—that in which Faust seduces the Duchess of Parma, and in which Mephistopheles is invoked simply as the courier of their dead child and the falsifier of Faust's hopes of immortality. The difficulties the composer experienced over this opera were first of all related to the choice of subject. In 1911 he had met d'Annunzio (incidentally a very strong partisan of the idea of a new Italian music drawing its inspiration from remote, classical or baroque sources) and had been eagerly solicited to do an opera with Leonardo da Vinci as the subject—the Italian 'Faust', as d'Annunzio called him. But the poet was beset with doubts when it came to the planning stage, his Wagnerism and his feeling that Leonardo was perhaps too lacking in passion ('a skeleton with a torch for a head') eventually putting paid to the scheme. Busoni then became enamoured of the figure of Merlin, and even had the temerity to consider a second opera on the personality of Don Giovanni. By 1914, however, he had settled on *Faust* and sketched out the libretto in a mere six days (he wrote the libretti for each of his operas himself). It would be impossible, within the confines of this short essay, to describe the subtleties of Busoni's opera in detail. But we should mention again the importance he attached to the large gaps in the action which were filled by purposive music—intended in some cases to point up Faust's fear, in other cases to create the atmosphere of exorcism during the act in which this religious rite is attempted. The vocal lines are, by this time, however, fully contrapuntal, and tension is generated by making each line climb higher in register than the last. There is a scenic intermezzo set in an ancient chapel; a festival garden scene (later turned into a ballet); and a continuous use of bells to engender feelings of ill-omen or rejoicing. Altogether, then, *Doktor Faust* is an opera that makes a determined attempt to satisfy the singers without sacrificing Busoni's concern for a heightened musical background of close to absolute interest.

From the standpoint of Busoni the composer, the failure of his operas to become a regular part of the repertory was a tragedy. It still is, despite the occasional hearings they are nowadays given. But it is to Busoni the theorist that many of us have turned for guidance when attempting to evaluate the shifting philosophies that lie behind modern music. So far, it may have been inferred that the composer was an unqualified supporter of 'newness'. But as his micro-tonal and other experiments failed, he found himself drawn more and more to classicism as an ideal. 'Futurism must wait for the moment,' he said, a little reluctantly, and turned his attention to the instrumental past. As may be imagined, he regarded the past, not as a field for unlimited pillaging as some members of 'Les Six' were to do, but as a repository of standards, something which one could hope to emulate. As he phrased it:

> First, before we begin a new way, can we do everything in the old way as well as it has been done in the past? Secondly, in addition to this have we the talent?[1]

His neo-classicism, then, began with a scholarly and utterly un-biased attempt to interpret the heritage. Being a great pianist, the works he first looked at were inevitably compositions for that instrument; and the extent of his self-confidence may be gauged from the fact that Bach himself was not immune from scrutiny and ultimate rearrangement. From 1905–15 he had worked on bringing out his famous edition of the *Well-Tempered Clavier*, and felt therefore that he had earned the right to consider transcribing a good deal of Bach's music. Liszt, whom he revered both as a musician and a pianist, gave him the idea for this. Impressed by the uncanny ability Liszt had shown for extracting the essence of an orchestral or vocal work and reproducing it on the keyboard, Busoni became convinced that music, if it were good enough, did not need to depend on a chosen instrument. He said, sincerely:

> I learnt the truth that good and great universal music re-mains the same through whatever medium it is sounded.[2]

Not all musicians would agree on this point. But Busoni was never a man to withdraw a conviction once it had been reached. He accordingly transcribed, much as Liszt had done, the great organ

---

[1] See *The Essence of Music* (Dover Books, 1957).
[2] Op. cit., p. 87.

works of Bach for piano, and brought up to date the Toccatas by imbuing them with new figuration.

As usual, the composer's strong powers of logic enabled him to rebut several of the charges hurled against him, commenting acidulously:

> *Arrangements* are not permitted because they change the original, whereas the *variation* is permitted although it *does change* the original.[1] (Busoni's italics)

Though he was disinclined to go as far as, say, Stokowski, in his Bach transcriptions, Busoni was certainly capable of extremes as his proposal for a dramatic presentation of the St Matthew Passion indicates.[2] In this event, he would cheerfully have cut the arias and speeded up the action in a manner that would have made Bruno Walter ill. Again, he was not above complaining about the tenuousness of the connection between prelude and fugue in many of the 48—a criticism César Frank would possibly have endorsed, since he used his 'Choral' as a means of separating the two in his own music. Busoni's other transcriptions (such as Liszt's *Spanish Rhapsody* and Weber's *Polonaise*) produced much less in the way of public outcry, perhaps because the composers concerned did not induce the same feeling of reverence. But it is always fascinating to read Busoni's views on other composers. They are every bit as unconventional as Debussy's. What is more, they are delivered with much the same weary self-assurance. For Busoni, middle-period Beethoven was mere 'filling'—the *Appassionata* being in his view much weaker than the *Pathétique*. Only the first and third periods merited serious consideration. (This is, of course, conservative when set beside Debussy's opinion that Beethoven wrote badly for the piano throughout!) Mozart was a composer he adored, however, with more or less total absence of discrimination. His Mozartean aphorisms are well worth remembering—for instance, 'He did not remain simple, yet never became cunning' or 'He is as young as a boy and as wise as an old man.' Saint-Saëns he respected for his level of accomplishment, but he rated Strauss as factitious. Boito was his favourite Italian, and Liszt his champion in the sphere of modernity. The 'Faust' Symphony held a magnetic attraction for him that never wore off.

---

[1] See 'The Value of Transcription' in *The Essence of Music* (Dover, 1957).

[2] It is interesting to compare this notion with Debussy's actual mounting of *Le Martyre de St Sébastien* on the Paris stage. He brought down the wrath of the Archbishop as well as a number of Catholic writers like Péguy. Debussy's librettist was, of course, the decadent d'Annunzio.

Though a trifle outside our scope, it may be worth commenting briefly on Busoni's contribution to the pianist's art. Here his classicism showed in the inexorability of his playing, his steadfast monumentalism. Despite his reputation as a Lisztian, his method of execution was unromantic, and he was among the first to lay the foundations of that strict, anti-rubato style we associate with players of the Schnabel cast. From listening to the rolls of his playing (not always a reliable guide), his method did not spring as much from detachment as from an idea of purity, of linear unbrokenness, which was in some respects a tribute to his feeling for beauty and not just another testimonial to his intellect. It is unfortunate that so many imitators of Busoni and Schnabel have chosen to avoid romantic gestures without being able to maintain these artists' extraordinary loftiness of conception. Busoni's pupil, Egon Petri, was an exception in this respect, and was one of the few to approach his master's standards. My own teacher, the late Mark Hambourg, told me that Busoni had very thin, long hands, not entirely suited to the piano. They were probably rather like those of Michelangeli, the best Italian pianist since the composer of *Arlecchino*. Such hands have great potentialities for sensitivity, but are not usually considered the best to have for executing massive works of the order of the Bach transcriptions and *Hammerklavier* sonata, the staples of Busoni's repertory. He considered the piano the greatest of all instruments, nevertheless, and perhaps it is no co-incidence that his successor in Italian neo-classicism, Casella, was also a pianist above all else. Busoni's rules for pianists remind us very much of Schumann's rules for musicians. They each emphasize the need to practise always as if a listener were present; and each lays great store upon general culture. Technique was a necessary but not a sufficient condition for being a great pianist in Busoni's eyes, and he would have agreed with Andor Foldes who argues, in his book *Keys to the Keyboard* (O.U.P. 1950), that it is wrong to give in to temperament. Yet he was opposed to routine, and demanded the same freedom of expression in performing as he sought in composing. Apparent paradoxes of this kind are what make Busoni so formidable a figure to understand.

When the composer died in 1924, the task of de-throning the more melodramatic rulers of Italian opera was still far from complete. Indeed, the unconscious exile of Busoni in Berlin and Zürich had meant that most of the back-breaking work of opposing native sloth and tastelessness fell to other men, of whom Casella and Malipiero were the most prominent. The former, being the more combative of the two, also resorted to expatriation as a reaction to his initial rebuffs, but he eventually returned and

exercised a powerful effect on his juniors. The latter, having been
brought up in closer contact with the nineteenth-century tradition,
stayed on in Italy with a minimal rebelliousness in his heart. It is
to him, however, that the nation owes its present knowledge of the
baroque instrumental heritage, as well as the opera of the pre-
classicists. Older men—Sgambati for instance—had made their
protests, but they hardly carried conviction. Malipiero, once he
had heard Monteverdi's *L'Incoronazione di Poppaea* in 1902,
decided that he would devote some years to editing the works of
this great early Italian master and his compatriot, Vivaldi.[1] Casella
in the meantime had fled to France, where he expected to be met
with a more progressive artistic climate. In 1896 he had joined
Fauré's composition class, and later on he helped to found the
Société Musicale Indépendante (or S.M.I. as it was better known)
which catered for the works of men like Ravel, Koechlin and himself. Casella was in Paris for a total of eighteen years—tours
excepted—and hence remained until the outbreak of the First
World War. Between 1906 and 1909, he toured with the Société
des Instruments Anciens, really an ensemble for giving concerts
of the older music. Casella himself acted as the harpsichordist.
The group visited Russia, where he met Balakirev (whose *Islamey*
he transcribed for orchestra), Rimsky-Korsakov and Stravinsky.
The last had a profound influence on him, especially in persuading
him to adopt a difficult, percussive style of piano writing. A tour of
Germany also resulted in a meeting with Mahler, so that Casella's
works of this period are unintentionally eclectic; his symphonies
of 1906 and 1908 being, so to speak, out of Rimsky by Mahler.

By 1909, when he had returned from his tours, Casella had
resolved to write in the older styles (for example, his Suite in C),
but was rather tormented by the folk-music urge at the same time.
The latter posed the possibility of a different kind of nationalism
from that of Verdi and his followers. To understand Casella's
infatuation, it is necessary to realize that folk-song had been
traditionally excluded from serious, symphonic music in Italy, and
hence its employment in this context was something revolutionary.
The rhapsody *Italia* was an early essay in this vein which did not
succeed. Much later in his life, Casella attempted a ballet, *La
Giara* in which his infatuation made a brief re-appearance. Otherwise, his principal leaning was towards a classical simplicity or
'pandiatonicism' as Nicholas Slonimsky has called it. This
appeared particularly obvious in works like the popular *Pezzi*

---

[1] It is noteworthy that at much the same time Vincent d'Indy was
reviving both Monteverdi and Marc-Antoine Charpentier at the Schola
Cantorum in Paris. The 'Back to . . .' had accordingly started in both
countries.

Infantili (1920), where there seems to be a predominance of white notes. These pieces are incidentally for children and represent a good introduction to modern music for the younger performer. When Casella returned to Italy in 1915, however, he was still very mixed in his attitudes. The Piano Sonata (1916) is a formidable work, hardly tonal and full of a rugged complexity that seems the reverse of Italian. This and the *Elegia Eroica* proclaimed a marked debt to Schönberg, under whose influence the composer had also fallen. His *A Notta Alta* for piano and orchestra again belongs to this phase, which spanned the years up to 1920, when a sudden period of musical bankruptcy was ushered in. Ultimately, it was broken up by the success of 'Les Six' in France, who encouraged him to write more lightly in the style he had originally favoured. The *Scarlattiana* for piano and small orchestra, and *Serenade* for five instruments, both written in 1926, placed him back on the avenue that led to a moderate, facile neo-classicism. The *Partita* of 1925 had contained ancient dance forms like the passacaglia, gagliarda and giga, and this work helped the composer to clarify his ideas once and for all. The *Concerto Romano* (1926) is not as vivacious a piece as the others he wrote in that year; but it was equally studious in its avoidance of romanticism. Its nearest ancient equivalent would be one of the more heavily contrapuntal concertos of Vivaldi.

It is worth recollecting that, despite his long stay in France, impressionism left Casella utterly unmoved. Perhaps this was because he did not wish to be taken for another Respighi. But one should recall that his Italianism was already a sufficient stimulus to his awareness of natural beauty. In his autobiography, written in 1939, the composer wrote:

> Tuscany impressed me enormously, not only with its art but, above all, for its wonderful Nature. I understood that an Italian can never be an impressionist, and that the transparent clarity of that landscape is that of our own art.[1]

One wonders whether Busoni, who had been born at Eboli in Tuscany, had reached a similar conclusion. At any rate, Casella had something of his great predecessor's disciplined sense of adventure, and impatience with anything that merely set out to titillate the senses. His remaining years were fairly prolific, not simply in musical terms, but in terms of pedagogy and musical analysis. He transcribed a great deal from Vivaldi and picked up Busoni's obsession for making piano arrangements of the works of

[1] See *Music in my Time* published by the University of Oklahoma Press (1955).

composers of all periods. There were no vastly significant changes in his style in the 1930's and '40's, for it had always been more eclectic than dogmatic. His attempts to combine the Schönbergian influence with his neo-classical simplicity resulted in what Roman Vlad has paradoxically described as 'dissonant diatonicism'—that is to say, music in which the intervals of a second and seventh are prominent and which leaves its triads unresolved, but which goes no further in the direction of atonality. Even this was more than most Italians of the period could stomach, and much of the composer's later life was marred by polemics with Bossi, Respighi and others, none of whom approved of him or his ideas. Toscanini was never known to conduct a single work of his. In his musical tastes, he continued to prefer Wagner to Verdi, and while continuing to endorse Stravinsky and 'Les Six' on account of their neo-classicism he could not help bearing them a grudge for their blasé cosmopolitanism. For all the dislike he incurred at home, Casella wanted to remain an Italian musician. His *Pro Pace* (1944), a mass for the dead of the Second World War, though it actually goes as far as to employ a twelve-tone theme, is really a work of patriotic sorrow, rooted in the bloodstained soil of his country.

The condition of Italian music since the heyday of Casella has been on the whole very promising. Malipiero, as we have noted, lent weight to the twentieth-century renaissance and achieved in works like his opera, *Favolo del figlio cambiato* (1934), based on the career of a changeling, and his cantata to Vergil's *Aeneid* (1946), the vocal equivalent of Casella's instrumental strides forward. Perhaps this was very desirable, since the aridity of much that Casella wrote must be set against the national preference for a 'cantando' style of some sort. Indeed, the function of composers like Petrassi and Dallapicola, for all their modernism, has been to bring back an element of lyricism that their countrymen had sorely missed during the period of reaction against opera. Petrassi's *Coro di Morto* (1940), for instance, is a splendidly choral setting of poems by Leopardi in which modal and percussive effects combine to produce something that resembles the *Symphony of Psalms* of the later, more religiously attuned Stravinsky. It was prepared for by the setting of Psalm IX (1936) which the composer made, and which helped re-instate the unearthly vocal beauty sought by Palestrina. By comparison, Dallapicola has stuck to his pantonality (a version of the twelve-tone technique) and has proved its capacity for generating tender voice parts in his settings of the Greek Lyrics (1946) and his moving opera, *Il Prigionero* (1944–8), another work inspired by the horrors of war. The Fascists, as may be imagined, banned overtly atonal music during their years of power, and Dallapicola suffered more than any other composer from this act.

Oddly, he claims to have derived his musical ideals not so much from Schönberg as from a reading of the great literary systematizers of our time, men such as Proust and Joyce. It is too early to say where all this is leading, since the very youngest generation of Italians is one of further contrasts. Maderna and Nono were both born in Venice—which now seems the musical capital—and both incline to advanced styles, in the former's case mathematically determined and in the latter's conditioned by strong social convictions. All Maderna's music takes the form of variants, relying on tension and relaxation as its poles in preference to melody and rhythm as conventionally understood. Nono, who was more self-taught and who has met with considerable opposition in his native land, has retaliated by dedicating many of his works to non-Italian causes—for instance, his *La Victoire de Guernica* and *Epitaffo per Garcia Lorca*.[1]

What seems likely during the last quarter of this, one of the most critical centuries in Italy's turbulent but magnificent history, is that there will be a gradual return to the expansive, lyric flow that seems so indigenous a part of the native genius, while upholding the stand against melodrama and sentimentality which did so much to discredit it in the time of Puccini, Mascagni, Leoncavallo and their associates. If only the nation could unite once more its love of order and symmetry (a love which has been apparent not only in its tradition of polyphonic music, but in its superb architectural decorum and masterpieces of Renaissance painting) with its obvious passion for animation, vivid declamation and melody, what triumphs would await it? As Luigi Barzini has written, in his perspicacious analysis of the national character:

> The unsolved problems inevitably pile up and produce catastrophes at regular intervals. The Italians always see the next one approaching with a clear eye, but, like sleepers in a nightmare, cannot do anything to ward it off. They can only play their amusing games, try to secure their families against the coming storm, and delude themselves for a time. They console themselves with the thought that, when the smoke clears, Italy can rise again like a phoenix from the ashes.[2]

Let us hope that this time they will be right and that cultural glories will once more serve to propel them to the heights of European and even world civilization.

---

[1] Perhaps the principal cause of the outburst against him was his opera *Intolleranza* (1960)—a patently anti-Fascist work that draws on texts from Brecht, Sartre and others.

[2] *The Italians* (Hamish Hamilton, 1964).

xv *Roussel and Orientalism*

After the flood of writings on Berlioz, it is hoped that English critics will find words left to commemorate the life and work of another great French composer whose centenary has now fallen due—Albert Roussel. Some might query the use of the term 'great' to describe so neglected a figure; yet it was through him as much as anyone that French music fulfilled its more conventional ideals, those which had been handed down by César Franck, d'Indy and the academics. That these ideals now give every appearance of having been swamped in the acclaim that attaches to Debussy and Messiaen hardly does much to alter the case. They remain for music what the classical principles have been for art and literature, a constant means of renewal.

Like so many others in Flanders, the Roussel family came of old bourgeois stock. The composer's great-uncle had served as a Minister under the Convention, while his father was to perish, along with several of his friends, in the Franco-Prussian War of 1870. When Albert was only seven, his mother's death made an orphan of him, and it may easily have been the need for self-reliance that propelled the lad in the direction of a naval career. Equally, it could just as easily have been the passionate liking he had for the novels of Jules Verne. Whatever the reasons for his decision, music did not appear on his horizon until he had begun an adventurous life at sea, and had travelled to such out-of-the-way places as Tunisia and Siam. These facts have led more than one commentator to see the composer as a kind of musical Joseph Conrad, a man of action forced to rub shoulders with fashion-conscious aesthetes. This is bound to be a trifle misleading, but it does contain the elements of an apt comparison: both artists despised popular taste, were sustained by unusual powers of independence, and devoted themselves mainly to the higher stylistic goals.

Born at Tourcoing on April 5th, 1869, Roussel received his first lessons in music from a Mlle Ducrême, an organist at the Church of Notre-Dame. It was she who prompted his interest in the art, and when he enrolled at the Collège Stanislas in Paris he encountered a second advocate in the pianist, Jules Stoltz. By attaching himself to Stoltz the young Roussel got to know the principal operas of the day, including *Carmen* and *Manon*, without in any way forfeiting his commitment to the Viennese masters. In 1887 he was accepted as a cadet at the École Navale, the result of his having passed the particularly gruelling examination. Not long afterwards he was given a taste of life on board ship. The spectacle of a serious-minded ensign putting in the time between watches studying the scores of Mozart and Beethoven could scarcely have been credible to the older officers, but it was typical that this particular recruit should pursue his hobby, indifferent to the opinion of others. Indeed, he went further and persuaded several of his colleagues to join him in an amateur chamber ensemble that gave concerts at the ports they visited. It was while he was still in the Navy that Roussel wrote his earliest known compositions—a *Marche Nuptiale*, some sketches for an Indian opera, and a *Fantaisie* for Violin and Piano. None of these works won him the slightest acclaim—indeed they were all later destroyed—but it was on the strength of them that he decided to resign his commission and return to Paris to study music.

As it turned out, he could not have made a wiser decision. For one thing, his health had been far from satisfactory; his later medical history tending to suggest that he would have been unable to withstand the strain of continuous service. For another, there was the joy of discovering his true vocation, and of mixing with people of similar interests. What the choice really signified for Roussel did not become apparent straight away, however, and he had to wait until 1898 before seeing the publication of his suite *Des Heures Passent*, the first of the piano collections he was to write in the years leading up to the First World War.[1] His teacher during the period following his demobilization was Fauré's friend, Eugène Gigout.

Having fixed his sights on the most rigorous forms of training,

---

[1] The suite was published, somewhat reluctantly, by Hamelle, who printed only a small number of copies on the grounds that the work was clumsy and discordant. He later tried to excuse his caution, in an article in *La Revue Musicale*, but it was well known that this publisher had strong financial reservations about most of the new works he issued; his treatment of both Fauré and Chausson was certainly less than equitable.

it was inevitable that Roussel would one day confront Vincent d'Indy, the austere director of the Schola Cantorum. In all such cases, there has to be a go-between, and in this instance it was Antoine Mariotte, a former naval instructor turned opera composer, who made the introduction. Roussel studied at the Schola until he was thirty-eight; but once d'Indy had taken his measure he eased the situation for him by making him professor of counterpoint. Again, the decision was sound in all respects, the composer going on to become one of the most brilliant teachers of the decade. His official pupils included Erik Satie (who impudently dubbed him 'Cadet Roussel' from their first meeting), Edgard Varèse and Roland-Manuel, all destined to achieve a permanent place in the nation's music. Before resigning from the institution in 1912 (by which time he had been caught too often in the crossfire between d'Indy and the Debussyistes, who had made a point of baiting him), he had laid the foundation of many a promising young musician's style. Later on, he was approached by Martinů, Conrad Beck and Jean Martinon for private lessons.

The next steps in the career of this versatile man are harder to make plain. Undaunted by the purely practical difficulties of writing music, he soon possessed a technique far beyond that which most composers were satisfied to adopt. It derived partly from his knowledge of instruments (he had been an inveterate experimenter with the stringed and wind instruments he had picked up in the East), but more particularly, perhaps, from the close study he had made of chamber music and its problems. Another spur, of course, was the formidable discipline that had formed part of his professional obligations. Taken together, these factors quickly placed Roussel in the class of super-musicians, the class to which men like Guy Ropartz and Paul Dukas are usually assigned. Like them, he was disinclined to make a great show of his learning. He simply wrote difficult works and expected the public to follow him, anticipating the tendencies of the 1950's. In the comfortable artistic climate of 1900–10 this was naturally an arduous if not impossible role to sustain. The upshot was that works like the orchestral tone-poem, *Résurrection* (characteristically inspired by Tolstoy's abstemious novel) aroused only spite and contempt in those who heard them. Further recriminations followed the First Symphony, sub-titled *Le Poème de la forêt* and completed in 1906. It was said that each of these works was too complex and dissonant.

What really lay at the root of Roussel's unpopularity? After all, the public had become accustomed to the opaque harmony of the Franckists, and had even extended a fairly cordial welcome to Debussy. Chiefly, one supposes, it was the singularly harsh idiom Roussel chose to adopt. It must be remembered that even the most advanced musicians (like Ravel, whose failure to gain the Prix de Rome in 1902, 1903 and 1905 had recently stirred up the avant-garde) were generally careful to preserve something of that respect for melody and euphony which had been so much of a fetish with their predecessors. Indeed, a pleasing surface charm had before most of the world become the accepted hallmark of French music; and it was precisely this reputation for jocosity that Roussel seemed bent on undermining. His reasons for doing so continue to be rather obscure. Those who dislike his music usually argue that he lacked any gift for melody, but several arresting tunes—such as the waltz from *Le Festin de l'Araignée* or the lament from the second tableau of *Bacchus et Ariane*—come close to disproving their contentions. It is true that these tunes occur more frequently in the compositions of the last period, but that constitutes no denial of the composer's propensities. A more likely explanation is that Roussel strove to emulate d'Indy by concentrating on the less hackneyed elements of music, notably rhythm and polyphony.

Probably the strongest impression his music leaves is one of rapid and subtle pulsation. Not only does he invent complicated cross-rhythms in the manner of Fauré (another victim of his own erudition) but there appears to be a constant ebb and flow of rhythmic vitality in his work, an unending struggle to alter the beat without halting or impeding the design. Sometimes his penchant is for angular, tipsy-sounding rhythms which seem to have been suggested to him by his nautical experience; at other times he joins with de Séverac, Canteloube and the Schola's other regional musicians in presenting folk-dances of a sprightly or bucolic character. These, however, do not often comprise borrowed material.[1] By comparison, the polyphonic element reveals itself in a certain thickening of the texture, which causes the untrained listener to lose his way, and which consorts oddly with the invitation to high spirits.

As an example of the composer's ingenious handling of rhythm, let us consider briefly the *Danse au bord de l'eau*—a short piano piece in 5/8 time intended to depict the sway of some water-nymphs as they proceed in imitative procession. Marked 'très souplé', the music is notable for its semi-division of the bar into three quavers and a triplet (meant to be played in the time of two quavers), and this combination forms a sort of ostinato accompaniment throughout. Along with the euphonious sixths go a variety of bare fourths, giving to the piece a quaint mixture of the seductive and the severe. In certain respects, it is a rather Satiesque

---

[1] A notable exception is the *Rapsodie Flamande* (1936), in which the composer uses five Netherlands folk-tunes. Despite this, he was never in any sense a regional musician.

piece, despite having been written some years before Satie became the composer's pupil. Its principal features also pre-figure many later tendencies in Roussel's work—the jagged intervals that permeate the symphonies (especially Nos. 3 and 4) and the asymmetrical preference for five, seven or nine notes to each measure. It seems unfair that Roussel was denied the credit for these innovations, for not only were they to re-appear a good deal less audaciously in Debussy and Ravel, but they became the stock-in-trade of the Stravinsky of the 1920's and '30's. Again, the glimpses of bitonality in these early works pre-date *Le Sacre du Printemps* and the various compositions in which Milhaud experimented with the device. All these things go to show how soon and how confidently the composer succeeded in anticipating the trends of the post-war period. What he seemed unable to do at this stage, however, was to weld these elements into a coherent, fully recognizable style.

Hence, it is possible to regard most of the music he wrote before 1914 as in one way or another paradoxical. We have already noted the emotional ambiguity that arose out of suddenly switching from one device to another, from hovering uncertainly between the arid and the vivacious. Another work that illustrates these failings (though it remains, perhaps, the best work of its kind the composer wrote in his first period) is the 'Divertissement' of 1906. Despite its light-hearted title, this composition is much sterner in its craftsmanship and more refined in its intentions than, say, Ibert's work of the same title. Its harmonies are again thoroughly astringent (with chords built up on successions of fourths) and its instrumental colouring seems determined to avoid the charge of blatancy. For these reasons, the work's very real grace may tend to be overlooked. Quite possibly, Roussel lost potential adherents by sticking to the smaller forms and refusing to branch out into any of the dramatic media being favoured by his contemporaries. The piano works, continuing with 'Rustiques' (1904-6) in which the water-nymph tableau may be found, significantly failed to interest a public on the point of responding to Diaghilev and his musicians, and the composer was unable to enlist a champion of the type of Ricardo Vinès to popularize them.

An instance of their typical strengths and weaknesses may be sought in the F sharp minor Suite, Op. 14 (1909-10), which has some splendid ideas, exhaustively worked out, but which suffers from its excessive elaboration. It shows too great a concern with what Debussy would have called 'les dessous' (the inner parts). The Sicilienne, in particular, exhibits this trait. It strives hard to be elegant and charming, but the pianism is neither buoyant nor slender enough to match the metre. Complaints of a similar kind can be levelled at the Sonatine (1912), which is not nearly so ingratiating a specimen as Ravel's. Blanche Selva, one of Roussel's colleagues at the Schola, wrote some scathing remarks about its 'wrong-note' harmony; but somehow this criticism does not really get at the root of the trouble. The Auric Piano Sonata is even fuller plagued with such harmonies, yet it is by no means an unsuccessful work. The comparative failure of the Roussel piece relates in greater degree to its handling of registers, and the dullness of its 'moto perpetuo' sections (e.g. the section marked 'Vif et Très Léger'—$\mathdollar = 200$ ocurring the middle of the first movement). The late Norman Demuth, in his biography of the composer, was another critic to have expressed his dislike of the work, saying:

> The material is interesting and well thought-out; the form is clear and hangs together well, but the pianism is so clumsy that considerable care is needed to make it sound clean and not overcrowded. Every composer, no matter how great, has a blind spot when he fails to see that he is not expressing himself in the right manner. This Sonatine is Roussel's blind spot, the only one he had.[1]

It would not entirely surprise me, however, if it did not re-enter the repertory at some future date. It has been recorded—and made to sound reasonably convincing—by both Françoise Petit and Lucette Descaves, and was included in the Cheltenham Festival's Roussel celebrations of 1969.

Fortunately, a turning-point in the composer's style occurred sometime after a visit he and his wife paid to the Orient in 1909. Up to this time, his music had been very French, even though he had made the acquaintance of several Far Eastern countries in his capacity as a naval officer. Now, however, he was determined to make a serious study of the various cultures of the countries he was touring, in the hope of injecting a more cosmopolitan note into his compositions. Obviously, he was inspired by the variety of the Eastern ragas, and had been struck by the effect gamelan orchestras were having on the works of Debussy and Ravel. When he returned from his trip, then, Roussel possessed an exciting new range of devices which he was anxious to assimilate into his music. As may be expected, he had no intention of doing this in any cheap or imitative fashion, preferring to extend his entire tonal and rhythmic idiom by a complete re-consideration of the territory it covered. The drift towards impressionism had been apparent in his music ever since *Rustiques*. What now took place was a full-scale acceptance of the atmospheric possibilities offered by his art.

[1] See his book *Albert Roussel* (United Music Publishers, 1947). Chapter nine (pp. 94–101) is devoted entirely to the piano works.

The change was clearly displayed in the orchestral triptych *Evocations* (1910), one of the brightest jewels in the entire crown of French music, and a work unaccountably neglected by present-day promoters. It is a shade long for concert performance (about twice as long as Debussy's *Nocturnes*, which it otherwise closely resembles), but has an irresistibly beautiful last movement entitled *Aux bords du fleuve sacré*, in which the location is the Ganges and the musical matter a long choral invocation to the Sun. Of course, Roussel was not alone in this infatuation with Eastern themes—one only has to recall d'Indy's *Istar*, Ravel's *Shéhérazade* and Dukas's *La Péri*, all of which belong to much the same period—but he differed from each of these contemporaries in wishing to go beyond the search for local colour.

His greatest step away from the provincialism of Europe came with his opera-ballet, *Padmâvatî* (1914–18). This astonishing work, which critics have not hesitated to compare to *Pelléas* and *Wozzeck*, is without doubt the most authentic oriental music-drama to have been written by a Western musician. In it Roussel treated the theme of marriage ritual in thirteenth-century India. Act I presents us with the entry of a Mongol king into the city of his enemies at Tchitor. Ratan-Sen, the ruler of the city, hopes to conclude a peace-treaty, but is prevented from doing so by the Sultan's openly-proclaimed designs on his queen, Padmâvatî. Having retired to the Temple of Siva in Act II, Ratan-Sen and Padmâvatî discuss whether it is better to give in to the demands made on their love, or be a witness to the butchering of their people. After a bitter inner struggle, Ratan-Sen decides to hand over his queen, but to save him from the sacriligious breaking of their marriage-vows that this would entail, she stabs him to death. Finally, as was the custom, she immolates herself on her husband's funeral pyre, while the original invader looks on in bafflement and frustration. The dramatic peaks of the work are all contained in the ballet scenes, the earliest of which work up to a pitch of voluptuousness as the appearance of Padmâvatî is awaited; while the latter assume all the macabre qualities needed to depict the queen's descent into the funeral crypt. The work's concluding scene, in particular, rises to a lament that seems far more real than theatrical.

Padmâvatî, however, was a work that took four years to be composed, and a further five to be mounted. (It was given at the Paris Opéra in June 1923.) Meanwhile, Roussel had won a moderate success for himself by a lesser theatrical work he had been commissioned to do shortly before the war. The impresario, Jacques Rouché, had been greatly stimulated by the triumphs of Diaghilev in France, and lost no time in trying to emulate them. It was he who had mounted Ravel's *Ma Mère L'Oye* in January

1912 (and later, after he gravitated to the very important post of Director of the Opéra, had consented to include *Padmâvatî* in the repertory). Towards the end of the same year as he succeeded with the Ravel work, he approached Roussel to write a ballet using as his scenario an insect play by Gilbert de Voisins. The play, in turn, had been based on Fabre's well-known *Souvenirs Entomologiques*. Though not frightfully interested in complying with this commission, the composer dashed off a score containing a good deal of popular-sounding music. He had no idea that, when the ballet was performed at the Théâtre des Arts in April, 1913, it would be the making of his reputation. But *Le Festin de l'Araignée*, as it became known, was the occasion of a striking coup-de-théâtre such as very few musicians are fated to enjoy. Roussel became a name to conjure with in musical circles, and the whole venture had the effect of tickling the public's fancy to a much greater extent than he had ever expected. Later on in his life, he even came to regret his success a little, since he was constantly being upbraided for not sticking to the vocabulary he had chosen for it, which foreshadowed that of the lighter Prokofiev. The various episodes of *Le Festin* were also hard to live down: the miniature march of the ants and the funeral of the day-fly possessed that kind of instant appeal that soon leads to a composer becoming stereotyped. What persuaded the composer to jettison this popular manner was the change of climate brought about by the 1914–18 War, in which he served as an ambulance driver on the Somme. The spectacle of seeing hundreds of his comrades slaughtered drove out all thoughts of further charades, and it became obvious that his post-war music would be a good deal more spare and chilling than any that had appeared before.

That this proved to be the case is apparent from a glance at the Second Symphony in B flat (1920), a work that makes a few concessions to the non-musician. Here we begin to encounter another Roussel, mercilessly intent on purging his music of all its evocativeness and impurity, and forcing himself to be brief to the point of brusqueness. The well-known trademarks of the later symphonies (neither of which lasts more than 23 minutes) emerge as the work gathers momentum—wide-skipping intervals coupled with terrific, stunning accents. The listener is left with the feeling of having been mildly pulverized. Uncompromising as the symphony was, it is most important that we distinguish it from the facile productions of 'Les Six', also aimed at reviving the ancient guidelines and bent on being cosmopolitan in a lesser, derogatory sense. The truth is that Roussel's neo-classicism did not spring, like Poulenc's, from a series of publicity-seeking gimmicks, nor was it as purely academic a formula as d'Indy had worked out for himself. Still less could it be equated with 'a rare species of kleptomania'—which is how Stravinsky later had the temerity to describe his obsession. Rather, it reflected the artist's genuine terseness of outlook, his preference for the gritty and the concise. During the years ahead, Roussel was to compose two more symphonies (1930 and 1934, respectively) and each, in its own way, is a superb work. The Third crossed the Atlantic for its première under the baton of Koussevitsky, and it was this wonderfully virile, human essay that led Mitropoulos to regard Roussel as the greatest French musician of the age and one of the two or three greatest symphonists since Beethoven. It is significant that in each of the last two symphonies, it is the slow movement that carries the main burden of the composer's musical thought. That of No. 3 is a masterly construction, beginning with a tenuously beautiful adagio on the strings and reaching a climax in a brilliant fugato passage in which the first voice steals in on the piccolo. Neither of these compositions is heard often enough in our concert halls today, a fact that stands very much to our disgrace.

From 1921 to almost the end of his life, Roussel occupied a quiet villa near the sea at Varengeville, a few miles from Dieppe. Here he and his wife escaped from the metropolitan existence they disliked, and basked instead in the simple pleasures of the country-side. As long as he could walk along the cliffs—his substitute quarter-deck—Roussel remained happy. He did an immense amount of work for the various musical societies then on the point of becoming active. The S.M.I. (Société Musicale Indépendante) which had been founded by Fauré, Koechlin and Vuillermoz was one. Another was the International Society for Contemporary Music, in which the composer was particularly interested. It is significant that each of these societies had as its aim the breaking down of barriers—cultural and political—between nations, and stood in sharp contrast to the older Société Nationale, founded by Saint-Saëns and Franck, which had been more specifically French in its exclusiveness. Though Roussel was still not as well-established a figure as he deserved to be, he did not hesitate to withdraw his own works from the concerts organized by these societies in favour of those of younger artists. In the 'twenties, the composer also suffered a number of breakdowns in health—partly the result of having taken on too onerous a job in the war during which he was in his late forties—but these detracted very little from the efforts he put into composition. The Suite in F (1926) continued the trend towards abstraction which had been a feature of the earliest post-war works; its hard edges and driving rhythms expelled the last vestiges of the composer's impressionism. A piano concerto, completed in the following year, was less successful, being to some extent vitiated by Roussel's old ineptness in dealing with the instrument. It has failed to secure a place in the repertory. Much better was his setting of Psalm LXXX for tenor, chorus and orchestra, a work that formed the peak of the 60th birthday celebrations held in 1929. Roussel hoped that this would prove popular in England, a country he admired very much, but the response it has received would hardly have pleased him.

About this time, too, the composer's contribution to the solo song (or mélodie) became recognized. He had always been acute in his literary responses, and a few of his early songs (notably, *Le Jardin Mouillé* and *Le Bachelier de Salamanque*) had shown he possessed a real aptitude for the medium. It is interesting that he should have decided to continue by settings of the blues (*Jazz dans la Nuit*) and of James Joyce (*A Flower Given to My Daughter*). As if these were not cosmopolitan enough, he rounded off his production with two poems from the Chinese ('Favorite abandonée' and 'Vois, de belles filles'), and some of Leconte de Lisle's translations from Theocritus and Moskhos, coming to rest with the four René Chalupt songs for which he is, perhaps, best known. None of these works is particularly forceful, like the orchestral music, but rather the opposite. The Chinese settings are fragile in the extreme, making use of delicate clashes of appoggiaturas instead of the more typical chordal superimpositions. Though Chalupt is associated with Satie as a collaborator, it is of Fauré that Roussel's settings of his work remind us. Perhaps we should not press his claims as a songwriter too hard, however, except to say that his handling of the piano in them is usually more idiomatic than when he resorts to the instrument on its own. This is a confession Poulenc also made in relation to his œuvre—though in his case he may have been doing himself an injustice. Roussel's only other attempt to come to grips with the piano as a solo instrument was with the *Trois Pièces*, Op. 49, published by Durand in 1934. These pieces—or at least the first and third of them—are hard on the ear, and sound a little like Hindemith at his most ascetic. The second piece, an Allegro Grazioso in waltz time, is curiously enough much sweeter and more graceful; so much so that it almost carries us back to *Le Festin de l' Araignée* and what David Drew has wickedly called Auric's 'old sprigs of lavender'. Comparing the *Trois Pièces* with the works of the pre-1914 period, there can be no doubt that Roussel eventually acquired some degree of mastery of the instrument even if he cannot be classed alongside Debussy, Fauré or Ravel.

Not entirely surprisingly, in view of what we have been saying, the last phase of the composer's life—which ran from 1930 to 1936—was marked by a resurgence of interest in the stage. The

ballet, *Bacchus et Ariane*, which deals with the same legend as
Strauss's famous opera, made use of the talents of Lifar as choreographer and dancer and appeared in 1931. Basil Deane has
described it quite justly as 'one of the supreme masterpieces of the
twentieth century'.[1] No one who has heard either of the orchestral
suites derived from it will be quick to challenge this opinion,
neither can they very well dispute the remarkable brilliance the
music seems to exude. Roussel's carefully-linked rhythms are now
built into such sweeping melodic paragraphs that not even the
great pagan ballets of Debussy and Ravel can astonish us more.
Instrumentally, the work is a colossal achievement, the various
brass and woodwind strands standing out like colours on a litho-
graphic plate. All the composer's dynamism has been retained—as
the concluding Bacchanale testifies—yet there is a hint of tenderness in Ariadne's music it would be hard to find in any previous
score. The change from Greek to Roman mythology involved in
the next and last ballet, the seldom heard *Aenéas*, brought a corresponding inflation of theme and, although the choir adds a few
fine touches, the work is both musically and emotionally more
restricted. It was first performed under Scherchen in Brussels in
1935. Actually, the last of the composer's stage works to be performed was the comic-opera, *Le Testament de Tante Caroline*
(1933), a typical story of intrigue and mistaken identity which did
not reach the boards till March, 1937, only six months before the
composer was struck down with a heart attack. It has had a
number of recent revivals, even one in England, and shows that
Roussel, no less than his master d'Indy, had his humorous side.

Other works confirm that the last phase was probably the most
fruitful. It was particularly prolific in chamber works, another
genre in which the composer might well have specialized to further
advantage. As it stands, the String Quartet (1932), the popular
Sinfonietta for small orchestra (1934) and the String Trio (1937)
combine to indicate what mastery Roussel had over the intimate
forms. In them, as in all the mature works of this admirable man
and musician, we should salute the qualities that have helped to
make France a great European nation.

[1] See *Albert Roussel* (Barrie & Rockliff, 1961), a book based on Mr
Deane's Ph.D. thesis submitted at the University of Glasgow.

xvi Russia, Rachmaninov and the Exiled Virtuoso

Vaughan-Williams, in a rare burst of spite, once remarked—quite unjustly in my opinion—that Mahler represented for him 'a fair imitation of a composer'. This remark, if it were applied to a variety of other modern musicians, might produce an interesting series of reactions from the critics and public. I suspect a good many of the former would consider it an appropriate epithet to lodge against Sergei Rachmaninov, whose high standing with the typical concert-goer is equalled only by the extreme contempt that is regularly showered upon him by the cognoscenti. Though younger than either Sibelius or Roussel, and only a year older than Schönberg, he has entered the repertory with far greater ease than all three; yet has been dismissed from the pantheon of modern composers with a summariness that is almost suspicious and which suggests that he has been the victim of an instant critical conspiracy. Joseph Machlis, for example, in his influential study *An Introduction to Contemporary Music* (Norton, 1961) writes candidly:

> Rachmaninov has no proper place in a book on contemporary music. He was a traditionalist who moved within the orbit of late nineteenth century romanticism, following in the footsteps of his idol Tschaikovsky.

Such an admission does not prevent Mr Machlis from devoting some thirty pages of his book to Mahler, Strauss, Sibelius and Scriabin, each of whom 'moved within the orbit of late nineteenth-century romanticism' to a degree many would think every bit as comfortable. A much older critic, Vyacheslav Karatygin, put the case against Rachmaninov more succinctly as far back as 1913 when he commented:

> The public worships Rachmaninov because he has hit the very centre of average philistine taste . . .

The question that really poses itself, as far as I can ascertain, is whether or not Rachmaninov *did* become the kind of composer he was by deliberate intent; and if not, what was the reason that led him to take the path he took? If we can answer this successfully, we may be able to say, with some semblance of justice, whether it is the waxworks image established by the critics or the more sincere and benevolent one created by the public that comes nearest to being a true portrait of the composer.

As with the other composers we have studied, it is necessary to begin, in a purely biographical fashion, by describing the sort of background out of which Rachmaninov emerged. As the child of a rich (but, as it turned out, improvident) father, with a huge country estate near Novgorod, he had no difficulty in being admitted to the Moscow Conservatory, where he was the contemporary of the pianists Scriabin and Siloti. His musical talents would, in any case, have brought him to the attention of scholars whatever part of Russia he had come from. The academics who ruled over the institution in which he worked were Taneyev (a pupil of Tschaikovsky's) and Arensky (who had worked, like Stravinsky was to do, with Rimsky-Korsakov). Rachmaninov's progress at the Conservatory was as startling a phenomenon as any in the history of music. Not only was any and every piece of piano music child's play under his long, talented fingers, but his prowess as a composer and conductor rapidly assumed legendary proportions. All three activities occupied his time to advantage, but he soon ran into the snag that he could not excel at all at one and the same time. Even more than other versatile musicians, he found it imperative to pause between different activities, and the history of his next fifty years shows quite clearly that while he was succeeding at one of these concerns he was either failing or impotent at the others. This represents a fact of cardinal importance to anyone who wishes to understand why the composer was relatively unproductive in his later, American period, when he had become recognized as one of the world's leading pianists and was being expected to give recitals all over Europe and the U.S.A. At the Conservatory, he accelerated to the point of graduating in 1892— at the age of nineteen—and by the following year had written an opera, a set of piano pieces, Op. 3 and his Piano Concerto No. 1.

This was an incredible beginning to a career, and it is hardly surprising to learn that he left the Conservatory in possession of the Grand Gold Medal, the highest award the institution could offer. Despite these achievements, life became far from a bed of roses for Rachmaninov, as the years from 1893–1900 were to reveal. His troubles had started even before graduation, since by the middle of the 1880's the composer's father had frittered away most of the holdings he had possessed, and the family had been forced to move into a crowded flat in St Petersburg. While there, Rachmaninov's sister, Sophia, had died of diphtheria and an atmo-sphere of depression loomed over the entire household, redeemed a little by the boy's grandmother, Butakova, of whom he remained passionately fond. Since Rachmaninov is widely and rightly regarded as a melancholy composer, it is sensible to pay some attention to these early and very probably traumatic experiences he endured. The loss of the estate (a very Chekhovian situation made more ironical by the composer's actual collaboration with that dramatist in his tone-poem, *Crag*, based on the short-story called *Along the Way*) was perhaps the event that left the deepest scar on the young man's consciousness, so that even in middle and old age he was to recall, with understandable nostalgia, the haven of civilized pleasure from which he had been suddenly and in-explicably withdrawn. The composer's biographers, Bertensson and Leyda, paint a vivid picture of the spacious house and grounds he was compelled to leave behind:

> A landscape of the Russian north country stretching to a rugged horizon, threaded by the breadth of the Volkhov River; the odours of new-mown hay and the smoke of fishermen's bonfires; a great house near enough to ancient Novgorod to catch the echoes of its old bells; a family that filled the house with exciting, pleasant motion —an over kind and expansive father, a loving but strict mother, the noise and gallop of children and horses through the vast acreage and, most vivid of all, a protec-tive grandmother who defended all Seryozha's pranks and mischief from the punishment that was due him: these are the impressions that Sergei Rachmaninov would always recall when he tried to recapture the lovely, sunny blurred memory of his childhood on the estate of Oneg.[1]

Perhaps it was this decline in the family fortunes that led the composer to adopt a pose of lassitude and disenchantment even before his time at the Conservatory had reached its end. Though brilliantly clever, he was morose and indolent to the point that Siloti and his other friends had to push him into action; so that he was anything but student-like in his reactions to the factionalism and jockeying for position that inevitably went on. At no time during his training did Rachmaninov join in cliques or respond to displays of affection on the part of his teachers. (The origin of the

[1] See *Sergei Rachmaninov* by Sergei Bertensson and Jay Leyda (Allen & Unwin, 1965). This is an indispensable work, if only for the 500 pre-1917 letters and entire American archive it draws upon.

notorious grimace which remained with him to the end of his days
lay in his determination to disabuse Safonov, a later Director of
the Conservatory, of the idea that he was out to curry favour.)
Even the group students formed to listen to Wagner—then very
much the property of the avant-garde in Russia as in most
countries—won only the laziest allegiance from him. Leonid
Sabaneiev has described how the composer would trudge along to
meetings with his customary expression of weariness:

> Rachmaninov did not take part in any of the demonstra-
> tions; he sat in the corner in a rocking-chair, with a huge
> orchestral score on his knees. From time to time we would
> hear, coming from his corner, some gloomy remark in his
> deep voice: 'A thousand pages more!' An hour later, more
> gloomily: 'Eight hundred and eighty pages to go!'

It was Tschaikovsky, as Professor Machlis has claimed, who more
than anyone lighted a faint spark in him. The composer of *The
Queen of Spades* (which Rachmaninov incidentally travelled to
St Petersburg to hear) was very much the darling of Moscow
society at that time, the other members of 'The Five' either
residing in Russia's second city or else, emulating Borodin's
chemistry ambitions, shutting themselves indoors. Later on,
Rachmaninov came to admire Rimsky-Korsakov a good deal,
particularly when he realized how sensitive that benevolent artist
was to orchestral textures, and how acute were his responses to
theatrical style. Otherwise, it was Arensky (who held 'free composers' sessions in place of classes) and Liadov (a charming and
utterly un-self-seeking person) who seemed to incur his greatest
approval.

It was not until he had left the Conservatory that Rachmaninov
ran into the series of disasters that were destined to complete the
process of disillusionment already begun. Though *Aleko* (his early
opera) was played with moderate success at the Bolshoi, it was as
a symphonist that the composer saw himself at this particular stage
of his career. The bulk of his efforts around the middle of the
1890's accordingly went into the writing of his Symphony No. 1
in D minor, a work that had its notorious première (a night
Rachmaninov was never to forget) on May 15th, 1897, with
Glazounov conducting. This event turned out to be the greatest
failure imaginable, leaving the composer so neurotic and embittered
that he became the enemy of the entire musical fraternity.[1]
The circumstances surrounding the performance remain largely

---

[1] The composer tore up the score after the première, so upset was he.
It was, however, unearthed and pieced together again in 1942 at Lenin-
grad, and has since been played again in the U.S.S.R.

obscure. All we know is that Glazounov gave what was evidently an atrociously bad reading of the score, making it sound much worse than it really was. Rimsky-Korsakov, who was present, did not care at all for it, while César Cui became so vindictive that he was unable to resist writing a thoroughly damning notice for one of the city's journals in which he claimed:

> If there's a Conservatory in Hell, and one of its gifted pupils should be given the problem of writing a program-matic symphony on the Seven Plagues of Egypt, and if he should write a symphony resembling Mr Rachmani-nov's—his problem would have been carried out bril-liantly and he would enchant all the inmates of Hell.

On the whole, the professional critics were no kinder, using expressions like 'modern trash' (curious this, in view of the com-poser's later reputation for being reactionary) and 'sickly harmonic perversity'. The only one to offer anything like a charitable judgment was Findeisen, writing in the *Russkaya Muzkalynaya Gazeta*, who commented:

> Rachmaninov's symphony is the product of a composer who has not yet fully found himself. At this point, he could become either a musical crackpot or a Brahms.

What was the real reason underlying this strange catastrophe? Stravinsky (who *may* have been prejudiced in his remarks) has said in his *Conversations* that Glazounov was an habitual drunkard, as well as being anti-progressive to an almost pathological degree. Probably we can safely discount the influence of the second factor, since he would hardly have consented to conduct a work in which he totally disbelieved. But the possibility that he was inebriated during the performance is one that remains a realistic, if unproven, explanation. At all events, this is how things must have sounded to Rachmaninov, who could hardly credit the evidence of his ears.

That the result of the débâcle was to dissuade the composer from further ventures of the same kind is pungently illustrated in his recollections:

> After that symphony I composed nothing for about three years. I felt like a man who had suffered a stroke, and for a long time had lost the use of his head and hands.

Instead of doing more composing, then, Rachmaninov turned to the second of his three accomplishments—conducting. For long periods to follow, he directed operas at the Bolshoi—including Glinka's *A Life for the Czar* and Moussorgsky's *Boris*—and it was during these sessions that his friendship with Chaliapin blossomed.

This was one of the few lasting attachments the composer formed in the course of a long, public career. Both artists visited Tolstoy at Yasnaya Polyana in 1900, and not long afterwards Rachmaninov paid a second call in the hope of receiving some guidance from the man who, at that time, was generally regarded as the world's foremost living sage. Unfortunately, he could not have picked on a worse person to advise him, since Tolstoy, after writing *What is Art?*, had relapsed into that naïve belief that all art should be designed so as to be intelligible to the mass of the people, especially the peasants to whom he evidently considered he owed an unpayable debt. His advice to Rachmaninov therefore took the form of rhetorical questions such as:

> Is such music as yours needed by anybody? What is most needed by man, scholarly music or folk-music? Beethoven is nonsense . . .

After listening to a few hours of *this* nonsense, it is hardly surprising that Rachmaninov departed in an even more depressed state than that in which he had arrived. The two men did not meet again, but it is possible that their brief conversations had a mildly damaging effect on the composer's attitude to his art. At least, they would seem to explain his appalling popularity.

This may be the right point at which to state, however, that whereas it is easy to discern a Russian element in Rachmaninov's music, it is not so easy to relate this to any consciously-held nationalist beliefs.[1] The composer's nationalism—if it exists—was the direct consequence of his temperament and youthful nostalgia. It was quite unaccompanied by that devotion to the common folk that can be pointed to in the Russian writers of the period, like Gorky and Babel. Even Tolstoy's own Russianism and elevation of peasant life was in a sense contradicted by the universalism of his beliefs on religion, education and marriage. So that in dealing with the composer's national urges, it is clear that we are concerned with something that is neither political nor musical, but psychological. On this count, it is worth remarking that Rachmaninov suffered a severe nervous breakdown shortly after his first meeting with Tolstoy, and it was only by means of the hypnosis treatment given him by a Dr Dahl, a neighbour who combined a love of music with a knowledge of clinical psychiatry, that he recovered his former powers. The nowadays hackneyed Piano Concerto No. 2 was the direct product of Dahl's treatment, and

---

[1] In this connection, Wilfrid Mellers in *Man & His Music* (Barrie & Rockliff, 1962) goes as far as to say: 'For all the Russian quality of his pessimism, nostalgia and instability, Rachmaninov is hardly a national composer.'

the composer even went as far as to get the doctor to take the ovation at its première. The success of this work, marking a turning-point for the better in Rachmaninov's career, led him to contemplate a more normal way of life; and in 1902 he married his cousin Natalia and settled down to a period of high musical productivity. Between the years 1902–17, he wrote two more short operas, two cantatas, a setting of Edgar Allan Poe's *The Bells*, about forty piano pieces, fifty songs, the Second Symphony and the Third Piano Concerto. Compared with this mighty outpouring, the composer's catalogue for the twenty-six years he spent in exile reveals a mere five works of importance, only one of which has really entered the repertory.

Perhaps the largest spur to his international acclaim came with the performance of the Second Concerto with the Vienna Philharmonic in 1903. Safonov—whom he always disliked—conducted this concert, and whatever may be said against him he did not make the same mess as Glazounov had done with the Symphony. Previously, Rachmaninov had played in England, where the Chekovian tone-poem (it presents a typical 'slice of life' involving two travellers who meet briefly in sympathy at an Inn in winter) was not well liked, but where the famous Prelude in C sharp minor, which had been part of the Op. 3 set of pieces, was greeted with deafening rapture.

The years that followed were probably the happiest Rachmaninov enjoyed, if we except those of his childhood at Oneg. In 1904, he produced his cantata on Pushkin's *The Miserly Knight* and thus matched the achievement of his other work for choir and orchestra, entitled *Spring*, which had won him a Glinka award. The political unrest of 1905–6 left him relatively unmoved, though it put a temporary brake on his activities in all fields. Afterwards, Diaghilev invited him to Paris with a possible view to collaboration; but the two men did not hit it off at all well. This was hardly surprising, since it would be difficult to imagine two personalities more unalike. However, Rachmaninov revelled in his stay in the French capital, he, Rimsky and Scriabin all meeting at the Café de la Paix for a grand re-union, the senior of the three expounding his views on the interpretation of *Le Coq d'Or* with a glass of liqueur at his elbow. Scriabin, though his pianism was almost as extraordinary as Rachmaninov's, was a shade too wild and mystical for either of his companions, for all their friendship, and Rimsky eventually reached the conclusion—to which many have since consented—that the author of the *Poem of Ecstasy* was heading for lunacy.[1] It is interesting to compare Scriabin with Rachmaninov

[1] As it happened, he died of blood poisoning in 1914, at the age of 43. Rachmaninov recounts in one of his letters how he and the other Russians

as a pianist; and both with the young Josef Hofmann, who was also a success in Russia from this time onwards. Rachmaninov's playing was always perfectly controlled and polished. His strengths lay in his long-range architectural sense; his power of shaping a phrase with genuine finesse; and his almost god-like technical infallibility. Scriabin, on the contrary, played with Chopinesque emotion; was 'inspired'; and could indulge in extraordinary flights of poetry. Of the three, Hofmann may have been the greatest perfectionist, investing all his work with the sort of meticulous observance of dynamics we associate with a later generation. His colouring and vitality prevented him from being a pedant; but he looked forward more to the school of Schnabel, whereas Rachmaninov had much in common with the great nineteenth-century virtuosi and, at his best, would probably have been a match for Liszt.

A word or two on the training of pianists in Russia might not come amiss at this point. Unlike Western institutions, the Russian Conservatories tended (and still do tend) to nurture their young virtuosi on the romantic and post-romantic repertoires, avoiding the classics almost exclusively. The present writer's own teacher, the late Mark Hambourg, has testified how little attention was paid to the sort of grounding in Bach, Mozart and Beethoven that all British and German pianists have to go through. More recently, Vladimir Ashkenazy has made much the same points. In a recent television interview, he confessed that Mozart had been virtually unknown to him till he emigrated to the West ("Too easy for children, too hard for adults' was the comment of another great Eastern European player, Artur Rubinstein). Even Beethoven was apparently regarded as 'a bit square' at Moscow, where it was assumed that the path to pianistic perfection was through such composers as Liszt, Chopin, Scriabin, Liapounov, Balakirev and their successors. That this régime has resulted in a fantastic crop of keyboard masters is evident from the simplest glance. Men of the calibre of Rachmaninov, Lhévinne, Horowitz, Moiseiwitsch and Brailowsky were not produced by accident. They were products of a school of fabulous technicians which has all but died out since the introduction of a more scholarly, textually-biased style of playing in the 1930's. A few of the vanishing breed are still left— the most notable being the amazing Sviatoslav Richter. It will be interesting—at least to those of us who still believe the piano has a future—to see whether we have witnessed the last of the great virtuosi, or whether there will be a reaction against the correct, classical style at present exemplified in older players of the type of Backhaus, Kempff and Serkin and their younger counterparts,

of their acquaintance attended his funeral in the pouring rain, Taneyev catching pneumonia and dying as a result.

Brendel, Geza Anda and Ingrid Haebler. The point it is necessary to make in relation to Rachmaninov is that, despite his fame, the years of his American exile were in reality the years when the style of playing he so perfectly embodied—which in a sense may be compared to the style of the old actor-managers in the theatre— was being surreptitiously replaced.

From the time of his return from Paris to the eve of the Revolution, Rachmaninov led an increasingly busy and fêted existence. In 1907 he completed his Second Symphony—a long, lyrical work that at last shows signs of being popular in the way the Concertos have been. He considered other operatic projects, including one on Flaubert's *Salammbo* (it will be recalled that Debussy made a tentative start on the same work when he was a Prix de Rome scholar at the Villa Medici, but like Rachmaninov dropped the idea at an early stage) and another on Chekhov's play, *Uncle Vanya*. Neither of these came to fruition, but the composer's realization of Böcklin's picture, *The Isle of the Dead*, which he saw in a black-and-white reproduction and not in colour, resulted in a tone-poem of nearly unequalled intensity. In the same year, Rimsky-Korsakov died (1908) and Rachmaninov felt, as a great many others did, that an era in Russian music was about to come to an end:

> Rimsky-Korsakov is dead, and Russian music has been orphaned. In the realm of opera a great void has been left by the death of the composer of *The Snow Maiden*

These sentiments, strangely enough, were echoed most tremulously of all by Stravinsky, a musician who has little in common, in the public mind, with the composer of the Second Piano Concerto and the *Rhapsody on a Theme of Paganini*. Though they were both to leave Russia within the next decade, and even become neighbours in California, they evidently did not allow their common regrets over the demise of the Old Russia, or their common hatred of Glazounov, to become the means of engendering a proper friendship. Writing of Rachmaninov in his book, *Conversations* (Faber, 1959), Stravinsky relates:

> I remember Rachmaninov's earliest compositions. They were 'water-colour' songs and piano pieces freshly influenced by Tschaikovsky's. Then at twenty-five he turned to 'oils' and became a very old composer indeed. Do not expect me to spit on him for that, however: he was, as I have said, an awesome man, and besides, there are too many others to be spat upon before him. As I think about him, his silence looms as a noble contrast to the self-approbations which are the only conversation of all performing and most other musicians.

Not very heart-warming words, but perhaps the warmest it was possible to summon up about the 'six and a half foot scowl' Rachmaninov had by then become.

Though he went to live at Dresden in 1909, the composer returned to Russia periodically to conduct his own and other people's works, and engineered a major American tour in 1910 which enabled him to give recitals at Pittsburgh, Boston and Cincinnati. He also used the occasion to present his Third Piano Concerto (surely his best?) under Walter Damrosch and the New York Philharmonic. It was also given under Mahler. His playing of this and the Second Concerto gained him comparatively indifferent reviews, however, his real American triumphs not coming until later. Aldrich, of the *New York Times*, for example, took exception to the lugubrious character of the composer's music in a more than averagely caustic notice:

> Russian music and Rachmaninov's music in particular is weighted down with melancholy which seems to be racial in its insistence.

The interesting feature of this review is contained in the last few words. Everyone knows that at that time America was in the throes of an immigrant problem, and it was accordingly common for its writers to attribute national stereotypes of the kind we are currently reading about in England. Moreover, it was the America of Teddy Roosevelt and his bully-boys and a certain backlash was being directed at the foreigner. Later on, when the absorption of immigrants became a fact, America became less frontier conscious, less keyed up with 'Go West, young man!' slogans of the kind Horace Greeley and his kind had been preaching in The Gilded Age and which were still being bandied about in the 1900's. When this happened, there was a more determined effort to appreciate the cultural products of the Old Europe. In the visual arts, this led to the genteel plundering operations of Mrs Jack Gardner and Peggy Guggenheim; while in the musical domain it gave rise to a vogue for foreign musicians that was greatly stimulated by critics like James Huneker and Paul Rosenfeld. Though Rachmaninov did not benefit directly from the comments of these men (Rosenfeld complained of a certain lack of individuality in his work), it nevertheless became much easier for foreigners to take possession of the various musical citadels. One only has to reflect on the successes of men like Koussevitzky, Stokowski, Kreisler, Zimbalist and Heifetz to appreciate how rapidly the tide rose in their favour.

Back in Russia, Rachmaninov gradually shed his commitments as conductor at the Bolshoi, and as may be expected developed further as a composer in consequence. The famous song *Lilacs*,

Op. 21, added appreciably to his popularity around this time, and it was evidently inspired by the habit a mysterious well-wisher had contracted of sending the composer a bouquet of these flowers at the end of each of his concerts. Rachmaninov never discovered the identity of the sender until long after he had quitted the land of his birth. Apparently, she was a Mme Rousseau, and she was deeply affected by the composer's expatriation. In 1911, Rachmaninov also completed his set of *Etudes Tableaux*, nine in all though he published only six. These and the second book of *Preludes*, Op. 32, were played by him on his second London tour. It was generally felt, however, that his songs, beautiful though many of them were, had too strongly pianistic a basis; while the actual piano works were so redolent of Chopin that it sometimes became hard to tell whether or not they had been composed by the Polish pianist.[1] Examined in detail, there are, however, distinct stylistic differences. Rachmaninov's *Preludes* are longer and more polyphonic, and they do not cohere into a single large work in the way that Chopin's do. In the view of most, the first book, Op. 23, is the better of the two. It contains the impetuous G minor, with it tender, flowing middle section, which has proved the second most popular piece Rachmaninov wrote for the instrument. The easier and more contrapuntal Prelude in E flat from the same book is just as fine, however, and recalls the mood of the Second Piano Concerto. Otherwise, the best of the first set is probably the deceptively tricky D major, which requires a soft cantabile touch at the same time as it poses some awkward leaps and crossings of hands. Benno Moiseiwitsch, who was the composer's brother-in-law, always regarded the B minor Prelude of Bk. II as the gem of the entire series, and the present writer can remember the emotion with which he played it on the afternoon that he learned of Rachmaninov's death—as an encore to a recital he was giving at the Empire Theatre, Cardiff, on March 28th, 1943.

Among the other important pre-war events in the composer's life, two stand out. One was the composition of 'The Bells' and the other the friendship concluded with the young poetess, Marietta Shaginyan. The former may have been inspired by Debussy's interest in Poe (the French composer had been at work on an opera based on *The Fall of the House of Usher* for a number of years, though he died without having written more than a few pages of the music), since there are hints that Rachmaninov was envious of Debussy's success with the avant-garde. He was also getting

---

[1] It is a pity, in a way, that Rachmaninov did not make a more strenuous effort to assist in creating a Russian tradition of song worthy of the Moussorgsky cycles. On the whole, he chose uninteresting poets and poems, though possessing a natural flair for the medium.

extremely restive at the suggestions being thrown out that he was finished as a composer, having got nothing more to say. *The Bells*, which was first given in Moscow in 1914, *did* say something new, however, and is possibly Rachmaninov's finest composition. It was greeted warmly, and earned the inevitable floral tribute from *White Lilacs*. Evidence of the work's quality may be gauged from the fact that English choral conductors (it is actually a kind of choral symphony) quickly spotted it and gave it at Sheffield before the year was out. The text, as we have stated, was by Poe, but one cannot help feeling the work itself reflected the composer's life-long infatuation with the wide spectrum of sounds—ranging from the lightest tinkling to the sternest tolling—emanating from the great Russian belfries at Novgorod, Moscow, Kiev and a dozen other cities. Using a translation of Poe's poem by Balfont (who was also his collaborator in several of the songs) Rachmaninov expressed in this labour of love all the joy and mourning, the earthiness and spirituality, of Mother Russia as she existed under the Czars. Still thinking in the terms we described earlier, *The Bells* is easily the composer's most nationalist work, and could not conceivably have been written in the country of the poet whose verses it nominally employed. It was at the time of writing this glorious effusion that Rachmaninov came under the spell of his twenty-three year old poetess, whom he affectionately nicknamed 'Re'. Many of his songs were written for her—she was a cello student as well as a writer—but it remains impossible to say how deep their relationship really went. The composer saw her for the last time at Rostov in 1917, a matter of months before he slipped, almost unnoticed, out of the country.

The cause of his emigration was clearly the February uprising that was the prelude to the October Revolution. But Rachmaninov had been feeling for some time that his efforts as a pianist were not meeting with success in Russia. The year 1915 had been a bad one for him in this respect, since he suffered throughout it by being unfavourably compared with the dead Scriabin. A year or so later Prokofiev—another tremendous virtuoso, but of a much more steely and percussive breed—began to attract notice; and though he was hardly a competitor for Rachmaninov in keyboard terms, his ideas about the repertoire were patently different and more progressive. The young Prokofiev has recorded how he would sit, bored to extinction, at Rachmaninov's recitals—usually rounding up a few friends and clearing out when it came to the interval. The dislike was, of course, reciprocated, and both Rachmaninov and his friend Medtner (another extremely good pianist and composer of the traditional sort—his *Fairy Tales* are still occasionally heard at recitals) were confirmed in their feelings when they heard

Prokofiev's cycle of poems by Anna Akmatova in 1917. Rachmaninov was right in his supposition that America would take more kindly to his playing than the new school of Russians, and it must have given him some satisfaction when Prokofiev, who followed him to that country, failed utterly to win over the audiences there. It was therefore a combination of premonitions that led the composer to decide in December 1917 to get out by using the ruse that he was going to give a series of twelve recitals in Sweden. He did in fact sail to Stockholm and play the concerts for which he was booked; but what he neglected to tell the authorities was that after completing them he intended catching a second boat to take him to New York. This he did, arriving in November, 1918, just in time to participate in the hectic Armistice celebrations. Unfortunately, he had been forced to leave most of his belongings at home, including a large quantity of his music—it would have looked suspicious had he taken them with him on his trip. But some of these eventually turned up, and it was not long before the composer became a silent member of the West Coast expatriate colony along with so many others.

The last two-thirds of his life, while they offer material for the student of piano technique and its history, have very little to tell us about Rachmaninov the composer. In this capacity, he was a literal case of H. G. Wells's man who 'walked into the future backwards'. That is to say, he became more and more retrospective as his American position consolidated itself. He was accepted, quite correctly, as the greatest pianist of his time, and spent the active years that were left to him embarking upon tour after tour, always to the most vociferous applause. It was a curious situation in a way, since he rose to greatness as an executant by the unique and unprecedented method of deciding, at forty-five years of age, to refurbish his technique, re-learn the stock works in the repertoire and join the 'travelling circus', as Busoni once put it. The interest he took in the mechanics of the piano was stimulated by the friendship he contracted with Frederick Steinway, maker of the wonderful instruments on which he played, and by the jocular rivalry he entered into with Hofmann, who by this time had established a flourishing school of piano students at the Curtis, and one or two other Institutes set up by wealthy American donors. Despite being a poor mixer, Rachmaninov managed to move about fairly freely in U.S. musical circles, allowing himself to serve on juries at competitions and even taking the occasional pupil. It is interesting to note that his attitude to young American composers who came to see him with their works was quite old-fashioned in the sense that the advice he gave them was invariably to think in terms of 'correctness or incorrectness'. He did not seem to grasp the point that a new country like America would (and, of course, in the end did) produce a new musical aesthetic that would have its own laws and rules, its own special virtues. When Henry Cowell, for example, left one of his compositions with Rachmaninov for comment, all he got in reply was: 'Your piece has forty-two wrong notes!' That this was the way he approached the writing of his own scores is clear from a glance at one of the Preludes or Concertos. Aside from the ideas—and I am prepared to say that I do not think Rachmaninov has ever been accorded the credit he merits for the beauty of his ideas—they are all built-up by small increments. They are essentially compilations rather than compositions.

That the composer was not unaware of his conservatism tends to be an established fact. When interviewed by Olin Downes, for instance, and asked:

> Do you believe that a composer can have real genius, sincerity, profundity and at the same time be popular?

the cutting answer given was:

> Yes, I believe it is possible to be very serious, to have something to say and at the same time be popular. I believe that others do not. They think—what *you* think!

In 1927, Rachmaninov tried to prove his point by writing a Fourth Concerto, but his heart was not really in it. The work remains factitious to the extent that it tried too hard to impose 'modern' material (whole-tone scales, metric reversals) on an essentially out-of-date romantic sub-structure. The public predictably enjoyed it, while the critics—especially Lawrence Gilman and Samuel Chotzinoff—assumed a frankly sceptical air. Frequent European tours now became necessary to supplement the composer's income, and these proved almost farcical in their repetitiveness. When his manager once cautioned him that large numbers of ticket-holders at one concert had paid to hear the great man give one of his solemn renderings of the infamous Prelude in C sharp minor, Rachmaninov answered stoically: 'I do not need to be reminded of my duty.' Aside from such minor ventures as the *Corelli Variations*, nothing else in the way of composition was heard from him till 1934, when the far-acclaimed *Rhapsody on a Theme of Paganini* unexpectedly appeared. Bruno Walter gave the New York première with the Philharmonic (it had first been tried out in Baltimore) with the composer himself at the keyboard. Not surprisingly, it did well, since of all the composer's works it is the most contemporary in style. The motor rhythms and driving percussive techniques of the new Russian school make a brief appearance, though the presence of the mournful *Dies Irae* theme (as well as the one Schumann, Brahms and now Lutoslawski appropriated from Paganini) shows how strongly the Old Russia was still beckoning to him even at this late phase. The Third Symphony (1936) and Symphonic Dances (1940) brought the composer's canon to an end without further changes of style, mood or musical apparatus, and at the time of writing they are comparatively seldom handled by orchestras in any country.

What moral, if any, can we draw from the life of a man with Rachmaninov's staggering gifts and withdrawn temperament. That, as in the case of Duparc, psychological obstacles will in the last resort rob an artist of all chance of fulfilling his potentialities? That the artist, even if he is not a natural revolutionary, cannot afford merely to stand still? That it is impossible to achieve success —real success—on more than one plane? All these are possible explanations for the composer's ultimate failure. Yet it is surely wrong to assume from them that Rachmaninov was an insincere figure, a man out for cheap acclaim at all costs, who found it did not pay in the end. On the contrary, it was his very sincerity—accompanied by a certain wrong-headedness—that led him to acquiesce in the fact that he had been born out of his time. It is sometimes said by historians: 'The hour brings forth the man'—citing cases like Robespierre's or Lenin's to illustrate the point. But the opposite often occurs too, and people make their entry on to the stage of history a trifle early or late. Musically, it would have been better for France, for instance, if both Berlioz and César Franck had been born twenty or thirty years later than they were. They would then have had scope to express the works they were confined to imagining. Similarly, it might have been better for Rachmaninov had he been a contemporary of 'The Five' and of Anton Rubinstein. Then he would surely have given vent to the nationalism he was only permitted to reproduce nostalgically. No doubt he could have *attempted* to write in a more up-to-date fashion, and a truly insincere composer would have done just that—and reaped the usual bouquets from the trend-conscious critics. Rachmaninov preferred to relapse into silence, an action for which he merits respect rather than desecration. Perhaps, in any case, he was not really a composer; in which case he was at least justified in finding this fact out for himself. To me, it is significant that, without expressing a thought for the future of his music, Rachmaninov's last words, as he lay dying of cancer in the Samaritan's Hospital, were: 'My hands! Farewell, my poor hands!'

xvii De Falla in
European Terms

So far we have been using the terms 'nationalist' and 'national' almost as if they were synonymous; or at least we have made no proper attempt to distinguish them. It is therefore high time we became a little more specific in our use of these expressions, so that we may be able to call upon the finer discrimination necessary when discussing the work of musicians of similar nationality but slightly different aims. As we saw in the case of Sibelius, an artist may choose to make use of cultural devices that are only understood completely by the inhabitants of his own nation. He may, moreover, go further and permit these devices to become the means of political sloganeering or tourist attractiveness. On the other hand, all composers have had to begin by working within the styles or forms laid down by their previous compatriots, and it is no limitation for them to retain these styles or forms if they can in some way universalize them; or modify them in such a way as to make them acceptable to a wider world. In this sense, Sibelius moved from being a 'nationalist' composer to being a 'national' composer—though it was questionable whether he ever became the fully universal or cosmopolitan composer that the late Rachmaninov and Stravinsky became. As a matter of fact, this issue presented itself in a more artificial guise somewhat earlier in the history of music. A Polish composer like Stanislav Moniuszko (1819–1872), for instance, had an enormous following in his own country; but he did not create an 'image' of Polish music in the way that Chopin (1810–49) did. Nor, later still, did Leos Janáček (1854–1928) find it easy to add anything to the stereotype of Czech music that Antonin Dvořák (1841–1904) had established before him. This problem of being 'nationalist' as opposed to 'national' took a most acute form in Spain through the work of men like Pedrell, Albéniz, Granados and, finally, Manuel de Falla.

Everyone knows that Spanish music appears to have a distinct flavour which sets it apart from all others. We are told that each province has its separate and characteristic song or dance form, usually taking its name from its place of origin. Andalusia has, for instance, its famous 'cante jondo'—a generic term used to include polo, martinetes, poleares and others—while Aragón prides itself on its lively 'jota'. Thus the terms 'Andalusia' and 'Aragónesa' can mean almost any piece bearing the characteristics common to the region. 'Flamenco' is another such wide-ranging term, usually taken to denote a form of singing in which exists a special use of the appoggiatura or acciaccatura, and in which the intervals may be smaller than a semi-tone. Malagueñas, granadinas, rondeñas, sevillanas and peteneras—once more betraying through their titles their places of origin—are frequently heard in flamenco, which really derives from a mixture of oriental and occidental techniques. Clearly, Byzantine, Arabic and Hebraic influences have each played some part in shaping the musical styles one hears in various parts of that deceptively large peninsula. From the wider European standpoint, very few of these styles are familiar, what *we* mean by Spanish music often turning out to be one of the variants of the 'cante jondo' of Andalusia, commonly regarded as the most romantic of the provinces. It was to this province that Manuel de Falla owed his greatest allegiance, though long periods of his life were spent away from it. But before we examine the form this allegiance took, and the extent to which it became overlaid by non-Spanish attachments, we owe it to ourselves to provide a brief prelude outlining the particular problems that faced Spanish music as a whole at the time he was born (1876) and even delving back into history a little so as to indicate the relationship of Spanish to European music in past ages.

Most people are aware that a golden age of Spanish music occurred in the sixteenth century, with composers like Vittoria rivalling Palestrina and his contemporaries in Italy. But the wonderful choral works of this period had passed, like those of Byrd and his school in England, into something close to oblivion. Hence, in the eighteenth century the major influence in Spain was Italian, the musical Esperanto as far as most European countries went at that time. Domenico Scarlatti, for example, spent forty years of his life at the Escorial Palace in Madrid, where he acted as harpsichordist to the court; while Farinelli, the famous castrato, is known to have sung nightly arias to King Philip V, and even retained his hold on that monarch's successor, Ferdinand VI. By 1768, Boccherini had arrived in the country, he too spending a total of some thirty-seven years there. During that time, his was the dominant musical influence on the courts of Charles III and IV.

In the theatre, the Italian troupes, though at first meeting with comparatively little success, soon became a powerful source of rivalry as far as the native, vernacular entertainment was concerned. With the advent of the grander Italian operas, such local entertainments were put very much in the shade. The reaction to these foreign intrusions, when it came, took two forms. The first was the zarzuela, a kind of Spanish operetta in which spoken dialogue was permitted, and which often descended to rather crude, popular levels. The second was the tonadilla or sung interlude in a spoken play. Both these forms persisted to the point where they eventually ousted the Italian element, at least in the interests of the people; though it should be remembered that a continuation of Italianism may be detected in the work of Scarlatti's pupil, Padre Antonio Soler (1729–83) and in the work of the various musicians who had come under Boccherini's influence. Soler, however, who wrote extensively for the keyboard, was also imbued with Spanish blood and his compositions are therefore not to be construed as mere imitation Scarlatti. Probably Spanish music reached its nadir at the time of the Napoleonic conquest, when no musician of the stature we attach to Goya in art made an appearance.

The first great name to be significant as far as modern Spanish music goes was that of Felipe Pedrell (1841–1922), who lived long enough to absorb most of the knowledge available about previous nationalist styles (especially in the area of folk-music) and also to come under the spell of Wagner and other world-renowned founders of the late nineteenth and early twentieth-century philosophies of composition. By the time Pedrell had established himself, traces of the old Italian influence were becoming rare, and a new self-conscious range of sentiments was beginning to replace them. Though a notable composer, Pedrell's greatest contribution was made through teaching and research. By the end of the nineteenth century, he was the leading scholar at the Madrid Conservatory, where he was carrying out the most exhaustive studies of the various species of folk-song we have briefly described. Slightly younger than Pedrell, and very different from him in temperament, were the two colourful romantic composers Albéniz (1860–1909) and Granados (1867–1916) who, between them, were writing flamboyant piano pieces that owed a great deal to Liszt, but which managed to incorporate in a stylized fashion some of the typical Spanish ornamental and rhythmic inflections so much enjoyed by Western audiences. These composers were doing, in a sense, what Tschaikovsky and Balakirev were doing for Russia—that is to say, presenting the world with a slightly Westernized version of their nation's musical idiom. Albéniz had led a fairly meandering and disreputable life, earning his living as a popular pianist, but late in life he wrote the suite *Iberia*, which is a far more truly wild bit of flamenco in its hard, dissonant virtuosity than anything that had previously appeared from the pen of a serious musician. It influenced both Debussy and Ravel (who was only prevented from orchestrating it by Arbos, who had staked a prior claim) and became the means of preserving its composer's good name at the Schola Cantorum, where he was for a short time a teacher. Granados's contributions came later, principally in the decorative and sombre *Goyescas* inspired by the great Spanish artist's paintings, and he might have continued to be a force in Spanish music if he had not gone down with the Sussex on returning from an American tour.

De Falla, who was born at Cádiz and given early tuition in piano playing by his mother, had more of the scholarly than the artistic temperament—which is not to say that he failed to turn out a true artist. His first real acquaintance with good music came through a hearing of Haydn's *Seven Last Words* at the Cathedral for which they were originally written. After that, he was determined to become a musician, and was fortunate in being put into Pedrell's capable hands at Madrid for his training. While there he also had piano lessons from José Trago. Despite Pedrell's unquestioned influence over him, de Falla struck out on his own in some respects, since he was not altogether convinced that a literal approach to his country's musical forms was the right one to adopt. Without having that taste for the picture-postcard exoticism displayed in Albéniz's early pieces, he remained equally ill at ease with the prescriptions of the extreme nationalists. In other words, he harboured a mild distrust of village music as the basis of art. Certainly he would have disagreed with Bartók who once claimed that a peasant song, perfectly articulated, was as fine a work of art as a Bach fugue. De Falla was really something of a moderate. He was not against folk-music by any means; but he felt something needed to be added to it if it were to amount to anything in aesthetic terms. What he really wanted to do was to write his own folk-music, compounded of native urges and the sophisticated influences he had absorbed from his study of the great masters. To this extent, he would perhaps have applauded the remark Villa-Lobos was once alleged to have made, when he was asked to define folk-music for an interviewer. 'I am folk-music' the ebullient composer of the *Prolo do Bébé* replied, much to his companion's astonishment. But de Falla was never as forthright in his responses as his Latin American counterpart, and was inhibited by the high degree of reserve that is sometimes an aspect of the Spanish character.

Indeed, it may be worth emphasizing from the outset that

de Falla was an extraordinarily shy man—according to Stravinsky 'as modest and withdrawn as an oyster'.[1] In his middle years, he apparently looked painfully fragile and tiny, his skin waxen in colour but possessed of deep, piercing eyes. If he went out, it was never without his funereal, black suit and supporting cane. Lincoln Kerstein once wrote of him:

> He had the fanatic, suppressed asceticism of a St Francis as imagined by El Greco.[2]

In fact he was for the better part of his life an incorrigible hypochondriac who lived in constant dread of catching pneumonia or some other fatal disease. Doctors were seldom very far from his house, wherever he happened to be living, and an hermetic gloom seemed to have pervaded all his residences. His sister so rarely left him that it was said she never had the opportunity to go out and buy new clothes, and during the composer's final years, when he was living in Villa del Lago in Argentina, he could not bring himself to instal a piano in his home. When friends found him one in the nearby town of Carlos Paz, the dusty journey and the prospect of having it removed a distance of seven kilometres was too much for him, and he declined the offer. Facts such as these, while they should not be interpreted to mean that de Falla was half-crazy, indicate what a shockingly nervous constitution he had, what gigantic difficulties he encountered in all forms of human communication.

But as a student at Madrid in the early 1900's, the composer was in all probability at the point of maximum adjustment to life. At any rate, he attended classes without embarrassment and won not only the piano prize, but also the award for composition with his opera, *La Vida Breve*, at the Real Academia de Bellas Artes. This work, as one might have expected, made extensive use of the Andalusian techniques passed on to the composer by Pedrell, and to that degree is probably his most nationalist study. However, there are traces of Wagner's influence to be found in it (especially in the Tristan-like harmonies that occasionally obtrude) and it should be considered a fairly eclectic work to have emerged from Spain at that time (1905). The work's popularity was greatly enhanced by the ballets in Act II, de Falla from the beginning possessing a strong sense of movement and action. This sense was

---

[1] The judgment is again contained in the Russian composer's voluminous memoirs, an indispensable if often biased source-book for character studies of twentieth-century musicians. See *Memories and Commentaries* (Faber, 1960), pp. 80-1.

[2] See *The New Book of Modern Composers* ed. D. Ewen (Knopf, N.Y., 1961).

to reach a peak in the compositions of the middle period, then mysteriously die away in those of the third. One interpretation for this phenomenon is that as the composer shed his nationalist zest he reverted to a more passive style resembling that of the French impressionists. But it may equally have been the case that, as with so many composers, the last period was a period of calm resignation in the face of death, resulting in music full of hesitancy and withdrawal. Anyway, the success of *La Vida Breve* (which was incidentally not *performed* in Spain at this time, having to wait until 1914 for its home première) led de Falla to consider further study abroad. Paris was the choice that straightaway imposed itself on him, and from 1907 till the outbreak of the Second World War he resided in the French capital, learning all he could from such masters as Dukas and Debussy. Ravel also became his friend and was instrumental in getting *La Vida Breve* its first performance in Nice in 1913 and at the Paris Opéra-Comique later in the same year.[1]

The influence of Debussy made itself felt immediately in de Falla's infatuation with new orchestral sonorities. He was very much impressed with the French composer's *Nocturnes* for orchestra and choir, and it was this quietly flowing style that eventually showed up most obviously in his work. He also had no compunction about congratulating Debussy and Ravel on their attempts at 'espagnolerie'. For instance, when he first heard the second of the *Estampes* for piano—the piece called *La Soirée dans Grenade*—he was generous enough to admit that it was the best composition ever written with a Spanish background. This was an utterly astonishing compliment to have conferred, for it testified both to Debussy's mastery of what was essentially a foreign idiom (he had never been south of San Sebastien!) and to de Falla's willingness to judge a piece of music on musical as well as nationalist premisses. Other bits of Hispanic writing, like the preludes *La Puerta del Vino* and *La Sérénade Intérrompue*, he regarded as equally fine and absolutely authentic. It is surprising that he felt no sense of envy about these achievements. One cannot help feeling that he was secretly pleased that someone from outside Spain was at last writing the kind of Spanish music that stood up as music and not simply as either patriotism or tricksiness. The effect of Dukas's tuition was also significant. Not being an impressionist, Dukas wrote heavily-scored brassy music which was nevertheless faultlessly constructed and in the best possible taste. It was he who gave de Falla the equipment to be able to write the strident, climactic

[1] Perhaps it should be emphasized that, in addition to the influence of Pedrell and Wagner, *La Vida Breve* also proclaims a debt to the zarzuela, especially in the style of Francisco Barbieri (1823–94).

music of *El Amor Brujo* (1915) and the other works of the middle
period, which are distinguished by the sweep and brilliance of
their orchestration. These are still the most fetching of de Falla's
compositions, even if we only hear them in the form of suites or
single transcribed numbers for the instrumental virtuoso.

Nights in the Gardens of Spain (1915) is, of course, always heard
complete, though it divides itself into three short sections—'In the
Generalife', 'Distant Dance' and 'In the Gardens of Sierra
Cordoba'. The title sounds romantic enough coming from a
composer already notorious for his austerity. But the music is not
in the least indulgent. It hardly offers us anything resembling
a melody in its entire length. Impressionistic, atmospheric,
evocative—it is all these things without ever rising to the climax it
constantly seems on the point of proposing. Its antecedents are no
doubt the three panels in Debussy's 1900 triptych (*Jeux* had not
been written when the composer began work on it; and it lacks the
dynamism of *La Mer*). It is a tremulous, unassertive piece, neither
classical nor romantic in tone. Unlike in a proper Concerto, the
piano is treated primus inter pares, very much as it is in d'Indy's
Symphonie Cévenole. This last French work is possibly even closer
in form and spirit than any of Debussy's. Evoking as it does the
region around the Ardèches in Southern France, its chief point of
difference seems to be one of dialect. Both d'Indy's and de Falla's
works were forward-looking, prophetic of the tendency to incorporate the piano into the orchestra as just one more addition to the
rapidly expanding family of instruments. Fauré's late *Fantaisie*,
Richard Strauss's *Burlesque* and even *Petruschka* may all be
regarded as having contributed to the same end, which was only
completely fulfilled in such later works as Bartók's *Music for
Strings, Celeste and Percussion* and Stravinsky's *Symphony in Three
Movements*. The dangers of impressionism such as we get in the
Nights in the Gardens of Spain must have been apparent to de
Falla fairly soon after he had written it, however, as they were to
Debussy by the time he had reached his Cello Sonata and Sonata
for Flute, Harp and Viola. The chief danger was that textural
fragments would be so loosely strung together that they would
obviate altogether the need for form. Debussy did not live long
enough to witness the poor face-lifted rococo styles forced into
motion by Cocteau and his disciples in post-war France, and it is
exceedingly questionable whether he would have approved of them.
De Falla, who lived on till 1946, postponed as long as he could the
task of confronting them.

El Amor Brujo (usually translated as 'Love the Magician') was
an opera divided into short scenes, with the gypsy element well to
the fore. Both realistic and surrealistic, it tells the story of a

beautiful gypsy girl, Candelas, who is pursued by the ghost of her dead lover. The setting is in Granada. Her new lover, Carmelo, seems powerless to ward off the evil spirit, so she calls on her girl friend, Lucia, to entice the spectre away. This she is successful in doing, and while the ghost's seduction is completed in a night of dancing and ritual exorcism, the hero and heroine, Cantelas and Carmelo, awake to the prospect of unblighted love. The score itself contains a great deal of de Falla's best-known music—the *Dance of Terror*, for instance, and the now rather hackneyed *Ritual Fire Dance*, which had the original function of casting an hypnotic spell aimed at breaking the power of the evil spirit. That is why so much of the piece turns on repetitive phraseology and steady, grinding rhythms. It is *not* heard to best advantage in piano transcription, despite the stupendous elbow-raised technique invented for it by Artur Rubinstein. Other points to notice in this most forceful of de Falla's works are the fanciful pieces of ornamentation that regularly appear in it, and the expressive use of cante jondo to the swaying accompaniment of oboe and strings. In fact, almost all the Andalusian devices are again brought into play for *El Amor Brujo*, but with the added difference that they are embedded in a thoroughly modern, European orchestral technique. In some ways, the next stage work the composer wrote, *El Sombrero de Tres Picos* (1919), which was a ballet commissioned by Diaghilev, was an advance, since it contained more humour and yet was every bit as skilled in its instrumentation. Based on the play *The Magistrate and the Miller* by Alarcón (the same Hugo Wolf had used for his opera *Der Corregidor*), it turned out to be a witty and sparkling success, full of unforgettable tunes. The miller's 'Farruca', the wife's 'Fandango' and the final 'Jota' remain the best known of these. The introduction of the guitar marked a special departure in the orchestral department, and one could say that this work brought the composer's Andalusian period to a close. It may have been influenced, musically and dramatically, by Ravel's scurrilous *L'Heure Espagnole* (1907).

The *Tricorne*, as it became known in France, was a turning point in its composer's career in many ways. Despite its Spanish theme and instrumentation, it contained a good deal of music that was more or less indistinguishable from that being written by Debussy's successors. When, for example, Stravinsky praised the score on the grounds that its best parts were not necessarily those that were most Spanish, he knew this would be compliment in the composer's eyes. Such remarks, he felt, were helping to rid him of the label 'greatest Spanish composer', which he did not much care for—especially since there were scarcely any others over whom it posed his superiority. De Falla, however, produced a work for piano in

the same year, 1919, which still carried overtones of Andalusia in
its title if hardly anywhere else. This was the *Fantasîa Bética*, a
longish rhapsody in which many listeners can detect no trace of a
Spanish accent. Actually the phrase 'Provincia Baetica' was the old
Roman name for de Falla's native province, and there *are* Andalusian figures in the piece, even vaguely ambiguous reminiscences of
Seville! But the domination of orthodox scales and rhythms
(including some Phrygian modes) is such that the whole work
seemed like de Falla's most deliberate attempt to discover a
flexible, all-embracing style that would be suited to other kinds of
compositions besides the brightly-hued operas and ballets upon
which he had formerly been concentrating. To anyone looking
at this intimidating score—which is seldom played even by
Spanish pianists—there can seem no common ground with the
rippling lyricism of, say, Granados's *Goyescas*. The *Fantasîa* is
difficult in the way Casella's early works are difficult—thick,
dissonant and full of accidentals. It is accordingly quite unfair to
say, as some critics have done, that Spain failed to produce a
Moussorgsky and had to be content with three Rimsky-Korsakovs.
De Falla was not nationalist like Moussorgsky, but he was not, at
least in his post-war works, merely decorative like Rimsky. He was
internationalist and abstract. For pianists who want an easier and
more geographically-orientated introduction to his work for that
instrument, one is inclined to recommend the *Pièces Espagnoles*,
which are at least diverting and full of local colour.

Viewed from the purely mechanical angle, it is remarkable that
a country like Spain ever gave rise to a great tradition of piano
literature. After all, the piano does not react well to the near-
tropical temperatures of Southern Spain, and it must have been a
common occurrence to have the best of them split their sound-
boards or jam their actions through excessive heat and changes of
humidity. Today, the best firms—like Steinway, Blüthner and
Bechstein—go to an immense amount of trouble to insure their
instruments against the sort of damage that was probably regularly
inflicted on them in Albéniz's day. It is thus quite remarkable that
he and his successors should have produced a body of music which,
if it does not quite possess the originality and exquisiteness of that
of the French impressionists, is nonetheless almost unequalled in
the twentieth century for its vitality, richness and exuberance.
Indeed, the whole tradition seems doubly remarkable when one
considers that in the guitar Spain already had an instrument that
partook of many of the qualities of the piano, and was capable of
the greatest subtlety and imitativeness. Yet Segovia and other
masters have, on the whole, found it more difficult to elicit a
genuine guitar repertory than their opposite numbers, Iturbi and

Alicia de Larrocha, have to summon up a quantity of high level piano music. Perhaps the explanation lies with the foundations laid by Scarlatti and Soler, who may have appeared to Spanish piano composers of the modern era in much the same stimulating guise as the clavecinistes appeared to Debussy and Ravel. An examination of all these various styles makes this explanation less rather than more credible, however, since whereas one can see a clear link between, say, Couperin and Ravel (one the latter composer was generous enough to point out himself), it is much harder to see Albéniz, Granados or de Falla as lateral descendants of Scarlatti or Soler. The matter is as enigmatic today as it was in de Falla's day. One can only suggest (and this is borne out to some extent by *social* histories of the piano like Loessler's and Theodore Steinway's) that the piano sometimes succeeded best where conditions were least civilized, it being regarded, in a very positive sense, as an adjunct to civilization This is how it may have appeared to villagers of Southern Spain.

The ending of the War had made it possible for de Falla to return to Paris, but he expressed no desire to do so except in the most cursory and peripatetic fashion. His connections with the well-to-do patrons of the musical life in that city nevertheless provoked him into writing a small work many consider to be his finest. This was the puppet-opera, *El Retablo de Maese Pedro* (or 'Master Peter's Puppet Show'), commissioned for performance at the Princesse de Polignac's private theatre. According to Julio Jaenisch, the composer read deeply into Cervantes to acquire the background for this work, which recounts an episode from *Don Quixote*.[1] The episode is the one in which the Knight and his Squire are entertained in the courtyard of an Inn by a group of puppet players. The story which is enacted for their benefit deals with Don Gayferos and the beautiful maiden, Melisendra. It was an old Spanish tale, familiar enough to students of the country's mythology, but since it had originated in Castile (not de Falla's native province) the composer was obliged to research rather more conscientiously than usual to get his material right. *El Retablo* is an absolutely unique form of chamber opera in that it makes use of a double set of puppets—large ones for Don Quixote and Sancho Panza and smaller ones for the ballad characters. When the Don decides to intervene in the story, at the point where the Moors are about to assault Melisendra, the two sets of characters meet, so that three levels of reality are momentarily reduced to two. The work opens with a long, symphonic prelude—presumably intended to perform the function of an overture. The vocal parts are then dubbed from the pit, a tricky operation which may be one of the

[1] See *Manuel de Falla und die Spanische Musik*, Zürich, 1952.

reasons the opera is so rarely put on. There are some folk-songs
used in it (e.g. the Xmas song), but also much original, modern-
sounding music. An old romance, however, is chosen for Melisendra's reverie in Act II, which marks one of the score's high points.
The whole composition ends with a peroration on the duties of
knighthood, delivered by the Don. Very few performances of this
masterly little work have ever been mounted, one of the most
important being that organized by the American League of
Composers in New York in 1926. It was this effort that placed a
wider seal on it, and it is unfortunate that more countries have not
followed suit.

Among the players of the instrumental section of *El Retablo* was
the harpsichordist, Wanda Landowska, and it was she who proposed to de Falla that his next work should be a Harpsichord
Concerto. Nothing of this sort had been written since the days of
the 'style galant', as they both knew. What led them to decide on
such a collaboration is accordingly rather conjectural. The Scarlatti
influence, which we have already described, was of course quite
prominent in de Falla's mind as in that of all sensitive Spanish
musicians. But we should not forget that, ever since the turn of the
century determined efforts had been made by people like Landowska and her husband to restore the ancient instruments to a position
of prestige, to enjoy them without embarrassment in works in
which they seemed, by virtue of their generally lighter tone-
qualities, better adapted to securing authentic performances. This
was very much the case with the harpsichord *vis-à-vis* the
piano. Landowska had tried every means in her power to re-instate
the instrument for Bach, Couperin and Rameau.[1] From this, it
was only a short step to commissioning new works, and the Concertos of de Falla and Poulenc (who incidentally was also present
at the Princesse de Polignac's party and received a similar invitation from Landowska at the end of it) were among the earliest
attempts to compose modern music for an old instrument. As it
turned out, she was not as pleased with the Spanish composer's piece
as she was with the Frenchman's. The reason is perhaps not hard
to seek. De Falla's Concerto is a typically abstract and dignified
work, lacking a little in joie de vivre. Written in combination with
flute, oboe, clarinet, violin and cello, it confined itself to smaller
proportions than Poulenc's fully-scored *Concert Champêtre*. The
first movement is an Allegro, based on a sixteenth-century song by
Juan Vázquez, entitled *De los alamos vengo, madre*. To follow
comes a Lento, which turns out to be a canonic processional.

[1] See *Landowska on Music* edited by Denise Rideout (Stein & Day,
1966). This selection from Landowska's own writings tells the whole
story of her musicological campaigns.

Finally, the closing Vivace, marked by its sweeping arpeggios and adroit spacing of chords, alternates rhythmically between a 3/4 and a 6/8 metre. Composed in 1923, the Concerto was not performed until 1926—still some years before Poulenc's. Many have disagreed with Landowska and seen it as de Falla's crowning achievement.

The remaining years of the composer's life were painfully uneventful in the musical sense. He suffered a slight withering of the creative faculties not unlike that which had overtaken Sibelius and Rachmaninov. His fame rests on about half a dozen works, despite his having survived to be seventy. What marks him out as slightly special in this connection is that, like his mentor Dukas, he was successful in each form he took up and each one tended to be different. The situation in Spain in the 'thirties naturally helps to explain some of his unproductiveness. Ranging himself on the side of Franco against the Republicans (whose anti-religious attitudes he deplored), de Falla emerged from the Civil War as Spain's most esteemed composer—at least in the eyes of the Government. It rewarded him for his loyalty by making him President of the Institute, the highest honour a composer might receive. But after a year or so in office, de Falla found he could no longer sympathize with the régime. He became particularly disillusioned over the treatment meted out to political prisoners, and in 1939 Jaime Pahissa assisted him to escape to the Argentine, where he remained for the seven years left to him.[1] The province he chose to live in was called Alta Gracia, a district of Córdoba. By this time, plenty of commissions were flooding in from all parts of the world, including England and the U.S.A. But his health prevented him from making much of a start on any of them. Bronchial trouble seemed a persistent source of misery to him, and rather than try and work his way through it he contented himself on the income from about two or three annual concerts he gave in Buenos Aires. The one magnum opus upon which he exercised his talents was a tremendous oratorio called *La Atlántida*, which he certainly worked hard and feverishly upon when he felt fit enough to do so. Unfortunately, it was a longer project than he had time for, and he died in November, 1946, without completing it. However, the sketches he left were extremely extensive, and posed the possibility of completion by another hand. This was eventually what took place, the composer's pupil, Ernesto Halffter spending years of his own valuable career pursuing de Falla's vague directions until he had in his possession something that probably bears a very close resemblance to what might have been written.

[1] For the details, see *Manuel de Falla: his life and works*, translated by J. Wagstaff, London, Museum Press, 1954.

It cannot be one of the purposes of this essay to unravel the problems of original score versus accretion in *La Atlántida*; any more than it was in the brief appendix we attached to the Mahler essay, reporting the work Deryck Cooke put into finishing the Tenth Symphony. Such functions belong to the musicologist.[1] What we still have to determine on behalf of de Falla is the extent to which his musical philosophy cut free from the sources that originally bound it. Machlis has commented: 'De Falla belonged to that group of nationalist composers who felt that their imagination was constrained by the use of existing folk-songs.' This judgment seems to me utterly irrefutable. The composer's Paris period alone lifted him clear of the burdens of national consciousness. As he himself said:

> Without Paris, I should have remained buried in Madrid, submerged and forgotten, dragging out an obscure existence, living miserably by giving a few lessons, with the prize certificate framed as a family memento and the score of my opera in a cupboard.

One is not sure whether the last remark is one to which he should have committed himself; for de Falla had too introverted a temperament ever to have become an operatic composer of the first rank. The works by which he deserves to live are the Harpsichord Concerto, and possibly the little *El Retablo* in which the emotions are scaled down to a level on which he could meet his audience. Even so, it remains interesting to reflect on how inhibited, how unproductive, he really was. Santiago Kastner has recorded that de Falla, in the right mood, could have out-talked a Sibelius or a Vaughan-Williams; while another of his admirers, Massimo Mila, considered him capable of a far wider and larger output. The greatest of all Spanish authorities on modern music, Adolfo Salazar, has on the contrary been evasive and guarded in his evaluation of de Falla's achievements, possibly on account of the political judgments that might be involved. In this sense, the composer may be contrasted with, for instance, Pablo Casals, whose stand against intolerance has aroused far less qualified admiration. In the end, de Falla found his freedom in a different way; in the power he evolved of using or not using Spanish forms in accordance with the purely musical criteria he had acquired. His life-work was the justification of his motto: 'Truth without authenticity.'

[1] A preliminary study is Vincente Salas Viu's 'The Mystery of M. de Falla and "La Atlántida" ', *Inter-American Music Bulletin*, No. 33, Jan., 1963.

xviii The Anguished Itinerary of Bartók

Bartók was not the most prolific composer of his age, but he was so successful in mastering a variety of forms—the String Quartet, the Concerto, Opera, Ballet and the Piano Miniature among them —that it would be sheer impertinence to attempt a thorough summing-up of his musical achievements. As with the other musicians we have relegated to this section of the book, however, he can be profitably considered from the standpoint of nationalism; and more particularly from that of nationalism corrupted by a succession of independent, dissimilar influences. One of these influences is implied in the title of the essay, since no one will dispute that of all the forces to have disrupted national musical life during the first half of the twentieth century none has been more catastrophic than the political exile imposed by two World Wars. This, as we know from the attitude taken up by a moderate like Strauss, eventually led to a crushing of the spirit that had its repercussions on the composer's purely aesthetic and professional standing. When we come to a figure like Bartók, whose nationalism was from the beginning tinged with fanaticism, the story is apt to display complex, rancorous and puzzling aspects of a kind that have so far escaped our attention. It will accordingly be the function of this chapter to estimate the significance of Bartók's agonized journey from the Old to the New World, and incidentally to examine what role, if any, nationalism can still enact in modern music.

Most readers will scarcely need reminding that Bartók was born in Hungary at a time when the Austro-Hungarian Empire was in its heyday. From a very early age, therefore, the composer was subjected to the same rather frivolous tastes as the typical bourgeois inhabitant of Vienna. Because the capital of his country was

Budapest, however, and not the city of the Habsburgs, he was unable to react in quite the same fashion as, say, Schönberg or Alban Berg, who not only inherited a great tradition of serious music but who were fully at liberty to ignore or otherwise expressively adapt the music of the cafés and the streets. This gave them the advantage over Bartók who, on the contrary, was surrounded by people who knew only the lighter Viennese classics (which had no appeal to his rather solemn nature) or the debased 'gypsy-fiddle' styles that the great masters from Haydn to Brahms had occasionally intruded into their music in order to import what they imagined to be a little local colour. As Martin Cooper has said in regard to Brahms, folk-music was treated as a mere form of escapism into which he periodically retreated without feeling any need for scholarship or authentication:

> The hankering after escape in this direction had already showed itself in so staunchly traditional a composer as Brahms who, beside his interest in folk-song and old polyphonic music, showed his 'practical' interest in gypsy music in his 'Hungarian' pieces. These were, in his case, a mere side-show to the main musical spectacle.[1]

The concluding sentence could be made with almost as much accuracy about Liszt, who was fully Hungarian by birth but who had lost no time in becoming a celebrated cosmopolite, far more at home in Paris or Weimar than in the land in which he had grown up. His mature efforts to sound Hungarian were numerous but always mildly corrupted by his desire for widespread acclaim. Apart from the Hungarian Rhapsodies, there are transcriptions of operas by Mosonyi, a Hungarian Coronation Mass, a Hungarian 'Fantasia' and a host of other apparently nationalist works listed in his *catalogue raisonné*. There is even a musicological tome entitled *Die Zigeuner und ihre Musik in Ungarn* (1859), which was issued in Hungarian as well as German, and translated into English by Edwin Evans in 1926. But not only are the compositions more exotic than nationalistic, but the book was devoid of field-work and is apparently ethnologically unsound.

It was against this sort of background that Bartók directed the full force of his animus while a young man. His birth-place had been a little town called Nagyszentmiklós (now included in Rumania), but he had moved about a good deal after his father's death in 1888. Young Béla was only seven when this event took place, and the years of his later childhood and adolescence were spent accompanying his mother to the various towns where she set

[1] The quotation is taken from the author's book *Ideas and Music* (Barrie & Rockliff, 1966).

up in practice as a piano teacher. One of these towns was Nagyszol-
los, in Northern Hungary, and another, Pozsony, the birth-place
of Dohnányi and a very well esteemed academic centre. From
there, the composer at first looked like going on to the Vienna
Conservatory, where he had actually been promised a scholarship.
But Dohnányi's influence caused him to decide after all in favour
of the Budapest Royal Academy of Music, to which he repaired in
January, 1899. In one sense, he had made a sound decision, since
it was this institution rather than the other which eventually became the repository of the authentic Hungarian music he so much
admired. But at the time of his entry to it, the amount of control
exercised by German-trained musicians was immeasurably great.
In fact, nearly all the top posts in Hungarian colleges of music
were held by such men—the Volkmanns, Herzfelds, Koesslers,
Thománs and others. Bartók was thus placed in the awkward
position of having to placate these 'rootless' scholars at the same
time as he was trying to conduct a serious investigation into the
origins and characteristics of Hungarian music proper. Fortunately,
he was not too harshly treated by them, partly because he had
developed into a brilliant pianist of virtuoso calibre and partly because he was naturally shy and unrebellious in the outward sense.

Like many seemingly timid individuals, however, Bartók was a
mass of tensions and hatreds underneath the surface. He had contracted asthma as a child (often brought on by frustrated rage or
some kind of emotional deprivation) and gave every appearance of
being in fragile health. This appearance was to remain with him
all his life, photographs taken at successive stages all showing the
same cerebrotonic, ectomorphic features. Large staring eyes pro-
trude from a seemingly egg-shell skull, while the thin body and
slender fingers proclaim the eternal sensitive scholar. That he *was*
a considerable scholar is not in doubt. But the more emotional
side of him was less controlled and controllable than the ordinary
person might have guessed. For example, he responded in the way
few scholars did to Richard Strauss's early works—especially the
tone-poem *Also Sprach Zarathustra*—so that when he came to
write his *Kossuth* Symphony (1903) he was already committed to
a paradoxical musical philosophy. This was compounded mainly
of authentic Hungarian urges, but also contained typically Straus-
sian expressionist elements. One can hardly help viewing it as a
most curious kind of compromise for Bartók to have reached; since
it was the German influence on Hungary that had been so artistically pernicious. Possibly the ambiguity of the work was responsible
for the rather mixed reception it got from the various professors
to whom the composer showed it at the Academy. Thománs liked
it, presumably because he was fairly sympathetic to the theme—a

Hungarian *Hero's Life* in ten episodes, centred upon the War of Independence of 1848-9. Koessler, on the other hand, objected to the absence of those stock romantic devices found in the music of Schumann's day. It is an interesting comment that he was equally critical of Dohnányi's more 'lush' music, and one can hardly blame Bartók for having been annoyed at this attempt on the part of his teacher to pooh-pooh both the old *and* the new. For all that, *Kossuth* was played at home with gratifying success (Bartók appearing on the platform in national costume) and the following year Richter even went as far as to give it a hearing in Manchester!

In 1905, the composer decided to follow up this modest triumph by competing for the Rubinstein prize in Paris, entering for piano as well as composition. Unhappily, he failed in each of his ambitions, the piano prize going to Backhaus and the judges curiously witholding the composition award, despite their close reading of the *Rhapsody* Bartók had submitted. The effect of the latter decision was absolutely shattering as far as he was concerned. He was roused to a point of fury by it. While no doubt justified in his wrath, the incident shows what a pronounced conceit Bartók had as a young man. Indeed, it was not only as a youngster that it burst forth. All through his life, there were to be episodes marked by the most unlikeable vanity, episodes that did much to offset his obvious integrity and industry as an artist. For instance, he behaved very much like the dictators he professed to despise within the confines of his own household, and was quite indifferent to the sufferings he often inflicted on members of his family. The story of his marriage to Martha Ziegler—a sixteen-year-old pupil— makes distressing reading, so utterly heartless does it seem.[1] Bartók returned to Paris with his bride during the year of their marriage, and while there was considerably less than courteous to many of his hosts. It is true that Vincent d'Indy was rude about his music ('Il faut choisir les thèmes . . .' was his comment on what he saw of it), but other French musicians went out of their way to introduce him to people of influence. However, he declined to renew his acquaintance with Saint-Saëns, and declared that there was only one composer he would like to meet—Debussy. On being informed that Debussy was a horrid man in his personal relations and would probably insult him, Bartók replied 'Well, let

[1] On the day of their wedding, in 1909, he neglected to tell his mother, and after conducting the usual lesson casually remarked: 'Martha will stay. She is my wife.' When Dohnányi—also excluded from the secret —wired his congratulations, Bartok was furious with him for his alleged intrusiveness. In 1923, he got his wife to consent to a divorce so that he could marry another young pupil, Ditta Pasztory, by resorting to the old argument that it was better for one person to be unhappy than three.

him insult me!' Unfortunately, the meeting did not come about, in consequence of which history has possibly been deprived of a memorable exchange. Debussy nevertheless became a profound influence on Bartók; without this influence his music might never have attained wide appeal.

Back in Budapest, the composer had already achieved some of the more mundane aims other men might have found it hard to achieve. For example, he had no difficulty in getting a grant to pursue his folk-song researches. Kodály (who had been slightly ahead of him, gaining his Ph.D. for a thesis published in *Ethnographia* in 1905) accompanied the composer on these trips into the villages which he made, and between them the two men recorded something like 8,000 songs on their 'cylinder phonograph'. It is worth stressing that, even at this early stage, Bartók was not what one might have called a 'contained' nationalist. He was deeply drawn to Arabic music, as well as Hungarian, and his collection in the end included Slovakian, Turkish and Serbo-Croatian melodies. To this extent, there were elements in his outlook that transcended the parochial forms of nationalism and looked ahead to a kind of universalism. For instance, in a letter to Beu he wrote:

> My true guiding idea, which has possessed me completely ever since I began to compose, is that of the brotherhood of peoples, of their brotherhood despite all war, all conflict . . .

Such unexceptionable sentiments are hard to digest from a man who did not scruple to reciprocate the dislike his own 'Hungarian oxen' (his terminology) had for him and his music; and whose vicious attacks on the bourgeoisie ('Let them drown in *The Merry Widow!*') bore all the signs of a lasting misogyny. They seem even more insincere when one reflects on the perverse ingratitude he showed to those Americans who did their best to help him adjust to musical conditions in a new Continent after the Second World War had driven him from Europe.

The other piece of good fortune he enjoyed in Hungary at the time of his collaboration with Kodály was his appointment to the Professorship of Piano at the Budapest Royal Academy. Despite his failure in Paris, he was by all accounts an astonishingly good pianist, both as an exponent of his own music and that of other composers. His Bach was evidently unique for the clarity of the part-playing, while he was enough of a virtuoso to be able to do justice to all the more difficult works of Liszt. His pupils, Andor Foldes and Georgy Sandor, have testified to the remarkable prowess he invariably displayed at the instrument, and he was seemingly more tolerant of the work of interpreters than composers. Foldes has described how he was told by Bartok that his interpretation of the Sonatina (1915) was rather too flamboyant, the work being in reality little more than a string of Transylvanian folk-tunes. Yet his remarks contained little in the way of admonition; the composer willingly granting him the right to play it in his own way and even conceding that it could be made to sound better by being performed with more brilliance than he had intended. Bartók held the post of Professor of Piano from 1907 until 1934, though a good deal of his time was mortgaged to other concerns—composition, folk-music research, and the various aspects of botany and entomology in which he had developed a passionate interest. His second wife being herself an excellent pianist, much of their private life was devoted to the study of duet music for the instrument and the tremendously exciting *Sonata for Two Pianos and Percussion* (1937) was just one of the fruits of their hobby.

A close scrutiny of the music for solo piano will also reveal how incredible was the contribution Bartók made to keyboard writing in this century. Of course, his approach was far more percussive than that of any of the French group of composers with whom he is sometimes bracketed; and the jaggedness of his folk-song intervals made his pieces much less easy on the ear. But an impressionist influence appears in the titles of a great number of his piano works, especially of the middle and later periods. Early works, such as the Bagatelles, Op. 6, have been taken to reflect the impact of Schönberg's *Klavierstücke*, Op. 11—despite the occasional French designation. Similarly, the set of pieces entitled *For Children* (1908-9), though they are roughly contemporary with Debussy's *Children's Corner Suite*, actually take their departure from sources closer to home—namely, the Slovakian and Hungarian idioms perceived in the composer's collection of ethnological finds. What one discovers in them is a persistent pre-occupation with pentatonic scales, Phrygian, Aeolian, Dorian and Mixolydian modes, Magyar harmonies involving chords of the fourth and so on. It is to the sets like *Out of Doors* (1926), rather than the better-known *Rumanian Folk-Dances* (1915) and *Fifteen Hungarian Peasant Songs* (1914-17), that we must turn if we want to see how far Bartók allowed himself to move away from the nationalist obsessions with which he is continuously credited and learn from the more general, European currents of thought about the piano. The 'night music' in the first of these suites is clearly indebted to the innovations of Debussy and Ravel, while remaining quintessential Bartók. Again, in several of the pieces grouped together as *Mikrokosmos* (1926-39)—one called *Melody in the Mists* comes immediately to mind—we can detect the extent to which the composer's ambience was becoming increasingly French and the German influence fast disappearing.[1]

The very same French pressures were brought to bear on the composer's orchestral music, and on the music he wrote for the theatre. The one-act Opera called in English *Bluebeard's Castle* (1911) is a surprisingly early manifestation of what these pressures could result in. Though the libretto was by Béla Balázs (whose communist sympathies were instrumental in getting the work shelved until 1918), the play on which he had based it was the same drama of Maeterlinck's that had attracted Dukas four or five years earlier. What is most interesting about the work from our chosen standpoint is its unmistakably Debussyan orchestration—soft trills, tremolos, slides, a deliberate attempt to blur the texture from time to time, with the woodwind and strings doing most of the work. Apart from this, there is a distinct effort to reproduce in Hungarian the kind of speech-rhythms Debussy had used so undemonstratively in *Pelléas et Mélisande*. Bartók's *Bluebeard* is a similarly subdued, resigned sort of work. Aside from such gruesome effects of the sliding of the doors behind which lurk the various secrets Bluebeard wished to conceal from his Judith (blood, jewels, his previous wives) and the clammy sounds emanating from the dungeons, it is *not* a horrific work. Its object was certainly not to frighten the audience. On the contrary, the moral the opera seeks to get across is that privacy must be inviolable; that to search (either into the past or present of an individual) is to destroy. Kodály was perhaps misleading when he described the work as 'a musical volcano erupting for sixty minutes of tragic intensity'. The tragic intensity is there all right, but 'volcanic' is far too strong a term for what is essentially a composition of unspeakable sadness. Interpretations will continue to vary, some critics regarding Judith as the villainess for her unwillingness to love Bluebeard for what he is, and not to care what has taken place in the past. Others have argued that by denying her the right any wife has to *know* the man she is marrying, Bluebeard himself becomes the domineering and dishonest partner. Whichever construction we put on it, Istvan Kertesz is surely right when he says:

> Essentially it's a drama about the relationship of two people. That is why audiences are always so moved by it. Listen to the music of the Sixth Door, for instance. Tears, tears, says Bluebeard, and one hears the whole sorrow of human life.

[1] For an interesting account of Debussy's influence on Bartók, see the article 'Debussy and Bartók' in *The Musical Times* among the series that journal devoted to Debussy in 1967. This particular article, by Anthony Cross, appeared in Vol. 108, pp. 125–9.

Even the remaining stage-works Bartók wrote—the ballets *The Wooden Prince* (1914–16) and *The Miraculous Mandarin* (1919)—betray, to a marked degree, the pre-occupations of a different man from the rural realist of the earliest songs and the researches. Both reveal the influence of Stravinsky. The former ballet, also based on a scenario by Balázs, invokes fairy-tale elements such as the group of senior Russians known as 'The Five' liked to incorporate into their works. But the technique of invention is much more reminiscent of *The Firebird*. The story tells of a Princess who has fallen in love with a dummy Prince, whose finery and noble bearing have lit her imagination. It then becomes the task of the real Prince (there is always a real Prince, even in the folk-ridden Bartók!) to smash the gallant image that threatens to defeat him. Writing of the skills that went into the work, Halsey Stevens, Bartók's major biographer, says:

> Stravinsky, in *'The Firebird'*, found himself confronted with a similar problem in the representation of natural and super-natural elements . . . Bartók's solution does not entirely parallel Stravinsky's. The Prince and the Princess are, like those in *The Firebird*, portrayed in folklike terms, though not with actual folk themes; *The Wooden Prince* in frenetic, fantastic colours not unrelated to those of Kaschei in the Stravinsky ballet. . . .[1]

By contrast, *The Miraculous Mandarin* is so lurid that it incurred the disapproval of the censors throughout the whole of its composer's lifetime. It describes how a prostitute lures men to her room in the city, in order that they may be beaten up and robbed by the sly thugs who are her accomplices. When a rich oriental is picked up, he refuses to bleed on being beaten. The thugs continue to molest him till the prostitute can stand no more. She then falls in love with her victim, at which point he slowly begins to bleed and die. A frightful 'expressionist' fantasy, *The Mandarin* proved one of Bartók's most cacophonous scores. It has far more in common with *The Rite of Spring* than the works Stravinsky wrote under the influence of Rimsky-Korsakov. Its message is—to use the phrase of a current film-maker—that 'hell is a city'; and can thus be construed as an anti-urban parable. But it also teaches us that love, where it exists, can still triumph over greed.

If *The Miraculous Mandarin* proved too tough for audiences

---

[1] See *The Life and Music of Bela Bartók* (O.U.P. revised edition, 1964). This work is incidentally notable for providing a full bibliography on the composer, including works in Hungarian.

right up until the late 1940's, Bartók at least had some compensation in the fact that *The Wooden Prince* was an instant success. *Bluebeard*, too, was well received in Budapest in 1918, but the communist troubles that city endured for about eighteen months afterwards turned the composer away from the theatre, and even from his folk researches, towards a more encapsulated life at the Academy. For all his protestations in the name of 'the folk', Bartók was not really happy in their company once they emerged from the primeval state in which they had existed in the villages. In this, he was typical of his class, and resembles many of the upper-middle class socialists of today who shrink, Frankenstein-like, at the monsters they appear to have invented. The composer's life during the 1920's was accordingly somewhat uneventful. He engaged in many more recitals as a concert pianist, always with huge success. His interest in chamber-music also reached its peak in this decade, the Third and Fourth String Quartets appearing in 1929. The former was another shrill expressionist work, but the latter marked a new point of departure in its relentless employment of the principle of symmetry. It is almost Schönbergian again in its processing of motives. Neither possessed the slow, lyrical beauty of No. 1, which dated back to 1909, nor even the occasional moments of calm restraint of No. 2 (1917). It is tempting to believe that Bartók's first wife brought out more in the way of warmth and pleasure in his art and character than did the newly-installed Ditta. Certainly the two Violin Sonatas of 1921 and 1922 —which were presumably written on the threshold of his first marriage's break-up—are hard music, both aesthetically and technically, while the Piano Sonata of 1926 represents that more or less continuously fierce onslaught on the instrument that young people today have come to like but which pianists of Rachmaninov's school made a point of shunning. Much the most ingratiating specimen of Bartók's art to have been written in the 'twenties was the popular *Dance Suite* (1924), a bundle of light, rhythmically stimulating movements that rarely fails to delight the most unsophisticated assembly.

The 1930's, being a pre-eminently political decade, saw the commencement of the larger, social sorrows that made the composer's final ten years or so the worst he had ever endured. The decade began promisingly enough from the musical standpoint with the *Cantata Profana* (1930), a work many consider to be Bartók's best. Though a choral composition not designed for the stage, it has characteristics that link it with the ballets. The most pronounced of these is the story element. Another fairy-tale, it repeats the legend of a father whose sons turned into stags and who is narrowly prevented from hunting them down in the forest over which he rules. Serge Moreux, Bartók's French admirer, has placed a political interpretation on the work, arguing that it is:

> . . . a protest against the suppression of liberty by the Hungarian dictator, Horthy.[1]

It has also been regarded as a kind of 'secular Passion', and there certainly seem to be pantheistic, naturalistic features in it that help to give it this kind of dimension. Nature is celebrated at every turn in words reminiscent of the eighteenth century. By this time, Bartók had got to know a lot about physical nature, the plants, trees, animals and insects of the Hungarian countryside. But his understanding of human nature remained almost comically defective, and the brothers in this story amount to no more than a composite of Rousseau's noble savage. It might have done Bartók some good to have read another eighteenth-century writer on Nature, the horrifyingly realistic Marquis de Sade, whose views were not coloured by any misconceptions as to how much brutality the natural world needed in order to ensure its survival. But we must credit Bartók with an amazing gift for simulating the sounds of night. His nocturnes are infinitely more of the genuine article than the graceful salon pieces usually subsumed under that title. The slow movement of the Second Piano Concerto (1931), for example, abounds in wonderful minuscule noises—tiny, whirring ostinati', brief woodwind shrieks, slithering chromatics—all designed to render audible the creatures of the night. Yet, in the end, we are bound to feel that Bartók sought refuge from people in insects, that he was a democrat who blanched at the consequences of democracy.

Whether genuine or false, however, the composer's views on politics clearly differed from those of the Nazis whose territorial ambitions had increased, by the end of the decade, to a point where every country in Europe felt itself threatened. As soon as Austria capitulated, Bartók realized the time had come for him to quit. That he did not do so immediately may be attributed to his feeling of concern for his mother, who was too old to contemplate the upheaval involved. It took her death at Xmas 1939 to convince the composer that he had nothing left to keep him in the Old World. 1936 and 1937 had been great years for him, musically speaking, since they had seen the composition of the *Music for Strings, Celeste and Percussion* and the Violin Concerto No. 2 respectively—both by any reckoning among his very finest works. So that his fame, while still lagging well behind that of previous expatriates like Stravinsky and Schönberg, was now sufficient to elicit offers from abroad, one of which from Columbia University

[1] See the author's *Béla Bartók* (Richard-Masse, 1955).

seemed too strong a temptation to resist. In 1940, therefore, he and Ditta made their way across the Atlantic to America, never to see their beloved Hungary again.[1] Bartók's reactions to the U.S.A. might have been predicted, in a sense, for the stamp of commercialism everywhere to be observed in that country was the precise anathema to which he had drawn attention in Europe. Yet no one could have foreseen the ugliness of the abuse he showered on the single nation which had provided him with sanctuary from the extremes of totalitarianism. Agatha Fassett, whose book relates the day-to-day doings of the Bartóks in their new surroundings, went out of her way to make the transition as smooth as possible, providing a temporary home for the immigrants and handling the difficult chores involved in importing their music, furniture and precious belongings from Europe.[2] The response to her efforts was frequently acrimonious, and one cannot help believing that Bartók took out on her many of the contemptuous sensations he found welling up in himself as a result of his acquaintance with the country as a whole.

Though his appointment at Columbia (a research associateship which involved the classifying and cataloguing of that university's large collection of mid-European folk music) was originally set for six months, its tenure was in fact extended to the point when Bartók died. It is true, the stipend was not a very handsome one, and during the moments when it looked as if it might be withdrawn the couple were rendered frantic by the thought of possible poverty. As it was, they could not afford a grand apartment, and the second piano which they had for duet work (they possessed a baby grand and a small upright) was re-possessed by the finance company from whom they had acquired it, leaving them without the possibility of practising for concerts. In any case, Bartók's music was still very much disliked for what seemed to be its harshness and noisiness ('Bartókery' was the name the prejudiced James Agate gave to all modern music which rose to higher than average decibel levels!). Accordingly, nearly all the American orchestras declined to include any of his works in their pro-grammes. This must have been a terrible blow to his pride, as well as his finances. It stands to his credit, therefore, that he still went on composing. Undoubtedly the most inviting prospect he was offered was to write a Concerto for Koussevitzky for a fee of one thousand dollars. This was in the summer of 1943. But by that

---

[1] Actually, Bartók himself returned, very briefly, from a preliminary visit he made to the U.S. in April, 1940, to give a concert with Szigeti, and he and Ditta did not make the final crossing till the October.

[2] *The Naked Face of Genius* by Agatha Fassett (Houghton-Mifflin, 1958).

time Bartók's fatal disease (leukemia, or cancer of the blood cells) was beginning to affect his health, and he was having to spend periodic spells in hospital, a factor that imposed an additional financial burden. In the end, he completed the work and called it his *Concerto for Orchestra* (1944). It was performed triumphantly in Boston in the December of that year, and has remained a staple work in the repertory of all the larger orchestras. Admirers of the more severe Bartók (and the composer had admirers in most countries by this time—Walter Wiora, Willi Reich, John Weissmann and Colin Mason being only a few) are apt to consider this work too popular, having made the same complaint about the other American compositions like the Piano Concerto No. 3 and the unfinished Viola Concerto. Without doubt, it is easier to assimilate than nearly all the products of the 1920's and '30's.

Considered from the standpoint of our thesis that Bartók gradually moved away from nationalism towards a complex universal language, it is simpler to claim that the *Concerto for Orchestra* and the other American works are sophisticated and eclectic to a degree the composer would never have tolerated in his youth. The Concerto, though it has moments of national ruggedness, is really an orchestral showpiece which, by turning the beautiful Hungarian theme of the Intermezzo into an essay in nostalgia, converts a living tradition into a mummified corpse. Moreover, the parody of Shostakovitch (a composer whose formalist betrayals Bartók regarded with contempt) hints at that sort of chi-chi banter only to be found in musicians whose orbit is essentially professional, if not commercial. Hence, Bartók succumbed, to a greater extent than he realized, to the forces he began by vilifying. The Third Piano Concerto (1945), though less of a blatantly virtuoso work, concedes almost as much through the translucent delicacy of its orchestration and the gentle, Ravellian contours of its piano writing. This is not to say that such works are sub-standard Bartók. It is merely that they are a far cry indeed from the Bartók of the *Allegro Barbaro* (1911) or the *Fifteen Hungarian Peasant Songs* (1914–17). But the more one examines the composer's output as a whole, the more one appreciates that these concessions to popularity and cosmopolitanism were already apparent in much of the music he had written in the final years in Europe. The *Divertimento* (1939), for example, is as 'written down' as anything that came later; while a comparison of the two last Quartets (1934 and 1939) shows an almost unaccountable stylistic gap that cannot be explained away by reference to the encroachment of war and the increasing need for human solidarity. Again, it is arguable that the Sixth is the finer work; but to say that it is the more Hungarian of the two is surely to be in error. Perhaps what Bartók eventually arrived at was the 'measured balance' he confessed to desiring. But one is left with a large question mark when asked to appraise his complete development as an artist.

The composer's death came very much as predicted. The progress of his disease had become so marked by the end of the war that there was no possible likelihood of his returning. On September 21st, 1945, after having abandoned the Viola Concerto commissioned by William Primrose, he was moved from the small apartment on 57th Street to the West Side Hospital, where he died five days later.[1] What his life has to tell us is not easy to spell out in simple phrases. To understand it fully, we first have to ask ourselves a host of questions to which it is possible there will never be straight answers. Did he, for instance, really *want* to write his later works, or were they, as happened in Prokofiev's case a sacrifice to 'the bitch-goddess, success'? What moral are we to draw from the fact that Bartók loved Hungary, yet Hungary (as he himself knew only too well) continued to prefer Franz Lehár? Is it possible that Bartók lacked both the philosophy and personality to be the major figure he strove to be? Colin Wilson, in his perceptive essay on the composer entitled 'The Tragedy of Bartók' (reprinted in *Colin Wilson on Music*, Pan, 1967), asks:

> . . . How far is it necessary for a great composer to be a great man? The self-evident answer must be that a great composer *must* be a great man in some sense, since a composer is a human being, or an aspect of one.

I think this point has been appreciated, to a certain extent, in relation to Strauss, but (though it is a dangerous game to play) it is tempting to embark on it when it comes to one or two other modern composers. Bartók is one of the chief cases one might consider. It is not so much that, like Strauss, he failed to be heroic and slid into a disastrously commonplace way of life. Rather, he represents the case of a man who perhaps did not realize the full implications of folk-culture in an age that has long recognized a split between mass tastes and others. The fact that attempts are now being made to heal this split (cf. Mr Pleasants's comments in the Introduction) has not yet proved a justification of Bartók's particular solution; unless one happens to enjoy the ease of a middlebrow, mid-oceanic civilization, one that Bartók himself, the real Bartók, would scarcely have welcomed.

[1] The Concerto was completed by Tibor Serly, a pupil, after Bartók's death, and is now a regular, if disputed, item in the repertory.

xix Stravinsky as Littérateur

Notwithstanding the alliance proclaimed between music and literature, it must seem to the historian that the arts have always been a rather specialized business. Just as it is hard to think of many novelists or poets to whom music was anything but an innocent diversion, so it is easy to comb practically the entire history of Western music without bringing to light more than a handful of composers who really excelled at the art of writing. Schumann, Berlioz, Wagner, Debussy—these certainly displayed a rich and vigorous penmanship, as varied in style and subject-matter as their respective musical leanings. Yet the pressures that led them to write rarely seem to have been purely literary. Often inspired by a desire to publicize the work of one of their idols—in Wagner's case himself—their writings in the main served merely to extend the range of musical polemics in which they indulged. It is true that numerous great musicians expressed themselves nobly in their correspondence, but letter-writing was so much a standard part of previous cultures as to belie any special claim to status. What is missing from the personalities of most literate composers is any ambition to be recollected in and through their writings—if you like, any hint of that deviousness by which the bookman has traditionally attempted to fix his image for posterity. It is only with the carefully edited conversations of Igor Stravinsky—demolishing any Boswellian pretensions on the part of his disciple, Robert Craft—that we first recognize this element of calculation in a member of the musical élite.

Perhaps it should be reckoned typical of those who have attained both distinction and longevity to spend their declining years worrying about the place they will occupy in history. Elderly reserves were not meant to withstand the strains of adulation, and the temptation to anticipate history's verdict is one that frequently appears insufficiently resisted. This demands a tightening of sceptical resolution on the part of the reader, who must remain constantly on his guard against any tendency to subject life to a touching-up process and who must be able to detect at once when wish-fulfilment is beginning to displace a regard for the truth. Having made these things clear, it would be ungrateful to regret that the habit of self-portraiture has implanted itself on such a lavish scale in the man who is the greatest musician of our times. The five volumes Stravinsky has given us in collaboration with Mr Craft, along with the much earlier *Chroniques de ma Vie*, not only survey the twentieth-century musical scene in unprecedented richness and depth, but also furnish us with a series of projective psychological documents, the like of which we are unable to set against the personality of any previous composer. Considered in case-history terms, these documents are easily among the most important a modern artist has seen fit to publish, offering the reader the same sort of challenge he meets when confronted by the Trotsky papers or the Bertrand Russell file.

As with the self-revelations of these great contemporaries, the Stravinsky memoirs do not yield easily to comparative scrutiny. The different formats in which they have appeared make any search for contradictions doubly difficult. The *Chroniques* amount to little more than an academic essay of the kind that has attracted many a non-literary celebrity, being composed of straight narrative interspersed with tactful vignettes of important acquaintances. The succeeding volumes, on the contrary, employ a neo-Platonic style of presentation, and consist of passages of continuous dialogue in which the composer is subjected to questions from his disciple. These passages occasionally culminate in a brief selection of letters and documents which, although printed with the minimum of commentary, often serve as the excuse for a derogatory anecdote or two from the author. Both forms of writing create opportunities for obliquity—the first by the cloaking of facts in a web of belles-lettres; and the second through its deliberate invitation to manipulation. To this extent, the reader of the *Chroniques* is inclined to come away with the feeling that a good deal of literary distance has been put between him and the real emotions of the writer, while the impression left by the *Conversations* (and all subsequent volumes) is that the questions and answers have been studiously rehearsed beforehand. Method apart, however, the two sets of writings can be subjected to a rough process of collation. They describe the same happenings and portray the same characters, with the proviso that the post-war works obviously carry the narrative several stages further and are able, in virtue of their larger bulk, to offer a wider range of musical opinion.

At first glance, it might be supposed that such discrepancies as appear between the early and late memoirs reflect different stages in the composer's path to maturity. This explanation gains credence from the sterner pithiness and rigour of the recent books. But it must be recalled that the composer was well past fifty before he set down the first of his reminiscences; so that these can hardly be written off as the product of a certain amount of callowness. What seems far more believable—and the internal evidence goes a long way towards corroborating the notion—is that during the interval separating his writings Stravinsky devoted much thought to how he might re-shape his profile so that it would fit more neatly the new aspirations he had acquired. That he may even have realized the incongruities that would result from such a plan is suggested by the disingenuous reference to the *Chroniques* that we find on p. 134 of *Expositions and Developments* (1962). In a footnote correcting a mistake made over the location of one of his former residences, the composer blandly states:

> My autobiography and *Poetics of music*, both written
> through other people incidentally—Walter Nouvel and
> Roland-Manuel, respectively—are much less like me, in
> all my faults, than my *Conversations*; or so I think.

While it would be foolish to underestimate the part played by Stravinsky's two ghost writers in contributing to the changes we have been describing—and it is significant that even the admiring Eric Walter White has no hesitation in calling the *Chroniques* a trifle poker-faced—there is nevertheless much more to this casual admission than meets the eye. No one reading the complete autobiographical works can fail to be struck by the contrasting interpretations occasionally put upon the same events; the radical amendments in the portrayal of certain individuals; the many revised musical judgments; and, most of all, the impression of widespread personality-changes having taken place in the author himself. It is to these perplexities, and not to matters of factual detail, that historians of the future would be well advised to address themselves.

Rather than try to assess the significance of Stravinsky's prolonged 'graphomania', let us consider the chief features of the composer's literary persona and comment on the means he uses to to dispense judgment upon his colleagues in the profession. That these aspects are not unrelated may be gathered from asking ourselves how far the former do tend to derive from the latter. One feels immediately on turning to the *Conversations* that there is a

new and sudden deftness of attack in the approach to the composer's rivals, which coalesces into the device used to re-mould
those temperamental characteristics with which he had become
dissatisfied. The scathing, jaundiced façade he offers us in the
later books is a superb literary invention that cannot help contrasting with the timid and slightly cowed image that peeps out from
innumerable early photographs. It is hardly a secret that the composer's exceptionally short stature and crabbed looks combined to
render him painfully self-conscious while a young man. Though
he makes scarcely any reference to the fact in any of his books, it
is obvious that he must have been the butt of those mindless but
handsome extraverts who went to flatter and abet Diaghilev in the
years just before and after the First World War. One can scarcely
avoid the conclusion that in discovering himself as a writer
Stravinsky at last hit upon a weapon with which to strike back at
those who had made fun of him. Tamara Karsavina, who had
always been sympathetic and understanding towards the composer,
has described in her own memoirs how 'spontaneous and primitive'
his gestures often were; and how his body 'seemed to vibrate to the
rhythm of his own music'—each of these characteristics standing
in sharp contrast to the figure of the spectacled dandy he otherwise
presented. It is hard to avoid acknowledging a similar dichotomy
between the writer and the patriarch of more recent times.

A perfect illustration of the pent-up force that seems to expel
itself from the post-1959 writings can be found in the treatment
accorded to Diaghilev himself. The relationship between this
great musical impresario and his compatriot was unusually complex and ambivalent; that no one would deny. In the *Chroniques*,
it is clear that, despite their eventual rupture, the bonds that
linked the two men received preference in Stravinsky's thinking.
His account of the grief he felt on learning of Diaghilev's death
from diabetes forms one of the few moving episodes in that otherwise dry narrative. 'His loss moved me so profoundly that it
dwarfs in my memory all the other events of that year' is how he
expresses his reactions. Again, a few pages later, he adds: 'What
a terrible void was created by the disappearance of this colossal
figure, whose greatness can only be measured fully by the fact
that it is impossible to replace him.' Finally, he echoes the words
of the painter, Constantine Korovine, who had once gone up to
Diaghilev and thanked him merely for being alive. These effusive
sentiments are hard to reconcile with the remarks contained in
the chapter, 'Diaghilev and his Dancers', which forms part of the
later *Memories and Commentaries* (1960). Here the emphasis falls on
the showman's 'abnormal psychology', his 'odd and impractical
ideas', and the 'indomitable sexual prejudice' with which he judged

the talents of his entourage. He is moreover described as being 'self-destructively vain' and 'in no sense an intellectual'; while practically a whole paragraph is devoted to mocking the poor man's fear of death. It does not take much acumen to observe that it is Stravinsky's own fears which are most in evidence in this undisguised volte-face. Having spent his entire early life being subservient to Diaghilev's slightest whim, it has taken him thirty years to pluck up the courage to get his grudges off his chest. The pattern of this episode is not untypical of Stravinsky's manner of reacting. It can be seen duplicated in the responses made to other key figures. The generous praise accorded to Prokofiev, Auric, Milhaud and Poulenc in the *Chroniques*, for example, is belied by the contemptuous dismissal of all later Diaghilev protégés in the books that follow. It would be simple to collect similar instances from among the various scenic artists and ballet-masters belonging to the company, most of whose portraits take on increasingly garish and sordid colours as time goes by.

Much less spite seems to have been evoked by the older generation of Russians, those under whom Stravinsky pursued a smooth tutelage in the years before the Revolution. The sketches of Rimsky-Korsakov, Liadov, Tschaikovsky and Arensky are uniformly loving and respectful, proving that the composer's scornful attitude to his fellow artists is in certain cases permanently relaxed. The Tsarist musical world clearly provided Stravinsky with the stability and calm appreciation of which he felt himself so abruptly deprived in his years of exile. It is fascinating to speculate on how far the chameleon-like tactics displayed in the composer's later career can be attributed to the feelings of insecurity he experienced following the death of Rimsky-Korsakov. Without question, it was the passing of this liberal father-figure— and the elevation in his stead of the reactionary Glazounov—that first gave rise to acrimony in the young man. The menace of Rimsky's successor seems to have haunted Stravinsky throughout the bulk of his long life, even appearing as a spectre at the feast during the composer's recent acclamations by the Soviet. What was it that he so abominated in Glazounov? And how much of this hatred was retrospective? The *Chroniques* again refer only to an innocuous sort of conservatism, such as any young genius expects to find in the person of his Conservatoire director. Indeed, on p. 22 of the Norton library translation of this work there is an astonishingly laudatory reference to the man who, more than anyone, seems to have been the composer's all-time arch enemy:

Glazounov reigned supreme in the science of the symphony. Each new production of his was received as a musical event of the first order, so greatly were the perfections of his form, the purity of his counterpoint and the ease and assurance of his writing appreciated. At that time, I shared whole-heartedly this admiration, fascinated by the astonishing mastery of this scholar. It was, therefore, quite natural that side by side with other influences (Tschaikovsky, Wagner, Rimsky-Korsakov) his predominated, and that in my symphony I modelled myself particularly on him.

Yet by the time we reach the *Conversations* (1959) there are indications of a change in Stravinsky's recollections of his attitude. On p. 37 of this book the composer recalls having attended the première of a Glazounov symphony, and adds: 'I was not inspired by this concert.' In the few asides contained in *Memories and Commentaries*, he carefully completes the process of denunciation.

One important clue to the mystery may be sought in the attitude of the Rimsky-Korsakov family. Stravinsky tells us that while attending the funeral of his teacher, Rimsky's widow came up and said: 'Why so unhappy? We still have Glazounov.' This rather dreadful remark cut deeply into the young man's consciousness. Equally traumatic seems to have been the action of Rimsky-Korsakov's son, Andrei, who turned the family's affections away from Stravinsky in the years that followed his father's demise. It followed that Glazounov came to occupy a central position in their admiration instead. This process took some time to become apparent, however, and perhaps only became clear to the composer after he had written *The Firebird* in 1910. Probably the buffetings the composer's reputation underwent during his French and American expatriation drove him to take an increasingly embittered view of the break-up of his Russian idyll. Robert Craft, when reporting the events of Stravinsky's homecoming in *Dialogues and a Diary* (1968), was taken aback by the force of patriotism still left in the composer. This aspect of his character also came as a shock to those critics who had rejoiced at the anti-Soviet sniping in which he had formerly indulged. It must have cost Stravinsky a real effort to admit to such feelings, especially when he encountered Glazounov's hated visage looking down at him from a plaque of honour—a sign that the academicism against which the composer had unsuccessfully inveighed forty-eight years earlier was still in the ascendancy. These occurrences show conclusively what a complex amalgam of national and musical sentiments must have raged in Stravinsky's breast throughout the greater portion of his career. Anxious to recapture the serenity of his Czarist days, he was nevertheless too clever not to

have recognized the formalist betrayals in which they had culmin-
ated; while his disgust at Soviet materialism did nothing to lessen
the nostalgia evoked by the prospect of his native land. To have
lived so long and productively in the presence of such a conflict
adds further testimony to the composer's reputation for endurance.
Lesser men would have relapsed into impotence.

In view of these revelations, it should not surprise us to discover
that other and younger Russian composers, including some who
belonged to his own generation, are generally turned into objects
of Stravinsky's denigration. At all times, the author of *Memories
and Commentaries*—the book where these tirades are mostly
located—implies that he stood as a lion amid the jackals. His
savaging of Scriabin, Rachmaninov and Prokofiev is partly
provoked by the disdain he has privately reserved for the tribe of
performing musicians. At one time, all the evidence suggested
that this prejudice was being kept firmly under control. Klemperer,
Toscanini, Reiner, Hofmann, Artur Rubinstein and others all
emerge from the earliest memoirs with a refreshingly clean bill of
health. In the later volumes, however, there is hardly a single
unbarbed reference to them or their profession. The *Expositions*
puts forward the theory that composers are alone competent to
wield the baton; all others are jeered at as 'those pathetic people,
the career conductors'. The same scoffing attitude is bestowed on
pianists, even the best of whom are not infrequently found to be
blockheads. Some of this disenchantment no doubt has its genuine-
ness, reflecting the composer's justifiable impatience with those
who have continued to manhandle his scores. But it is also well
known that Stravinsky has been irritated by his failure to maintain
a succcesful dual career, his ventures as conductor or pianist
never having met with public approval. Hence, one suspects a
touch of envy in the remark that 'Prokofiev's depths were engaged
only when he played chess', or the comment that Rachmaninov
was the only pianist who refrained from grimacing at the keyboard.
Even so, it is clear that he does not think much of either of these
men as composers. His evaluation of the latter is as patronizing as
we should expect, given the great popularity of his music with the
ordinary concert-goer. Scriabin seems to have aroused his animosity
for different reasons, no less personal one would imagine. (There
is some evidence to suggest that his mother alienated him by
believing that her son never quite attained Scriabin's particular
eminence among the White Russian class.) Unable to denounce
this composer for being popular in both East and West, he is
forced to fall back on abuse, saying that his music is 'bombastic'
when what he means is that it is different from that of the neo-
classicists or serialists he admires. Many of these judgments

strike a crude note in view of the composer's expressed ideal of objectivity.

What nevertheless raises Stravinsky's memoirs so much above the level of petulance, placing them on a higher literary pedestal than anything written by his competitors, is their almost unbelievable cultural self-assurance. It has been claimed that the composer's obsession with the stylistic exercise lays him open to the charge of dilettantism as a musician. If this is true, it only remains to suggest that this offence has quite definitely enriched the character of his writings. The devouring curiosity Stravinsky displays about art, literature, philosophy, architecture and religion —to say nothing of the globe-trotting in which he is well known for indulging—renders what he writes astonishingly catholic in tone. There is no other musician whose writings do not seem provincial by comparison. It is not simply that the composer has made friends with virtually every important artist and thinker of the last fifty years, but that he has clearly been able to keep up with each and every one of these illuminati on their own subjects. Having inherited his father's love of books, he had already read Shakespeare, Dante and Tolstoy in his 'teens; going on to acquaint himself with Gorky, Dostoievsky, Ibsen and Strindberg during his university years, which were ostensibly supposed to be devoted to law. This capacity to be fired by literary enthusiasm has never deserted the composer, since his house in California contains whole shelves given over to modern writers like D. H. Lawrence, T. S. Eliot, W. H. Auden and Dylan Thomas. Moreover, his mastery of French and German has enabled him to get to grips with the works of André Gide, Paul Valéry, Thomas Mann and Franz Werfel, all of whom rated among his friends in the 1930's and after. A brief glance at the roll of his literary collaborators would put most other musicians (except, perhaps, Britten, about whom he has recently been typically snide) to shame.

Such an enviable background in the written word goes far towards explaining the peculiar virtuosity of Stravinsky the writer —a virtuosity it would hardly be too fanciful to compare to that of his fellow-exile, Vladimir Nabokov. Naturally, there are no obvious links between the styles of these sceptical ex-Russians beyond their common asperity of tone. What marks them out as special is that each has endeavoured to transcend the basic aim of communication, coming to look upon their adopted language much as a gymnast might look upon a new and challenging piece of apparatus. In Stravinsky's case, it is incredible that English seems to have been his fourth modern language. Unlike Nabokov—or for that matter, Joseph Conrad, another case of total assimilation— Stravinsky has steered clear of the pitfalls of mandarin prose. His

diction is neither elaborate nor highly-tinctured. The only form
of conceit he permits himself is a slight but recognizable preference
for the pun—a common weakness in experienced linguists. Otherwise, his skills are not in the least ostentatious. They reside chiefly
in the wit and trenchancy in which even his most casual observations are clothed. Whether he is describing the odours of old St
Petersburg, the warblings of Adelina Patti, the colour of the mayon-
naise at one of Lord Berners's luncheon parties or the exact extent
of d'Annunzio's baldness, there is the same swift, economical
concentration on the essence of what he was trying to convey. A
good specimen of the author's deadpan manner can be seen in the
quick thumb-nail sketch he does of the stage-designer, Léon
Bakst, contained in the *Conversations*:

> No one could describe him as concisely as Cocteau has
> done in his caricature. We were friends from our first
> meeting in St Petersburg, in 1909, though our conver-
> sation was largely Bakst's accounts of his exploits in the
> conquest of women, and my incredulity: 'Now Lev . . .
> you couldn't have done all that.' Bakst wore elegant hats,
> canes, spats, etc., but I think these were meant to detract
> from his Venetian comedy-mask nose. Like other
> dandies, Bakst was sensitive—and privately mysterious.
> Roerich told me that 'Bakst' was a Jewish word meaning
> 'little umbrella'. Roerich said he discovered this one day
> in Minsk, when he was caught in a thunder-shower and
> heard people sending their children home for 'Baksts',
> which then turned out to be what he said they were.

Most of Stravinsky's qualities as a writer are present in that
passage—his disbelieving tone, the wicked power of depiction he
possesses, his willingness to be side-tracked by some quite bizarre
piece of intelligence.

How do those qualities reflect on the author's activities as a
composer? Once again we are brought into contact with the more
tangible, inescapable aspects of the musician's existence, those the
inspirational type of composer would not consider worth mentioning. We are told, for instance, exactly how the germ of an idea
implants itself in the composer's mind, after which he is used to
experimenting with various 'building materials' drawn from his
vast library of classical scores. Only when the theme is clearly
conceived, and the form decided, does Stravinsky set about the
real business of composition—an activity he equates with 'further
expansion' and 'organization' of the material in hand. This he
usually undertakes at the piano, believing that nothing can replace
the actual physical sounds made by the notes. Sometimes, as

happened during the composition of *Le Sacre du Printemps*, the composer finds himself unable to discover the correct notation of what he has been playing. When this occurs, prolonged trial and error follows. Often he has to use the well-known aids to musical calligraphy contained in his meticulously-organized workshop. These include a wide range of coloured inks, his famous 'Stravigor' ruler (a device for drawing the lines of a stave), numerous timing aids and all manner of pens, pencils and engraving tools. Not only is the reader frankly invited to inspect this method of working, but he is drawn into a lengthy debate on musical resources. Electronics, stereophony, aleatory composition, the use of quarter-tones, Klangfarbenmelodie—all these twentieth-century techniques pass quickly beneath his gaze, each being summed up in a brisk, epigrammatic phrase. There are even drawings, reproduced in the text of the *Conversations*, which aim at clarifying the music of Bach, Wagner, Webern ('a perpetual Pentecost') and Stravinsky himself. All this stands in marked opposition to earlier musical memoirs, in which technical discussion was generally put aside in favour of vague, spiritual exhortation. It is only necessary to recollect how much more pompous and inflated were the 'confessions' of the German romantics to appreciate that, for all his prickly self-esteem, Stravinsky's way is the humbler.

This conclusion is re-inforced by every encounter the reader makes with the composer's religious spirit, never far from the surface when he is enumerating the trials of his vocation. Asked what role religion has played in his life and work, Stravinsky confesses to the many puzzling divagations his critics have noticed in the attitudes he has taken up towards the Church. It is common knowledge, for example, that the composer renounced all religious affiliations from the time he left the gymnasium till he reached the age of forty. Moreover, when he did decide to re-enter the Russian Orthodox Church, he did so with hereditary or linguistic reasons in mind, and not out of any sense of theological conviction. There is even the paradox that he afterwards wrote a Roman Catholic Mass. To all these lapses, Stravinsky has little in the way of contrition to add. Yet he remains certain that his inspiration is rooted in religious emotions. How can we account for this apparent contradiction? In the first place, it is clear that, as with his friend Erik Satie, there is a quasi-religious distaste for worldliness in the composer's thinking about music.[1] His efforts have always been directed against relapsing into mere brio. More obviously, he harbours a distinct nostalgia—which never becomes

---

[1] This common unworldliness hardly extends beyond the musical plane. Satie, who was nicknamed 'Monsieur Pauvre' was known to have turned down commissions because the fee was too high; whereas in

self-pitying—for the disciplines which used to be imposed by the church on its musicians. As he himself has put it:

> Whether or not the church was the wisest patron—
> though I think it was: we commit fewer musical sins
> in church—it was rich in musical forms.

Part of that acerbity one detects in the composer's attitude to his fellow musicians seems to have its origin in his awareness of the slow betrayal in which most of them have concurred. Not that the musician is invariably made to take the blame; the church, too, is sometimes condemned for the ignorance of its attacks on the polyphonic tradition. But when it comes to deciding whether or not to draw back from religious authority, it is quite patent which way the composer will jump. Unlike Beethoven, the music of humanity offers him small consolation.

It would be presumptuous to suppose that our observations have provided more than an assortment of keys by which to continue the task of probing the composer's character. Contradictions will probably be evident for a long time to come. These, if they do not succeed in exploding the stereotypes that have already gathered about the figure of the composer, will at least pose the possibility of a final image very different from the one many of us now hold. It will include the idea of a cosmopolitan who excoriates every reference to the sleek and mondain standards of the cultural establishment; an orthodox churchman who cheerfully vituperates against a sizeable portion of mankind; a patriot who jealously reserves to himself the right to criticize his own country; and, most apparent of all, a vigorous elder who finds nothing undignified in acting out the role of a perpetual pupil. Each of these pairs of irreconcilables contains an unfashionable element, even a hint of some deliberate perversity. The single quality no critic would want to deny this phenomenal musician is his hawk-like artist's acumen which, like that of Crispin in the poem by Wallace Stevens, seeks:

> To drive away
> The shadows of his fellows from the skies,
> And from their stale intelligence released,
> To make a new intelligence prevail.[1]

Stravinsky's case the reverse has not been unusual. In the case of *Sports et Divertissements*, it happened that each composer was approached independently, and the difference in the fee demanded was allegedly enormous.

[1] *The Comedian as the Letter C* by Wallace Stevens, from the *Collected Poems* (1955), published by Faber & Faber.

xx Martinů and the Brotherhood of Man

Ever since Beethoven set to music Schiller's *Ode to Joy* as part of his Ninth Symphony, composers have dallied with the idea of using their music as a means of uniting the peoples of the world, of strengthening in a more fundamental fashion those commercial or professional ties we normally consider as the cement of human relations. In the series of television lectures he gave for the B.B.C. on the theme of *Civilization* in 1969, Sir Kenneth Clark singled out Beethoven and Byron as the two nineteenth-century artists who never renounced their belief in man, his right to dignity and freedom. The others, Sir Kenneth suggested, turned away in disgust at man's ever-increasing inhumanity to man, ending by a withdrawal into 'art for art's sake'—or as D. H. Lawrence later expressed it 'art for *my* sake', which is not perhaps quite as unsubtle a philosophy as it sounds. To continue, for a moment, with the case of literature, Sir Kenneth's lectures traced most convincingly the steady decline in optimism that took place between Turner's poem, *The Fallacies of Hope* and Yeats's well-known defeatist sonnet, *The Second Coming*. While music, by its very nature, cannot express such concrete sentiments, it too can be essentially affirmative or negative in its tone, and we have already devoted several essays in the earlier part of this book to showing how men like Wagner, Mahler and Berg spent much of their lives hovering between these poles of acceptance and denial. On the whole, one might even say that, as in literature, the music of the late nineteenth and early twentieth centuries became patently more gloomy as time went on, the most popular works tending to be those written by men who sought to avoid the dilemma. Yet by the pressurized tactics of the Soviet State, musicians were paradoxically made to write joyful music once again, some of it so bursting

247

with solidarity as to sound both vulgar and insincere. The dilemma is accordingly a complex and long-standing one, and it is one to which Bohuslav Martinů devoted a large segment of his energies to solving.

Being born as late as 1890, Martinů reached maturity at the moment when Europe was about to be plunged into a major war, and was all set to follow it by a man-against-man struggle between Fascism and Communism. The gay interlude we know as the 'twenties was never regarded by him as anything more than a frivolous respite from the larger continuation of human dissension which had been a feature of his life almost since he had finished his formal schooling. It will be seen that I am describing an essentially serious man whose wish it was to become thoroughly involved in the great national and political issues of his time. The point is worth making from the very beginning, since the image of the composer that still persists in the minds of many Westerners is that attaching to the writer of *Half-time* (a half-humorous evocation of a crowd scene at an international soccer match between France and Czechoslovakia written in 1918, under the influence of the style Constant Lambert designated as 'Mechanical Romanticism'). Also, the brisk, athletic manner of several of the composer's neo-classical pieces (the Sinfonietta Giocosa is a good example) automatically conjures up a vision of someone rather like a slightly lightweight Hindemith—in other words a conscientious craftsman not too bowed under the cares of worldly strife. The difficulty with Martinů is that the craftsmanlike element is there all right (as the total of some 150 works testifies) but is complicated, in a quite unique way, by deeply spiritual and humane tensions. The evident lack of sentimentality in his music (which rarely displays anything like a Wagnerian pathos) should not be confused with either academicism or jocosity, neither of these latter qualities ever seeming to arouse his approval. Despite the faint suggestion of uniformity which clings to both him and his music, there has never been anyone remotely like Martinů during this century in any country. He was a true individual caught in the mass.

Perhaps it is as well to begin our study of him by reminding the reader of the outstanding characteristics of Czech music in the past—or we should say Bohemian or Moravian music, since the Czech state did not come into existence by that name until 1918. The land now occupied by the Czechs (or at least nominally occupied them, in view of the contemporary control being exercised by the U.S.S.R.) has produced an extraordinary number of fine musicians, and is without question one of the most musical Europe has to show. Besides Smetana and Dvořák, whom we all feel we know, there has been an additional list of composers, many of whom have been every bit as gifted but much less familiar. It includes Stamitz, Richter, Dussek, Tomaschek, Fibich, Suk, Novák, Ostrčil, Janáček, Alois Hába and Weinberger, the last famous for his Polka from *Schwanda* if for nothing else he wrote. These men comprised a tradition that streched back to the eighteenth century in more or less unbroken fashion, and several of them were so cultivated in their tastes as to have given their country a far more cosmopolitan façade in music than was apparent with most other states of Central Europe. Hence, we ought not to think of Martinů's problems as being quite so closely bound up with the nationalist versus non-nationalist dilemma as were those of most of the other musicians we have been treating. Assuredly, he *did* have nationalist problems to worry him, but he dealt with these firmly enough. Weinberger, who approved of a more restrictive philosophy, became his chief obstacle in this sense. But there were long periods in Martinů's life when nationalist questions were brushed completely aside in the interests of his broad, human concerns. What might be profitably emphasized at this point is that most Czech musicians, by the time Martinů had appeared, had developed an expansive, lyrical style of composition, notable for its clear textures and springy rhythms. They clung to this style as often as not as a reaction to the suggestion that they should take their directions from the members of the Second Viennese School. Certainly there was no backwardness in Czechoslovakia, and such research into folk material as seemed necessary had already been carried out by Erben in his comprehensive anthology of poetry and legend. It is true that no one had done for music what Erben had done for the other arts, but recent researches, like those of Racek and Sychra, have revealed that a gradual process of absorption had enabled composers to make free use of indigenous song and dance forms from quite an early stage.

Martinů was born in Eastern Bohemia, in the town of Politschka, where his father was a shoe-maker. One of the most astonishing facts about his childhood is that it was spent in a small apartment at the top of a bell-tower. So that until he was about six, the world must have appeared to him very much as a microcosm, other people resembling tiny dots in a landscape composed of row upon row of featureless cornfields. It was up and down the stone steps of this tower that the composer's hearty father carried him once he had been allowed periodic visits to places outside his home. At the age of eight, it became obvious that he had a remarkable flair for music, especially taking to the violin. This, of course, was an instrument at which Czechs have traditionally excelled, no doubt as a result of its frequent use in village fêtes. At this time,

too, Jan Kubelik (father of the present conductor) was widely
regarded as the world's finest player of the instrument, so that
every young Czech of musical ambitions felt slight leanings in this
direction. Martinů went on to become a renowned violinist and
was leader of the Czech Philharmonic Orchestra for ten years.
Before that, however, he was despatched to the Prague Conservatory, where he was considered a difficult and rebellious student.
Indeed, he was twice expelled from that institution for questioning
the competence of his teachers. It must be said that, from the
outset of his career, Martinů showed little patience with people of
only moderate musical capabilities. He himself was so fluent, so
quick at picking up the rudiments of harmony, orchestration and
the like, that he became bored and jaded at the prospect of listening
to such things being explained in an elementary fashion. When he
had been at the Conservatory for about six years, he heard Debussy's *La Mer*, and the sheer mechanics of this brilliant work convinced him that French composers were probably much better
equipped to teach him what he wanted to know. He continued,
despite this revelation, to remain in Prague, however, winning
prizes for composition but confining his studies more to a private
examination of the scores of Strauss and Debussy. So independent
was he in this habit, that it has sometimes been alleged, not quite
correctly, that Martinů was a self-taught composer.[1]

It was not until after the war that the composer faced the
serious decision as to whether or not he should emigrate to Paris
and participate in a fuller musical life than his homeland was
perhaps able to offer him. In 1923, he made up his mind to go,
becoming the first Czech composer to be a fully-fledged expatriate
in the fashionable manner of the day. For the next seventeen
years, therefore, Martinů was a member of that mixed but on the
whole distinguished colony of artists, writers and musicians which
helped to make Paris such a cultural Mecca between the wars. His
first line of approach (Debussy having died, and Fauré being on
the point of death) was to Roussel, who shared with Ravel the
distinction of being the finest French composer then alive. I think
it fairly obvious why Martinů elected to study under the former
rather than the latter. Roussel, who had taught counterpoint at the
Schola, had the reputation of being an enormously erudite, serious
and yet avant-garde figure. Ravel, on the contrary, was not only
renowned for his flippancy, but had retired to his diminutive villa
at Montfort L'Amaury in the Île-de-France, where he was determined to make himself less accessible to the ordinary visitor.

---

[1] The incorrectness ostensibly reveals itself in the fact that, disengaged
though he appeared to be, the composer also took a brief course of lessons
(typically dropped halfway along) from Suk in 1922.

Besides, he hated teaching, as was borne out by his refusal to accept Gershwin as a pupil in 1928. Martinů accordingly wended his way to Varengeville for guidance from the composer of *Padmâvatî*, or else lingered in Paris in his slightly truculent, self-supporting fashion. Roussel was a revelation to him, as Debussy had been. Never before had Martinů met anyone so capable of turning him inside out, musically speaking, and he was humble enough to be grateful for, rather than irritated by, the experience. The clique he found most objectionable was predictably 'Les Six'. Honegger apart, he found the entire circle wanting in purposiveness. They seemed too intent on pleasing the tastemakers to merit respect. In any case, he had absorbed most of what they had to give before coming to Paris, his ballet *Istar* (based on the same Assyrian legend as d'Indy's variations for orchestra) having had a moderate *succès d'estime* as early as 1922.

The principal works of the composer's French years were cast in the neo-classical style of the late Roussel. Perhaps they were neither so weighty nor so driving as those of his teacher. The Piano Concerto No. 1 (1925) was his first big essay; but it has never proved as popular as the much later Violin Concerto (1941) in which all Martinů's specialized knowledge, acquired with the Czech Philharmonic, was put to practical use.[1] More characteristic were the bewilderingly large numbers of compositions for intimate media—String Quartets, Quintets, Sextets, Violin Sonatas and Cello Sonatas. In addition to these, the composer wrote a variety of works for extended but still relatively small ensembles, like the *Partita* (1931) and the three *Ricercari* (1938). These were eventually followed by his *Sonata da Camera* (1939) for cello and chamber orchestra. Some proved far more lyrical than their titles imply, suggesting that Czech tunefulness was still a factor in the composer's musical make-up. The *Serenade* (1930)—admittedly given a more frankly pleasurable designation—is a surprisingly flowing and ingratiating work to have sprung from the pen of a musician so scholastic as Martinů was then bent on becoming. It might be said of him, therefore, that throughout this phase he alternated uneasily between the severity proposed by the neo-classical idioms he was using and the impulsiveness inflicted on him by his nationality and temperament. With the Debussy influence still inclined to assert itself now and again, Martinů was apt to relapse into a style one jaundiced critic satirically described as 'impressionist baroque'. Yet he was also writing programme music in the 'thirties. But even in 1927 he reverted to the manner

---

[1] Generally, however, Martinů preferred to accept the old Concerto Grosso form, with its assertion of ritornello over thematic development, and its avoidance of the solo instrument.

of *Half-Time* in his *La Bagarre* (first performed in New York by
Koussevitzky) which explored crowd-psychology in music once
more.[1] Similarly, the *Allegro Symphonique* was originally written
as a *Military Symphony* as far back as 1929. By the middle of the
1930's, he was unashamed in his assertion of humanist ideals in
music, and the culmination of this came with his famous *Mass
at Camp* (1940) inspired by the fate of Czech soldiers after
Munich.

It is to the chamber works that we must look for the real Martinů
of the middle period, however, and it must be conceded that they
add up to an impressive and efficiently-written corpus. Players
liked them, since they always seemed to contain parts of interest
for each instrument—this despite Martinů's difficulty in transferring from a homophonic to a polyphonic style. The best
products of his imagination in this sector were characterized by
long, clean melodic lines, strongly kinetic rhythms and a distinctly
expressive quality that triumphed, in the last resort, over mere
technique. Perhaps the worst that can be said about them was that
they employed too much light and not enough in the way of tonal
contrast, using the last term in its non-musical context. One is
reminded of Diaghilev's comment on Prokofiev—a composer who
possessed certain features in common with Martinů. After listening to the Russian's ballet music, the astute impresario said:

> He would not have understood the remark Mallarmé
> made to a man who once congratulated him on the clarity
> of one of his lectures—namely, 'next time I shall have to
> add a few shadows!'

If this seems to contradict what we have formerly said about
Martinů's contempt for the passionate love of 'la clarté' professed
by 'Les Six', then we can only add that whereas they took lightness
as a mandate for humour, and even high jinks, he regarded it as a
straight ideal. There is a difference. I think it is true to say that
Martinů genuinely admired French goût at its finest; but he
considered it as the obverse of German ponderousness and not as
a synonym for mirth. In particular, he was disappointed in the
banal choice of themes of composers such as Poulenc and Auric
(shades of d'Indy here!) and by the aura of artificiality that clung
to the ballet Russe in general. Stravinsky, however, continued
to arouse ambivalent emotions in him, chiefly favourable.

If we may digress for a short while on the nature of Martinů's
character, it must be made clear that at this stage he was firmly
opposed to irony and paradox in music—typical French ingredi-

[1] This time the reactions to Lindbergh's Atlantic flight in the plane
'The Southern Cross'.

ents in the eyes of many. He was also opposed to anything that might set him apart from the common man. Hence, although earnest he was strangely opposed to excessive self-analysis or philosophizing. Music, he thought, should arise out of the subject-matter and should reflect the general experience of mankind. It was not best served by being too infected with personal concerns, neither was it likely to stem from the god of pure artifice. As he once said quite simply and sincerely:

> I do not like placing the creative process under a microscope, to explain a work, to look at the molecules (so to speak) instead of examining the body as a whole.

No one can fail to see how this notion of music as a gestalt or complete pattern helped to place Martinů outside the pale as far as the academic critic was concerned. Then again, his refusal to regard art as something separate from life must have incurred the wrath of those who regard the two as having different objectives. The composer once characteristically remarked: 'No part of the living world can be known by itself alone.' Not only does this presuppose a far more liberal approach to musical education than was current in his day, or even in ours, but it tended to be the sort of remark that misleadingly placed the composer as an upholder of the Mahlerian doctrine that music must be the repository of all the world's troubles including those of the artist. An examination of the work of these two musicians would show, on the contrary, that whereas they might have shared common ground on the general, experiential component, they could never have met on the psychological or personal issue. Not only would Martinů have wished to express his experience in a less naked and undisguised fashion, but he would have preferred to suppress altogether the nightmarish self-pity, the phantasmagoria of the ego, that marked out the great Viennese conductor–composer.

Undeniably, one of art's greatest dilemmas has centred around just this problem—as to whether or not the artist is entitled to intrude or project his own inner compulsions. Renaissance painters and composers subjected their own feelings to religious or universal expression, and often regarded their art as an exercise in pattern-making (albeit on the grand scale of a Raphael or a Palestrina). Later figures, on the other hand, have not hesitated to exchange positions—making their problems the world's problems. A Van Gogh or a Wagner stands out in verification of this habit. Perhaps we should see it as a clear indication of Martinů's answer to the dilemma that in 1956 he wrote a series of compositions entitled *Frescoes of Pierra della Francesca*, dedicated to his friend Rafael Kubelik. For everyone appreciates that this early Italian painter, like the Dutchman Vermeer, seemed to exclude the personal in favour of the universal; making geometry and symmetry do the work romantic artists were subsequently to make over to anguish of line or tension of colour. Yet those who probe deeply into Martinů's style will find its abstractness continually mitigated by human emotion and depth of commitment; presented not in the form of Beethovenian self-assertion or Mahlerian spiritual neurosis but in the form of a global identification with the species. This might lead some commentators to see the composer as a conventional socialist expressing what are more or less undifferentiated sentiments, and there is a faint grain of truth in this assumption. Mankind interested Martinů in the mass, and his ideals moved more towards universal brotherhood than towards feelings of compassion for particular individuals or groups. He looked forward, almost in a Soviet way, to an era of unalloyed progress and happiness for all. While such sentiments have recently gained fresh expression (for instance, through student-worker alliances and the general levelling out of educational differences), they were not as fashionable as might be supposed in the 1930's, when socialism often arose out of a sense of noblesse oblige on the part of the upper-middle classes or out of straight ideology.

Hence, Martinů, despite his pioneering of people's opera and his ready acceptance of the amenities designed to bring about cultural improvements in the tastes of the masses, was not so much a child of *his* time as a child of *our* time. A typical instance of this may be found in his urge to create a form of opera in which *participation*, from the highest to the lowest, was to be the guiding rule. He was not satisfied with good singers and a highly-trained orchestra, but demanded a virtual corps of technicians, directors, designers, actors, costumiers, administrators and people responsible for opening up the channels of communication in the new media. At first glance, this may recall the Wagnerian gesamt-kuntswerk again; but actually what the composer had in mind was much less exalted, much more what we should nowadays associate with a 'local theatre group'. His attempts to resuscitate Czech opera rested on a combination of the 'folk' element and a very determined 'modernism'—half-cultural and half-political. During the period when he was technically a resident of Paris, he never ceased to experiment, from time to time, at home. His two radio operas—*The Voice of the Forest* (1935) and *Comedy on a Bridge* (1936)—were written for sample people's audiences, using ensembles more like those of Britten than Wagner. They were pioneering works in that they were not intended for stage performance, and that the latter used what was then a new medium for satirical as well as musical purposes. At about the same time, however, Martinů reverted to a harlequinade for his other Czech opera, which *did* reflect his own experiences in a curious and unexpected manner. Entitled *The Theatre Behind the Tower* (1935), the work is a kind of re-enactment of the artificial world the composer inhabited in his early boyhood, when play with toys and miniature dramas formed the only possible substitutes for the natural, outdoor existence he was denied. Such a theme uneasily pre-figures theatrical successes of the type of Tennessee Williams's *The Glass Menagerie* and Lillian Hellmann's *The Toys in the Attic*. The difference lies in the fact that Martinů's opera refrains from drawing the Freudian morals commonly ascribed to the American plays, which tend to view the fantasies they describe as productive of a near-psychotic after-life. Martinů was content merely to invoke his childhood with the affectionate nostalgia—now grave, now gay, even occasionally rumbustious—of a man who had become thoroughly adjusted to life.

This normality notwithstanding, it is tempting to regard the composer's works from about 1933 to the beginning of the Second World War as indicative of an increasingly shrill element. They move, not always in logical sequence, towards the break-up of that utilitarian neo-classicism which had sufficed during the 1920's. For instance, *The Miracle of Our Lady* (1934) embodies yet another sort of operatic ideal, being in reality a mystery play in three independent scenes. Two of these—one depicting the Nativity and the other Sister Pascalina—drew their material from Czech religious texts of ancient or popular vintage. The other part, actually Part I of the triptych, is on the contrary called *Mariken of Nimwegen*, and is based on the literary reconstructions of Henri Ghéon. It was this work, far more than either of the radio operas or the self-written *Theatre Behind the Tower*, that began the process of involving the composer in a more emotional aesthetic. Up to this time, he might have been expected to concur in the well-known theory—subscribed to by both Hindemith and Stravinsky—that music was powerless to express emotion. At least, this would have been a fair inference to have made from listening to his works. But several witnesses have testified to the warmth of his reactions to *The Miracle* when it was rehearsed in Prague in 1934. Warmth is perhaps an appropriate term to use, since according to one of these witnesses, Šafránek, the composer was not only deeply moved but bitterly irate at the conventionality of the performers. They were attacked with a ferocity of which one would scarcely have believed him capable:

In these outbursts of anger, I found the true character-istics of Martinů's personality, his deep convictions and

artistic greatness of stature . . . Putting himself in the
place of others, in the widest sense, he came into the open
and reached a definite expression of artistic truth,
emotionally as well as rationally . . .[1]

From this time on, Martinů in fact developed much more 'expressive' views on opera. Though not advocating naturalism—which
would have implied for him an illusion impossible to sustain—he
demanded emotion through gesture, facial movement and posture.
Again unlike Wagner, he relegated the orchestra to a secondary role.[2]

The greatest of Martinů's twelve operas is without doubt
Juliette, a key work in more than one sense. Written in 1938, it
appeared at precisely the moment when several important crises
in the composer's life were coming to a head. Aside from the dire
political situation in Munich, and the emergence of his musical
personality from beneath its previous colourless façade, there
were domestic upheavals generally ignored by the composer's
more circumspect critics. The young Czech girl Vítězslava
Kaprálová, whose technique of composition had been based on
that of Martinů, suddenly emerged as a sensationally gifted figure
in the nation's music at this juncture. Her *Military Sinfonietta* was
heard in London in that fateful year, while her *Partita* for piano
and strings reproduced the best of her mentor's qualities. Though
married, Martinů could hardly help being touched by the devotion of his imitator, and one senses in his portrayal of *Juliette*
some of the admiration she elicited from him. The work, incidentally, is no *Village Romeo and Juliet* in the fashion of Delius's
opera, dealing with the loves of Gottfried Keller's Swiss peasants.
It is, on the contrary, 'grand opera' (yet another departure for
the changeable and versatile Martinů) and strives to reach the
heights of Shakespearian passion. What would have happened to
Martinů and Vítězslava had the war not intervened continues to
be problematical. As it turned out, he and his wife left for the
U.S.A. in 1940, the same year as the Bartóks, and the two musicians—one in his late forties and the other in her early twenties—
never met again. Bernard Stevens has said of her: 'There is no
doubt that had she lived she would have become one of the greatest
women composers in Europe.'[3] But she died in a Nazi concen-

---

[1] For an account of this incident and many others in the composer's
life, see the official biography *Bohuslav Martinů* by Milos Šafránek
(Alfred Knopf, N.Y., 1942).

[2] It will be recalled from the earliest chapters of this book that Cosima
Wagner, in particular, was also insistent upon stylized gesture as a mean to
emotional truth, though her husband's music tended to render it less vital.

[3] See his essay in *European Music of the Twentieth Century* ed.
H. Hartog (Pelican Books, 1961).

tration camp, leaving Martinů to bewail the passing of their friendship and the crushing of Czechoslovakia's most promising musical
talent.

Setting aside his critical personal difficulties, and even the
shadow of Fascism, there were good reasons why the composer
should have departed for the States at this time. *Juliette* had
perhaps convinced him of the impossibility of realizing the intimate
opera ideal at home; for what it seems to have suggested is an
abandonment of the procedures that had gone into the writing
and producing of *The Miracle of our Lady* and the other smaller
works, and a plain reversion to nineteenth-century operatic
speech. Martinů was too much ahead of his age with his 'do-it-
yourself' concepts, and he may accordingly have thought Americans would respond more quickly to them. Certainly he was
correct in this assumption as far as radio opera went, since the
multiplicity of local stations in the U.S.A. made this form far more
of a practical proposition for the humbler composer. Though he
could hardly have realized it at that point, the birth of television
opera was also just around the corner, the 1950's giving rise to the
remarkable series of breakthroughs by Menotti and his followers.
In time Martinů was to make his own contributions to these
advances. His T.V. opera *The Marriage* (based on a story by Gogol)
was mounted by the N.B.C. Opera Company as early as 1953,
while only three years afterwards it was followed by another,
entitled *What Men Live By*, resorting to Tolstoy's well-known
tale for its subject. America had also been kind to Martinů in his
Paris years, the Elizabeth Sprague Coolidge Foundation having
awarded him 1st Prize in a competition for one of his String
Quartets. So that in addition to becoming a place of political and
psychological refuge for him, it also promised to be a land in which
commissions would be forthcoming. And come they did. One of
the most lucrative was, as usual, from Koussevitzky and the Boston
Philharmonic Society, which demanded a symphony from the
composer—a form he had never previously attempted. In 1942,
only a couple of years after his arrival in the new country, this
work was performed with moderate acclaim. It is by no means his
best work in this vein, the Second (a work that has earned the title
of 'Pastoral') and the Sixth (the last in his catalogue) being stronger
contenders for that honour.

To the average person, it may seem hard to envisage this determined European, with his background of rolling Czechoslovakian
fields and faint memories of the bell-tower life at Politschka,
coasting along the New Jersey Turnpike in a large American car
on his way to the television studios each day. But it was a style
of life far more adapted to Martinů's populist sympathies than one

might suppose. He found in the U.S.A. a resolution of many of the problems that had troubled him deeply in his native land; and if we are inclined to regard this resolution as facile or unworthy, we should remember that the composer had never at any time been a fastidious introvert, like Bartók, to whom all manifestations of progress were anathema. Quite to the contrary, the typical American love of materialism, 'group membership' and new ideas reflected much that he himself admired. At any rate, he was a success in American terms, and had little difficulty in 'making it', to resort to Norman Podhoretz's abhorred phrase. Possibly on account of the sympathy most Americans had for the plight of those trapped in the Nazi sector of Europe, Martinů had nothing but praise for the various memorial works he wrote during the middle years of the war—especially for the moving tribute to the citizens of Lidice, destroyed as a foul act of reprisal by the brutal Heydrich. The same commendation was lavished upon him for his Double Concerto, written much earlier in 1940, which came to seem an elegy for the fate of his native land and for all that Americans valued in the Old Europe. Both works were as sincere as they were unanguished, yet again demonstrated the composer's capacity for responding to traumatic events in what would seem to have been a calm if not detached manner. The Violin Concerto (1943), to which we have already referred, was less of an emotional investment for him, as was the skilfully-written Concerto for Two Pianos of the same year. The former was first performed by the late Mischa Elman and the latter by the duettists Pierre Luboshutz and Genia Nemenov. Yet in both works (especially the Violin Concerto) there are strains of mourning, brief lyrical interludes, that hint strongly at fresh dimensions of sensibility.

While in America, Martinů assumed academic responsibilities, chiefly at Princeton University, where his discovery of the manuscript of Haydn's *Sinfonia Concertante* delighted him beyond measure. This work had been known and loved by him ever since his youth, and its sudden re-appearance at this time sparked off another succession of neo-classical compositions, including one with the same title as Haydn's, scored for piano, strings and four solo instruments. It is a piece that successfully emulates the Viennese master's brisk, happy, commonly-enjoyed manner. Other late works 'dans le style ancien' were the *Toccata and Two Canzoni for Piano and Chamber Orchestra* (1946) and the *Concerto for Orchestra* (1947), the last-named being nothing like the stunning virtuoso tour-de-force with which Bartók had crowned his achievements. But these were written before the Haydn discovery. The additional Symphonies and Quartets were also less of a product of new musicological interests than of the composer's naturally prolific gifts, which continued unimpaired despite occasional hankerings to return to Czechoslovakia. The Piano Quartet (1942) was an American work, but the Sixth String Quartet (1947) and the Quartet for piano, oboe, violin and cello (1949) were both written after Martinů had returned to Europe. On the whole, the Quartets bear no comparison with those of Bartók, while the Symphonies suffer from too much repetition, superfluous passage-work and static harmony.[1] They are nevertheless competent essays in media that held a constant attraction for the composer. The Sixth Symphony (1955) was particularly admired by Ansermet, who conducted it on numerous occasions.

This great, lamented chef d'orchestre also had a high opinion of Martinů's last three operas. *La Locandiera* (1954), written around a play by the eighteenth-century dramatist Goldoni, whom the rococo composers had often called upon for wit, was the first of these. The second, based upon the Greek Passion after Nikos Kazantzakes (1956), is a greater work, spiritually gripping and unrelated to the pagan Greece of the third, *Ariadne*, in which the librettist was Georges Neveux, who had collaborated on *Juliette*. Together, these large stage-works form an impressive conclusion to the career of a musician whose high productivity, like Milhaud's, poses the difficulty of deciding upon what will endure and what will revert to being mere musical wastage. At present, it seems too early to say with any great confidence where his final acclaim will lie. Martinů's return to Prague as Professor of Composition at the Conservatory was made almost immediately after the cessation of hostilities. It shows that, however much he was attached to the American way of life, the pull of nationality and the desire to see once again the unspoiled beauty of his fields and hedgerows (to say nothing of the enchanting capital) proved too great a temptation for him to resist. Yet how tragic and ironical must his feelings have been on re-visiting the scenes of former love, previous displays of carefree rebelliousness, knowing that such venues somehow remained inseparable from his present desires yet were inhabited by ghostly figures from out of the past, his own included, who would forever preserve their muteness in the face of his puzzled, ageing stare? Martinů's death in 1959, the year after the Hungarian uprising, released him at last from that quest for human brotherhood which, had he lived on till today, would surely have given him less cause for hope than at any point in his wracked and turbulent lifetime.

[1] For detailed criticism of the composer's work in these forms, see John Clapham's 'Martinů's Instrumental Style' (*Music Review*, Vol. XXIX, 1963) and Peter Evan's 'Martinů the Symphonist' (*Tempo*, Nos. 55/56, 1960).

xxi Prokofiev's Western Sojourn

Russia's dependence on the West for its cultural forms throughout the whole of the eighteenth and most of the nineteenth centuries is a well documented fact. In the musical field, Glinka
absorbed a good many of his ideas from Rossini, despite the
authentic national flavour which clung to his work, while most of
his successors were in one way or another powerfully indebted to
their opposite numbers in Germany, Poland or Hungary. There is
a touch of Mendelssohn in César Cui, for example, and more than
a hint of Chopin in Liadov. Most fruitful of all the importations
made in this way was probably Liszt's decorative style of keyboard
writing, which reproduced itself in the piano works of Balakirev,
Liapounov and, of course, Anton Rubinstein. With the establishment of 'The Five', however, Russia achieved something resembling a national identity of a quite separate kind, its features
being carved out once and for all in Moussorgsky's *Boris* and
Pictures at an Exhibition. One consequence of this was the building
up of a strong, if conservatively-based, tradition in the nation's
acadamies. The reason why this tradition retained its formalist
character for a long while after the Revolution (some would say
up to the present time!) was that it had only just taken hold when
Lenin and his followers rose to power; and even revolutionaries
are apt to accept a thing if it gives the appearance of being new. In
this sense, the artistic revolutionaries (and Prokofiev was among
the first of them) were a good deal more ready with their fire than
those of the political breed. Hence, 'old-fashioned' romantic ideas
(even if they *were* dressed in Russian national costume) were
energetically promulgated by senior composers like Glière and
Miaskovsky with the full approval of the Soviet bosses, while so-
called 'servile and corrupt' conservatives like Stravinsky were
laughing themselves sick at their archaisms in Paris or Zürich.

But it should be remembered that one aspect of the Russian character had always been indolent and supine. This aspect was satirized in literature in the fat figure of Oblomov, and is illustrated in countless characters from among the stories and plays of Chekhov. Peter Ustinov, who is related to the composer Tcherepnin, has even jokingly remarked on the way most paintings of Russian musicians are inclined to show them in near-horizontal postures—as in the famous Glinka portrait—whereas German musicians seem invariably to be discovered standing briskly to attention, as if poised for a quick sprint to the music-room. But no reader of Russian musical activities over the last half-century can seriously entertain the notion that *all* that country's composers have been marked by their preference for inactivity. On the contrary, the complement to Glinka's hypochondriac fatigue must be sought in the back-breaking drive of a Prokofiev or a Shostakovitch, men whose characters were shaped less by the land-owning sloth of White Russia than by the bounding industry of an United People's Republic. This is not to say that Prokofiev, in particular, was born to a spirit of revolution. As it happens, he lived through much the same sort of régime at the St Petersburg Conservatory as Rachmaninov had already done at Moscow. But there was a difference of age, a generation-gap, that inevitably led to a new set of assumptions on the part of the younger of the two men, a set of assumptions to which the older would never have pledged his consent.

Born at Sontsovka in the Ukraine in 1891, Prokofiev came from a slightly less well-to-do family, though still very much middle class. His father had been trained in Moscow as an agricultural expert, and had accordingly set up a model farm in this remote and beautiful province, once the terrain over which the Scyths and the Mongols had flayed their noble animals. The composer's mother, on the other hand, was from St Petersburg and had much more artistic leanings. She played the piano well—mostly Chopin, Schumann, Grieg and the like—and encouraged young Sergei's gifts. That he was keenly, unusually gifted is proved by his composition of a 'galop' for piano at the age of five and a half, and by his immediate prowess at his mother's instrument. In 1900, when the boy was only nine, his parents took him to Moscow to hear *Faust* and *Prince Igor*. He also attended a performance of Tschaikovsky's *The Sleeping Beauty* at the Bolshoi Theatre. Perhaps it is worth remarking that of these three experiences it was the hearing of *Faust* that made the strongest impression on him. After returning home, he dreamt of nothing but writing operas, and it is one important key to Prokofiev's history to reflect that, though he has up till the present been regarded primarily as an instrumental composer, he himself always thought he would be remembered for his operas. But that particular dilemma was not to worry him for many years yet. At the turn of the century, the more pressing question was where he was to go for instruction. A temporary solution was found in following the advice of Taneyev, who heard the lad in 1902 and was duly impressed by his abilities. His proposal was to invest in a private teacher for a while. This is what happened and Glière and Taneyev himself took turns to do the instructing. Prokofiev got on well with both these men—far better than he was to do with the seemingly more progressive figures he met at the St Petersburg Conservatory in 1904. During the years between, he pursued his studies happily, even persuading Glière to come down to Sontsovka to play duets and spend the summer holidays.

On entering the St Petersburg school, of which Glazounov was then Director, Prokofiev found the teachers much less to his liking. It was not as if the institution was short on highly-qualified personnel; Rimsky-Korsakov, Winkler and the older Tcherepnin (Nicholai) were all members of the faculty. But none of these men was terribly sympathetic to him, including Glazounov—though the composer's official Soviet biographer, Israel Nestyev tries hard to make a case for that unpopular scholar's benevolence.[1] Even allowing for the drop in interest, all might still have gone well had the young student not fallen foul of Liadov—a gentle enough soul whom Stravinsky (also working at St Petersburg as a private pupil of Rimsky-Korsakov at this time) has referred to as 'a darling man'. It is difficult to know which man was at fault here. Liadov was not by any means a reactionary in the Glazounov sense. He was, for instance, an ardent champion of Scriabin's music, then in bad odour with many of the old guard. And anyone who knows his own *Biroulki* suite and other pieces for the piano will appreciate what an exquisite harmonic sense he possessed. Yet within the classroom, he could be a bit of a pedant. Certainly he exercised a fair amount of dogmatism over the writing of exemplary music in the styles of the various contrapuntal composers. Canon, fugue and the other baroque forms became Prokofiev's staple diet throughout most of 1907 and 1908 until he reached a point of deliberate rebelliousness, causing his teacher to remark bitingly:

> I suppose I should be studying with you, not you with me. Why don't you go to Richard Strauss or Debussy?

[1] The work is simply entitled *Prokofiev*, and an English translation appeared from Oxford University Press in 1961, done by Florence Jonas. It appears to be a factually accurate, but politically biased book.

There was no answer forthcoming, as far as the last question was concerned, since Prokofiev never really brought himself to admire either of these undoubted moderns. (Debussy he referred to as 'mere jelly', while Strauss was obviously not astringent enough to comply with his essentially brusque early manner.) He did, however, express his grievances in a letter to his old private teacher, Glière, which pinpoints the objections he had to Conservatory training:

> Liadov holds firmly to the old, tranquil music and values most good voice-leading and logical progression. He rails at new music with interesting harmonies. Since my latest things fall precisely into this category, I prefer not to show them to him at all.

The truth is that Prokofiev had a pronounced classical streak in him, but it did not take the orthodox form. Mozart and Haydn were the older composers with whom he had most in common, but what he disliked about them was the tameness of their harmony. About Mozart he would say irreverently: 'What harmonies are these—I, IV, V!' It is obvious to anyone who examines the Classical Symphony (1917) that it is an awkward work to classify in terms of genre and style. Contrary to what is commonly supposed, the work is not just a pastiche invented with the object of poking fun at the Viennese masters. It is a curious kind of semi-ironical homage paid to them by a modern artist who appreciated quite sincerely their grace, wit and charm; but who nevertheless delighted in giving reign to the imp of the perverse. The Gavotte, in particular, shows Prokofiev's method of working. It is a straightforward four-in-the-bar piece of rococo with spiced-up harmonies and chromatic passing notes added. As William Austin has truly remarked, it sounds like an ordinary diatonic movement that has somehow side-slipped without affecting the tonality.[1] Though it was to Winkler he went for piano, Prokofiev had similar criticisms to make on that score. As we have related, in our essay on Rachmaninov, the training in piano at the Russian Conservatories tended to centre upon the Romantic and post-Romantic schools. Hence the composer found the perennial round of recitals that filled the city's concert schedules all too predictable for his more advanced tastes. 'They say you can't give a piano recital without including Chopin!' he grumbled with some justification. It was in matters such as these that he differed sharply from Rachmaninov, who never sickened of the works of the great pianist-composers of the period 1830-80. When Prokofiev himself gave a recital (and he was a brilliant, if rather metallic, player, who became notable for the ease with which he managed eccentric

[1] See *Music in the Twentieth Century* (Norton, 1966) pp. 454 et seq.

skips, contrary motion runs and hammering discordant chordal sequences, 'sans pédale'), he was apt to include a work like his own *Suggestions Diaboliques*—which one critic not inaptly compared to 'a wild Sabbath of dirty-faced devils dancing in Hell' and 'a violent brawl between two enraged gorillas'.

The hostility that separated Prokofiev and Rachmaninov was in the last resort traceable to temperamental imponderables. But it also reflected that enmity between the young and the not-so-young that is more than ever a feature of life in artistic and educational establishments in general. It sprang, on Prokofiev's part, from a determination to rebel against what he took to be the stale academic mindlessness typical of most such establishments. Rachmaninov, though he had begun by reacting equally unfavourably to, say, Glazounov's particular brand of conservatism, was on the contrary convinced that a tough dose of the classics (or Romantics if one happened to be a pianist) was a more or less indispensable training if ever the student were to be able to present his talents in a thoroughly professional way. That elements in the average Conservatory curriculum were stupid, reactionary or unjust was a fact he would probably not have denied; but he did not consider the remedy lay in anarchy or a deliberately shocking use of dissonance. Indeed, Rachmaninov held views not unlike those associated with many dons today—namely, that the whole business of revolt could easily become a crashing bore and would as likely as not end in nothing more edifying than a lot of noise and tumult. In Prokofiev's case, he was mistaken to the extent that this was one of those exceedingly rare cases in which the rebel had something beyond mere vituperation to offer. Funny though it may sound to call it by that name, he possessed that rarity recognized as style. Even Stravinsky, who was by no means unqualified in his praise of the young man, found that Prokofiev was invariably a convincing exponent of his own works. He brought a unique power of occasion to them, making the audience sit bolt upright in their seats as if aware that here was something both pungent and futuristic. Not all of the composer's pieces were harsh and stunning, however, as a glance at the *Fairy Tale*, also belonging to his first group of piano works, will confirm.

A close analysis would reveal that Prokofiev's musical personality was a complex one. His language contained a number of separate and many would think irreconcilable elements. We have already noted the neo-classical element, which was not much different from that later employed by Poulenc—though it had little in common with the sincere simplicity of that father of French anti-Romanticism, Erik Satie, which he regarded with contempt. Also like Poulenc, however, Prokofiev harboured melodic or lyrical talents of a somewhat unsuspected kind. These were kept firmly in abeyance during most of his early period, but emerged very strongly in such late works as *Romeo and Juliet* and *Cinderella*. Looked at from one angle. the explanation for the composer's ultimate abandonment of the role of enfant terrible and his return to Russia in the guise of what Lawrence and Elisabeth Hanson have called 'the prodigal son', lay in the incredible gift for melody he possessed. This was something he knew would appeal to the Soviet people and, to put a less discreditable motive on it, appealed in a paradoxical way to one aspect of his *own* character. The reason he generally got himself into trouble, both in the East and the West, was because this melodic strain of his was inextricably mixed with other, less acceptable, predilections. For example, he was animated by a characteristic motor quality which sometimes went beyond the limits set by Stravinsky and Ravel. In the *Scythian Suite* (1914-15), and the set of *Sarcasms* published for piano by Jurgenson in 1916, Prokofiev gave full vent to this side of his nature, and these works have never attracted worshippers from any quarter. Then again, 'grotesquerie' played a significant part in his make-up. One senses this in the ballet *Chout* (or *The Buffoon*) dating from 1921, and still more clearly in the opera, *The Love for Three Oranges*, written earlier but produced in the same year. These works are full of a mocking, ribald satirical spirit, far too much like that of Gogol to have suited the Western peoples for which they were written, but equally removed from the clamped-down atmosphere of Soviet art during the days when Commissar Zhdanov ruled the roost. Ordinary Russians, when they were not admirers of Prokofiev's lyrical vein, responded better to his knock-about manner than to his occasional outbursts of savagery. Indeed, he eventually became known as 'the football composer' among the more sophisticated working-classes.[1]

But to return to our chronicle of the composer's early doings, he stuck it out at the Conservatory in St Petersburg until 1914, winning First Prize for piano. As he was exempt from military service, the War did not affect him very much, and he was able to continue his now excitingly notorious recitals. His eventual acceptance as a pianist was based partly on the additional training he had from Essipova, who taught him stock works like the Liszt B minor Sonata in the ampler style of the popular virtuosi. He

[1] An oddly appropriate designation in some ways, since it also reflected the composer's personal profile. One rather clever analyst of facial characteristics once described Prokofiev as looking like 'a cross between a Lutheran pastor and a soccer player'. Incidentally, both Auric and Poulenc were also lampooned for their alleged importation of athletic qualities into their art, being collectively dubbed 'les sportifs de la musique'.

also did a little conducting (though not as much as Rachmaninov) and became acquainted with the works of Wagner, Reger and Strauss. Being non-political (and incidentally anti-clerical), the Revolution left him with no great feelings of shock or triumph, and the only real contact he had with the régime was when Lunarcharsky, the People's Commissar for Education, congratulated him on the première of the *Classical Symphony* in what had become Petrograd in 1918. Lunarcharsky was exceedingly liberal, considering his position, and he was more regretful than punitive when Prokoviev broached with him the possibility of emigrating to Paris, or else the United States. It was the latter country, with its forward-looking technology, its receptivity to new ideas and its superb, well-financed orchestras that finally gained his vote. So, in the Spring of 1918, the composer made his way to New York, via Vladivostock and Tokio, without arousing as much as a flutter in the hearts of the iron men in the Kremlin. On the boat on the way over, Prokofiev had already worked out ideas for an opera-buffa (his first operatic work, *The Gambler*, based on the short novel by Dostoievsky, had been scheduled for performance at the Maryinsky Theatre in 1917, but had proved too difficult for the performers and had to wait till 1929 for its première in Brussels) and this turned out to be *The Love for Three Oranges*, which he confidently expected to be his first American triumph.

The work, however, ran into a series of difficulties, not all of which were attributable to its music. Campanini, the producer, agreed to a Chicago opening, but died before he could honour his promise. Prokofiev tried to recover his losses by appearing as a recitalist, but discovered, somewhat to his amazement, that Americans much preferred the standard works in the repertoire. Not having the 'god-like' standing of Rachmaninov with Damrosch, Steinway and other influential New Yorkers, he found himself curiously adrift in a country he assumed would be entirely hospitable to him. At his Aeolian Hall recital, he was stigmatized as 'a musical Bolshevik'—hardly a fair comment since he had just quitted the scene of revolution. The *Scythian Suite* was received in Chicago with kinder notices, but as Prokofiev had appropriated the style contained in this work very largely from his idol, Stravinsky, it was obvious that he would be up against a superior competitor if he persevered with it. Instead, he hoped that his Concertos would find favour with the larger orchestras, and that he could appear with them as soloist. But it was not to be. Writing of this period in his life at a later date, he complained:

I wandered through the enormous park in the centre of New York and, looking up at the skyscrapers that bordered

it, thought with cold fury of the marvellous American
orchestras that cared nothing for my music, of the critics
who baulked so violently at anything new, of the managers who arranged long tours for artists playing the same
old hackneyed programmes fifty times over ...

In poverty and desperation, therefore, Prokofiev gradually made
up his mind to leave America and seek a fresh start once more in
Paris, where the activities of Picasso, Diaghilev, Ravel (who began
by saying 'Please do not call me "maître"!') and their colleagues at
least ensured that a modernist ferment was in motion.

Here the composer was considerably more successful. Diaghilev,
always on the look-out for some new, preferably scandalous,
protégé, was quick to notice his possibilities. They were fellow
countrymen, of course, and each also had a high regard for Stravinsky. The ballet *Chout* was accordingly dredged up out of
Prokoviev's files (where it had lain since 1915) and used to open
the 1921 season. Its plot has all the elements of a black comedy and
concerns the efforts of a village confidence man (the *Buffoon* of the
title) to wheedle money out of his neighbours on the pretence that
he possesses the power to raise the dead. Some of the villagers
take him up on this challenge, using their wives as the experimental material. Predictably, these poor females remain inert at
the conclusion of the experiment, and the Buffoon has to disguise
himself as a maid in order to escape his creditors. While dressed in
this feminine attire, he attracts the unwelcome attentions of a rich
merchant, and only just manages to avoid being seduced by the
expedient of leaping from a second storey window. Instead of
breaking his neck, however, the Buffoon survives, changes back
into his normal clothes and brings along a platoon of policemen
to arrest the merchant for the murder and rape of 'his sister'.
The score of this alternately comic and gruesome work abounds in
the sort of savage harmonies and shrieking orchestral effects the
composer was compelled to renounce once he had returned to
accept the Soviet laureateship. Lots of the tunes are folk-ditties
garnished with frolicsome or ghastly intrusions in the authentic
Prokofiev manner. The grace notes and sudden discordant leaps
are particularly characteristic, while the piano and percussion
provide constant noises-off in the form of sweeping glissandi and
ear-splitting crashes of indeterminate pitch. Muted trumpets and
strings played sul ponticello add to the vital richness and sinister
exuberance of the orchestration. The whole work represents an
unrepeatable tour de force.

Meanwhile, the ill-fated opera, *The Love for Three Oranges* had
found a new American sponsor in the singer Mary Garden, who

had created the part of Mélisande in Debussy's famous work. She, too, chose Chicago rather than New York, for the première, which came about in the autumn of 1921. Prokofiev himself had to go back and act as régisseur and the whole venture was very difficult indeed to mount. Based on a comedy by Gozzi, it lacked the element of contemporaneity in the theatrical sense; but the composer more than made up for this by the modernism of his music. Very deliberately factitious in plot, the play divides its characters into Tragedians, Comedians, Lyricists and Empty-Heads; and may thus be regarded as a kind of self-satire. As Nestyev has put it:

> The Tragedians wanted Weltschmerz, misery and murders; the Comedians demanded wholesome, joyous laughter; the Lyricists argued for 'romantic love, moons, tender kisses'; and the Empty-Heads insisted on 'entertaining nonsense, witty double-entendres, fine costumes'! . . .

This section forms the prologue to a romantic comedy about the King of Clubs and his son, the Prince, who has fallen into a state of hypochondria from which no one seems able to retrieve him. While debating what is to be done, a conspiracy is hatched by the King's niece, Clarissa, and the Prime Minister, Leandro. Together, these plan to take over the state. Other characters include a magician named Celio, whose function it is to be the King's protector, and an evil witch, Fata Morgana, who plays a similar role on behalf of Leandro. When it comes to curing the Prince, the doctors at first prescribe laughter; so that the initial scenes involve Truffaldino, the Court Jester, and his efforts. These proving unsuccessful, Fata Morgana causes the Prince to break out into laughter by falling down, with the result that she puts a curse on him that involves travel in search of three oranges. Eventually, the Prince finds these in the ancient castle of Creonta—and one of them contains the beautiful Princess Ninetta, whom he brings back and marries. Like *Chout*, the opera offered Prokofiev limitless opportunities for drollery and horseplay, and the treatment he gave it contrasts markedly with his late fairy-tale stage works. Though enjoyed in Chicago, it lost 130,000 dollars in New York—which, as one critic drily noted, worked out at about 43,000 an orange.

After this, Prokofiev became more convinced than ever that his future lay in France. Still deeply enamoured of the stage, he continued to think in terms of another opera or ballet. But despite the relative success of *Chout*, Diaghilev was not altogether pleased with his new protégé. For one thing, he considered him too unreceptive to extra-musical influences. After introducing the composer to most of the painters, littérateurs and leftists who made up the impresario's famous circle, he reached he conclusion that Prokofiev was a little wanting in general culture. The remarks the composer had made about *Chout* sowed the seeds of doubt in Diaghilev's mind, as is apparent from the letter the producer wrote to Stravinsky:

> The music, as he says, does not look for Russianism, it is just music. Precisely, just music, and very bad. Now we have to start all over again, and for this we have to be kindly with him and keep him with us for two or three months. Am counting on your help...[1]

It would be unwise to attach too much importance to Diaghilev's musical opinions, however, since his own culture did not embrace music to any very technical degree. What is significant about this letter is that it shows Prokofiev's limitations as a cosmopolite and hints at a reason for the inability he revealed to maintain his position with the avant-garde in Paris. The composer, for all his driving, extravert music, was actually a fairly reserved person, who preferred mechanical or puzzle-type hobbies to 'arty' conversation. He was, for example, a magnificent chess player, just below grand master level in his capabilities. It was therefore only to be expected that he would find many of Diaghilev's more bizarre associates a shade raddled or freakish. Stravinsky, too, had reservations about him, again partly on account of his dourness and lack of interest in wider subjects and partly because of his feeling that Prokofiev was merely imitating him. This last supposition was true, up to a point. Then again, Stravinsky disliked Prokofiev's somewhat communist attitudes to the church. It was not as though the older composer had himself developed much further towards his ultimate religious phase at this point; but he regarded Prokofiev's atheism as crude. The outcome of all this was that further success on the stage was more or less denied him.

At any rate, the breach between him and Diaghilev was firmly established by about 1922, though later on in that frivolous decade Prokofiev's talents were twice reluctantly re-invoked. Once for *Le Pas d'Acier* (1928), translatable as *The Leap of Steel*, and finally for *The Prodigal Son* (1929), a most unfrivolous ending to the two men's partnership. Unbelievably, in view of Diaghilev's increasingly unsavoury reputation in Soviet Russia, he chose *Le Pas d'Acier* as an illustration of the Bolshevist State in action.[2] It

---

[1] See *Memories and Commentaries* by Igor Stravinsky and Robert Craft (Faber, 1960), Chapter III.

[2] During the early 'twenties Diaghilev had been the target of much abuse in the Soviet press, which described him, in its inimitable way, as 'a degenerate blackguard, anti-Russian lackey of the Western bourgeoisie'.

was almost a 'ballet mécanique' in its reliance on constructivist as opposed to decorative sets (they were done by another Russian exile, Yakulov, using the principles first demonstrated by Meyerhold) and revolved around a presentation of factory life with the din of its generators and the intermittent roar of steam-hammers. Actually, the whole thing was a piece of sheer exoticism in that it reflected only the sophisticated Parisian's conception of what Russian life was really like. Elegantly dressed châtelaines, who had never set foot in any place East of Marienbad called out 'charmant', 'épatant' and so on, in their loud upper-class accents. The London papers were more guarded, though even they seemed to regard the ballet as somehow expressive of the great Future that Shaw and the Webbs had always been gabbling about. Prokofiev himself had the gravest doubts about it all, knowing full well that French composers like Auric or Milhaud could probably have made a better job of it, viewed in Diaghilev's terms. *The Prodigal Son*, which follwed, was a far cry from the phoney Russianism of *Le Pas d'Acier*, and took its inspiration from the vogue for Biblical scenes already in force in the Western cinema. By this time, cubism and surrealism were becoming tiresome to a surfeited public, and Picasso and Stravinsky had moved on to neo-classical themes. Rouault was accordingly engaged to do the designs and Lifar appeared as the Son, with the choreography left in the capable hands of Balanchine. The result was a little more pleasing to the composer, and revealed a less stormy side to his character. Rachmaninov was present at the première, and it is symptomatic that he found it the best of the Prokofiev ballets.

By far the finest theatrical work Prokofiev attempted to put on in the West, however, was his opera, *The Flaming Angel*, which had taken him from 1919 to 1927 to complete, much of it having been composed near the Bavarian monastery of Ettal, where he had sought retreat from Paris's noisy decadence.[1] Unfortunately, it was never staged during his lifetime (the première being given in Venice as late as 1955) and the composer had to be content with reducing it to the dimensions of an orchestral suite. Bruno Walter offered to mount it, but was prevented in the last resort from doing so. In June, 1928, excerpts were given by Koussevitsky in Paris instead. The opera's story is one of witchcraft and possession, derived from a novel by Valery Briussov, and the setting is in medieval times. The knight Ruprecht, who is the hero, falls in love with a possessed girl named Renata, and together they set out

[1] For a sympathetic account of this work, see Alan Jefferson's article 'The Angel of Fire' in *Music & Musicians*, Vol. XIII, No. 13, August, 1965.

to enlist the aid of an angel to whom the latter had turned for help when a child. In the course of their travels, Ruprecht has to fight a duel with Mephistopheles and Renata is sentenced to be burnt by an Inquisitor. Before the threat can be carried out, Ruprecht goes to visit an old philosopher, Cornelius Agrippa, who disclaims any magical powers but who is contradicted by a skeleton that leaps up and screams 'Liar!' at him. Finally, the two men, knight and philosopher, conspire to end the plot against Renata and drive out the forces of the devil, having to rely on Divine intervention to assist them. It goes without saying that such an opera presented every possible opportunity for Prokofiev's cruel grotesquerie to express itself; but, more than that, it also gave him a chance to depict scenes of tenderness and grief, especially where Renata was concerned. It thus helped the composer to realize the full range of his gifts, and despite Nestyev's contemptuous dismissal, will probably go down in history as his masterpiece. Sadly, its vocal excesses still make it fearsome to perform, and the canonizing of the late (and very straight) opera *War and Peace* in the Soviet Union has only had the effect of making it more difficult for this brilliant earlier work to be heard to proper advantage. As an evocation of the horror and superstition that lay behind the old Germany of Dürer's woodcuts and the legend of Dr Faustus, it will probably remain unrivalled.

From 1927 to 1933, the composer made frequent trips back to Russia in the hope of meeting with a more favourable artistic climate for his work. He had never ceased, since his quarrel with Diaghilev, to correspond with certain friends in Moscow, and it may be that they put the final pressure on him to return for good. But there is clearly more to Prokofiev's repatriation than meets the eye. Many different explanations have been offered for it, some of which will already have been deduced by the reader. It is obvious, for instance, that though his personality was a good deal less nostalgic than Rachmaninov's, he was not able to adapt to European, and especially American, styles of life as well as his senior. His bent for satire, coupled with the unique combination of savagery and solemnity he exhibited, made him an enigma to the gay, unthinking 1920's. Perhaps these qualities would have caused him to be more acceptable today, when 'high camp' tastes and a certain pessimistic mockery lie all around. Stravinsky, whose immediate thoughts always centred upon finance, attributed Prokofiev's departure to nothing more complicated than commercial failure; seeing his subsequent success as a typical 'sell-out' to Russian propagandist music. There is possibly some truth in this. For many of the works the composer wrote on being re-admitted to a position of prestige in his native land bear the stamp of sentimentality or mass-appeal. For example, the film scores for *Lieutenant Kije* and *Alexander Nevsky*, good as they are, seem hardly a substitute for the shattering operas the composer *might* have written if he had gone on in the vein of *The Flaming Angel*. Yet it remains true that a surprisingly large number of his so-called 'Western' scores were fairly fully sketched out by him before his emigration. This was the case with *Chout*, *The Love for Three Oranges* and even the delightful *Tales of the old Grandmother* for piano, to say nothing of the neglected Dostoievsky opera. What needs underlining here is that, whereas these works may have been conceived in Russia, they would probably have had even less chance of being performed there than they had in Europe. The example of Shostakovitch's *Katerina Izmailova* is instructive in this respect. Hence, what Paris did for Prokofiev was to give him limited scope for the development of ideas that were certainly being frowned upon in his own country, and would probably have resulted in an even more rapid crushing of his spirit had he attempted to express them there.

The difficulties of repatriation and gradual climb to favour are aspects of the composer's history that we shall not be concerned with here. They belong in a more comprehensive biography, or else in a more direct account of the influence of politics on music. Perhaps, however, it is worth remarking in Prokofiev's favour that when he was asked to recant, and to affirm the new principles of Soviet art which exalted above all such criteria as popularity and intelligibility, he was not being entirely insincere in his replies. Solicited for a statement of his beliefs in 1941, the period approaching maximum Soviet solidarity, the composer complied by saying:

> I strive for greater simplicity and more melody. Of course I have used dissonance in my time, but there has been too much dissonance. Bach used dissonance as good salt for his music. Others applied pepper, seasoned the dishes more and more highly, till all healthy appetites were sick and until music was nothing but pepper. I think society has had enough of that. We want a simpler and more melodic style for music, a simpler, less complicated emotional state, and dissonance once again relegated to its proper place as one element in music, contingent principally on the meeting of melodic lines ...[1]

[1] A statement given to the American critic, Olin Downes, and reprinted in *The New Book of Modern Composers*, edited by David Ewen (3rd revised edition, A Knopf & Co., New York, 1961). But see also Alexander Werth's book *Musical Uproar in Moscow* (Hamilton, 1949) for a full account of the censorship issue.

At first analysis, that sounds very much like the statement of an artist with a gun pointed at his back, and a far cry indeed from the angry manifestoes of the composer's youth. But, hard though it may be for us to accept, I cannot help feeling that it represents one aspect of Prokofiev's complex individuality speaking the truth; and that the gun which is almost certainly there is not being held by any People's Commissar but by the composer's lyrical alter-ego, the gentler if no less determined writer of the Second and Third Piano Sonatas and the music for Hans Andersen's '*The Ugly Duckling*', which last creature embodies so aptly many of the traits of this strange and paradoxical man.

Thus far in our chronicle of twentieth-century music, America has seemed a place of refuge for European composers, a handy New World into which to disappear when the military eruptions of the Old World became too terrifying to endure. That facilities for music-making in the United States had much to commend them was a fact all knowledgeable musicians took for granted. But few had given any thought to the possibility that there might be American composers in the offing, men capable of using the facilities brought about by the country's wealth to impressive advantage. In literature, even so prophetic a figure as Matthew Arnold had patronizingly assumed—in the face of works like *Moby Dick* and *Leaves of Grass*—that American novels and poems were non-existent commodities, there being only one cultural product of the English language and that being the entity colloquially referred to as 'Eng. Lit.'. Obviously, things were not quite the same in music, since there was no real need for Americans to depend on English models, and indeed there were few worthwhile English models upon which to depend. Yet the urge to take their cultural orders from the Old World, so to speak, ran strong in the veins of Americans of the period 1900 and thereabouts in all of the arts. Musically, this usually meant an acceptance of German or Italian forms, as may be confirmed by reflecting on the great popularity of the symphony in cities like Boston and Philadelphia and the immense prestige enjoyed by the Italian operas in which Melba, Caruso and Farrar appeared at the Met. On the other hand, one or two serious-minded American composers—Daniel Gregory Mason of the famous piano firm of Mason & Hamlin was a typical case—found their salvation in Paris, placing themselves under the strict guidance of a d'Indy. In most cases, however, the notion of Americans becoming composers of serious music was about as fondly regarded as that of Englishmen becoming occupants of the Wild West.

A little later on, when the streams of popular art began to pour forth from across the Atlantic, it was conceded that the people who lived on that side of the ocean had a definite gift for 'lowbrow' musical forms, among which the popular song and the instrumental jazz number rated as the most acceptable. As a matter of fact, popular song had had a reasonably long history in the States, as anyone who had followed the events of the latter half of the nineteenth century must have realized. The wonderfully expressive Civil War songs easily surpass any that have been written for later wars, even those for the First World War, which were inclined to be too patently jingoish or sentimental. Again, who in Europe had written such perfect specimens of the parlour ballad as Stephen Foster—composer of *I dream of Jeanie with the light brown hair*—or would produce such thunderingly good marches as Sousa's *Liberty Bell* or *Washington Post*? It is all very well for Professor Wilfrid Mellers to say that 'Tin Pan Alley was spawned in the gutters of Vienna'—a true enough statement as far as it goes—but many of these early musical populists that America gave birth to were a good deal less dependent on European masters than, say, our own Sir Arthur Sullivan, whose reliance on Schubert, Mendelssohn and other great creators of melody hardly needs underlining today.[1] Moreover, Tin Pan Alley had not been invented at the time they wrote, so that it is their successors who really deserve the sting of Professor Mellers's lash. Gottschalk, an indefatigable pianist and composer of light classics, was the composer of the older generation who perhaps owed most to the professionalism of Europe (he had learnt his swashbuckling Hungarian-type virtuosity from the example of Liszt himself), and yet even he derived from his native New Orleans the Creole rhythms and cake-walk melodies that were to differentiate him, in the last resort, from his opposite numbers in France and Germany, the countries of his parental ancestry.

What Santayana called 'the genteel tradition' also had its place in American music, and this tradition—as had been the case with literature—*did* build more on the English example. Composers like the much-feared Horatio Parker (1863–1919) of Yale University may be quite justly compared with our own Parry (whose disciple he was) or Stanford, and did his damnedest to inculcate a similar fore-correctness. That he was not altogether unopposed in

[1] I am aware that Sousa played under Offenbach, when the Frenchman toured the States, but I hesitate to think his achievements should be attributed to the encounter.

carrying out his policies was suggested by the presence of natural
rebels of the type of Charles Ives (1874–1954), almost certainly the
greatest and most futuristic of his pupils, and of other and more
benevolent teachers like Edward Macdowell (1861–1908), who
forsook the stolid, oratorio-based training in favour of a milder
Romanticism reminiscent of Grieg. Macdowell, however, was a
more interesting and advanced composer than this description
might imply, and while he is conservative enough in such favourites
as *To a Wild Rose* and *A.D. 1620* the Piano Sonatas and other
works have an architectural grandeur more likely to recall Brahms
as he was in his youthful, heroic world. To describe him as 'a
miniaturist of charm and sensibility'—as Joseph Machlis does—is
to commit a cardinal error one would hardly have expected from
a fellow-American. Nevertheless, both Parker and Macdowell were
Europe-orientated in one way or another, and Aaron Copland was
quite correct when he wrote, much later on, that a much more
indigenous music had to be formed before anything of great value
would emerge. His actual words are worth quoting:

> A true musical culture never has been and never can be
> solely based upon the importation of foreign artists and
> foreign music, and the art of music in America will always
> be essentially a museum art until we are able to develop a
> school of composers who can speak directly to the Ameri-
> can public in a musical language which expresses fully
> the deepest reactions of the American consciousness to
> the American scene.[1]

Again, to resort to a literary analogy, Philip Rahv once divided
American writers into what he called 'palefaces' and 'redskins'—
his assumption being much the same as Mr Copland's, namely
that it is the native response that one wants and not the European
echo. Most critics would agree that in the middle of the twentieth
century America had established enough 'redskin' musicians
to constitute a native school different from any to be found
abroad.

The business of bringing this school to birth was a lengthy one,
and we can only take a selective view of it. But in choosing to
comment on the career of Virgil Thomson, we shall be singling
out a figure as American as Edison or Henry Ford, yet who has
had the sophistication to spend much of his long life window-
shopping in Europe and who possesses a degree of articulacy so

[1] See *Our New Music*, Whittlesey, New York, 1941. Aaron Copland's
more recent books, including *Music and Imagination* (Harvard University
Press, 1952), are also worth reading for their acute analysis of the dilemma
of the American composer.

uncommon among musicians as to have made him a veritably unique spokesman for his country and its myriad difficulties over art, affluence and communication. Thomson, unlike Copland, was also a country boy—a bright young lad from Missouri who surprised his townsfolk by winning a scholarship to Harvard. He accordingly exemplifies a particularly American dream, that of rising from a humble and parochial background to a position of eminence in one of the large East coast citadels of power or learning. Like most of the men to whom this dream became an actuality —men like Harry Truman in the political sphere and Carl Sandburg in literature—Thomson was pre-eminently a good mixer, a natural 'joiner and belonger' as the Americans say, whose professional zeal has always been coupled with a genuine taste for the club-room and the journalists' den. In addition to writing large quantities of music, he has penned a sizeable collection of books (including an enormously readable and witty autobiography), uncountable articles for periodicals at home and abroad, and was music correspondent for the New York Herald Tribune from 1940 to 1954, during which time his column was probably the most trenchant source of cultural gossip to have subsisted throughout the entire continent. His decision to relinquish the post in order to devote more time to composing struck Americans as the saddest journalistic deprivation they had suffered since the loss of Alexander Woolcott and H. L. Mencken.[1] I have used the term 'cultural gossip' rather deliberately, since America has never produced quite such a well-rounded musician as Thomson, who was the intimate of painters like Christian Bérard and Maurice Grossier and the boon companion of writers like Hemingway, Joyce, Pound and Gertrude Stein. A composite photograph taken very recently shows him enjoying a hearty chuckle with his old friends Nadia Boulanger, Walter Piston and Aaron Copland—a mirthful, rubicund figure, tightly squeezed into a dress suit, revelling in every second of his seventy-fifth year.

Every comfortable elder has his beginnings in childhood, however, and Thomson's was spent in the Baptist-dominated suburbs of Kansas City, where hymns, Civil War songs and parlour ballads formed the only fare calculated to do anything to stimulate this remarkably eager and brilliant lad's musical imagination. Such music has predictably remained with him all his life, not just as a wry memory, but as the mainstay of his creative energies. Indeed, there is something especially splendid and American in his determination to cling on to his home town heritage despite all the cosmopolitanism to which he was canny enough to expose himself

[1] A selection from his reviews has now appeared under the title *Music Reviewed* (Vintage Books, 1966).

on reaching the age of twenty-one. It is as if he were saying:
'What's good enough for Kansas City ought to be good enough for
you, whoever you are!' And that is probably what he sincerely felt,
even after entering upon his fifteen-year sojourn in Paris, since
he expressed as much in saying:

> I wrote in Paris music that was always, in one way or
> another, about Kansas City. I wanted Paris to know
> Kansas City, to understand the ways we like to think
> and feel on the banks of the Kaw and the Missouri.[1]

But before he could think up such sentiments he first had to serve
his time in the First World War, and it was only after two years in
the Army that he was able to settle down to a comfortable existence
in the Harvard Music School from 1919 to 1923. E. B. Hill was his
teacher there—not another Parker, but a musical 'paleface' of the
breed for which the ebullient Thomson reserved a sturdy Middle
Western scepticism. From Harvard, he went on to the Juilliard
School of Music in New York, working for a year with Rosario
Scalero. During these long academic sessions, the young composer
managed to win himself brief interludes in Paris in the form of
fellowships and the occasional semester absences. Much of the
time he spent abroad was as an 'auditeur' at Nadia Boulanger's
famous American school at Fontainebleau. Even after he had
severed all connections with his native land, he remained a frequent
guest at these gatherings and can be said to have sat around her
lectures from 1921 to 1927 and beyond. How he survived after the
expiration of his fellowships remains a mystery, for he was not rich.
As he characteristically put it to a friend who was wondering the
same thing: 'There's nothing like starving where the food is good!'

Perhaps the first thing to understand about Thomson's approach
to music was that it remained utterly open-minded and pragmatic.
He had no theories to impart, and he showed no great anxiety to
adopt any from among those offered him by his seniors. His wish,
he said, was that his music would resemble:

> . . . a large railway station, not particularly attractive,
> though details of it were interesting, but massive and full
> of variety, with many people going in and out of it.[2]

Such a frank admission of unintellectualism should not be misunderstood. Thomson was no fool, and knew better than most of
his highbrow mentors the shallowness that can arise out of systems.
Moreover, his candour was much like that of Erik Satie, of whom
he became an intense admirer—that is to say, it was a form of
absolute sincerity designed to rid music of the quasi-philosophical

[1] See *The State of Music* (Vintage Books, New York).
[2] See op. cit.

props with which a good many untalented people were attempting to hold it up. To begin with, he liked most kinds of music—popular café-tunes, jazz, Bach, anything lively and unpretentious with a good tune to it. What he most disliked was emotionally-laden romantic music of the type Wagner had initiated, and any sort of pseudo-profound music of the kind he sometimes attributed (not without occasional mistakes) to the younger Germans. Two particularly deeply rooted tastes he had were for brass band music and for the ordinary chapel tunes he had heard sung by choirs or else played on the organ as a boy. Again, the temptation imposes itself to say: 'How banal!' But it should be recalled that Ives, too, had begun with a passion for the bands, and the superimposition of one strand of band music over another that one gets in works like his *Three Places in New England* and Fourth Symphony was one of his most significant ways of creating an independent New World atonalism. Thomson never went as far in this direction as Ives, being content to disrupt what appear to be straightforward diatonic movements, full of open brass choir chords, with the odd crushing dissonance. The effect is often more startling than one obtains from Ives, whose mixing of tonalities creates an immediate impression of chaos. A similar patch of montage can frequently be ascertained in the composer's otherwise simplistic religious music, slightly suggestive of a Baptist service gone awry.

As with Satie, humour played some part in these surrealist exercises, the difference being that the Frenchman's intentions were as often as not 'anti-pompier', as he would have put it, whereas Thomson's were just plain bluff. As may be expected, the latter began his Parisian period by succumbing to the worship of antiquity, his Sonata da Chiesa (1926) for clarinet, trumpet, viola, horn and trombone being his most substantial contribution to the prankish researches of Cocteau, Auric and Poulenc. But Americans are apt to tune in more easily to the present, and it is not surprising that Thomson soon declared his antipathy to 'rigid neo-classicism', preferring after all to go back to the simplified romanticism of the ordinary citizen's life as currently lived. Satie's *Messe des Pauvres* in this sense made a far greater impression on him than that composer's academic parodies of Clementi or post-Schola tomfoolery. One cannot see Virgil Thomson as the upholder of anything so hieratical as the Rose-Croix cult out of which Satie's Mass had sprung; but the spirit of religion as felt by the man in the street was an aspect of life to which he responded regardless of colour or creed. Even his Sonata had contained phrases suggested to him by a Negro preacher's intoning of the service, while the Chorale that appears in it seems to have more in common with nonconformist hymnology than with the liturgical practices of seventeenth-century

Leipzig. But of course Thomson was a farceur—at least in this period—as well, and it should not be assumed that any of the more pointedly religious pieces he wrote would have been acceptable to the worthy folk who wended their way to chapel every Sunday morning at home. The *Variations and Fugues on Sunday School Tunes* for organ (1928-9) were really sharp take-offs on the sort of community-bound complacency with which he had been so familiar as a child. They abound in shocking 'wrong-notes', polytonal zig-zag effects and other devices intended to make the (imaginary) congregation leap out of their pews in stupefaction. The composer's *Symphony on a Hymn Tune* (1929) invites one to make similar observations, though the intention in this case was clearly not quite so flippant.

A second Symphony followed in 1931, and two String Quartets in the year after. These make use of American folk material, and show how expressively he could handle the inflections of traditional mid-Western melody as well as how competently he had mastered set classical forms. Thomson's best stroke of good fortune came out of his collaboration with Gertrude Stein, however, and this was something that had begun as early as 1927. Their *Capital, Capitals* for four male voices and piano was a mock-up or burlesque intended to poke fun at the European reverence for cities. It was one of Stein's delusions that she, too, was an all-American small-town sceptic, and it must be admitted in her favour that she had done more than anyone to divorce formal English (as spoken in Europe and the best circles of the Eastern seaboard of America) from the natural, vivid speech of the United States working man or woman.[1] Her book, *The Making of Americans*, was to prove an important sociological and liguistic document in that it listed (rather like Mencken's tome on *The American Language*, only less systematically) the now familiar contractions of phraseology we associate with the slangy phase of American life and letters. Today, when jargon and officialese have taken the place of raciness of expression, it is doubtful whether either Stein's or Mencken's work has the validity once attached to it. But Hemingway and other American writers certainly learned much from Gertrude Stein's habit of plain writing—without the adjectives and fancy adverbial clauses of the littérateur. Her well-known saying 'A rose is a rose is a rose' illustrates the philosophy that lay behind her short-lived reforms. What a lady of this pugnacious normality was doing living in Paris alongside sophisticates like Scott Fitzgerald and Ezra Pound

---

[1] Actually, she had been brought up in Baltimore in a well-to-do Jewish family, who sent her first of all to Johns Hopkins Medical School, where she tried, unsuccessfully, to become a doctor. Her brother Leo has several times punctured her pretensions to proletarianism.

remains a good question. But it was one that Thomson never bothered to ask, since he was satisfied at last to have discovered a possible librettist who could supply him with the earthy speech rhythms he knew so well how to set to music. Their opera, *Four Saints in Three Acts* (1928) was inspired, curiously enough, by a most un-American theme—namely, the lives of Saint Theresa of Avila and Ignatius Loyola, to which were added incarnations in the course of the writing. But the fame it quickly acquired helped to pave the way for further expressions of the partnership, and in itself it has remained a freak masterpiece neither author nor composer quite predicted.

The fantastic success of the work (it ran in America for an unprecedently long time, considering its irreverently modern title) seems all the more astonishing in view of the fact that its orchestration was omitted from the Paris performances (mostly private) and had to be undertaken in a few days for the benefit of the New York première in 1933. It provides a peculiar insight into Thomson's methods of working that he should have left such an important task to the last minute, and then accomplished it with the aid of a number of artist and writer friends who copied the parts without the composer checking them on the piano. Over 600 pages of score were gone over in this fashion, and the results were as much of a surprise to the composer as to the public. The instrumentation, he later wrote '. . . turned out to give a strange sound indeed . . . a strangeness I was not to know until the first rehearsal. When I did hear it, I was shocked, then got used to it.'[1] The plot of the opera was more or less non-existent; Gertrude Stein's firmest belief was in the destruction of narrative as the basis of art. It has a *theme* rather than a plot, and this is to be construed as the opposition of intellect (personified by Loyola) to feeling (represented by Saint Theresa). Each saint appears in two guises, however, hence the title. Scenes are repeated (as happens after the death of Saint Ignatius) and a symbolic marriage is enacted. But what really holds the audience's attention is the constant play on language; the detailed working out of puns and humorous verbal juxtapositions. To anyone familiar with Gertrude Stein's books, all this will be familiar to the point of boredom, for it was one of her weaknesses that once the joke had worn off there was nothing at which to direct the interest. Her verbal quips—like the famous 'pigeons on the grass, alas!', which came from this opera—went the rounds of sophisticated America and inspired amusing stylistic parodies from James Thurber and others. But they all died a natural death with the passing of the years; whereas Thomson's music, despite its

[1] See *Virgil Thomson* by Virgil Thomson (the titling is Steinian still) published by Weidenfeld & Nicholson, 1967.

rushed and purely aural character, has survived very well. At least, his fragmentary street songs, homespun triads and naïve hymns continue to possess a certain childlike charm, though heard against the black and white abstract décor (intended to convey immobility) they seem almost provocatively anachronistic.

This final contradiction is really the crux of any analysis that might be made of the collaboration of these two strangely dissimilar spirits. For Gertrude Stein, despite her poker-faced, wise-cracking manner was in reality far more deeply immersed in the gangrenous post-war decadence of Paris than even she herself believed. Her friends Derain and Picasso were primitive in their origins only, their art being, like Stravinsky's music of the period, a junk-heap of pointless experimentalism. And they all relied heavily on the power to shock as a means of preventing their reputations from withering. Stein herself was soon classed alongside Joyce as one of the great literary mystifiers, and in her case once the mystery was cleared up nothing but a blank wall remained. When, twenty years later, Thomson essayed another Steinian opera, *The Mother of us All* (1947), it was in America and two decades away from the chance encounter which had led to their fluke success. Here was no more mingling of religious symbolism with 1920 chic, but an opera far more truly representative of 'the making of Americans'. The figures it contains are sometimes drawn from history, at other times from the imaginary present or recent past. The division into scenes is once more entirely arbitrary, and the repetition principle (later admired by John Cage) still more rigorously re-inforced. But this time each scene has a moving true-to-life aspect to it, with a feeling for small-town mores not unlike that displayed by Thornton Wilder in his New England context. There is Uncle Joe playing the organ at his wife's funeral; Aunt Emily making a fuss over Billy's graduation; a local marriage ritual—all perfect cameos from a passing age, old snapshots to be pasted away in the family album. Thomson's music for such episodes was beautifully adapted to its purpose, his Wedding March and Funeral Hymn having just the right degree of commonplace elation and compassion. Perhaps a better literary parallel to these sketches would be the Middle West lyrics of Edgar Lee Masters who, without Wilder's obtrusive intelligence, makes even more credible the basic, raw-material quality of life in a land not so long ago inhabited by pioneers and frontiersmen. On Stein's death in 1949, Thomson wrote an elegy for wind band, entitled *A Solemn Music*, which testifies to the regard in which he held her right up to the end.

During the years between 1934 (after his New York acclaim for *Four Saints in Three Acts*) and 1940, Thomson divided his time between Paris and America. He became involved with Orson

Welles in the Federal Theatre Project, and wrote the music for a number of successful Broadway plays. From there, he triumphed by providing the score for the controversial Negro *Macbeth* and ultimately went on to do the famous series of documentaries with which his name is still most frequently linked. These—in order of production—were Pare Lorenz's *The Plough that Broke the Plains* (1936) and *The River* (1937); Hemingway's *The Spanish Earth* (1937), in which his collaborator was Marc Blitzstein, a pioneer of the new-type highbrow musical nowadays associated with Leonard Bernstein; and, most significantly of all, Robert Flaherty's *Louisiana Story* (1948). This last score undoubtedly contains Thomson's best music for the cinema, possibly because the theme yet again rested on the experiences of a young boy growing up into a world he does not understand. Thinking of illustrating the impact of the giant oil industry on one of the most jungular of the Southern States, Flaherty chose the boy canoeing his way through 'bayou' country to convey his message. There are four scenes in the suite made from Thomson's score. The first aims at depicting the clear sky and fresh earth of the boy's birthplace, his paddling down the river in search of alligator's eggs. The mood music here is impressionist and unremarkable. A modal cor anglais tune forms the basis. Next, we are shown the boy suddenly confronted with the oil derrick. A folk-song is abruptly replaced by a chorale (featuring a twelve-tone theme) to render the thrust of the steel tower against the sky, and to hint at the switch of emotions experienced by the watcher as he gazes in wonder and bewilderment. The third section enacts the robbing of the alligator's nest, employing a conventional passacaglia. It is only in the fourth and final section that bassoons, trombones and even a tuba are invoked to create a growling fugue indicative of the combat between boy and beast. Here the suspenseful piling up of subject and counter-subject dramatically offsets the 5/4 ground bass of the preceding episode, rounding off the work with a thoroughly epic climax. In the entire score we sense Thomson's unconscious identification with the hard wilderness from which all Americans have sprung.

Among the other music Thomson wrote, songs and tone-poems have formed the chief offerings. His setting of *Five Songs from William Blake* might have been thought a trifle unexpected in view of his obvious penchant for clarity and simplicity. But these represent the innocent Blake, the poor engraver who met with such contempt from Reynolds and his quizzical friends at the Academy. They do not touch upon the mystical Blake of the Apocalyptic books. Set for baritone and orchestra, they include several attractive portraits. *The Divine Image*, for example, is an unpretentious revelation of 'the heart of the common lot' and expresses itself chiefly in the language of eighteenth-century hymnody. The famous, *Tiger, Tiger* gives the composer scope for harsher treatment, and the song is characterized by its insistence on stony fifths and an ominous march-like rhythm. Lyricism breaks through in the middle section, but acts as a temporary refuge. In *The Land of Dreams* the free-association technique Stein had used in language is adapted towards musical ends, the song comprising improvisatory-like elements that lead into bitonality, unprepared modulations and parallel chromatic scales. The fourth song is called *The Little Black Boy*—another theme virtually made for Thomson—and recounts the stern mother's rebuking of her naughty child on his return from an escapade. This is the most tuneful of the lyrics, with the mother's recitative being offset by gay violin obligato music and the gentle strum of a harp somewhere in the background. The same violin, played Kentucky or turkey-trot style, appears curiously in the final song, *And did those feet*. That this could not be more different from Parry's famous *Jerusalem* (the same poem) hardly needs underlining. Thomson's aim is to create a kind of 'hot gospel' fervour, the voice and harmonium contributing an overlay of religious piety and determination. It seems a pity in view of America's own rich heritage of poetry that something more closely resembling a native lieder tradition has not grown up across the Atlantic. Copland's Emily Dickinson settings have proposed a promising start to such a tradition; but where Thomson is concerned one can appreciate that New England puritanism lacks the joy of the eighteenth-century English revivalist poetry and there was no other source to which he could have turned.

Of the purely orchestral works, most are impressionist in character and evoke the static landscapes the composer had learned to admire from his painter friends. *Wheat Field at Noon* uses square blocks of chords, mainly diatonic but occasionally overlapping to produce minor dislocations of the pattern. It is an exact musical equivalent of the visual concept. There is no suggestion of loneliness in it, however, having none of the terrifying implications of human remoteness one perceives, say, in the pictures of Andrew Wyeth or in such a stock Middle Western novel as Willa Cather's *My Antonia*. *Sea Piece with Birds* is another of these straight naturalistic pieces, the whole-tone scales of which are slightly reminiscent of Debussy's *Voiles*. Indeed, it is clearly with the great French master of tonal values that Thomson seeks to ally himself in works such as these. His portrait of *The Seine at Night* does not hark back to his semi-expatriate days, but is a post-Second World War study that implies a continuing infatuation with the Gallic world and all its scenic and harmonic attributes. It is to this style that Thomson resorts when he is not busy reproducing the bugle-calls, the zipping of the banjo or the wailing religious homophony of his beloved Missouri. The largest work he has attempted in recent years, however, is rooted in his homeland and yet manages to be serious in a new way. It is the *Missa Pro Defunctis* (1960) for chorus and orchestra, which seems to aim at a musical and religious limbo in that it breaks away both from the flat harmonic collages of his gospel style and the sliding chromatics of his more pagan, Debussyan music. True, references to various New Orleans effects percolate the surface of the music from time to time—as in the jazzed-up *Sanctus*—but it seems that for once Thomson has produced a work for genuine liturgical use, though what church could possibly sponsor it remains an enigma. Perhaps he is anticipating the feeling of the young everywhere that churches are in any case an encumbrance, and that such spiritual needs as may be experienced in the future will be best catered for by works that combine the assorted devices of all the religious faiths of our Christian civilization. To this end, Thomson's Mass may be regarded as the typical hippie's requiem or plaint for an age of disenchantment.

It remains only to say a few words about the remarkable autobiography in which the composer has set down all the impressions his eventful life has left him with. Most moving are the descriptions of life in Kansas City at the turn of the century, with the composer's tribe of relatives bringing a constant flood of gaiety into his modest Baptist home. His grandmother's eye-rolling stories of the Civil War, his cousin Lela's alluring glances from the piano, the whole family, including his Post-Office worker father, getting together to sing *Darling Nelly Grey*—these memories are recounted in prose that seems to render all fiction statuesque. Reminiscences also abound of the composer's days at college, his hearing of Mary Garden in French opera at Chicago (the spur to his desire for 'abroad') and the rough-and-tumble life among the doughboys of the First World War. Later in the book come his revelations of the Parisian scene between the wars, and these chapters do not seem as free from the spite and ambition that made those years so poisonous to so many as they might have been. A certain malice attends his descriptions of the eternal feuds between artists, musicians and writers; yet throughout it all there runs the implicit assumption that Paris meant music and music meant Paris. Nothing that happened anywhere else was of real significance. The hatred, for instance, of German innovations emerges quite prejudiced and undisguised:

> I believed then (1928) and still do, that German music, after being blessed above all others and having led

the world for two hundred years, had failed to keep contact with our century, that it had long since become
self-centred, self-regarding and self-indulgent . . . For
modern harmony the Germans seemed to me tone-deaf,
and as for rhythm, children.[1]

About Gertrude Stein he is affectionate without being tremulous,
and concerning his seemingly endless stint as reviewer and critic
he at last appears to have reached a point of weary cynicism:

> The orchestras play off pitch, and the singers sing off
> pitch; no one bothers to blend, to balance, or to get the
> rhythm right . . . Go to a concert today and look at the
> faces. Music can make them applaud or shout; but it
> never seems to lift them up, give joy.[2]

Yet it is the lift and joy of music that have sustained this cherub
of modernism throughout his entire existence, and one feels they
will go on sustaining him to the end.

[1] *Music Reviewed* (Vintage Books), 1966.
[2] Op. cit.

English music, though as distinguished as any during the period of Byrd, Tallis and Weelkes—and later on that of Purcell—slid, as most people are aware, into the doldrums until Elgar and one or two of his contemporaries restored it to a position of honour in the present century. What is so surprising about this overlong intermission is that, contrary to what is sometimes alleged, it was not followed by a continuation of the programme, so to speak, but by something utterly foreign to our previous ways. To speak, as Frank Howes has recently done, of an English musical 'renaissance' accordingly seems misleading, if not downright absurd. Elgar and Delius, the leading spirits in the English musical world at the turn of the century, when things began looking up again, were each entirely removed by temper and influence from the establishment view of English music as expressed through the person of the late E. J. Dent at Cambridge; and Stanford at London. No one could have hated more than Elgar that alternately febrile and jolly style, derived from madrigal and motet, which had been lauded by the Doctors of Music at the ancient, scorned universities; while Delius, though perhaps one might see some tenuous connection between his music and Stanford's Irish folksiness would have shuddered at the possibility of joining that breezy academic at his pedagogical pursuits. True, Stanford was German-trained and had a certain admiration for composers like Wagner and Brahms; but he chose to settle in Britain where he ignored Delius and hated the late Elgar. The influence of the sixteenth-century English composers made itself felt strongest in the music of men such as Vaughan Williams (the *Fantasia on a Theme by Thomas Tallis* dates from 1910), but these men were not the artists who put Britain back on the map, musically speaking, neither were they to lead into anything much more than a provincial cul-de-sac. Compared to the Schumann-worshipping Elgar and the self-sufficient Delius they were comparative latecomers of minimal talent.

Unfortunately, the view spread during the 1920's and '30's that Vaughan Williams, Sir Arnold Bax, John Ireland and their friends had been responsible for a mighty musical revival. What, in fact, they did was to obscure the tremendous achievements of Elgar (for some reason regarded at that time as a jingoistic bore) and Delius (vaguely disliked for his atheism, Nietzschean philosophizing and air of independence). As Michael Kennedy's brilliant and illuminating study has now made clear, Elgar was for the most part of his life a victim, and not an advocate, of jingoism; while Delius, whatever one may think of his political or religious views, was shown by Professor Arthur Hutchings and others, just after the Second World War, to have written perhaps the best English music of his time. The late Sir Thomas Beecham, usually right in most of his musical judgments, would have added 'of all time'. But this was not what the academic pundits wanted by any means. They looked forward to a new English music that would be compounded of sixteenth-century counterpoint à la Byrd, some Purcellian declamation, and the sort of folk-song indigenousness to be found in Cecil Sharp's collection of melodies. When one looks hard enough for a certain combination of qualities one is sure to find them in someone, however, and I suppose we ought not to be too surprised to find 'great' English composers appearing by the dozen in the period between the wars. It was only with the crop of real youngsters that had grown up *after* the war—I am thinking especially of Alexander Goehr, Richard Rodney Bennett and their contemporaries—that the idea got around that English music may have been a bit parochial in the years leading up to 1939. The reaction has predictably been a shade too fierce, leading some of our under-thirties to regard Darmstadt as the focal point of the Southern counties and Boulez as the greatest living Englishman. The invention of new musical resources has, if anything, exacerbated this situation, with the result that no national style at all will be evident unless more care is taken to express at least a few of the qualities for which this island has earned its musical reputation. But just what *are* those qualities? And are they capable of expression in so international a climate as now exists? These are questions we shall have to come to presently.

Meanwhile, we have not mentioned the name of the composer who has unquestionably acquired the highest prestige, both at home and abroad, accorded to an English musician, and who has been rightly credited with having revived English opera, Delius's limited achievements in that sphere notwithstanding. Britten has at least three qualities that mark him out from all other native composers of his generation. (He was born, incidentally, at Lowestoft, Suffolk, in 1913.) These are an amazingly assured technical facility; a determination, rather like Poulenc's abroad, to remain within the bounds of the tonal system and to avoid excessive Central European intellectualism; and finally a warm attachment to the Suffolk landscape and to the older English way of life in general. This last attribute should not be misunderstood. It would, for example, be quite wrong to regard him as a disciple of Vaughan Williams. His teacher at the Royal College of Music (where he distinguished himself as a youthful but prolific composer of songs and chamber music) was the more sophisticated, some would say dilettante, Frank Bridge. Hence his acceptance of folk-song—and he and his friend Peter Pears have become famous the world over for their slightly modern and skittish arrangements of favourites like *The Plough Boy* and *The Foggy, Foggy Dew*—was from the beginning tempered by a love of the best English literature, much of which he has set with great distinction. His own Crabbe, for instance, made a profound impression on him (especially after reading Auden's critique of that Suffolk poet), while his cycles *The Holy Sonnets of John Donne* (1945) and *Winter Words* (1953), the latter drawing its material from the work of that unrivalled countryman, Thomas Hardy, were among the first indications of a rising interest in, for want of a better term, we shall have to call the art-song. Britten has accordingly struck a successful middle path between the too homespun course followed by his seniors and the die-hard cosmopolitanism of some of his juniors. At least, this is the popular image of the composer that comes across to most listeners. The actual line of development he has pursued has been slightly at odds with this image, and before examining his American operas, *Billy Budd* and *The Turn of the Screw* in particular, it will do us no harm to glance briefly at one or two significant pointers from within his early career.

I shall pass over, without much comment, the phase during which the composer worked for the G.P.O. Film Unit and acquired the knack of writing fairly complex orchestral music to order. This was pre-eminently a phase of professionalization, a period of learning how to do what he wanted to do quickly and under pressure. Not all great composers learn to execute the commands of their imagination in this way, but it is a great advantage if one can do it. By 1939, Britten was about as professional a composer as it was possible to become. The only other pointers of importance were his stirring of political conscience (evident at the time of the Spanish War) and the friendships he formed with various writers, including Auden, Isherwood, Spender, Day Lewis and MacNeice

—at that time regarded as the most talented in England. I believe the first of these pointers has had a considerable, though not highly publicized, influence on Britten's choice of themes for operatic and other works, while the second has helped to equip him with the literary taste to select these themes from the works of outstandingly great writers of the past and present. As a pacifist, the composer quitted England in the summer of 1939 and settled temporarily in New York. He may have been influenced by the similar decision Auden had made a few months previously. Though his stay in America was not an especially happy one (he was criticized at home for having departed hastily at the onset of war, and was at that time hardly prepared for the more swift and impersonal tone of American society), it is my belief that many American attitudes were unconsciously absorbed by him during the two years or so he remained in that country. His desire to return to England in the middle of the war indicates that it was no lack of bravery that had caused his tentative emigration, the home crossing being difficult to obtain and a calculated risk, to some extent, into the bargain. It was ostensibly sparked off by a reading of one of E. M. Forster's essays on Crabbe which, if it did not immediately suggest *Peter Grimes*, certainly filled the composer with a deep nostalgia for the Suffolk countryside and a rapidly developing conviction that, come what might, his real place lay in England. It was not that he had failed to compose in the U.S.A. Works like the Violin Concerto, the Rimbaud song-cycle, *Les Illuminations* (now much criticized for its misunderstanding of French accentuation) and the Sinfonia da Requiem were all products of the New World sojourn.[1]

The two effects of his stay that I am most inclined to think influential for his future development were, first of all, the taking over of certain stock American literary themes to add to his English based preferences; and, secondly, the tendency begun in the Rimbaud poems to look outside England for extensions to his vocal technique. Looking at these questions separately, it will be conceded that one of Britten's major themes (indeed, unkind critics like Colin Wilson have said his *only* theme) seems to be the corruption of innocence by experience. This is not a theme upon which Americans have a monopoly, by any means, as the *Songs of Innocence and Experience* by Blake reveal. But any keen reader of American literature will be able to demonstrate how obsessive an aspect of that country's literature it has become. It was Mark

---

[1] The chief errors in the Rimbaud settings occur in stressing, say, the first and third syllables of 'après-midi' instead of the second and fourth and similar 'howlers'. But French is almost as arbitrary as English in some of these matters.

Twain's great theme in *Tom Sawyer* and *Huckleberry Finn*—
though in his case one feels that innocence can always win out by
sheer avoidance of the issues presented by a not *too* corrupt and
expanding civilization. Melville, who was more of a natural
pessimist, given to solemn biblical allegory, shows in works like
Moby Dick, Billy Budd, Pierre or the Ambiguities and so on, that
man's apparent progress is from happiness and ignorance to
despair and cynicism. By the time we reach Henry James's later
works—*The Wings of the Dove* and *The Golden Bowl* in particular—
evil presents itself as a horrible spectre that lurks behind almost
every human relationship and is certainly to be connected with the
typically American desire for possessions, picked up from decadent
Old Europe. Indeed, even in such early works by James as *The
American* and *The Portrait of a Lady*, we are confronted with a
young, energetic and brilliant traveller to Europe who meets, in
each case, with nothing but guilt, dissimulation and world-
weariness. In choosing *Billy Budd* of Melville's and *The Turn of
the Screw* of James's for his later operas, Britten was consequently
accepting a pair of works in which the same disillusioning moral
was apt to be drawn, in which a similar range of innocent and
guilty characters could be met with. As to the vocal extension, it
seems to me that the style of the early vocal works underwent a
necessary change to meet the dream of innocence shattered and
violated which had always existed alongside what William Dean
Howells once called 'the smiling aspects of American life'.

Arthur Jacobs, in his study of the modern period in Denis
Stevens's compendious *History of Song* (Hutchinson, 1960), has
identified three major devices by which Britten has helped to
enrich English song:

> First, by an enlargement of harmonic resource, particu-
> larly by a simultaneous combination of tonic and
> dominant harmony; second, by the florid 'Purcellian'
> treatment of melody, especially the extension of a single
> syllable (not necessarily in an emotional world) over a
> long run of notes; third, by the building of accompani-
> ments not through the extensions of chords into
> continuous flowing lines, but through the use of short,
> melodic motives often contrapuntally used and having
> both thematic and expressive value.

Such devices have also been attributed to the composer by Donald
Mitchell and Hans Keller in their well-known symposium.[1] The
first writer quoted also finds it a feature of the 1940's and '50's

[1] *Benjamin Britten* ed. Donald Mitchell and Hans Keller (Barrie &
Rockliff, 1952).

that the single song (as formerly practised by musicians like Roger Quilter and Peter Warlock) becomes replaced by the song-cycle— a development more in keeping with German or French music. Britten was one of several English musicians who assisted in this development, others being Alan Bush, Michael Tippett and Lennox Berkeley, to say nothing of the much-lamented Finzi. Berkeley had, of course, been trained in France under Nadia Boulanger and so was thoroughly conversant with the song-cycles of Fauré, Debussy, Ravel and Poulenc. What the cycle permits is something beyond the expression of a single mood or character study, something in fact like a miniature opera. It stands to the lone song as the novel does to the short story. It is easy to see from this line of reasoning how Britten's operatic genius was enhanced by the various experiments he conducted with unified groups of songs, like the Michelangelo, Donne and Hardy settings. The experience thus gained enabled the composer to move away from the set numbers, arioso passages and ensembles of *Peter Grimes* towards that continuously-connected style, supported by orchestral interludes, that distinguishes the later operas. With such recent cycles as the *Six Hölderlin Fragments* (1958), the *Songs from the Chinese* (1958) and the Pushkin-based *The Poet's Echo*, written especially for Galina Vishnevskaya to sing at the time of the new building at the Maltings, we may hope to see further refinements of the composer's operatic manner.

When Britten returned from America, he scored what many critics still take to be his greatest triumph in *Peter Grimes*, adapted from Crabbe's poem by Montague Slater. Afterwards, the composer went to live at Aldeburgh, where he has remained to this day. At first this set him firmly apart from the centre of metropolitan culture. But it is doubtful whether it was ever his intention to retreat, Thoreau-like, into the Suffolk wilderness. Much as he loved the wild sea-breakers, he immediately entertained ambitions —necessarily difficult to fulfil without greater financial resources than he then possessed—of turning his home locale into a venue for the type of summer international festival which has nowadays become a commonplace, but which was then only associated with such cities as Edinburgh. Britten's goal was not fully achieved until the building of the Snape concert hall (at this moment severely damaged by fire) was completed in 1968. But his dream of mounting his own operas at Aldeburgh was realized earlier. Setting aside the children's opera, *The Little Sweep*, he managed to secure his *A Midsummer Night's Dream* première at the Jubilee Hall, Aldeburgh in 1960, the first big step forward. Once the concert hall was finished, it became obvious that it was not intended merely as a vehicle for Britten's own music. The works of French, German and Russian composers were rapidly given prominence there, as were the talents of the great musical executants of these nations. The Russians Vishnevskaya, Rostropovitch and Sviatoslav Richter were among the first to be invited. Hence, the national element in Britten, while indubitably present in his great love of Purcell, the madrigalists and the entire English tradition of pre-Elgarian times, has not turned out to be as all-consuming as certain of his commentators have either hoped or feared. As far as his operas went, it is worth noting that, after *Peter Grimes*, the next to have specifically English connections was the relatively late *Gloriana*, tepidly received in 1951. In the meantime, *The Rape, Albert Herring* (a tragic tale as conceived by Maupassant very much enlivened by Eric Crozier's libretto) and *Billy Budd* all drew their inspiration from foreign sources. It is only with the last of these that we shall be concerned for the present; but since most critics consider it the best of the three we should not be too inclined to feel that we may be by-passing important advances in the composer's technique.

The story of *Billy Budd* (1951), the first of the American operas, is a curious one and its meaning is difficult to make clear.[1] It was set down as a short novel (or 'nouvelle' in Jamesian terminology) by Melville in the last years of his life, not being completed till within three months of his death. In view of the many allegorical meanings that have been attached to it, perhaps it is just as well to make clear at the outset that the author derived the tale from a real event, the hanging of one Philip Spencer aboard the brig *Somers* in 1842, almost fifty years before Melville wrote his book. The reason the tale came to his ears was that his cousin, Guert Gansevoort, had been one of the officers at the tribunal and had consequently spent a large part of what was left of his life deep in misery at the thought of the decision for which he had been partly responsible. Similarly, the character of Claggart, the master-at-arms whose false allegations send Billy Budd (the handsome sailor based upon the figure of Spencer) to the gallows, can be traced back to one Jack Chase, a fellow mariner of Melville's, or alternatively to a corresponding figure in the same author's earlier novel, *White-Jacket*, a man named Bland. It has been suggested that the captain of the ship, the humanitarian but regulation-bound de Vere, was modelled on Melville himself. Unhappily, the matter cannot be resolved quite that simply. For although Britten (and his librettists E. M. Forster and Eric Crozier) encases his opera between a prologue and an epilogue, so to speak, each scene of which deals with the aged Captain de Vere reflecting sadly on the

---

[1] I omit reference to the unpublished *Paul Bunyan* (1942) written in collaboration with Auden.

execution, Melville's Captain de Vere is not shown apart from the
action and is killed off by a bullet from the French attacking ship,
the *Athéiste*, with Billy's name on his lips as he dies. Moreover,
there have been allegorically-minded literary critics, like the late
Richard Chase, who have argued that de Vere is a corruption of
'vir', the Latin word for man; which suggests the character was
conceived along Everyman lines. Billy, again, is constantly claimed
as handsome beyond belief, Melville going as far as to write
that, in the nude, 'he might have posed for a statue of young
Adam before the Fall'. One hardly needs to be reminded of the
significance of this Adamic symbolism for Americans, R. W. B.
Lewis and others considering it the chief element in American
literature.

In his widely admired critical study of Melville, Professor
Newton Arvin delves into the allegorical structure further and
adduces some formidable, if occasionally speculative, evidence.
He writes, for instance:

> If Billy is the Adam of this naval Eden, Claggart is, of
> course, its Satan. Malign as he is, Claggart, like the great
> Enemy in 'Paradise Lost', has a certain nobility of form
> and type . . . his depravity is inherent and terrible but
> it does not express itself in what are called vices or small
> sins. As a naval officer, Claggart is a model of dutifulness
> and patriotism, and intellectually he is a man of marked
> superiority.

This view, if accepted, seems to dispose of the notion that Claggart's charges against Billy spring from a shallow homosexuality or
even from a brutish desire to make the splendid and the innocent
suffer. It pre-supposes a more profound evil, at least as abstract as
that of Iago in *Othello*. Indeed, when Captain de Vere and Billy
pick up Claggart's body (the latter having struck him a death-blow
in anger at the false charges), Melville describes the raising of his
corpse as 'like the handling of a dead snake'. In the book, too,
there is much cogitation on the significance of the deed, which
seems to have sprung from Billy's one defect (another Shakespearian concept?) of being unable to answer questions as a result
of a stammer. Arvin goes on to complete his thesis by stressing the
similarity between de Vere's reluctant decision to hang Billy and
Abraham's sacrifice of Isaac. Britten's handling of this whole
scene is different from Melville's. Firstly, he has Billy quickly
removed to an antinomous position, not allowing him to assist in
the business of dragging the dead Claggart away and depriving
him of the book's powerful cry: 'Struck dead by an angel of God!'

This last remark once more tends to buttress Professor Arvin's interpretation. But there are points to be made for the other side. On his own admission, Arvin considers Melville's prose 'stiff-jointed' and comments that there is a 'torpidity of movement and an excess of commentary' in the scene described. It is probable, therefore, that Britten wished to prevent his opera from becoming bogged down in metaphysical speculation. In any case, the allegorical argument is not completely proven (where, for instance, is the Eve of this alleged Eden?) and it has to be remembered that Melville himself transferred the action to an English 'man-o-war' so as to avail himself of the realism of the Spithead mutiny.

The outstanding features of the opera, as opposed to the book, may be listed in various ways. Aside from the intrusion of prologue and epilogue, it seems as if speed and continuity of action have been Britten's principal objectives; whereas Melville allowed himself an excess of digression even within the short novel form. No one can doubt that Britten was right to adopt the course he did. Otherwise, the work would have been a theatrical failure. In particular, the shipboard scenes all move with incredible rapidity and conviction, the dramatic conflicts being well brought out in the music. The choruses which accompany the setting sail of the vessel and the fight between Billy and Squeak (deliberately set up by Claggart to foster the impression of the former's mutinousness) give the composer excellent opportunities to display his flair for rousing maritime music of the traditional kind. So do the various dances to pipe and drum that also occur in Act I (I am assuming a division into two acts, and not four as originally envisaged). Set against these are the more ominous sounds that break through de Vere's equable temper—for instance, Claggart's semi-tonal theme, with its strong implications of menace and lies, and the off-stage shanties which hint ambivalently at the alternately loyal and threatening presence of the men below. The command of mood in the cabin scenes is particularly notable from the moment when the officers are at dinner, uneasily discussing the possibility of a 'French' revolution taking place in England. There are also some highly original touches of instrumentation—as when the Novice is flogged to the background of a saxophone melody, which returns at a faster tempo as part of the funeral march leading up to Billy's execution. Incidentally, this scene merges adroitly into the Epilogue, in which de Vere asks: 'O what have I done?' and the rocking B flat major chords—symbolic of the smoothness of the sea and the inexorableness of duty—gradually replace the tense B flat minor of his self-questioning. It is interesting that Melville himself chose to extend Billy's feelings rather than de Vere's, for in addition to the sailor's

dying cry of 'God Bless Captain de Vere!' he wrote for him a brief
dream-poem, entitled *Billy in the Darbies* which ends:

> Fathoms down, fathoms down, how I'll dream fast asleep.
> I feel it stealing now. Sentry are you there?
> Just ease these darbies at the wrist,
> And roll me over fair.
> I am sleepy, and the oozy weeds about me twist.

Three years separated *Billy Budd* from *The Turn of the Screw*,
Britten's next American opera, which received its première at the
Teatro La Fenice, Venice, 1954. Oddly enough, this was another
case of a story written by an American but set in an English locale.
The story is so familiar it scarcely bears further repeating, at least in
detail. It was given to James in the form of a 'donnée' by an Archbishop with whom he shared a club. The essence of it rests with
the trials of a young governess, who is charged by an attractive but
distant guardian to look after two young children at Bly House in
the south of England. Briefly, the governess finds the children
(Miles and Flora) delightful, though their relationship seems
clouded by the spirits of the previous servants of the house, a man
named Peter Quint and the governess's predecessor, a Miss Jessel,
who was evidently his mistress. The present housekeeper, Mrs
Grose, claims that both Quint and Miss Jessel are now dead; yet
appears to think they may still be exercising some corrupting
influence upon the children, one of whom, the boy, has already
been sent down from his preparatory school. Thus far, it seems as
if we are about to hear another of James's famous ghost stories—a
tale in the tradition of *Sir Edmund Orme* or *The Beast in the
Jungle*. But literary critics—most notably Edmund Wilson in his
book *The Triple Thinkers* (Lehmann, 1948)—have conspired to
throw doubt on the interpretation of *The Turn of the Screw* as a
straight 'ghost' study or thriller. They have argued that the presence
of Quint and Miss Jessel (who *do* apparently come alive during the
tale, with horrifying effect) can in each case be traced to a delusion
on the part of the governess, whose love for her remote employer
and desire to protect the children have combined to render her a
neurotic witness. This essay is not the place in which to argue out
the respective claims of the 'story-telling' school and the psycho-
analytic critics. Wilson's claims are, to some extent, vitiated by the
fact that Mrs Grose recognizes Quint from the description the
governess gives of the apparition she has seen, thus posing the need
for two delusive characters and not one. On the other hand, the
sexual imagery of the story is quite astonishingly Freudian—the
governess first seeing Quint atop a huge tower; Flora claiming to

see Miss Jessel across a lake; and the children constantly playing games in which pieces of wood are forced through holes.

As Miss Patricia Howard has stated, in her penetrating book on Britten's operas, *The Turn of the Screw* is one of the few works the composer treated asymmetrically.[1] Though there is a prologue, as in *Billy Budd*, this merely has the function of setting the scene, and what follows is a sequence of fifteen Variations. A remarkable innovation for the rather insular Britten is the introduction of a twelve-tone theme of rising fourths and falling fifths that serves as a sort of overture. But perhaps we ought to have been prepared for something of this kind, since we have already been to some pains to show that the composer's 'Englishry' was never quite what it seemed. (An indication of this can be had from the fact that as early as his Royal College of Music days he had expressed a wish to study with Alban Berg—a wish the college authorities refused to grant him, very much to his perpetual annoyance.) One of the best scenes in this chamber opera (the libretto, by the way, was the work of Myfanwy Piper) is the one in which the governess rides down to Bly and meets the children. Miss Howard says of the latter—'they are surely Britten's most successful operatic children'—which is saying a good deal. Yet one feels she is right in this assumption, for the boisterous and yet decorous play in which all engage perfectly captures the charm of the age, which was that just previous to the one in which James wrote the story (1898). One imagines they would have made a good subject, not so much for James's admired Lord Leighton, but for such a delicate portraitist as Julia Margaret Cameron. Curiously, Britten chose the celeste as the instrument to announce the presence of 'the devil, Quint'. Whether this is quite appropriate remains a matter of taste. I am inclined to feel that Britten all along shows more ability in depicting the children and their growing-up problems (after all, his strongest dramatic talent) than in conveying the very real atmosphere of horror that pervades the story. The apparition on the tower, for example, seems decidedly tame, and one cannot help imagining how much more terrifying a really great master of the grotesque, such as Debussy or the early Prokofiev, would have made it. Britten's macabre qualities, such as they are, seem better expressed through the children's puzzled musings—for instance, Flora's lullaby in Variation VI.

When the story itself develops to the point where the children are themselves exposed to the attentions of Quint and Miss Jessel, it becomes evident that Britten has accepted the conventional explanation of the tale—namely, that it is a ghost story with moral corollaries. We deduce this from the fact that Quint's music is

[1] *The Operas of Benjamin Britten* (Barrie & Rockliff, 1969).

invariably played to Miles and not the governess (the celeste perhaps being more likely to seduce a child into wrong-doing than it is to terrify an adult?). Similarly, Miss Jessel's music, which is of a gong-like character, is aimed directly at Flora. But it is noticeable that she (i.e. Miss Jessel) had been a victim of Quint herself, and is not classed as a collaborator in evil. Her music certainly lacks the element of enticement of Quint's, and to that extent creates an unconscious sense of anti-climax. The second act, if one must think of it in these terms, begins with Variation VIII. This ushers in a destructive desire to do away with the children altogether. No longer figures of immoral enchantment, the ghosts now become possible murderers, Quint exercising his demonic will over his mistress to hasten this dénouement. The change of mood is brought about partly by a change of instrumental means—the celeste, piano and glockenspiel giving way to deeper-toned woodwind colours. For instance, the canon between the bass clarinet and bass flute in Variation XI creates a stronger sense of threat than anything that has previously appeared, it no longer being a mere sinister inducement. As in the book, Mrs Grose is finally led to take Flora away, leaving the governess to fight her last battle for Miles's soul alone. Much ambiguity (Wilson's essay, by the way, was entitled *The Ambiguity of Henry James*) attends the climax. Has the governess gone so far in her attachment to Miles that she has projected on to him the love she feels for her employer? If so, the battalions of evil have been increased by one, and Miles is caught between two forces neither of which he can hope to combat on his own. On this reckoning, it is not merely Quint's obscene designs he has to worry about; it is also the governess's sublimated possessiveness. The latter's passacaglia illustrates very well the insistence of her hold on the boy, who indeed dies as a result of being crushed in her arms after Quint has made his escape. 'Together we have destroyed him!' shouts the governess in triumph. But it is Miles who has actually been destroyed.

The success, artistically speaking, of *The Turn of the Screw* was not repeated in any of Britten's subsequent operas, unless one makes an exception for *A Midsummer Night's Dream*. That the American theme of innocence defiled continues to press irresistibly on his imagination is proved by the desire he has recently shown to write another Jamesian opera—this time on the story *Owen Wingrave*. This was first produced in 1970, which is too near to us to elicit a complete judgment. The story upon which it was based comes from much the same late period of James's œuvre as the other, having been written in 1892. It tells of the sensitive, brilliant young son of a military family who refuses to take to the army as a career. A ghostly element is again present in that the boy is forced to spend a night in a bedroom alleged to be haunted by one of his ancestors, a combative individual who died in a fit of passion. Though disheartened by false accusations of cowardice, Owen spends the night as he is compelled to do, but is found dead in the morning. This time there has been no awkward literary exegesis for Britten to disentangle. It appears to be an ordinary tale of the supernatural; but like all such tales in James it points a meaning, if not such a complex one as Wilson has attributed to *The Turn of the Screw*. The parable on this occasion is perhaps more concerned with the failure of people to understand the nature of courage, and the difficulties which arise out of rejecting a natural legacy. Does Britten's choice imply yet another step on the road away from Englishness? I think not. At an early point in his career, he said:

> One of my chief aims is to try and restore to the musical setting of the English language a brilliance, freedom and vitality that have been curiously rare since the death of Purcell.[1]

That he has not chosen to achieve these aims by the simple expedient of folk-song with added counterpoint only testifies to the composer's intelligence and sophistication. He knew, even when he wrote those words, that a new English tradition would have to absorb, just as the old one did, a host of foreign influences if it were to stand any chance of survival. Paradoxically, it is by submitting himself to the influence of America and other countries that this great and gifted musician will stand his best chance of keeping English music alive and forceful.

[1] See the preface to *Peter Grimes* (Boosey & Hawkes, 1945).

PART THREE

PART THREE

The Death and
Re-birth of an Art

Just as we speculated at the outset of this book on how modern
composers would respond to the dissolution of Romanticism, so
we must now predict the reactions of our contemporaries to the
music they will be hearing in what remains of this century. We
have already debated the merits of atonality and neo-classicism,
and attempted to assess the health of nationalism as a musical
philosophy. The Schönbergs, Stravinskys and Bartóks are composers we ought by now to have assimilated. After all, two have
been dead for twenty years and more, while the third survives
precariously into his late eighties. Though it seems true that their
music still evokes shock, misunderstanding and shrill dislike in
many quarters, it is equally the case that it is making lifelong
devotees among the young. I fear, therefore, that we shall soon
have to accept it much as we accept Haydn's or Beethoven's. If we
have failed utterly to come to terms with it, what it suggests is a
lack of goodwill on our parts or a certain sluggishness on the part
of Time, which is not used to operating at the same pace as genius.
Henry James, whose books we have just been describing, once
remarked: 'It takes a lot of history to make a little literature.' His
remark seems doubly true when we consider that, musically
speaking, an element of the 'illiterate' clings to most of us. I do not
intend this as a swipe at the average willing listener. Anyone who
has read this book must be aware of the discrepancies that exist
between my ability to describe people and events and my powers
of explaining actual musical processes. Few people can count
themselves fortunate enough to possess equal fluency in both
languages. When they can, it is probable that they practise the one
and merely preach the other, or vice-versa. In any case are not
these languages becoming outdated almost as soon as they are

mastered? Whitehead used to argue that the great difference
between our age and those previous to it was the compression that
had taken place in the unit of change. Changes that once took a
hundred years to happen, now occur within the lifetime of a typical
individual, and may soon occur within a decade. Another writer,
Charles Péguy, who never lived beyond the First World War put
it this way: that more changes had taken place in the twentieth
century than in all those centuries that succeeded the death of
Christ.

What we must now ask ourselves, therefore, is what changes are
presently taking place on the musical scene? To answer this question, even cursorily, is not going to be easy, since there are so many
different sorts of change involved. Some appear to be technical,
others aesthetic. Some imply a psychological shift, others a purely
cultural transformation. Considering the technical revolution
first, much of the 'new music' (a term I shall employ for music
written after 1945) has sprung from the discovery of new means.
H. H. Stuckenschmidt has observed, as a rough guide to the problem, that from 1600 to 1750 music was primarily vocal in character.
Around the time of Mozart's birth it became chiefly instrumental,
and has remained that way up until the middle of the present
century. From 1950 onwards, however, we have been confronted
by repeated attempts to create music out of machines—i.e. objects
differentiated from instruments by being made to work by a force
such as electricity (or some other force of a non-human kind). The
tape-recorder, for example, has been able to reproduce a range of
sounds—some of them natural in origin—in a way not previously
possible; just as it has offered composers the possibility of musical
montage or laying of sound upon sound. Following this, electronic
machines came into existence which could produce unheard of
noises. Synthesizers and filters were added, by which certain
frequency bands could be mixed or extracted. Finally, we now have
the possibility of 'programming' sounds into a computer which
does the job of arranging these in the form of 'compositions'. This
last is not exactly a new source of sound material as much as a
new, technical means of creation, in which the personality of the
composer may be omitted. As an example of the last type of music-
making, we may quote the case of Professor Hiller's machine at the
Illinois Computer Center, Urbana, U.S.A., developed from the
Datatron (1957) of Klein and Bolitho, who used their 'mechanical
composer' to produce 4,000 tunes an hour. An analogy can be
drawn between this method of composition and the so-called art
of computer poetry. The advantages and disadvantages are the
same in both cases. Fresh combinations may have the effect of new
and interesting juxtapositions of words or tones; but it is difficult

to see how such a method can embody a human purpose or give rise to a genuine human impulse.

To assess the full significance of mechanical aids to composition, however, it is necessary to go back to the original introduction of tape sources in or around 1950. The key-figure in this development was probably Pierre Schaeffer, whose book *A la recherche d'une musique concrète* appeared in 1952 and who has exercised an enormous influence on composers coming after him. The very term 'musique concrète' is attributable to Schaeffer, and may be taken to mean any palette of noises derived from mechanical sources. Schaeffer's *Symphonie pour un homme seul* is nothing more than a collection of sounds such as any human being might make in the course of a day, reproduced on tape. Hence, noises of breathing, coughing, shouting, whistling, footsteps all occur in the course of the 'composition'. Some percussion is added, so that it is not entirely natural; but the effect is rather like a musical equivalent of Mr Bloom's day in Joyce's *Ulysses*. I should wish to point out one extremely important difference, however. This is that Bloom's day included his *thoughts* (hence the term 'stream-of-consciousness') and was not a mere phenomenological record. To that extent, it is easier to make a case for *Ulysses* as art than it is to make one for the *Symphonie pour un homme seul*. For thoughts imply meanings, whereas the noises of phenomena are meaningless. In order to accept Schaeffer's music, therefore, the listener must first accept the proposition that sound is interesting quâ sound. This proposition takes us a little further than, say, Debussy, whose sounds were intended to depict or imitate scenes of beauty; and it certainly takes us a long way from Beethoven to whom each sound was a part of some tonal sequence, some accepted musical grammar. Schaeffer, however, was able to demonstrate that a number of new things could be done with tape. In addition to what we have described, he pointed out that it could simplify notation by making note-durations measurable, not through crochets and quavers and the like, but through the 'revs' counter of the recorder. Similarly, dynamic changes, instead of having to be expressed crudely as ff or pp, could now, by adjustments to the volume control, be marked off in decibels. Again, by playing a piano piece backwards, for example, one could alter the instrument—making it a crescendo and not a diminuendo instrument. These were largely technical gains, but they were of some importance in terms of resources.

Schaeffer's opera, *Orphée* (1953) was made up of a series of musical collages, and in this sense he did not hesitate to combine unlikely sounds one with another. In one of his compositions, a motor-boat engine is heard as the background to an accordion solo and a Balinese priest's song. From about 1954 to 1957, Paris was

full of these 'concerts de bruits' and such conventional composers
as Milhaud, Sauguet and Varèse were interested in them. Varèse,
whose *Déserts* combined live sounds with musique concrète, was
perhaps more advanced in his outlook than Schaeffer; at least the
adjective 'conventional' applied to him only in the sense that he had
been writing pre-tape music for many years before the technical
revolution. As a matter of fact, it is surprising how many fairly well
established, and even conservative, figures sought to identify
themselves with this 'new music'. Scherchen, the conductor, made
himself the spearhead of the movement as executant, while
Malraux and Stravinsky looked on with interest. When in 1958,
Schaeffer wrote his *Etudes Allures* (which made use of bronze
Chinese bells) he immediately aroused the approval of Messiaen,
the doyen of the gamelan style. The movement was not confined
to France, however, and similar experiments were being carried
out at this time by Stockhausen and Eimert at Cologne. The
former's *Studio I* (1953) was based on the idea of 'sinus-tones'—
that is to say, tones without their overtones. Eimert went for the
reverse procedure, which was to use mixtures of harmonics.
Probably the culmination of the German experiments was reached
with Stockhausen's *Studio II* (1954) and *Klavierstück XI* (1956).
These works attempted to follow up Webern's idea of serializing
other elements than pitch, making use of electronics as an additional link. Stockhausen's biblical work, *Gesang der Jünglinge*
(1955–6), set up loudspeakers among the audience, while Krenek's
Whitsun oratorio, *Spiritus Intelligentiae Sanctus* (also 1955–6),
became the first electronic Mass! The text was from Kierkegaard,
who would certainly have been astonished at the result to which his
labours had been put. Other groups operated in Berlin under Boris
Blacher, who had an electronic/natural opera performed at Hamburg in 1966 (*Zwischenfälle bei einer Notlandung*) and in Milan
and Tokyo. Berio and Maderna were the leading spirits at the
former city, Toshiro Mayuzumi the main proponent at the latter.

Other composers resident in France in the '50's chose to exploit
an entirely different line. We have already mentioned Messiaen
and his influence as a teacher at the Conservatoire. His theories
were also expressed in book form, and the result was another indispensable handbook to the 'new music'. Written as early as 1944,
the *Technique de mon language musical* posed some of the most influential ideas to have been expressed in the present century. These
included:

1. Serial use of rhythm.
2. Non-retrograde rhythms, i.e. rhythms which read the same
   whether played forwards or backwards.

3. Non-invertible intervals, i.e. intervals that again remained tacitly unchanged when inverted, unlike the fourth which becomes the fifth, etc.
4. 'Valeur ajoutée'—which is a method of increasing the duration of notes asymmetrically instead of by augmentation.
5. The employment of 'ragas' and 'talas'—that is, oriental scales and rhythms.
6. The notion of the 'transposed' scale. This was of the first importance to Messiaen, who probably derived it from his teacher Tournemire. The idea was that an unconventional scale (i.e. one made up of unorthodox combinations of tones and semi-tones) was capable of only a limited number of transpositions. These could be assessed mathematically. Perhaps 'mode' is a better name for them than 'scale'. In any case, a mode of alternating tones and semi-tones can only be transposed twice, whereas a ten-note mode (such as Messiaen's No. 7) can be transposed four times. The whole concept may be regarded as an extension of the work of Fauré, Debussy and Roussel, each of whom experimented in this direction without going about it so systematically. Not all Messiaen's pupils accepted this element in his teaching, some asserting that 'tonal gravitation' occurred in much the same sense as Schönberg's unwanted 'tonal reminiscence'. Advocates of biological tonality, like Ansermet, were needless to say opposed to the procedure, *a priori*.

A composer who accepted the exotic element in Messiaen without necessarily committing himself to the 'modal transposition' idea was André Jolivet, musical director of the Comédie française, who had been associated with Messiaen and Daniel-Lesur in the group which had called itself 'La Jeune France'. Primitivism of a highly individual kind marked the music of Jolivet, who became noted for his striving after hypnotic effects (usually using the method of rhythmic ostinato) or effects of frenzy. His *Incantations* for flute had appeared as early as 1936, without arousing great interest. But contemporary with this work came the suite *Mana* for piano, which has made the composer far better known. *Mana* is atonal and its name signifies the force of heaven or the supernatural. The suite actually comprises six pieces, each intended to represent some *objet d'art* in the composer's collection. For example, *Beaujolais* is a copper doll, and *La Princesse de Bali* another South Pacific image or ikon. The five *Danses Rituelles* aim at a similar percussive, rhythmic style. The high point of this style came with the tremendously volatile Piano Sonata, dedicated to the memory of Bartók in 1945. A second

Sonata has since been added, equally brutal and uncompromising, and a Piano Concerto of immense technical difficulty. Oddly enough, in view of his position, Jolivet has composed little theatre music, seeming to be more interested in a sort of abstract impetuosity, comparable to the post-Nabi painters or the more design-minded Fauves. Naturally, the most famous of the descendants of the Messiaen group has been Pierre Boulez, whose attitudes have changed from early acceptance of the twelve-tone technique, as bequeathed by Webern and Leibowitz, to an uneven pursuit of the goals set by Debussy in works like *Jeux*. The melodic arabesque foreshadowed in some of Debussy's work has been extremely fruitful as far as he has been concerned, and of late he has been inclined to criticize sharply the obsession with formal rigidity he has noted in Schönberg and his followers. *Le Marteau sans Maître* (1955) was the work that really placed Boulez in the forefront of European composers (it is a cantata on poems by Réne Char) and the 'chirping, knocking, porcelain sounds' it exudes result from the unusual instrumentation—including flute, guitar, viola, xylophone and vibraphone. It is a very beautiful, though perhaps over-melismatic work.

Still concerning ourselves with technical innovation, one of the principal developments since the mid-century—though it actually goes back much further than this on analysis—has been a certain obsession with pseudo-mathematics as a basis for music. I am not, of course, referring to the tone-row, which at least derives its logic from the division of the octave into semi-tones, but the notions of mystical numerology that now appear to have reached Egyptian proportions with some composers. Berg's fetish over the number 23 has already been mentioned. But just as Vermeer and other painters became enamoured of the Greek idea of the Golden Section (the division of the line in such a way that the smaller section is to the larger section as the larger section is to the whole), so certain musicians have experimented with arbitrary combinations of figures as the meaningful element in their art. The concept of the Trinity is naturally to be found in much early music as a religious idea. Friedrich Smend and others attempted to establish a mathematical symbolism of this sort in Bach very many years ago, and d'Indy virtually essayed the same thing *vis-à-vis* César Franck. The chief exponent of the mathematical theory in modern times was the German expatriate Schillinger (1895–1943), who taught George Gershwin and who wrote a book on *The Mathematical Basis of the Arts* (1942). Had he lived long enough Schillinger would undoubtedly have welcomed the computer, since it would have enabled him to make the arduous calculations upon which he felt music should be founded. For instance, he thought up 65,535

different rhythmic configurations, and aimed at doing the same
for the other parameters of music—namely, melody and harmony.
This kind of pre-composing is open to the same kind of criticism
as Honegger made of pre-tonal architectonics. That is to say, it
precludes the element of inspiration. There is also a touch of
monkish scholasticism about the whole idea that seems slightly
silly and repellent. Messiaen himself is not wholly exempt from
this dabbling, and it is significant that both he and Stockhausen are
deeply religious men. The criticism that Boulez (and unquestionably Cage) would make of all this is that it also precludes another
important dimension of creativity—chance. Further criticisms
still relate to notation.

Chance is a word one comes across time and time again in all
discussions of modern music and it takes us away from our first
theme of technique and rationality to our second theme of ran-
domization. Like other intellectual disciplines—philosophy, for
instance, or psychology—music has lately turned again to the East
as a means of offsetting its too insistent reliance on logic and
systematization. The vogue for Zen Buddhism in the '50's had its
counterpart in the 'aleatoric' composition—which is to say the score
that contains in it an element of chance. This element can take
many forms. Either the composer can leave it to the performer to
improvise certain sections, as happens frequently in the work of
Cage, or he can set down a limited range of sequences that can be
played in any order, the last technique being regarded as a species
of 'guided chance'. The expression just quoted is actually Boulez's,
as is the original term 'aleatoric'. As will have been gathered from
what has gone before, one of the great objections Boulez has
lodged against the Viennese has been their pre-occupation with the
planned work. Flexibility, improvisation, spontaneity in general
mean more to him as ideals. But it should be stressed that they do
not mean everything to him. Unlike most of his extremist American
counterparts, Boulez has opted for a characteristically French
compromise—a music that partakes of chance at the same time as
its range of permutations remains strictly limited. On this whole
question, it is worth observing that physicists have run into a
similar dilemma over relativity. According to Heisenberg's
Principle of Indeterminacy, momentum and locality cannot be
measured simultaneously. In the same way, one would suppose, a
melody that moves forward cannot be mathematically analysed in
terms of its components without rendering it static. Keeping to the
philosophical analogy, music up to the present has been seen in a
more Hegelian light. Thesis is opposed by antithesis, which in
turn leads to synthesis. This is the dialectic behind the sonata form
and the fugue. To dispense with this in favour of pre-determined

aural events in sequence is to re-raise the difficulty of precisely notating such events, or precisely measuring their spatial concomitants. Chance, however, is not necessarily an artistic solution, for it is just as dependent on judgment as is precision.

Chance and mathematics both play some part in the music of a composer who had the curious distinction of being an assistant architect to Le Corbusier for twelve years (1947–59). He is Yannis Xenakis, who was born at Athens in 1922. Naturally enough, his training led him to think of music as something to be worked out on the drawing board, though he did study independently with both Milhaud and Messiaen while practising as an architect. Originally, Xenakis seemingly followed the twelve-tone method with some slavishness, but quite early on dropped it as being of no use. He considered it too linear and objected to the polyphonic density to which it inevitably gave rise. What he desired to put in its place was some sort of audio-mosaic, and a longish period of experiment was necessary before he could find a technique that would express his purpose. Moving away from Messiaen, as well as the twelve-toners, he found a model better suited to him in Varèse. The first pieces of Xenakis to attract serious attention were presented between 1955 and 1957. They included his 'Metastasis', which Scherchen performed at Donaueschingen, and which was scored for 63 strings. It became obvious from listening to this that the 'glissando' was a device into which the composer read a great deal. The notation tends to consist of straight lines with the pitches identified only at each end. The *Pithoprakta*, *Achorripsis* and *Diamorphoses* all followed in a short time, and were differentiated chiefly by being based on what the composer called 'probability-calculus' studies. The term he coined for such music was 'stochastic', and despite the suggestion of precise demarcation implied, the effect his music was intended to produce was global. In a book written in 1963, entitled *Musiques Formelles*, he argued much as Furtwängler, Hindemith and Ansermet had done—that atonal or twelve-tone music had no aural roots in human sensitivity. Ansermet's erudite but rather obscure tome, *Les Fondements de la musique dans la conscience humaine* (1961), had already expounded this view in scholarly detail. Since he, too, had been mathematically trained (he began life as a mathematics teacher at the 'lycée'), both his and Xenakis's books impose something of a burden on the student who is not fully numerate. While Furtwängler was always suspected of holding the views he did out of deference to Nazi opposition to atonalism. One cannot accuse Hindemith of such motives, however, and he is easier to read.

So far we have said nothing about Polish music in this century, and perhaps this is a good time to do so; since there are certain similarities between the glissandi techniques of Xenakis and the unconventional string effects in the work of a composer like Penderecki (born 1933). But before we come to his music, it is only fair to mention the contribution of an older Polish musician, Lutoslawski (born 1913), which has until recently been neglected in the West. Again a mathematics student (this time at Warsaw University), Lutoslawski did not carry his calculations into his music to any very noticeable effect, at least in the early years. Much of the music he wrote before the War sounds merely Eastern European, and is difficult to distinguish from that of Bartók or Martinů at their most natural. That Lutoslawski was a great admirer of Bartók is proved by the moving *Funeral Music* he wrote on that composer's death. It was this work, perhaps more than any other, that earned him universal applause. However, he soon moved on to adopt serial methods, and eventually fell prey to 'aleatoric' and Sprechstimme techniques. His *Trois Poèmes d'Henri Michaux* were the sensation of the Zagreb Biennale of 1963, and his large choral work, *Pensées*, scored for woodwind, two pianos, xylophone, harp, celeste and percussion in addition to voices, has added further to his reputation. Perhaps he is best known in Britain for his set of Paganini Variations (the same theme as was used by Schumann, Brahms and Rachmaninov!) for two pianos, which has been played here many times by John Ogdon and his wife Brenda Lucas. By contrast, Penderecki has concerned himself very much indeed with mathematical series. But, like Xenakis, he is fascinated by the range of colour to be had from a single family of instruments, namely the string family. In his *Canon* (1963), the instruments are struck, rubbed, played 'col legno' and so on, in the hope of achieving variety within unity. Despite the title of this last work, Penderecki cannot be regarded as a contrapuntal composer, his 'Hiroshima Threnody' and *Stabat Mater* both being characterized by use of homophonic chord-clusters. Lately, Penderecki has been attempting to bridge the gulf between his own Communist state and the West by writing further religious works, like the St Luke Passion which was first performed in Munster Cathedral in 1963.

But I imagine that most critics would consider Hans Werner Henze (born 1926) as the most important European composer of his generation, after Boulez. Being German, one might have expected Henze to take easily to the serial method, and so he did in many of his earliest works. But more recently he has had changes of heart (his is a case a little like Copland's in which a difficult early phase seems to have been replaced by a more relaxed, intelligible period). Fluency was a strong feature of Henze's music from the beginning, and with the exception of Britten he strikes

one as the most accomplished musician now writing. Though he
has written five symphonies, it is opera that seems to have interested
him most.[1] His *Boulevard Solitude* (1951) combined jazz elements with Sprechstimme and montage. The next opera he
wrote, however, the lesser known *König Hirsch*, was almost
melodious in the Italian bel-canto manner. Most listeners will have
heard his ballet music for *Undine* (1956), the famous water-sprite
depicted by both Debussy and Ravel, and few would deny that it
is pleasant and easy to assimilate. Some commentators have gently
rebuked the composer for having followed the path of Stravinsky
in *Apollon Musagète* and *Orpheus*, but actually these two composers
have crossed paths recently—Henze moving from twelve-tone
methods to a simple tonal style, while Stravinsky was giving up
his neo-classicism for the serialism of works like *Agon* and the
Mouvements. Understandably, Stravinsky has one or two snide
comments to make about Henze in his writings; but since he is
equally churlish towards most of his juniors ('I cannot make out
whether it is Nono who is holding up Venice, or the other way
around', etc.) there is little point in taking his criticisms too
seriously. At any rate, Henze seems sincere enough in his desire to
write directly for the more ordinary listener. 'I have needed all my
strength to write simply,' he remarked not long ago, and he rather
bravely denounced several of his dodecaphonic juniors in a recent
television interview as assisting in the 'de-humanization' of music
—a process he sees as leading back towards Fascism. The last two
of Henze's operas, *Elegy for Young Lovers* and *The Bassarids* (1966)
were composed to libretti by Auden and Kallmann, and the latter
was voted by a panel of critics here as the opera they most wanted
to see during 1969 at Covent Garden.

Finally, we come to America again, where, as its inhabitants
would be inclined to say 'the real action lies'. Despite the claims
of Ives, Babbitt, Sessions, Carter and the other important figures
to have created a distinctively transatlantic tradition in music,
interest seems more than ever to have centred upon the personality
and ideas of John Cage (born 1912, in Los Angeles), who has set an
example that younger composers appear to be following all over
the world. Long considered something of a charlatan, like Satie in
France, Cage has lately come into his own and proved that, even
if he is not the genius his admirers state, he is at any rate one of the
most influential composers of the second half of the twentieth
century. We have described Boulez's interest in 'guided chance',
but in Cage we experience a composer to whom indeterminacy has

[1] For a good analysis of the orchestral works, see 'Henze in the Concert
Hall' by Meirion Bowen in *Music and Musicians*, Dec. 1968, Vol. 17,
No. 4.

become the very life-blood of art. As long ago as 1938 his invention of a 'prepared' piano enabled him to write music that would be indeterminate both as to pitch and tone-colour.[1] By collaborating with the pianist David Tudor, Cage has since been able to compose works for this instrument which are not merely indecipherable but deliberately absurd. The Buddhist 'koan', or sudden flash of insight resulting from the bringing into conjunction of illogical sequences, lay at the back of Cage's thinking on this subject, so that what he has tried to do is to shock audiences into *experiencing* not just music but the whole aural universe in a new way. Europeans (and, of course, a good many Americans) have become a little sceptical of the claims of these oriental religious cults to create enlightenment—partly because they have been reared in a tradition which values rationalism and partly because some obvious confidence-tricksters have delighted in employing Cage's methods with hoax-like objectives. Some of the verbal 'koans' to which Zen writers have subjected us (e.g. 'We all know the sound of two hands clapping, but what is the sound of one hand clapping?') have, contrary to the original intention, caused us to feel an even greater respect for rationalism than we had before. On the other hand, there can be no question about Cage's own sincerity. His point that we often do not really listen to what we hear is also something that is hard to deny.

Some critics simply view Cage and his work as a reversion to the cult of Dada, popular in the 'twenties. But I do not believe it to be quite the same thing. True the composer has played some shameless games with the public. His idiotic composition 4'33"—which consists of simply raising the piano lid for that duration of time and then closing it again—seems to have no other object than getting the audience to listen to the random sounds that might emanate from the hall. On another occasion, Cage arranged a simultaneous concert at which some performers shot at painted balloons; others listened to Tannhäuser relayed on a loudspeaker; one had a shave; and the last sang *Parlez-moi d'amour*. Meanwhile, the composer himself stood in a corner and counted up to twenty-three. An even greater session of endurance took place in New York a few years back when Cage had Satie's *Vexations* (an early 'aleatoric' piece in which there are 840 repetitions) performed by twelve hired pianists. The performance went on for nearly two days. Reasonably enough, most of the composer's friends stayed away, but one wit who stuck it out was reported by *Time* magazine as yelling 'Encore' as the last of the marathon died away, incidentally waking up several less

[1] A prepared piano is one in which strips of metal or wood are inserted between the strings, or which has been tampered with in such a way as to falsify the original intentions.

hardy spirits who had succumbed to their customary nocturnal habits. 'Happenings' such as these hardly inspire one with great faith in the composer's integrity. But a conversation Cage had with David Sylvester on the B.B.C.'s Third Programme on June 7th, 1969, succeeded in clarifying his aims a little. In it, he argued that men like Mahler and Sibelius had merely been products of the machine-age, their works being the artistic equivalents of the blast-furnaces and coal-mines with which they were surrounded. His *own* music, he said, was a phenomenon more like weather. He was also interested, he added, in the vibrations stemming from ordinary objects. If people failed to hear these and appreciate how beautiful they were, it was only proof of their musical deafness. To me, such statements—though I regard them as invalid— seemed less discreditable than the suggestion the composer advanced that art had no other aim than to pass away the time. 'The goal of each activity is its obviation' is the way he put it. Or, falling back on one of his Japanese 'koans', 'By taking a nap, I pound the rice.' I am afraid I cannot see such suggestions in any but a nonsensical light.

If I understood him correctly, what Cage wanted to say was that some persons thought of works of art as priceless artefacts, whereas in his view it was the *activity* of composing or listening that was important. Schönberg, as a system-builder so called, was interested in the product. And this has been the attitude of most artists up to the present, including those whose art has had an admittedly functional bias, like architects. He cited the case of Mies van de Rohe, who was alleged to have gone up to some people in a building of his and taken away the flowers they were holding. It spoilt the effect of his building, he said. Whether this story is true or not I cannot presume to say. Certainly buildings are meant to be used by people and should not be regarded as large pieces of sculpture. But then I would place the architect in a different posi- tion from the musician or the painter, who (to my way of thinking) may legitimately aim at creating a thing of beauty, durable and untouchable. Beethoven's Ninth may be an artefact, in Cage's terminology, but it is an artefact that endures and gives people spiritual or aesthetic comfort as it stands. There is no guarantee that, if interfered with, these amenities would still be afforded. Furthermore, I am not sure that I can share Cage's continued assertion that art must be a social affair. If by 'social' he means 'participatory', my inclination would be to disagree. After all, with whom (except the author and his characters) does one participate when reading a novel? And does not the existence of 'hi-fi' in the home indicate that one may partake of music privately? Indeed, there are some musicians—Glenn Gould, for instance—who are arguing that the concert is a thing of the past, and that private listening can now call on facilities which make it preferable. Even if this last assumption is disallowed, who will dispute the right of an instrumentalist to play for his own pleasure? Perhaps this is what Cage means by 'passing the time'. If so, it only throws the question back a stage further to the point of asking whether one way of passing the time is more edifying than another. As for other implied meanings of the word 'social', I cannot see how a socialization of art will help to mitigate human suffering, which is I understand another of Cage's contentions. Such a task, surely more political than artistic, must depend on obligatory factors.

A detailed study of Cage's aesthetics would have to take proper account of the two books he published in 1968, giving full expression to his philosophy.[1] However, I think it can be said without prejudice that the composer believes the tradition of Western music as we know it is deservedly dead, and will not be resurrected. We have lived, he would say, through a period of assertive art, having as its aim the fabrication of a product. From now on, this will not hold good. What the future promises is an *activity*, purposeless in itself, but having the function of bringing people together to engage in a less brutal existence. Chance and trust in the instinctive life will enable us to maintain interest in this activity and the abandonment of all rules will free us from the constraints which are at present the main cause of human friction. To these stipulations, I should just like to add a brief commentary. First of all, as I have already hinted, I am an admirer of the finished product—always provided it is well enough finished. I have proved this to my own satisfaction in that the consolation I now derive from those works of art I admire is much the same as that I derived from them thirty years ago. I find this the major source of stability in an otherwise unstable world. Certainly I find it consolation enough. Secondly, I fail to see how a return to instinct, to an absence of rules, to a deification of the 'ab ovo' principle, can lead to anything but anarchy. As Professor Wilfrid Mellers recently reminded us: 'Art cannot be a rage of chaos.'[2] A retreat into infantilism—for that is what it really is—I consider to be a form of regression, Wordsworth and Rousseau notwithstanding. I am glad, also, that Professor Mellers has reminded us of the moral values that attach to art, and that such values are not won without struggle, discipline, repression. Indeed, I would go as far as to agree with Freud that repression is the price we pay for civilization, and that on the whole it is a price worth paying.[3] For Cage, it is

---

[1] *Silence* and *A Year from Monday* (Calder & Boyars, 1968).
[2] See *Caliban Reborn* (Gollancz, 1968).
[3] See *Civilisation and its Discontents* (Hogarth Press, 1930).

enough simply to be. But unless being is complementary to knowing nothing of any artistic value can possibly emerge.

What I am prepared to concede is that Cage has not only drawn around him an impressive range of disciples, but that he has been able to point to real disasters in the course music has taken in the West since the Second World War. One understands clearly why such talented composers as Earle Brown and Morton Feldman, Harry Partch and Lukas Foss, have been driven into accepting his philosophy. One important reason is that the cheapening of the artefact has brought with it a cheapening of the view that upholds the artefact. Composing in the academic fashion has become too easy, acclaim for mediocre talent become too common. Feldman, in a forthright article for the journal *Composer* (Winter, 1966) has noted how destructive has been the effect of university music-making in the United States, where 'productivity' rather than discrimination has resulted in a situation in which almost every piece of correctly written music, good or bad, gets its turn at one of the summer festivals and becomes the means of earning the cachet of 'composer'. As in their creative writing courses—which have almost sunk American literature by foisting on to it tons of worthless verse and fiction—American university music studies have evolved along pedestrian lines, the students and teachers forming their own mutual admiration society. Writing of the latter, Feldman goes on to say:

> It becomes increasingly obvious that to these fellows, music is *not* an art. It is a process of teaching teachers to teach teachers. In this process, it is only natural that the music of the teacher will be no different from that of the teacher he's teaching. Academic freedom seems to be the comfort of knowing one is free to be academic. A painter who continually turned out paintings like Jackson Pollock would soon be on his way to Rockland State Hospital. In music, they make him Head of the Department.

What Feldman omits to add is that much of this pointless grind is a part of the promotion race, and that music departments (instead of producing musicians) are *building* their student-image on the figure of the imitation-composer who in turn becomes the professor. 'Publish or perish' has long been the slogan in other departments. 'Compose or decompose' might be a suitable one for the 'new' music departments. To this kind of thing, Cage is almost preferable.

As in most academic matters, Europe ends by imitating America, and there are already several universities in Britain where to be a 'composer' is the path to scholastic preferment. Being a 'composer', it need hardly be added, means having had a few works performed at Cheltenham or commissioned by the B.B.C. As Milton Babbitt has said: 'It's a mad scramble for crumbs.' One can only hope that there will be a return to teaching music, just as one can only hope that 'creative writing' does not catch on in literature departments here. A similar dilemma, of course, attends the Art College—perhaps it is here that the dilemma has shown itself at its worst in Britain. For we have never had the kind of art colleges that teach the history of art and the aesthetics of art. What we have had have been schools for artists—which, almost by definition, become schools for non-artists. When an attempt was made, rather belatedly, to 'liberalize' the curriculum, it was met with hostility. Now, apparently, it is not bad enough to know no art history or aesthetics. One can become a designer, a commercial artist, a specialist in fabrics and so on. It is no wonder that, as John Lennon is reported to have said: 'The Mona Lisa is a load of crap.' Before long, we shall have a generation that has not heard of the Mona Lisa; just as the present path being pursued by music departments will end in a generation that has never heard of Beethoven. One may be sure, however, that its members will be 'composers'. It is almost impossible to foresee a way out of the coming impasse. All forms of art—music included—are rapidly becoming a form of do-it-yourself activity. I have even heard that 'kits' are now being supplied by certain firms, which may be assembled into 'symphonies' or 'sonatas' after the fashion of model aeroplanes. My difficulty, to return to the subject, is to know whether the Cage philosophy is a stimulus to, or a reaction against, this development. On the evidence of tirades like Feldman's, it would seem a protest. Yet if this is what it really is, can we rely on Cage's bland anti-formalism to give us a better lead? Speaking for myself, I believe the re-birth of music will depend on a compromise such as Boulez and his followers exemplify. Or else on an unsolicited gift, like Mozart's, from the Creator.

Bibliography

Dealing with so wide a field as modern music, this bibliography could not be expected to strive for completeness. It merely refers to the material consulted in the book's preparation. Fuller bibliographies may be found in Austin, Saltzman and others.

ABRAHAM, G.: 'The Bartók of the Quartets' in *Music and Letters*, XXVI, 1945
(ed.) *The Music of Sibelius* (Duckworth), 1947
ACKERE, J. VAN: *Ravel* (Elsevier, Brussels), 1957
ALDVOGEL, W.: 'The Story of Bayreuth' in *Music*, Vol. 3, No. 2, 1969
APRAHAMIAN, F. (ed.): *Essays on Music* (Cassell), 1968
AUSTIN, W.: *Music in the Twentieth Century* (Norton, N.Y.), 1967
BAREA, I: *Vienna* (Secker & Warburg), 1968
BARRICELLI, J.-P. & WEINSTEIN, L.: *Ernest Chausson* (University of Oklahoma Press), 1955
BARZINI, L.: *The Italians* (Hamish Hamilton), 1964
BARZUN, J.: *Darwin, Marx and Wagner* (Secker & Warburg), 1942
BAUDELAIRE, C.: *L'Art Romantique* (Conard, Paris), 1925
BLISS, SIR ARTHUR: 'Four Aspects of Music' in *Composer*, Winter, 1966–7
BOULEZ, P: 'Schönberg is Dead' in *The Score*, Vol. I, No. 6, 1952
BOWEN, M.: 'Henze in the Concert Hall' in *Music and Musicians*, Dec., 1968
BRADSHAW, S. & BENNETT, R. R.: 'In Search of Boulez' in *Music and Musicians*, Jan. and Aug., 1963.
BUSONI, F.: *The Essence of Music* (Dover Books), 1968
CAGE, J.: *Silence* (Middletown, Conn.), 1961
A Year from Monday (Calder & Boyars), 1968
CARDUS, SIR NEVILLE: *A Composer's Eleven* (*Cape*), 1958
Gustav Mahler, Vol. I (Gollancz), 1967
CASELLA, A.: *Music in my Time* (University of Oklahoma Press), 1955
CLAPHAM, J.: 'Martinů's Instrumental Style' in *Music Review*, XXIV, 1963
COLLAER, P.: *A History of Modern Music*, trans. Sally Abeles, Cleveland, 1961
COOPER, M.: *Ideas and Music* (Barrie & Rockliff), 1965
COPLAND, A.: *Our New Music* (Whittesley), 1941
Music and Imagination (Cambridge, Mass.), 1952
Music since 1900 (Spearman), 1969
CORKE, H. & LAWRENCE, D. H.: *The Trespasser* (Duckworth), 1922
CORTOT, A.: *French Piano Music*, Vol. I, trans. Hilda Andrews (O.U.P.), 1932
COX, D.: 'France' in *A History of Song* (ed. D. Stevens), (Hutchinson), 1960
CRAFT, R. & STONE, K.: 'Anton Webern' in *The Score*, Vol. I, No. 13, 1955
CROSS, A.: 'Debussy and Bartók' in *The Musical Times*, Dec., 1967

CULSHAW, J.: *Sergei Rachmaninov* (Dobson), 1959
CURTISS, M.: *Bizet and His World* (Mercury Books), 1959
DAVIES, L.: *The Gallic Muse* (Dent), 1967
    'Dutilleux—composer of tradition' in *Music and Musicians*, Sept., 1969
    César Franck and His Circle (Barrie & Rockliff), 1970
DEANE, B.: *Albert Roussel* (Barrie & Rockliff), 1961
DEMUTH, N.: *Maurice Ravel* (Dent), 1947
    Albert Roussel (United Music Publishers), 1947
    Vincent d'Indy—Champion of Classicism (Barrie & Rockliffe), 1951
    French Piano Music (Museum Press), 1960
DENT, E. J.: *Ferrucio Busoni* (O.U.P.), 1933
DONNINGTON, R.: *Wagner's Ring and its Symbols* (Faber), 1963
DREW, D.: 'French Music' in *European Music of the C20th*, ed. H. Hartog
    (Pelican Books), 1961
DUMESNIL, R.: *L'Aube de XXe siècle* (Armand Colin, Paris), 1958
EINSTEIN, A.: *Music in the Romantic Era* (Norton, N.Y.), 1947
ELGAR, F.: *Mondrian* (Thames & Hudson), 1969
EVANS, P.: 'Martinů the Symphonist' in *Tempo*, Nos. 55 & 56, 1960
EWEN, D. (ed.): *The New Book of Modern Composers* (Knopf N.Y.), 1961
FASSETT, A.: *The Naked Face of Genius* (Gollancz), 1948
FELDMAN, M.: 'Boola Boola' in *Composer*, 22, Winter, 1966–7
FOLDES, A.: 'Béla Bartók' in *Tempo*, No. 43, 1957
FREUD, S.: *Civilization and its Discontents* (Hogarth Press), 1930
GARTENBERG, E.: *Vienna: its musical heritage* (Pennsylvania State University Press), 1968
GLASENAPP, K. F.: *Life of Richard Wagner*, trans. by W. Ashton Ellis,
    2 vols., Wagner Society of London, 1911
GLASSCO, J.: *Under the Hill* (New English Library), 1968
GOLEA, A.: *Rencontres avec Pierre Boulez* (Belmond, Paris), 1968
GOLLANCZ, SIR VICTOR: *The Ring at Bayreuth* (Gollancz), 1965
GOSS, M.: *Bolero: a life of Maurice Ravel* (Tudor Publishing Company,
    N.Y.), 1940
GREENLAGH, J.: 'Boulez 1969 and Wagner 1850' in *Music and Musicians*,
    May, 1969
GRAY, C.: *A Survey of Contemporary Music* (O.U.P.), 1924
    Sibelius (O.U.P.), 1931
GROUT, D. J.: *A Short History of Opera* (Columbia University Press),
    2 vols., rev. ed., 1968
HANSLICK, E.: *Selections* (Peregrine Books), 1968
HANSON, L. & E.: *Prokofiev the Prodigal Son* (Cassell), 1966
HAYWORTH, P.: 'Old Klingsor and New Bayreuth' in *Encounter*, July, 1967
    'The Rise and Fall of Richard Strauss' in *Encounter*, Aug., 1968
HEINSHEIMER, H.: *Menagerie in F sharp* (Verlag-Zürich), 1953
HELL, H.: *Francis Poulenc* (Calder), 1959
HELM, E.: 'Malipiero' in *Musical America*, April, 1952
HODEIR, A.: *Since Debussy* (Secker & Warburg), 1961
HONEGGER, A.: *I am a Composer* (Faber), 1966
HOWARD, P.: *The Operas of Benjamin Britten* (Barrie & Rockliff), 1969
HUGHES, G.: *Pan Book of Great Composers* (Pan Books), 1965
    Sidelights on a Century of Music 1825–1924 (Macdonald), 1969
HUTCHINGS, A.: *Pelican History of Music*, Vol. 3 (Pelican Books), 1968
IRVINE, D.: *The Ring of the Nibelung and the Condition of Ideal Manhood*
    (Grant Richards), 1897
    Parsifal and Wagner's Christianity (Grant Richards), 1899
JAENISCH, J.: *Manuel de Falla und die Spanische Musik* (Verlag-Zürich), 1952

JANKELEVITCH, V.: *Ravel* (Calder), 1960
JEFFERSON, A.: 'The Angel of Fire' in *Music and Musicians*, Dec., 1965
JOHNSON, H.: *Sibelius* (Faber), 1960
JOUSLER, J.: *Music in the Twentieth Century—Schönberg to Penderecki* (Schunemann Verlag. Bremen), 1969
KAUFMANN, W.: *The Portable Nietzsche* (Viking Press), 1954
KELLER, H. & MITCHELL, D.: *Benjamin Britten—a symposium* (Barrie & Rockliff), 1952
KLEIN, J.: 'Wozzeck—a summing up' in *Music and Letters*, April, 1963
KOECHLIN, C.: *Gabriel Fauré*, trans., Leslie Orrey (Dobson), 1946
KOLNEDER, W.: *Anton Webern* (Faber), 1968
LAMBERT: *Music Ho!* new edn (Faber), 1968 (with preface by A. Hutchings)
LANG, P. H. (ed.): *Contemporary Music in Europe* (Dent), 1965
LAVIGNAC, A.: *Voyage Artistique à Bayreuth*, trans. as *The Music Dramas of Richard Wagner* by Esther Singleton (Dodd Mead, N.Y.), 1898
LAYTON, R.: *Sibelius* (Dent), 1965
LEHMANN, L.: *Singing with Strauss* (Hamish Hamilton), 1964
LEYDA, J. & BERTENSSEN, S.: *Sergei Rachmaninov* (Allen & Unwin), 1965
LOCKSPEISER, E.: *Debussy: His Life and Mind*, 2 vols. (Cassell), 1962–4
LONG, M.: *Au Piano avec Gabriel Fauré* (Julliard, Paris), 1963
MACDONALD, D.: *Against the American Grain* (Gollancz), 1962
MACHLIS, J.: *Introduction to Contemporary Music* (Norton, N.Y.), 1961
MAHLER, A.: *Memories and Letters*, new edn (Murray), 1969 (with preface by D. Mitchell)
MANN, T.: *Buddenbrooks*, trans. H. Lowe-Porter (Secker & Warburg), 1924
Essays of Three Decades, trans. H. Lowe-Porter (Secker & Warburg), 1947
Doctor Faustus, trans. H. Lowe-Porter (Secker & Warburg), 1954
MANN, W.: *Richard Strauss: a critical study of the operas* (Cassell), 1964
MAR, N. DEL: *Richard Strauss*, Vol. 2 (Barrie & Rockliff), 1969
MAREK, G.: *Richard Strauss—the life of a non-hero* (Gollancz), 1968
MASON, C.: 'Bartók through his quartets' in *Monthly Musical Record*, No. 80, 1950
'Webern's Later Chamber Music' in *Tempo*, No. 28, 1957
MCCABE, J.: 'Messiaen's Vingt Regards' in *Records and Recording*, Aug., 1969
MELLERS, W.: 'Romanticism and the Twentieth Century' in *Man and His Music* (Barrie & Rockliff), 1962
Music in a New Found Land (Barrie & Rockliff), 1964
Caliban Reborn (Gollancz), 1968
MENDES, C.: *Le Roi Vierge* (Paris), 1881
MILA, M.: *Manuel de Falla* (Milan), 1962
MOREUX, S.: *Bartók* (Richard Masse), 1953
MYERS, R.: *Erik Satie* (Dobson), 1948
Maurice Ravel: life and works (Duckworth), 1960
'Towards a New Music' in *Composer*, Winter, 1966–7
Chabrier and His Circle (Dent), 1969
NATHAN, B.: 'Twelve Tone Compositions of Dallapicola' in *The Musical Quarterly*, No. 45, 1958
NESTYEV, I.: *Prokofiev*, trans. Florence Jonas (Stanford University Press), 1961
NEWLIN, D.: *Bruckner, Mahler and Schönberg* (Owen), 1947
NEWMAN, E.: *A Study of Wagner* (Grant Richards), 1899
Wagner as Man and Artist (John Lane), 1925

Fact and Fiction about Richard Wagner (Gollancz), 1931
Life and Works of Richard Wagner (Cassell), 1933–47
Wagner Nights (Putnam), 1949
NEWSOM: G.: 'Electronic Odyssey' in *Composer*, Winter, 1967–8
NORTHCOTE, S.: *The Songs of Henri Duparc* (Dobson), 1949
NOSKE, F.: *La Mélodie Française de Berlioz à Duparc* (Presse Universitaire), 1954
PAHISSA, J.: *Manuel de Falla and His Works*, trans. J. Wagstaff (Museum Press), 1954
PAYNE, A.: *Schönberg* (O.U.P.), 1969
PERLE, G.: *Serial Composition and Atonality* (Faber), 1962
PERLEMUTER, V. & JOURDAN-MORHANGE, H.: *Ravel d'après Ravel* (Editions du Cervin, Lausanne), 1961
PIRIE, P.: 'Bantock and His Generation' in *The Musical Times*, Aug., 1968
PLEASANTS, H.: 'Who's Afraid of Pierre Boulez?' in *Encounter*, Feb., 1969
Serious Music and all that Jazz (Gollancz), 1969
POULENC, F.: *Moi et mes amis* (La Palatine, Paris–Génève), 1963
PRAEGER, F.: *Wagner as I Knew Him* (Longmans), 1891
REDLICH, H.: *Alban Berg: the man and his music* (Owen), 1957
Bruckner and Mahler (Dent), 1963
REICH, W.: *Alban Berg*, trans. C. Cardew (Thames & Hudson), 1965
RIDEOUT, D.: *Landowska on Music* (Stein & Day, N.Y.), 1966
RINGBOM, N.-E.: *Sibelius* (University of Oklahoma Press), 1954
ROLAND-MANUEL: *Maurice Ravel*, trans. C. Jolly (Dobson), 1947
RUNCIMAN, J. F.: *Wagner* (Longmans), 1913
SAFRANEK, M.: *Bohuslav Martinů*, trans. R. Finlayson-Samsourova (Dobson), 1962
SALTZMANN, E.: *Twentieth Century Music* (Prentice-Hall), 1967
SAMUEL, C.: *Entretiens avec Olivier Messiaen* (Belmond, Paris), 1968
SCHÖNBERG, A.: *Style and Idea* (Williams & Norgate), 1950
SEROFF, V.: *Rachmaninov* (Grove Press, N.Y.), 1950
SHAW, B.: *Music in London*, 3 vols., 1890–4 (Constable), 1922
The Perfect Wagnerite (Brentano), 1911
SIMPSON, R.: *The Symphony*, 2 vols. (Pelican Books), 1966
SKELTON, G.: *Wagner at Bayreuth* (Barrie & Rockliff), 1965
SOUSTER, T.: 'Schönberg and His Pupils' in *The Listener*, April 3rd, 1969
'Boulez and the Second Viennese School' in *The Musical Times*, May, 1969
STEVENS, H.: *The Life and Music of Béla Bartók* (O.U.P.), 1964
STEVENS, W.: *Collected Poems* (Faber), 1955
STRAUSS, F. & A.: *Briefwechsel Hugo von Hofmannsthal*, English trans. (Collins), 1961
STRAVINSKY, I. & CRAFT, R.: *Conversations with Igor Stravinsky* (Faber), 1959
Memories and Commentaries (Faber), 1960
Expositions and Developments (Faber), 1963
Dialogues and a Diary (Faber), 1969
STRAVINSKY, I.: *Chroniques de ma Vie*, trans. as *Autobiography* (Norton Library), 1960
STUCKENSCHMIDT, H. H.: *Arnold Schönberg*, trans. E. Roberts and H. Searle (Calder & Boyars), 1960
Twentieth Century Music (Weidenfeld & Nicholson), 1969
SUCKLING, N.: *Gabriel Fauré* (Dent), 1946
THOMSON, V.: *The State of Music* (Vintage Books), 1962
Music Reviewed (Vintage Books), 1966
Virgil Thomson (Weidenfeld & Nicholson), 1969

TOLSTOY, L.: *What is Art?* (O.U.P.), 1954
TURING, P.: *The New Bayreuth* (Spearman), 1969
VALLAS, L.: *César Franck* (Harrap), 1949
  Claude Debussy (O.U.P.), new edn., 1959
  The Theories of Claude Debussy (Dover Books), 1968
VIU, V. S.: 'The Mystery of Manuel de Falla and La Atlántida' in *Inter-American Music Bulletin*, 33, 1965
VUILLERMOZ, E.: *Gabriel Fauré* (Flammarion), 1960
WAGNER, R.: *My Life* (Constable), 1911
WALTER, B.: *Theme and Variations* (Hamish Hamilton), 1952
WARRACK, J.: 'Old Germany and New Bayreuth' in *Opera*, Nov., 1960
  'Berlioz's Mélodies' in *The Musical Times*, March, 1969
WEISSMANN, J. S.: 'Strauss on Stage' in *Music Review*, Feb., 1968
WERTH, A.: *Musical Uproar in Moscow* (Hamish Hamilton), 1949
WHITE, E. W.: *Stravinsky* (Faber), 1968
WHITTALL, D.: 'Sibelius's Eighth Symphony' in *Music Review*, Nov., 1964
WILDGANS, F.: *Anton Webern* (Owen), 1960
WILSON, C.: *Brandy of the Damned* (Baker), 1964
WILSON, E.: *The Triple Thinkers* (Lehmann), 1948
WRIGHT, K.: 'From Flop to Pop' in *Music*, Feb., 1969
YATES, P.: *Twentieth Century Music* (Allen & Unwin), 1968
ZUCKERMANN, E.: *A Hundred Years of Tristan* (Princeton University Press), 1965

Index

Adler, G., 73
Adler, O., 73n
Agate, J., 233
Albéniz, I., 136, 146, 210, 212–13, 219
Alkan (alias Valentin Morhange), 125n
Altenberg, P., 89
Amy, G., 137
Anda, G., 203
Andersen, O., 167–8
Annunzio, G. d', 176, 244
Ansermet, E., 82, 258, 310
Apollinaire, G., 119–20
Appia, A., 15, 33
Aprahamian, F., xiv, 69n, 81
Arensky, A., 196, 198, 239
Arvin, N., 294–5
Ashkenazy, V., 202
Auber, L., 100
Aubert, L., 130
Auric, G., 112, 127, 149, 189, 193, 265n

Babbitt, M., 312
Bach, J. S., 9, 51, 76, 128, 173, 177–9, 202, 213, 220, 227, 245, 272, 279, 308
Backhaus, W., 202, 226
Bahr, H., 41, 43
Bakst, L., 244
Bakunin, L., 20
Balakirev, L. M., 180, 202, 212
Balanchine, A., 270
Balázs, B., 229–30
Bantock, Sir G., 24, 165
Barbieri, F., 215n

Barraqué, J., xiv
Bartók, B., 72, 110, 158, 168, 213, 216, 223–35, 256, 258, 259, 303, 307–8, 310
Barzini, L., 183
Barzun, J., 2–3
Baudelaire, C., 11, 13, 26, 117, 118
Baudrier, Y., 123
Bax, Sir A., 25, 288
Beaumarchais, P., 42, 174
Beck, C., 186
Beethoven, L. van, xv, 4, 51, 61, 65, 139, 141, 200, 303, 305, 314, 317
Bellini, G. V., 169
Bérard, C., 277
Berg, A., vii, xii, xv, 16, 38, 62, 71, 75–6, 247, 308
Berio, L., 170, 306
Berkeley, L., 292
Berlioz, H., 5, 23, 56, 108, 113–14, 141, 151
Berners, Lord, 39, 244
Bernstein, L., xiii, 63, 69–70, 140
Béroff, M., 137
Bizet, G., 102, 107, 113, 144
Bliss, Sir A., xi
Böcklin, A., 29, 202
Bolitho, D., 304
Bordes, C., 106, 121
Borodin, A., 9, 117, 163, 198
Boughton, R., 24
Boulanger, N., 136, 277, 278, 292
Boulez, P., xii, 35–6, 52, 72, 76, 78, 80, 81, 85, 90, 112, 122–4, 127, 131, 137, 288, 308–9, 311
Brahms, J., 51, 76, 140, 144

Bréville, P. de, 106, 121, 126, 127–8
Brian, H., 24
Bridge, F., 289
Britten, B., 254, 287–99, 311
Brown, E., 316
Bruckner, A., xiv, 51, 57, 58, 65, 73, 162
Bruneau, A., 15, 107–8
Büchner, G., 41, 90–1
Bush, A., 292
Busoni, F., 77, 160, 171–81, 205
Byrd, W., 211

Cage, J., ix, 138, 282, 309, 312–14, 316, 317
Cairns, D., 142
Cameron, B., 167
Campanini, B., 265
Canteloube, J., 147, 187
Cardus, Sir N., xvi, 55, 139
Carpelan, Baron de, 164
Carter, E., 312
Caruso, E., 68, 274
Casals, P., 222
Casella, A., 170–82, 218
Castelnuovo-Tedesco, M., 170
Castillon, A. de, 116, 126
Cervantes, M. de, 219–20
Chabrier, E., 14–15, 107, 113, 133
Chaliapin, B., 68, 199
Char, R., 123–4, 308
Charpentier, G., 108, 121
Charpentier, M.-A., 180n
Chausson, E., 11, 15, 29, 101, 104, 105, 120–1, 128n, 145–6, 159, 185n
Chávez, C., xii
Cherubini, L., 101, 141, 169
Chotzinoff, S., 208
Claudel, P., 111, 116
Cocteau, J., 244
Colonne, E., 102
Cooke, D., 52, 54, 66n, 69, 72, 139, 222
Cooper, M., 121, 224
Copland, A., 276–7, 284, 311

Cornelius, P., 6
Cortot, A., 130, 145
Cowell, H., 208
Crabbe, G., 289–90, 292
Craft, R., 84, 236–46
Cui, C., 199, 260

Dahl, Dr., 200–1
Dallapicola, L., 170, 182
Damase, J. M., 136
Daniel-Lesur, Prof., 123, 136
Dankworth, J., 51n
Danreuther, E., 18
Debussy, C., 11, 13, 16, 64, 74, 78, 80–1, 84, 104, 108–9, 117–120, 121–50, 203, 228, 266
Del Mar, N., 45n
Delibes, L., 107
Delius, F., 24, 52, 54, 256, 288, 289
Demuth, N., 134, 137, 149, 189
Dent, E., 24, 287
Diaghilev, S., 111, 190, 239–40, 252, 267, 268–9, 270
Dohnányi, E., 225–6
Donington, R., 23
Downes, O., 166, 208, 272n
Drew, D., 134, 135n, 150, 193
Dukas, P., 11, 16, 109–10, 126–7, 128–9
Duparc, H., 15, 104, 105, 115, 116–17, 146
Dupont, G., 102, 121
Dutilleux, H., 112, 122–3, 127, 150–1
Dvořák, A., 139–40, 164, 210, 248

Elgar, Sir E., 24, 140, 157, 163, 287, 288
Eluard, P., 120, 123
Erede, A., 31
Essipova, Mme, 265

Falla, M. de, 210–22
Fantin-Latour, I, 13
Fargue, L.-P., 122
Fassett, A., 233

Fauré, G., 14, 110, 114–15, 116, 118, 121, 129–30, 131, 180, 185n
Feldman, M., 316–17
Fibich, Z., 249
Findeisen, C., 199
Flaherty, R., 283
Flaubert, G., 203
Flem, P. le, 147
Foldes, A., 179, 227–8
Ford, F. M., 18
Forster, E. M., 290, 293
Foss, L., 316
Foster, S., 275
Françaix, J., 136
Franck, C., 14, 63, 78, 104, 106, 116, 117, 125–7, 143, 144, 145, 178, 192, 209
Freud, S., 56, 59, 64, 73, 88n, 315
Furtwängler, W., 24, 31, 32, 310

Gallén-Kallela, G., 163
Galli-Marié, M., 103
Garden, M., 267–8, 285
Gartenberg, E., 70
Gautier, J., 11–12
Gautier, T., 12, 113
Genetz, E., 164
Gershwin, G., 251
Gigout, E., 185
Gill, A., 12
Gilman, L., 208
Giordano, U., 170
Glasco, J., 18n
Glasenapp, K., 5n
Glazounov, A., 198–9, 201, 240–1, 262, 264
Glière, R., 260, 262, 263
Glinka, M., 199, 260, 261
Goehr, A., 288
Goethe, J., 63, 64, 84, 176
Goldschmidt, B., 69
Gollancz, Sir V., 34–5
Gossec, F., 141, 151
Gould, G., 314
Granados, E., 210, 212–13, 218, 219
Gray, C., 39–40, 144, 157, 166
Greenlagh, J., 36n
Grétry, R., 5, 155

Grieg, E., 164, 261, 276
Gropius, W., 62n
Grout, D., 107
Grovlez, G., 131
Grunenwald, J-J., 136

Hába, A., 249
Halévy, F., 100, 103
Halfter, E., 221
Hambourg, M., 179, 202
Hammamdjian, A., 127
Hanslick, E., xiv
Hardy, T., 21
Harris, Sir A., 19–20
Hartmann, V., 48–9
Heinscheimer, H., 98
Heisenberg, A., 309
Henderson, W., 47
Henze, H., xii, 311–12
Herzfeld, F., 225
Heyworth, P., 3, 39n
Hill, E., 278
Hiller, L. A., 304
Hindemith, P., 82, 193, 248, 310
Hitler, A., 32, 34
Hodeir, A., xiv
Hofmann, J., 202, 207
Hofmannsthal, H. von, 40–50
Holbrooke, J., 24
Holmès, A., 12, 101
Holst, G., 24
Honnegger, A., x, 111, 135n, 148–149, 251
Horowitz, V., 202
Howard, P., 297
Howells, W. D., 291
Howes, F., 287
Hueffer, F., 18
Hughes, G., 38
Humperdinck, E., 6
Huneker, J., 204
Hutchings, A., 66, 288
Huysmans, J. K., 13

Ibert, J., 136
Indy, V. d', 15, 51, 63, 101, 104–5, 125–6, 145, 146, 180n, 191, 194, 216, 226

Ireland, J., 288
Irvine, D., 21–2
Ives, C., 276, 279, 312

Jacobs, A., 291
James, H., 158, 291–9, 300
Jammes, F., 116, 122
Janáček, L., 210, 249
Janssen, H., 32
Jarnach, P., 175
Jaubert, M., 122
Jeritza, M., 47
Johnson, H., 159, 163, 167
Jolivet, A., 112, 122, 123, 150, 307–8
Joyce, J., 53, 193, 277, 305
Jung, C., 34, 64
Jurgensburg, Baroness von, 161

Kajanus, R., 160, 164
Kaprálová, V., 256
Karatygin, V., 195
Karsavina, T., 239
Kassowitz, G., 94
Keller, G., 256
Keller, H., xi, 291
Kempff, W., 202
Kennedy, M., 288
Kerman, J., 108, 170
Kerstein, L., 214
Kertesz, I., xi, 229
Klee, P., 74
Kleiber, E., 98
Klein, E., 304
Klemperer, O., 60
Klindworth, W., 30
Klingsor, T., 116, 123
Knappertsbusch, H., 35, 39
Kodaly, Z., 227–8, 229
Koechlin, C., 121, 130, 133–5, 150, 180, 192
Koessler, 225–6
Kohl, G., 34n
Kokoschka, O., 62n, 74
Korovine, C., 239
Koussevitsky, S., 166, 192, 233, 252, 257, 270
Krafft-Ebing, R., 95

Kraus, K., 95
Krenek, E., 306
Kubelik, J., 250
Kubelik, R., 253

Lalo, E., 15, 107
Lambert, C., xiv, 81, 140, 144, 166, 248
Lamoureux, C., 11, 102, 146
Landowska, W., 220–1
Lavignac, A., 13
Lawrence, D. H., 21, 247
Layton, R., 161n
Lazzari, S., 16, 106, 121
Lehár, F., 48, 235
Lehmann, Lilli, 68
Lehmann, Lotte, 39, 42, 44
Leibowitz, R., 136, 308
Lekeu, G., 14, 77
Lennon, J., 317
Lenormand, R., 121
Lenya, L., 99
Leoncavallo, R., 103, 170, 183
Lewis, R., 294
Leyda, J., 197
Liadov, A., 198, 239, 260, 263
Liapounov, S., 202
Lifar, S., 270
Lindbergh, Colonel, 135n, 252n
Lisle, Leconte de, 114, 121, 193
List, E., 31
Liszt, F., 5, 17, 87, 101, 114, 140, 177–8, 224, 260
Lorenz, K., 283
Loriod, Y., 137
Louÿs, P., 121
Ludwig II, 6, 12, 26–7
Lully, J.-B., 139
Lunarcharsky, A., 266
Lutoslawski, W., 209, 311

Macdonald, D., xiii
Macdowell, E., 276
Machlis, J., 81, 195, 198, 222, 276
McVegh, D., 120
Maderna, B., 170, 183, 306
Magnard, A., 105, 135

Mahler, A., 59–60, 60n, 62–3, 68–9, 74, 98
Mahler, G., 51–70, 71, 73, 75, 76, 85, 88, 97, 139, 195, 204
Malipiero, G. F., 170–1, 179, 180, 182
Mallarmé, S., 119, 122, 124, 252
Malraux, A., 112, 306
Manduell, J., 142
Mann, T., 7–9, 98–9
Mann, W., 40–1
Marek, G., 39
Mariotte, A., 186
Martini, J., 113
Martinon, J., 186
Martinů, B., 135n, 186, 247–59, 311
Mascagni, P., 170, 183
Mason, C., 85, 234
Mason, D. G., 274
Massenet, J., 103–4, 107, 121
Masters, E. L., 282
Mauclair, C., 120
Mayer, W., 172
Mayuzurni, T., 306
Medtner, N., 206
Melchior, L., 24, 31
Mellers, W., 200n, 275, 315
Melville, H., 158, 291–9
Mencken, H. L., 277, 280
Mendès, C., 11
Mendelssohn, F., 17, 51, 126, 140, 260
Mengleberg, W., 68
Menotti, C., 257
Messiaen, O., 122–3, 136, 137–8, 151–2, 306–7, 309–10
Michelangeli, A. B., 179
Migot, G., 122–3
Mila, M., 222
Milhaud, D., 58, 111, 122, 134, 148, 188, 259
Mitchell, D., 60n, 80, 291
Mitropoulos, D., 192
Moiseiwitsch, B., 202, 205
Moniuzko, S., 210
Monteverdi, C., 169, 180
Moor, E., 173

Moore, G., 18
Moreux, S., 232
Moussorgsky, M., 9, 199, 205n, 260
Mozart, W. A., xv, 4, 40, 42, 108, 139, 263, 317
Muck, K., 30–1
Müller, W., 114
Myers, R., 138

Nestyev, I., 262, 268, 271
Newman, E., 5n, 22–3, 110
Newmarch, R., 164
Newson, G., xi
Nietzsche, F., 6–7, 13, 106
Nigg, S., 123
Nono, 183, 312
Noufflard, A., 20
Novák, V., 249

Offenbach, J., 46, 101, 275n
Ogdon, J., 137, 311
Orel, A., 34n
Ostrčil, C., 98, 249

Paganini, G. N., 209, 311
Paisiello, G., 155
Parker, H., 275
Parry, Sir H., 275, 284
Partch, H., 316
Pasternak, L., 56
Pasztory, D., 226n, 231, 233
Patissa, J., 221
Patti, A., 244
Payne, A., 79n
Pears, P., 289
Pedrell, A., 210, 213–15
Péguy, C., 178n, 304
Penderecki, K., 311
Petit, F., 189
Petit, R., 75
Petrassi, G., 170, 182
Petri, E., 179
Pfitzner, H., 6, 35, 68
Picasso, P., 267, 270, 282
Piper, M., 297
Pirie, P., 24
Pizzetti, I., 170

Pleasants, H., xii–xiii, xiv, 235
Podhoretz, N., 258
Poe, E. A., 109, 201, 205, 206
Pollak, J., 316
Poulenc, F., 107, 111, 112, 119–20,
    122
Praeger, F., 22
Preetorius, E., 33
Prokofiev, S., xii, 135, 158, 206–7,
    235, 242, 252, 260–73, 297
Puccini, G., 170, 171, 173, 175

Quilter, R., 292

Rachmaninov, S., 195–209, 242,
    264, 266, 270
Rackham, A., 18
Rahv, P., 276
Ravel, M., 110–11, 116, 119, 121,
    126, 129–30, 131–2, 137, 157,
    187, 190–1, 213, 215, 219, 267
Redlich, H., 57, 87
Reger, M., 127, 265
Régnier, H. de., 121, 132
Reich, W., 87, 90, 234
Reinhardt, M., 49
Respighi, O., 170, 181–2
Rethberg, E., 47
Reyer, E., 15, 102
Richter, H., 19, 68
Richter, M., 249
Rimbaud, A., 290
Rimsky-Korsakov, N., 104, 180,
    196, 198, 199, 201, 203, 240
Ringbom, N.-E., 167n
Rolland, R., 13
Rolleston, T. W., 18
Ropartz, G. de, 105, 145, 146, 186
Rosa, C., 17
Rosenfeld, P., 204
Rosenthal, H., 48
Rossini, G., 101, 103, 260
Roualt, G., 270
Rouché, J., 190
Roussel, A., 102, 145, 149–50,
    151, 175, 184–94, 250–1
Rubinstein, Artur, 202, 217
Rückert, F., 55, 62

Runciman, J. F., 22
Runeberg, J., 163
Ruskin, J., 5

Sabaneiev, L., 198
Safonov, V., 198, 201
Safránek, J., 255–6
Saint-Saens, C., 11, 16, 38, 101–2,
    104, 113, 127, 128–9, 142–3,
    172, 192, 226
Salazar, A., 222
Saltzman, E., ix
Samazeuilh, G., 127
Sandor, G., 227–8
Satie, E., 80, 107, 111, 122, 133–4,
    186, 193, 245n, 278, 279, 312
Sauguet, H., 111–12, 122, 149n
Sauvage, C., 123
Scalerio, A., 278
Scarlatti, A., 139
Scarlatti, D., 211
Schaeffer, P., 305–6
Schalk, O., 45, 69
Scherchen, H., 98, 194, 306, 310
Schillinger, J., 308–9
Schmend, B., 308
Schmitt, F., 130–1
Schnitzler, A., 41, 94–5
Schönberg, A., 16, 62, 65, 71–86,
    89, 98, 170, 173, 181, 183, 224,
    303
Schopenhauer, C., 3–5, 84
Schröder-Devrient, W., 29
Schubert, F., 6, 61–2, 78, 113,
    116
Schuman, W., xii
Schumann, R., xvi, 6, 51, 97, 115,
    126
Schweitzer, A., 9
Scriabin, A., 79, 196, 201–2, 242,
    262
Segovia, A., 218
Selva, B., 189
Serly, T., 235n
Sessions, R., 312
Séverac, D. de, 121, 128n, 147,
    187
Sgambati, J., 180

Shaw, B., 19–21
Shostakovitch, D., xii, 261, 272
Sibelius, A., 168
Sibelius, J., 52, 53, 155–68
Simpson, R., 139–40
Skelton, G., 32n
Slonimsky, N., 180
Smalley, R., xi
Smetana, B., 248
Soby, J. T., 96
Soler, A., 212, 219
Solti, G., 31
Souster, T., 75, 79, 90n
Souzay, G., 118n
Specht, R., 69
Spontini, G., 141, 169
Stamitz, K. J., 249
Stanford, Sir C., 275, 287
Stein, E., 98
Stein, G., 277, 280–6
Steiner, R., 84
Steinway, F., 207
Stevens, B., 256
Stevens, H., 230
Stevens, W., 80, 246
Stockhausen, K., 306, 309
Stokowski, L., 166, 178, 204
Stoltz, J., 185
Strauss, J., 39
Strauss, R., 31, 38–50, 52, 53,
    56–7, 165, 174, 216, 225, 235,
    263
Stravinsky, I., xiv, 46, 56, 58, 72,
    86, 111, 151, 180–2, 192, 196,
    199, 203, 214, 216–17, 236–46,
    260, 262, 269–70, 306, 312
Stuckenschmidt, H., ix, 304
Suckling, N., 51
Suk, J., 164, 249
Sullivan, J. W. N., 51
Swinburne, C., 18
Symons, A., 18

Taneyev, S., 196, 202n, 262
Tcherepnin, N., 262
Thalberg, A., 125
Thómans, M., 225
Thomas, A., 144

Thomson, V., 274–86
Tietjen, H., 15, 31–2
Tippett, Sir M., 292
Tolstoy, L., 8, 200
Tomaschek, J., 249
Tortelier, P., xi
Toscanini, A., 30–1, 60, 68, 182
Tournemire, C., 146
Tovey, Sir D., xvi, 51, 139
Trago, J., 213
Tschaikovsky, P., 196, 198, 212
Tudor, A., 75
Tudor, D., 138, 313
Turgenev, I., 9
Turing, P., 36n
Turner, J. M., 247

Ustinov, P., 261

Varèse, E., 186, 306
Vaughan Williams, R., 25, 195,
    222, 287, 288, 289
Verdi, G., 169, 174–5, 182
Vidal, P., 148
Villa-Lobos, H., 213
Vinès, R., 188
Vishnevskaya, G., 293
Vittoria, L., 211
Vivaldi, A., 180–1
Vlad, R., 182
Vuillemin, L., 131n

Wagner, Cossma, 29–31, 68, 256n
Wagner, R., xiv, 1–26, 73, 81–2,
    198, 236, 245, 253–4
Wagner, S., 29–31
Wagner, Wieland, 8, 23, 31–5
Wagner, Winifred, 30–3
Wagner, Wolfgang, 29, 35
Walter, B., 52, 53, 57, 60, 65, 69,
    84, 88, 178, 208, 270
Warlock, P., 292
Warrack, J., 5–6, 114n
Weber, C. M., 4, 5, 178
Webern, A., xv, 62, 71–86, 98,
    245, 308
Weelkes, T., 287
Weill, K., 38, 43, 93

Weinberger, K., 249
Weingartner, W., 69
Weissmann, J., 49n, 234
Welles, O., 282–3
Wellesz, E., 81
Werfel, F., 62n
Werth, A., 272n
White, E. W., 238
Whitehead, A. N., 304
Whittall, A., 167n
Wilde, O., 41
Wildgans, A., 87
Wilson, C., xiv, 235, 290
Wilson, E., 296, 298
Windgassen, W., 36
Winkler, F., 262–3

Wiora, W., 234
Wolf, H., xiv, 6, 61, 73, 217
Wood, Sir H., 165
Woolf, V., 22
Worner, K., 34n
Wright, K., 103n
Wyeth, A., 284
Wyzewa, T. de, 13

Xenakis, Y., 310

Yeats, W. B., 247

Zemlinsky, A. von, 62, 72–3
Ziegler, M., 226
Zimbalist, E., 204